Paul, the Law
and Justification

To Professor Ralph P. Martin
Scholar, mentor and friend

Paul, the Law and Justification

Colin G. Kruse

Lecturer in New Testament
Bible College of Victoria
Lilydale, Vic., Australia

 APOLLOS

APOLLOS (an imprint of Inter-Varsity Press)
38 De Montfort Street, Leicester LE1 7GP, England

First published 1996

British Library Cataloguing in Publication Data
A catalogue record for this book is available from the British Library.

ISBN 0–85111–441–5

Set in Times New Roman
Photoset by Parker Typesetting Service, Leicester
Printed in Great Britain by Clays Ltd, Bungay, Suffolk

Contents

Preface   19

Chief abbreviations   21

Introduction   24

1. Survey of selected monographs   27

Introduction   27

Earlier voices of protest   28

Claude G. Montefiore

George Foot Moore

Albert Schweitzer

W. D. Davies

H. J. Schoeps

Krister Stendahl

Development theories   33

John Drane

Hans Hübner

The new perspective   35
  E. P. Sanders
  Heikki Räisänen
  James D. G. Dunn

Recent responses   42
  Lloyd Gaston
  Stephen Westerholm
  Frank Thielman
  Brice L. Martin
  Peter J. Tomson
  N. T. Wright
  Thomas R. Schreiner

2. Galatians: the charter of freedom   54

Introduction   54

The situation in Galatia   55
  Paul's readers
  The 'troublers' of the Galatians

Paul's response: personal   57
  Independence and authenticity
      No immediate visit to Jerusalem after conversion
      The purpose of the visit after three years
      The purpose of the visit after fourteen years
      The significance of the Antioch incident
  Integrity
      Not a watered-down gospel
      Not seeking human approval

The ulterior motives of the Judaizers

They wanted to end Paul's friendship with the Galatians

They wanted to escape persecution

Paul's response: theological evaluations   64

Titus' experience in Jerusalem

The Antioch incident

Matters upon which Paul and Cephas agreed

Excursus: 'the works of the law' in Galatians

Matters about which Paul and Cephas disagreed

Concluding denial

Paul's response: theological arguments   72

The Galatians' own experience

The argument from Scripture

Those of faith and those of the works of the law

The curse of the law

Keeping the whole law

The law is not of faith

The application of Deuteronomy 21:23 to Christ

To whom does 'us' refer in 3:13?

The argument from human legal practice

The function of the law

Why then the law?

Is the law contrary to the promises?

The law as paidagōgos

The law as guardian or trustee

Argument from allegory: Sarah and Hagar

Paul's response: warnings and exhortations   100

The dire consequences of submission to circumcision

Being circumcised obliges people to observe the whole law

Circumcision means abandonment of the faith

The law summed up in a single commandment

Exhortation to walk by the Spirit

Bear one another's burdens and fulfil the law of Christ

Summary   107

The nature and function of the law

The law is not of faith

The law does not annul the promise

The law cannot make alive

The law as paidagōgos

Justification

Justification by faith in Christ

Justification and the hearing of faith

No changes to the means of justification

Justification rests upon redemption

Faith in Christ is incompatible with reliance on works

Justification by faith is incompatible with covenantal nomism

The law and the believer

Freedom from the law

No rebuilding what was torn down

Learning from the law

The law fulfilled in one word

Those led by the Spirit are not under the law

Fulfilling the law of Christ

3. 1 Corinthians: the regulation of freedom   115

Introduction   115

The background to 1 Corinthians   115

A case of incest   117

Judgment pronounced

The law provides a paradigm for purity of life

The law provides a paradigm for excommunication

The matter of litigation   119

You were . . . justified

Questions about marriage   121

Obedience to the command of the Lord

Obeying the commandments of God

Observing the rule laid down in all the churches

Things offered to idols   125

The law provides a paradigm for financial support

The command of the Lord and financial support

The law and Paul's accommodation to Jews and Gentiles

    Under the law of Christ

    Emulating Paul's practice of accommodation

    Was Paul inconsistent?

The law and Israel's experience in the wilderness

Women praying and prophesying   136

The law provides a paradigm for human relationships

Appeal to the universal practice of the churches

Speaking in tongues   138

The 'law' as a paradigm for the effect of tongues

Appeal to the command of the Lord

Women keeping silence   140

The law provides a paradigm for submission

Appeal to the universal practice of the churches

The resurrection   142

The defeat of death

The power of sin is the law

Summary   143

    The nature and function of the law

        The law as the power of sin

    Justification

        A central part of the experience of grace

    The law and the believer

        The law as a paradigm for Christian behaviour

        Freedom from the law

        Obeying the commandments of God

        Observing the commands of Christ

        Following the universal practices of the churches

4. 2 Corinthians: authentic ministry, the law and justification   149

Introduction   149

The background to 2 Corinthians   149

    The course of events

    Paul's opponents in 2 Corinthians

Two ministries compared and contrasted   152

    Negative functions of the law

    A positive function of the law

    Justification

Abstention from idolatrous worship   155

    The law provides a paradigm for the experience of God

The collection   156

    The law provides a paradigm for equality

Suffering, the mark of a true apostle   156

Observance of the law not incumbent upon believers

Summary   158

The nature and function of the law
The law brings condemnation and death
The temporary function of the law
The law as witness to Christ

Justification
A fundamental aspect of the ministry of the new covenant

The law and the believer
The law as a paradigm for Christian behaviour
Freedom from the law

5. Romans 1 – 5: justification apart from the law   162

Introduction   162

The purpose of Romans   163

A statement of the argument of 1:16 – 15:13

Relating the argument to the implied purpose
Response to a situation in the Roman church
Related to Paul's apostolic career
Emerging from both the above

Paul's theme: the gospel and the righteousness of God   169

The righteousness of God revealed in the gospel

A righteousness by faith

Paul's argument: no distinctions in sin or judgment   173

Human failure depicted with allusions to the law

Justification for the doers
Is judgment according to works?
Did the Gentiles keep what the law requires?

The Jews and the law

In defence of the righteousness of God

Has God abandoned his faithfulness to Israel?

Scriptural proof of universal sinfulness

Excursus: the meaning of 'the works of the law' in Romans

Paul's argument: no distinctions in the matter of salvation 187

The heart of Paul's gospel

The meaning of the term 'the righteousness of God'

The manifestation of the righteousness of God

The witness of the law and the prophets

The faithfulness of Christ and the righteousness of God

The faithfulness of Christ and his atoning sacrifice

The exclusion of boasting

Upholding the law

The case of Abraham

Justified by faith without works

Justified by faith without circumcision

The promise realized by faith without the law

Justification depends upon the Christ event

The fruits of justification by faith

The humanity-wide implications of Christ's death

Christ's obedience and believers' justification

The law given that sin might be reckoned

The law given to increase the trespass

6. Romans 6 – 15: answering objections and explaining implications
204

Introduction 204

Answering objections: morality and the law 204

Objections to Paul's thesis: moral standards

Objections to Paul's thesis: status of the law

Freedom from the law

The law and sin

The law and new life in the Spirit

The hope of believers

The emotive climax to Paul's argument so far

Answering objections: God's promises to Israel   221

The privileges of Israel

The pursuit of righteousness and the law

A striking paradox

Zeal without knowledge

The testimony of the law to faith

A special way of salvation for Israel?

The ethical implications of Paul's gospel   236

Love of fellow believers

Tolerance of the practice of other believers

Summary   239

The law and the Jewish people

Jewish advantage: possession of the law

The failure of the Jews despite their advantage

They pursued the law for righteousness

The works of the law

The nature and function of the law

The strength and weakness of the law

The function of the law

Limited time of the law's jurisdiction

Justification by faith for all

Revealed in the gospel apart from the law

To be received by faith

Based on the work of Christ

Grounded in God's election and calling

What justification involves

No Sonderweg *for the Jews*

The law and the believer

Freedom from the law

Fulfilling the law

Observing the law for the sake of the weak

Learning from the law

7. Law and justification in the other Pauline letters   250

Introduction   250

1 Thessalonians   250

Observing the commands of the Lord Jesus Christ

The wrath of God has come upon the Jews

2 Thessalonians   253

Keeping the charge given in the name of the Lord

Philippians   254

'Work out your own salvation with fear and trembling'

We put no confidence in the flesh

As to righteousness under the law, blameless

Two kinds of righteousness

Colossians   258

Christ the end of human traditions

The cross and the cancelling of the *cheirographon*

Ephesians   261

Salvation by faith and not by works

The abolition of the law

The first commandment with a promise

1 Timothy   265

   The law is not for 'the just'

   The justification of a notorious sinner

   The law provides a paradigm for financial support

Titus   267

   Justification by grace, not by deeds of righteousness

2 Timothy   269

   Saved by grace, not by works

   The positive role of the law

Summary   270

   Two kinds of righteousness

   As to the law, blameless

   The abolition of the law

   Christ removes the human sense of guilt

   The role of the law

   Paul and the Jews

8. General conclusions   273

A brief overview   273

   Galatians

   1 Corinthians

   2 Corinthians

   Romans

   The other Pauline letters

A summary   278

   The nature and function of the law

     The temporary role of the law

     The law does not annul the promise

The law cannot give life

The law brings condemnation

The law as a witness to the gospel

The law inferior to the promise

The law is holy, just, good and spiritual

The law is the unwilling ally of sin

Justification

Justification has always been, and still is, 'by faith'

Justification rests upon the redemptive action of Christ

Justification and inclusion among the people of God

Justification is incompatible with legalism and nomism

Justification is grounded in election and calling

The experience of justification

The place of justification in Paul's theology

The law and the believer

Freedom from the law

Learning from the law

The fulfilment of the law in the lives of believers

The law of Christ

Accommodation to those who live under the law

Keeping the commandments of God

Obedience to the commands of Christ

Observing the rules laid down in all the churches

The law and the Jewish people

Problems   287

The nature and function of the law

Ambiguous use of the term 'law'

Contradictory statements about the origin of the law

Problematic statements about law and sin

Contradictory statements about human ability to keep the law

The power of sin attributed to both Adam and the law

The law promised life, but lacks the power to provide it

A dramatic act needed to terminate a temporary expedient

Justification

Justification was merely a polemic doctrine

Contradictory statements about justification

The law and the believer

Inconsistencies in the matter of freedom from the law

Later letters correct mistakes in earlier ones

Inconsistency in the matter of accommodation

Jewish laws replaced by ecclesiastical practices

The law and the Jewish people

The place of the law in Jewish soteriology

Law and justification today   297

The experience of justification

No unnecessary barriers for converts

No unnecessary burdens for believers

The paradox of Christian living

Reading the Old Testament as a Christian

Accommodation

Robust holiness

Bibliography   300

Index of authors   319

Preface

The possibility of my writing a book on Paul and the law was first raised with me by the Rev. David Kingdon, the Theological Books Editor of IVP, in 1987. I am very grateful for his suggestion, and for the subsequent invitation from IVP to write this book. Most of my discretionary time for the last four years has been devoted to the task. It has been the most difficult writing assignment I have undertaken so far, and yet one of the most rewarding.

Many people have helped me in different ways to produce this book. I am grateful to the Council of Ridley College for granting me study leave in 1991 to work on this project, and to the Governors of the Australian Research Theology Foundation Inc. for assistance given in meeting the costs of study leave. I began work in earnest on the manuscript for this book during a six-month period spent at Tyndale House, Cambridge in 1991. I wish to thank the Warden, Bruce Winter, and his wife, Lyn Winter, and the staff of Tyndale House, together with other researchers in residence at that time, for their friendship and encouragement. I am grateful, too, that my wife, Rosemary, was again prepared to accept the disruptions to normal living that were involved in accompanying me on my study leave, and that our son, David, our daughter-in-law, Janet (then with a brand-new baby), and our daughter Elizabeth were willing to look after our home (and animals!) in Melbourne, while Rosemary and I were away. Also I wish to thank students in the second and third-level

New Testament class at Ridley College in 1994, who, by their interest, comments and questions, helped me to come to a clearer understanding of Paul's views about law and justification. I am grateful, too, for comments made on the first draft of this book by David Kingdon and by the other readers whose comments he solicited.

This book was begun when I was a member of the lecturing staff at Ridley College and completed during my first few months as a member of the faculty of the Bible College of Victoria. I want to take this opportunity to record my appreciation for the friendship and support given by colleagues and staff at Ridley College over the past sixteen years. Also I want to express my gratitude for the warm welcome given to Rosemary and me by the Council, Principal, faculty and staff of the Bible College of Victoria, and for the encouragement I have received to continue research and writing, alongside my other duties in the College.

I wish to dedicate this book to Professor Ralph P. Martin, who supervised me as a PhD student at Fuller Theological Seminary in the 1970s, whose careful scholarship continues to provide a model for me, and whose friendship and encouragement I have greatly valued from the time we first met.

March 1995

Colin G. Kruse
Bible College of Victoria
Lilydale, Vic., Australia

Chief abbreviations

AB	Anchor Bible
AJT	*Asia Journal of Theology*
AusBR	*Australian Biblical Review*
BA	*Biblical Archaeologist*
BAG	*A Greek–English Lexicon of the New Testament and Other Early Christian Literature*, by Walter Bauer, William F. Arndt and F. Wilbur Gingrich (Chicago: University of Chicago Press, 1957)
Bib	*Biblica*
Bijdr	*Bijdragen*
BBR	*Bulletin for Biblical Research*
BJRL	*Bulletin of the John Rylands University Library of Manchester*
BSac	*Bibliotheca Sacra*
BZ	*Biblische Zeitschrift*
CBQ	*Catholic Biblical Quarterly*
CTM	*Currents in Theology and Mission*
EKKNT	Evangelisch-katholischer Kommentar zum Neuen Testament
ET	English translation
ETL	*Ephemerides theologicae lovanienses*

ETR	*Etudes théologiques et religieuses*
EuroJTH	*European Journal of Theology*
EvK	Evangelische Kommentare
EvQ	*Evangelical Quarterly*
EvT	*Evangelische Theologie*
ExpT	*Expository Times*
FoiVie	*Foi et Vie*
GeistLeb	*Geist und Leben*
HBT	*Horizons in Biblical Theology*
HeyJ	*Heythrop Journal*
HR	*History of Religions*
HTKNT	Herders theologischer Kommentar zum Neuen Testament
HTR	*Harvard Theological Review*
ICC	International Critical Commentary
Int	*Interpretation*
JBL	*Journal of Biblical Literature*
JETS	*Journal of the Evangelical Theological Society*
JSNT	*Journal for the Study of the New Testament*
JSNTSup	Journal for the Study of the New Testament – Supplement Series
JTS	*Journal of Theological Studies*
Judaica	*Judaica: Beiträge zum Verständnis . . .*
KD	*Kerygma und Dogma*
KEK	Kritisch-exegetischer Kommentar über das Neue Testament (Meyer)
LD	Lectio divina
LS	*Louvain Studies*
LumVie	*Lumière et Vie*
LTJ	*Lutheran Theological Journal*
LXX	Septuagint (Greek version of the Old Testament)
MS	*Milltown Studies*
NCB	New Century Bible
Neot	*Neotestamentica*
NICNT	New International Commentary on the New Testament
NIGTC	The New International Greek Testament Commentary

NIV	New International Version
NovT	*Novum Testamentum*
NRSV	New Revised Standard Version
n.s.	new series
NTS	*New Testament Studies*
RB	*Revue biblique*
REB	Revised English Bible
RelSRev	*Religious Studies Review*
ResQ	*Restoration Quarterly*
RTR	*Reformed Theological Review*
SBLDS	SBL Dissertation Series
SEÅ	*Svensk exegetisk årsbok*
SJT	*Scottish Journal of Theology*
SNTSMS	Society for New Testament Studies Monograph Series
SR/SR	*Studies in Religion/Sciences Religieuses*
ST	*Studia theologica*
StudBib	Studia Biblica
THKNT	Theologischer Handkommentar zum Neuen Testament
TijdT	*Tijdschrift voor Theologie*
TP	*Theologie und Philosophie*
TrinJ	*Trinity Journal*
TS	*Theological Studies*
TT	*Teologisk Tidsskrift*
TynBul	*Tyndale Bulletin*
TZ	*Theologische Zeitschrift*
VoxRef	*Vox Reformata*
WBC	Word Biblical Commentary
WTJ	*Westminster Theological Journal*
ZAW	*Zeitschrift für die alttestamentliche Wissenschaft*
ZNW	*Zeitschrift für die neutestamentliche Wissenschaft*
ZTK	*Zeitschrift für Theologie und Kirche*

Introduction

From the time of the Reformation the exegesis of the Pauline letters (in Protestant scholarship especially) has been deeply influenced by Luther's 'discovery' of justification by faith. His understanding of Paul's views about the law and justification were coloured by his struggle with medieval Catholicism. Thus first-century Judaism, in and alongside of which Paul proclaimed and defended his gospel, was seen as analogous to medieval Catholicism – a religion in which salvation was earned by works of merit.

This approach has not been without its critics, Jewish as well as Christian. It was not until E. P. Sanders' book *Paul and Palestinian Judaism*[1] was published in 1977, however, that Christian attitudes to Judaism really began to change. It is now widely agreed that first-century Judaism was not, in principle, a religion in which salvation was dependent upon merit accumulated by obedience to the law, but rather a religion based upon God's election and grace.

One result of this revised view of the nature of Judaism has been, in more recent times, the expenditure of a great deal of energy in attempts to redefine Paul's understanding of the law and justification. In some cases such attempts have resulted in charges of inconsistencies in the apostle's thought and an

---

[1]E. P. Sanders, *Paul and Palestinian Judaism: A Comparison of Patterns of Religion* (London: SCM, 1977).

emasculation of the much cherished Reformation understanding of justification by faith.

Some scholars have argued that there are so many inconsistencies in Paul's statements about law and justification that it is impossible to put forward a coherent expression of the apostle's views on the subject. Others have tried to explain the inconsistencies in terms of a development in Paul's theology: the apostle realized the problems inherent in his earlier writings and sought to correct these in later writings. Another approach has been to understand Paul's negative statements about Judaism and the law, not as a critique of the law itself, but of Jewish exclusivism expressed in an insistence upon those demands of the law which function as the identity markers for Israel, *i.e.* circumcision, food laws and calendrical rules. These approaches, and others, are described in the next chapter, which surveys selected monographs published over the last 100 years.

In revisiting the letters of the Pauline corpus to look again at what is said in them about the law and justification, however, the issues of the current debate must not be allowed to set the agenda. It is important that whatever statements are made about this matter in the different letters be understood in the context of the concerns of each letter. By approaching the study in this way we have a better chance of understanding the significance of the various statements made about law and justification. To draw statements from the different letters and compare and contrast them without giving attention to the particular concerns of each letter is not only methodologically suspect, but increases the difficulty involved in seeking to understand those statements properly. By treating each letter in turn, not only is this problem minimized, but it also becomes possible to identify the particular emphases of each letter. This will in turn make it possible to evaluate the case for development in Paul's thinking about law and justification and the case for the existence of irreconcilable inconsistencies, both between the various letters and within the individual letters themselves.

Following the survey of selected monographs, then, successive chapters are devoted to the study of Galatians, 1 Corinthians, 2 Corinthians and Romans. While these letters contain most of the relevant data, the remaining letters of the Pauline corpus do contain some extra evidence which needs to be taken into account to complete the picture. For this reason a chapter is devoted to these other letters. Here again, each letter is taken in turn so as to allow any particular emphases each might have to emerge.

At the end of each of the chapters devoted to the study of the Pauline letters a summary of results is included so that the special emphases of each letter, as far as Paul's view of of law and justification is concerned, can be readily identified. A final chapter states the general conclusions of this study, relates these to the major issues in the recent debate, and suggests briefly some possible implications of Paul's teaching about law and justification for believers today.

1

Survey of selected monographs

Introduction

As noted in the previous chapter, the now widely held view of first-century Judaism as a religion based, not on human merit, but on God's election and grace, has raised questions about Paul's own understanding of the nature of first-century Judaism. In addition questions have been raised concerning his statements about the law and justification. These include such issues as the following. (i) Just how central to Paul's theology is his teaching about the law and justification? (ii) How he can say that people are justified by faith yet judged according to their works? (iii) What is his view concerning the ongoing role of the law for believers? (iv) Are there inconsistencies in his statements about the law and justification between his letters and even within particular letters? These questions, and others, have occupied many scholars in recent years.

A survey of selected monographs which have been influential in this debate helps to illustrate the key issues and to set the present study in context. The monographs surveyed include several which, long before Sanders' work, questioned the prevailing 'Lutheran' approach to Pauline studies. In addition, Sanders' own writing and the works of those who have built upon it or challenged it in one respect or another, are surveyed.

Earlier voices of protest

Claude G. Montefiore

In the first of two essays in a very significant monograph,[1] Montefiore asks: 'How far was Paul, up to his conversion, a Rabbinic Jew? Was Rabbinic Judaism the religion which he had known, believed in, and practiced?'[2] He argues that Paul's religion was very different from the rabinnic Judaism of AD 300–500 which is known in some detail; a religion which was rich, warm, joyous, and optimistic. Further, Montefiore is inclined to think that the rabbinic Judaism of AD 50 'was a better, happier, and more noble religion than one might infer from the writings of the Apostle'.[3] He is therefore suspicious of the statement of Acts that Paul was brought up in Jerusalem at the feet of Gamaliel.[4]

Montefiore argues that the rabbinic Judaism of AD 300–500, unlike the Judaism reflected in Paul's writings, taught an intensely personal God who, though great and aweful, was nevertheless merciful and loving. He provided Israel with a law, not that it should be a burden to them, but that they might be happy. Rabbinic Jews revelled in the 'joy of the commandments', and this did not normally lead to pride or self-righteousness. They believed they would inherit the world to come, though this had nothing to do with their own merits but would be the result of God's grace. They were conscious of their failures, but trusted in God's love towards repentant sinners, something underlined for them on the great annual Day of Atonement, when Israel's slate was wiped clean and every penitent was offered the chance of a fresh start.[5] The only noteworthy fault in rabbinic Judaism was its particularism.[6]

If rabbinic Judaism of AD 50 was like that of AD 300–500, then, Montefiore argues, it is inconceivable that Paul was a rabbinic Jew before his conversion. If he was, he could not have developed the theory of the law he elaborates in Romans, or ignored repentance as he does. He would not have needed to develop the mystic notions which he did, and would not have found it necessary to devise the soteriology found in his major epistles.[7]

All this leads Montefiore to conclude that Paul's pre-Christian religion was a

---

[1]C. G. Montefiore, 'The Genesis of the Religion of St Paul', *Judaism and St Paul: Two Essays* (London: Max Goschen, 1914), pp. 1–129.

[2]*Ibid.*, pp. 13–14.

[3]*Ibid.*, p. 87.

[4]*Ibid.*, p. 90.

[5]*Ibid.*, pp. 25–52.

[6]*Ibid.*, p. 53.

[7]*Ibid.*, pp. 59–60.

'colder, less intimate, less happy' religion because it was not rabbinic Judaism, but diaspora Judaism.[8]

Montefiore's essay continues to be of significance even though the clear distinction he made between rabbinic (Palestinian) and diaspora (Hellenistic) Judaism is no longer accepted. It continues to be significant because it still challenges Christian exegetes to do justice to the nature of first-century Judaism when interpreting the letters of Paul.

George Foot Moore

G. F. Moore's much quoted article, written in 1921,[9] must be noted, even though it is not part of a monograph. He shows that, from the earliest times until our own century, Christian interest in Jewish writings has been dominated by apologetic or polemic rather than historical concerns. Early Christian apologists such as Justin Martyr and Tertullian appear to have written not so much to convert Jews as to encourage Christians, and the Jewish opponents in their writings were but 'men of straw'. In the Middle Ages, Christian apologists could no longer deal with 'straw men'; they had to debate with learned defenders of Judaism, and therefore they had to gain some real knowledge of Jewish literature, both ancient and modern. Outstanding from this period is the work of Raimundus Martini entitled *Pugio Fidei*. Although this book was composed with a view to converting Jews, it did not vilify them, as many of the earlier Christian works had done. Moore says, 'Compared with much more recent anti-Judaic polemic it might almost be called gentle- manly.'[10] Reformation writers were not concerned to defend the doctrines of the church against Jewish attacks, but rather, having rejected the authority of the church and its traditions, they made use of Jewish literature to help develop their own systems of Christian doctrine based on Scripture alone. They appealed to Jewish writings to show that, on issues of debate between Catholics and Protestants, the Jews were on the side of the Protestants. It was in the seventeenth and early eighteenth centuries, Moore says, that Christian study of Jewish literature was first carried out with a view to portraying Judaism 'as it was, from its own literature, without apologetic, polemic, or dogmatic presuppositions or intentions.'[11] The works of some leading Christian scholars

---

[8]*Ibid.*, p. 93.

[9]George Foot Moore, 'Christian Writers on Judaism', *HTR* 14 (1921), pp. 197–254.

[10]*Ibid.*, p. 205.

[11]*Ibid.*, p. 225.

of the nineteenth and early twentieth centuries attract Moore's most critical comments, in particular the work of Emil Schürer, *Lehrbuch der neutestamentliche Zeitgeschichte* (1874); Ferdinand Weber, *System der altsynagogalen palästinischen Theologie* (1880), and W. Bousset, *Die Religion des Judentums im neutestamentlichen Zeitalter* (1903). Such scholars as these were responsible for criticizing Judaism as legalistic, a criticism no-one seems to have wanted to make prior to this time. Moore asks, 'What then brought legalism to the front in the new apologetic?' He answers his own question: 'Not a fresh and more thorough study of Judaism at the beginning of our era, but a new apologetic motive [*i.e.* the desire to find in Judaism an antithesis to what they believed was the teaching of Jesus], consequent on a different apprehension of Christianity on the part of the New Testament Theologians who now took up the task.'[12]

Albert Schweitzer

In his book *The Mysticism of Paul the Apostle*,[13] Schweitzer argued that the mysticism of the apostle is connected, not with a Hellenistic worldview but rather with a Jewish eschatological worldview. In accordance with such a worldview Paul believed that the law remained in force only until the beginning of the messianic age. Those who are 'in Christ' are free from the law. Schweitzer notes that Paul would have saved himself a lot of trouble if he could have then regarded the observance of the law as an *adiaphoron*, something indifferent, and look upon the activities of the Judaizing believers 'With a gentle smile, knowing and preaching that believers from among the Gentiles, who allowed themselves to be persuaded to take upon themselves circumcision and the Law, were merely burdening themselves unnecessarily'.[14] Paul, however, was not able to adopt this 'ironic' attitude to the problem. Instead, he argued that believers should maintain the *status quo* in respect of the law. Gentiles who became believers outside the law were not to subject themselves to the law. Jews who became believers under the law must continue to observe it.[15] While this might sound reasonable in theory, it created great problems for the apostle in practice, and these problems forced Paul to defend his position by arguing that justification was received by faith and not by the

---

[12]*Ibid.*, p. 253.

[13]Albert Schweitzer, *The Mysticism of Paul the Apostle* (London: A. and C. Black, 1931).

[14]*Ibid.*, pp. 192–193.

[15]*Ibid.*, pp. 193–195.

works of the law. It follows, then, that justification by faith is not the centre of Paul's teaching. Rather, at the centre is Paul's mystical doctrine of redemption. Schweitzer asserts, in words often quoted, that 'the doctrine of righteousness by faith is therefore a subsidiary crater, which has formed within the rim of the main crater – the mystical doctrine of redemption through the being-in-Christ.'[16]

W. D. Davies

In his seminal work *Paul and Rabbinic Judaism*,[17] W. D. Davies seeks 'to set certain pivotal aspects of Paul's life and thought against the background of the contemporary Rabbinic Judaism, so as to reveal how, despite his Apostleship to the Gentiles, he remained, as far as was possible, a Hebrew of the Hebrews, and baptised his Rabbinic heritage into Christ'.[18]

This involves two rebuttals. First, against C. G. Montefiore, Davies argues that Paul was not simply a Jew of the Dispersion, who was unacquainted with rabbinic Judaism as it was found in Palestine. Second, against those scholars who set Paul in an antithetical relationship to first-century Judaism, he argues that the apostle's life and thought were in fact determined by Pharisaic concepts which he baptized into Christ. Davies shows that a number of the key elements of Paul's understanding of the Christian dispensation are grounded in an essentially rabbinic world of thought. These include his understanding of the flesh and sin; the old and new humanity; the old and new Israel; the old and new man; the old and new Torah; the old and new obedience; and the old and new hope. In his conclusion Davies asserts that 'the gospel for Paul was not the annulling of Judaism but its completion, and as such it took up into itself the essential genius of Judaism.'[19] And he adds:

> Paul was a preacher of a New Exodus wrought by the 'merit' of Christ who was obedient unto death, but this New Exodus like the Old was constitutive of community, it served to establish the New Israel; it also led to the foot of a New Sinai, and Paul appeared before us as a catechist, the steward of a New Didache that imposed new demands. 'Torah', 'Obedience' and 'Community' then are integral to Pauline Christianity no less than to Judaism. The source of Pauline Christianity lies

---

[16] *Ibid.*, p. 225.

[17] W. D. Davies, *Paul and Rabbinic Judaism: Some Rabbinic Elements in Pauline Theology* (1948; Philadelphia: Fortress, 4th edn., 1980).

[18] *Ibid.*, p. xvii.

[19] *Ibid.*, p. 323.

in the fact of Christ, but in wrestling to interpret the full meaning and implication of that fact Paul constantly drew upon concepts derived from Rabbinic Judaism; it was these that formed the warp and woof if not the material of this thought.[20]

H. J. Schoeps

H. J. Schoeps' book on Paul[21] includes a long chapter on the apostle's teaching about law. Like Schweitzer, Schoeps insists that Paul's thought about the law can be understood only if we keep our attention 'focussed on Paul's consistently eschatological mode of thought'. Paul accepted the Jewish belief that the role of the Torah would come to an end with the dawning of the messianic era. Because he believed that the messianic era had been inaugurated by Jesus, he could say, 'Christ is the end of the law' (Rom. 10:4), a statement which 'is an absolutely exact inference from the standpoint of Jewish theological thought', although, of course, 'the rabbis did not share Paul's premise that the Messianic age had begun with the death and resurrection of Jesus'.[22]

Schoeps argues that Paul was guilty of legalistic moralization of the law, and of a failure to appreciate it as the seal of God's covenant with Israel. The *Berith-Torah* 'was reduced by him to the scope of ethical law, which he understands as a law intended to make righteous, and which, he concludes, it is unable to do, since man is not righteous but a sinner'.[23] Schoeps concludes:

> Because Paul had lost all understanding of the character of the Hebraic *berith* as a partnership involving mutual obligations, he failed to grasp the inner meaning of the Mosaic law, namely, that it is an instrument by which the covenant is realized. Hence the Pauline theology of the law and justification begins with the fateful misunderstanding in consequence of which he tears asunder covenant and law, and then represents Christ as the end of the law.[24]

---

[20]*Ibid.*

[21]H. J. Schoeps, *Paul: The Theology of the Apostle in the Light of Jewish Religious History* (ET, London: Lutterworth, 1961).

[22]*Ibid.*, p. 173.

[23]*Ibid.*, p. 198.

[24]*Ibid.*, p. 218.

Krister Stendahl

In his stimulating article 'Paul and the Introspective Conscience of the West',[25] Stendahl argues that western exegesis of Paul (beginning with Augustine, through Luther and down to the majority of Protestant scholars) is guilty of misreading the apostle. 'Where Paul was concerned about the possibility for Gentiles to be included in the messianic community, his statements are now read as answers to the quest for assurance about man's salvation out of a common human predicament.'[26] Stendahl argues that Paul was not plagued with a troubled conscience because he was unable to fulfil the demands of the law, and then found relief in the doctrine of justification by faith. On the contrary, Paul had a robust conscience. Prior to his conversion he regarded himself as blameless in respect of the law, and after his conversion his sense of remorse was related to his persecution of the church, not to his inability to live up to the standards of God's law.[27] Even Romans 7:19 ('I do not do the good I want, but the evil I do not want to do is what I do') is part of an argument that involves the acquittal of the *egō*, not abject contrition on the part of the *egō*. The purpose of the passage is not to provide an analysis of the human predicament, but rather to lay the blame for it at the feet of the flesh and sin, and in so doing to exonerate the law itself.[28] In conclusion Stendahl ventures to suggest 'that the West for centuries has wrongly surmised that the biblical writers were grappling with problems which no doubt are ours, but which never entered their consciousness'.[29]

Development theories

John Drane

In his monograph *Paul, Libertine or Legalist?*,[30] Drane sets out to trace the development of Paul's theology across his major epistles. He assumes that Galatians is the earliest of these, followed by 1 and 2 Corinthians and then

---

[25]Krister Stendahl, 'Paul and the Introspective Conscience of the West', *Paul Among Jews and Gentiles and Other Essays* (London: SCM, 1977), pp. 78–96. This is a revised edition of an article, 'Paulus och Samvetet', published in *SEÅ* 25 (1960), pp. 62–77.

[26]*Ibid.*, p. 86.

[27]*Ibid.*, pp. 89–91.

[28]*Ibid.*, pp. 92–93.

[29]*Ibid.*, pp. 94–95.

[30]John W. Drane, *Paul, Libertine or Legalist? A Study in the Theology of the Major Pauline Epistles* (London: SPCK, 1975).

Romans. He argues that Galatians represents a true but extreme presentation of the apostle's teaching which was elicited by the attacks of Judaizing opponents. In Galatians Paul stressed the bankruptcy of the law-principle of the Old Testament and argued for the complete spiritual freedom of the believer. When confronted by a Gnosticizing movement in Corinth, Paul did an about-face in his theological expression. Whereas he appears like a libertine in Galatians, he comes across as a legalist in 1 Corinthians as he imposes moral, social and ecclesiastical laws upon his converts. When responding to Jewish opposition in 2 Corinthians, however, the apostle modifies his approach and gives a somewhat different expression of his theology. This is a combination of the types of teaching found in Galatians and 1 Corinthians, and one in which there is a virtual absence of any direct moral instructions. This process of synthesization comes to its full fruition in Romans, for in this letter the apostle sought to give a completely balanced exposition of his theology, one which could not be misconstrued by either Judaizers or Gnosticisers.[31]

Hans Hübner

Professor Hübner notes that his work *Law in Paul's Thought*[32] runs parallel to Drane's thesis. Hübner argues that Paul's theology can be properly understood only in relationship to its development. He argues specifically that there is a significant shift in emphasis between Galatians and Romans. In Galatians, for example, the law is seen only in negative terms (it provokes sinful deeds, derives from the demonic angelic powers, and serves as a locus for enslavement).[33] But in Romans Paul speaks positively of the law. His doctrine of justification by faith, far from doing away with the law, actually upholds it, for the law itself indicates (in the case of Abraham) that justification does not come from the law.[34] In Galatians circumcision is of no value at all and those who are circumcised are severed from Christ and fall from grace. But in Romans circumcision is of value when accompanied by faith.[35] Hübner asserts that such differences in emphasis between Galatians and Romans are so great that they cannot be accounted for either by regarding Romans as a further

---

[31]*Ibid.*, pp. 123–124.

[32]Hans Hübner, *Law in Paul's Thought* (ET, Edinburgh: T. and T. Clark, 1984). Original German edition, *Das Gesetz bei Paulus: Ein Beitrag zum Werden der paulinischen Theologie* (Göttingen: Vandenhoeck und Ruprecht, 1978).

[33]*Ibid.*, p. 36.

[34]*Ibid.*, p. 53.

[35]*Ibid.*

explication of earlier ideas found in Galatians or by the different situations of the addressees, but only by recognizing that Paul had become aware of the inconsistencies in his thought. Having done so, there followed a far from trivial development in the apostle's theological thought, which is reflected in Romans.[36]

The new perspective

E. P. Sanders

E. P. Sanders' book *Paul and Palestinian Judaism*,[37] was published in 1977, and has come to be regarded as the most influential work of Pauline studies in recent times. The general aim of the book is to argue a case concerning Palestinian Judaism as a whole and to carry out a comparison of Pauline Christianity and Palestinian Judaism.

To achieve this, Sanders first makes an exhaustive study of Jewish sources which date from 200 BCE to 200 CE. These include the early rabbinic (Tannaitic) literature, the Dead Sea Scrolls and a selection of works from the Apocrypha and Pseudepigrapha. As a result of this study he concludes that Palestinian Judaism can be best described as 'covenantal nomism'. What is meant by this term is best described in his own words:

> The 'pattern' or 'structure' of covenantal nomism is this: (1) God has chosen Israel and (2) given the law. The law implies both (3) God's promise to maintain the election and (4) the requirement to obey. (5) God rewards obedience and punishes transgression. (6) The law provides for means of atonement, and atonement results in (7) maintenance or re-establishment of the covenantal relationship. (8) All those who are maintained in the covenant by obedience, atonement and God's mercy belong to the group which will be saved. An important interpretation of the first and last points is that election and ultimately salvation are considered to be by God's mercy rather than human achievement.[38]

The next step in Sanders' work is to describe the pattern of Paul's religion. To do this, he undertakes a careful investigation of the seven letters of Paul whose authenticity is unquestioned (Romans, 1 and 2 Corinthians, Galatians, Philippians, 1 Thessalonians and Philemon). The results of this investigation lead him to conclude that Paul's religion, unlike that of Palestinian Judaism,

---

[36]*Ibid.*, pp. 54–55.
[37]*Paul and Palestinian Judaism: A Comparison of Patterns of Religion* (London: SCM, 1977).
[38]*Ibid.*, p. 422.

cannot be described as covenantal nomism, but is best understood as participationist eschatology. Once again it is best to let Sanders speak for himself:

> The heart of Paul's thought is not that one ratifies and agrees to a covenant offered by God, becoming a member of a group with a covenantal relation with God and remaining in it on the condition of proper behaviour; but that one dies with Christ, obtaining new life and the initial transformation which leads to the resurrection and ultimate transformation, that one is a member of the body of Christ and one Spirit with him, and that one remains so unless one breaks the participatory union by forming another.[39]

In concluding this work, Sanders describes those features which do and do not specifically differentiate Palestinian Judaism from Pauline Christianity. The true contrast is not to be found in the matter of grace and works or in Paul's expectation of an imminent end. It is predominantly his understanding of righteousness which distinguishes Christianity from Judaism:

> To be righteous in Jewish literature means to obey the Torah and to repent of transgression, but in Paul it means to be saved by Christ. Most succinctly, righteousness in Judaism is a term which implies the maintenance of status among the group of the elect; in Paul it is a transfer term. In Judaism, that is, commitment to the covenant puts one 'in', while obedience (righteousness) subsequently keeps one in. In Paul's usage, 'be made righteous' ('be justified') is a term indicating getting in, not staying in the body of the saved. Thus when Paul says one cannot be made righteous by works of law, he means that one cannot, by works of law, 'transfer to the body of the saved'. When Judaism said that one is righteous who obeys the law, the meaning is that one thereby stays in the covenant. The debate about righteousness by faith or by works of law thus turns out to result from different usage of the 'righteous' word group.[40]

It follows, then, that as far as Paul is concerned, what is wrong with Judaism is not its zeal for the law or that it promotes a quest for self-righteousness based on the works of the law, but rather that it is unenlightened. In Sanders' oft-quoted words: 'In short, *this is what Paul finds wrong in Judaism: it is not Christianity.*'[41]

Many of the early reviews of *Paul and Palestinian Judaism* commend

---

[39] *Ibid.*, p. 514.
[40] *Ibid.*, p. 544.
[41] *Ibid.*, p. 552.

Sanders for having done his homework in the Jewish sources and for correcting a distorted view of first-century Judaism. There was, however, general criticism of his approach to the comparison of Palestinian Judaism with Pauline Christianity, on the grounds that the categories used ('getting in' and 'staying in') are inappropriate when applied to Judaism. They are not categories which emerge from the Jewish documents themselves, but rather are those shaped by Pauline scholarship.[42] Neusner in particular was critical of this aspect of Sanders' work, saying that 'in regard to Rabbinic Judaism, Sanders' book is so profoundly flawed as to be hopeless and, I regret to say it, useless in accomplishing its stated goals of systemic description and comparison'.[43] But Neusner commends Sanders for making an apologetic for rabbinic Judaism which combats the ignorance and malicious anti-Semitism of other accounts of it.

In 1985 Sanders produced another book, *Paul, the Law, and the Jewish People*,[44] in which he takes up in greater detail the two issues of Paul's attitude to the law, and Paul's relationship to contemporary Judaism.

In the first and longest part of the book Sanders makes three main points about Paul's attitude to the law. (i) When Paul was thinking about how a person enters the body of those who will be saved, it was always by faith in Christ and never by the works of the law. (ii) This then raises the question of the purpose for which God gave the law. Paul's main response was to say that the law was linked with sin in the purposes of God – either to enslave all people under sin that God might have mercy on all alike, or to restrain sin until Christ should come. But in Romans 7 the apostle adopts a different approach. Here it is implied that God's will is that the law be obeyed, but sin uses the law against the purposes of God to bring people into slavery. (iii) When it comes to the behaviour of his converts, Paul expected them to order their lives according to the will of God revealed in Scripture. The only explicit exceptions he makes are circumcision, sabbaths and food laws. While Sanders believes that there is no single unity which accounts for every statement Paul makes about the law, he disagrees with those who want to write off Paul's statements as merely inconsistent. Sanders prefers to say that 'Paul held a limited number of basic

---

[42]*Cf. e.g.* Jacob Neusner, 'Comparing Judaisms', *HR* 18 (1978), pp. 177–191; Thomas F. Best, 'The Apostle Paul and E. P. Sanders: The Significance of Paul and Palestinian Judaism', *ResQ* 25 (1982), pp. 65–74; Nils. A. Dahl and Samuel Sandmel, 'Review of *Paul and Palestinian Judaism: A Comparison of Patterns of Religion* by E. P. Sanders', *RelSRev* 4 (1978), pp. 153–160; W. Horbury, 'Paul and Judaism', *ExpT* 90 (1979), pp. 116–118.

[43]Comparing Judaisms', p. 191.

[44]E. P. Sanders, *Paul, the Law, and the Jewish People* (London: SCM, 1985).

convictions which, when applied to different problems, led him to say different things about the law'. [45] Thus, for example, Sanders says that the greatest shifts in Paul's thought take place in respect of the purpose and function of the law.[46]

In the second and briefer part of the book Sanders addresses the question of Paul's relationship to the Jewish people. Three main points emerge. (i) While Paul conceived of the church in terms of the fulfilment of the promises to Israel, and in that sense it was no new religion, nevertheless in his thought and especially his practice it was a third entity. Gentile and Jew alike were admitted to the body of Christ by faith in him, the admission rite was baptism (not circumcision) and the worship was not that of the synagogue. Gentile believers had to leave behind some of their behavioural patterns, and Jewish believers had to be prepared to give up certain aspects of the law in order to associate with Gentile believers.[47] (ii) Paul's mission was to the Gentiles, not to the Jews (the evidence of Acts that when Paul came to a new city he preached first in synagogues is not supported by the first-hand evidence of his letters).[48] (iii) Paul's persecution at the hands of the Jews signifies that he had not withdrawn from Judaism, otherwise he would not have attended synagogues where he received the forty lashes less one five times, nor would the Jews have administered such punishment if they considered him to be an outsider.[49] (iv) Faced with Israel's rejection of Christ, Paul sought a formula that would keep God's promises to Israel intact, without compromising his insistence on faith in Christ.[50]

Heikki Räisänen

Heikki Räisänen, in an early essay on Paul and the law,[51] argued that, far from resolving problems of the early Christians regarding the law, Paul's own thought about the matter is the real problem. Räisänen identifies ten anomalies in Paul's thought. (i) The concept of law oscillates between the Torah and

---

[45]*Ibid.*, p. 147.

[46]*Ibid.*, p. 149.

[47]*Ibid.*, pp. 171–179.

[48]*Ibid.*, pp. 179–190.

[49]*Ibid.*, pp. 190–192.

[50]*Ibid.*, pp. 192–198.

[51]Heiki Räisänen, 'Paul's Theological Difficulties with the Law', written for the Sixth International Congress on Biblical Studies held in Oxford in 1978, and now conveniently reproduced in the collection *The Torah and Christ: Essays in German and English on the Problem of the Law in Early Christianity* (Helsinki: Finnish Exegetical Society, 1986), pp. 3–24.

something else. (ii) The law is discussed as an undivided whole, yet it is often practically reduced to a moral law. (iii) The law has been abrogated, nevertheless its 'just requirement' (Rom. 8:4) is still in force and is met by Christians. (iv) Nobody can fulfil the law, and yet its requirements are fulfilled even by some non-Christian Gentiles. (v) The power of sin in the world is ascribed to Adam's fall on the one hand (Rom. 5) and to the law on the other (Rom. 7). (vi) The law was given 'for life' (Rom. 7:10), yet it lacked, even theoretically, life-giving power (Rom. 8:3; Gal. 3:21). (vii) The law was only a temporary addition to God's 'testament' (Gal. 3:15ff.), yet a dramatic act on God's part was needed to liberate men from its curse (Gal. 3:13). (viii) Paul's interpretation of the Old Testament in support of his position is arbitrary. (ix) The statement that the law (and only the law, as opposed, say, to the apostolic paraenesis) calls forth and multiplies sin, is problematic, to say the least. (x) Why should one have to fulfil the *whole law* in order to avoid the curse? Why is the possibility of repentance and forgiveness excluded.[52]

In a major work, *Paul and the Law*,[53] Räisänen, having acknowledged his debt to E. P. Sanders, goes on to examine in detail a number of the anomalies in Paul's thought. Paul, like other early Christian writers, takes the Christ event as the starting-point in his approach to the law. But, more than any of the others, he comes to the most radical and negative conclusions concerning the law. His actual attitude to the law amounts to its abrogation. Yet these negative statements are contradicted by other statements which the apostle makes, suggesting that Paul went further in the negative direction than he really intended.[54] Räisänen suggests that it was primarily Paul's missionary experience and the conflict with the 'Judaizers' that led the apostle to develop his radical position in relation to the law. In this context the apostle defended himself against charges that he was not taking the law as a whole seriously because he dispensed with certain of its demands. This led him to make his statements implying global rejection of the law to counteract the charges of unwarranted selectivity.[55]

Räisänen is one who 'calls a spade a spade', and his writings will have to be taken seriously in all subsequent works on Paul and the law. But the question that must be asked is whether it is good enough just to identify the anomalies and conclude that there are irreconcilable tensions in Paul's thought. Such an

---

[52]*Ibid.*, pp. 8–9.

[53]Heikki Räisänen, *Paul and the Law* (Philadelphia: Fortress, 1986).

[54]*Ibid.*, pp. 200–201.

[55]*Ibid.*, pp. 256–263.

approach sticks in the throats of conservatives who might well be accused of wanting to defend Paul's consistency at all costs. But Räisänen could be charged with taking the easy way out by accusing Paul of inconsistencies rather than wrestling with the text of his letters to see if there is not a more positive way of dealing with the anomalies.

James D. G. Dunn

In the essay[56] which marked his first foray into the debate about Paul and the law, James D. G. Dunn, like Heikki Räisänen, acknowledges his indebtedness to E. P. Sanders' book, *Paul and Palestinian Judaism*, for correcting the distorted image of first-century Judaism assumed in much Protestant exegesis. Dunn criticizes Sanders, however, for not taking the opportunity which that monumental work provided. He failed to explore the extent to which Paul's theology could be explained in terms of Judaism's covenantal nomism, being content instead to highlight the difference between Paul's pattern of religion and that of first-century Judaism.[57] Dunn acknowledges the advances Sanders made in his subsequent work, *Paul the Law, and the Jewish People*, but still contends that Sanders has Paul making an arbitrary jump from one system to another. Dunn believes that the new perspective on Paul, pioneered by Sanders, goes much further in making better sense of Paul in his Jewish context than Sanders himself realized.[58]

Dunn bases his own remarks on Galatians 2:16 and contends, against Sanders, that when Paul speaks of the 'works of the law' he has in mind, not all the law demands, but primarily circumcision, food laws and sabbath. These were the characteristic marks of faithful Jews which distinguished them (from the Gentiles), as members of the covenant people of God. Dunn says:

> The conclusion follows very strongly that when Paul denied the possibility of 'being justified by works of the law' it is precisely this basic Jewish self-understanding which Paul is attacking – the idea that God's acknowledgment of covenant status is bound up with, even dependent upon, observance of these particular regulations – the idea that God's verdict of acquittal hangs to any extent on

---

[56]James D. G. Dunn, 'The New Perspective on Paul', *BJRL* 65 (1983), pp. 95–122, now conveniently included in the collection, *Jesus, Paul and the Law: Studies in Mark and Galatians* (Louisville, KY: Westminster John Knox, 1990), pp. 183–206, to which subsequent references are made.

[57]*Ibid.*, p. 186.

[58]*Ibid.*, pp. 187–188.

the individual's having declared his membership of the covenant people by embracing these distinctively Jewish rites.[59]

The coming of Christ had ushered in a new era of fulfilment in which the covenant could no longer be conceived of in Jewish nationalistic or racial terms.

Thus Dunn argues that Paul did not simply make an arbitrary shift to another system of religion when he embraced Christianity. On the contrary, he was making a specific criticism of the first-century Judaism portrayed by Sanders, on the grounds of its exclusivism. Sanders failed to recognize this because he did not appreciate the significance of the expression 'the works of the law' in Paul's thought.

In the introduction to his collection of essays, *Jesus, Paul and the Law*, Dunn acknowledges that in 'The New Perspective on Paul' he 'did not make it clear enough that the "works of the law" do not mean *only* circumcision, food laws and sabbath, but the requirements of the law in general, or, more precisely, the requirements laid by the law on the Jewish people as their covenant obligation and as focussed in these specific statutes'.[60] In a subsequent essay,[61] then, Dunn explores the social function of the law in an attempt to broaden and deepen the argument set out in 'The New Perspective on Paul'. The thrust of Dunn's argument in this later essay is best summed up in his own words:

> The phrase *ta erga tou nomou* belongs to a complex of ideas in which the social function of the law is prominent. The law serves both to identify Israel as the people of the covenant and to mark them off as distinct from the (other) nations. 'Works of the law' denote all that the law requires of the devout Jew, but precisely because it is the law as identity and boundary marker which is in view, the law as Israel's law focuses on these rites which express Jewish distinctiveness most clearly. The conclusion of the previous section is thus confirmed: 'works of the law' refer not exclusively but particularly to those requirements which bring to sharp focus the distinctiveness of Israel's identity.[62]

Dunn argues that this recognition of the social function of the law, and especially the recognition of the 'works of the law' as a summary expression of the law's function as seen from within Judaism, goes a long way towards

---

[59]*Ibid.*, p. 194.

[60]*Ibid.*, p. 4.

[61]James D. G. Dunn, 'Works of the Law and the Curse of the Law (Galatians 3.10–14)', in *ibid.*, pp. 215–236.

[62]*Ibid.*, p. 223.

resolving the tensions and contradictions in Paul's thought encountered by Sanders and Räisänen. In particular, he argues that (i) it resolves the problem of the tension between Paul's negative and positive statements about the law in that it is the social function of the law which attracts his criticisms. Apart from that he is able to recognize the law's positive role. (ii) It shows why all attempts to account for the tensions in Paul's thought by positing a distinction between the ritual and moral aspects in his pronouncements about the law fail. They fail because Paul himself does not defend his position by dividing the law into acceptable and unacceptable elements. Rather, he attacks an attitude to the law as such – one which emphasizes its social function as distinguishing Jew from Gentile.[63]

Dunn's approach to Paul and the law (like Räisänen's and Sanders', but for different reasons) is one that modern interpreters of Paul must take seriously. It is a more sympathetic reading of Paul. It is one that has the apostle interacting in a meaningful fashion with first-century Judaism, and one which does not simply dismiss the apostle's statements about the law as inconsistent.

Recent responses

Lloyd Gaston

Gaston's book *Paul and the Torah*[64] consists of a collection of his essays written over a number of years, to which he has added a 'retrospective introduction'. The thesis of the book is stated in chapter 1 (which bears the same title as the book itself), and following chapters all deal with difficult texts which could be cited against his thesis. Gaston is concerned to deal with the problem of the anti-Semitism which appears to him to lie at the roots of Pauline theology, and in particular the Pauline abrogation of the law, one of the basic pillars of Judaism. He is also concerned about the problem of the apparent misrepresentation involved in Paul's critique of Judaism. Gaston rejects all the more usual resolutions of this problem (the denial of any misrepresentation; Paul attacked not Judaism but Jewish Christians; he attacked those Jews who, according to Acts, sought to frustrate his mission; he was involved with a battle within himself; he was critical of Hellenistic Judaism, but not Palestinian Judaism; he was a theologian of the messianic age in which there will be no more Torah).[65] Instead, Gaston argues, to understand Paul's polemic we need

---

[63] *Ibid.*, pp. 223–225.

[64] Lloyd Gaston, *Paul and the Torah* (Vancouver: University of British Columbia Press, 1987).

[65] *Ibid.*, pp. 19–21.

to recognize the existence of legalistic *Gentile* Judaizers. Paul's letters, all written for Gentile believers, attack not Judaism or Jewish Christians, but Gentile Judaizers. 'Legalism', he says, 'arose as a Gentile problem and not a Jewish problem at all. Salvation and God's grace are for all who are under the covenant and have not cast off the yoke of the Torah, but God-fearers *not* under the covenant must establish their righteousness by the performance of certain works.'[66] When Paul speaks (negatively) about those 'under the law' or of being 'under the law', he is speaking not about Jews or Jewish Christians, but rather about the situation of Gentiles who seek inclusion among the covenant people by placing themselves under the rule of the law.[67] It was against this latter belief, not against Judaism or the practice of Jewish Christians, that Paul employed his polemic. Paul came under the criticism of Jews only when it was believed that he was teaching other Jews to abandon their Judaism, something of which Gaston believes Paul was innocent. He goes so far as to say: 'Had all Israel followed Paul's example, it may be that we would have had a Gentile church loyal to the righteousness of God expressed in Jesus Christ and his fulfilment of the promises to Abraham, alongside an Israel loyal to the righteousness of God expressed in the Torah.'[68]

Stephen Westerholm

In the first part of his book *Israel's Law and the Church's Faith*,[69] Westerholm has provided one of the most readable reviews of the major contributors to the debate on Paul and the law. His survey begins with Luther, then moves on to those who regard Paul's teaching of law and justification as merely a polemic doctrine rather than its real centre (W. Wrede, A. Schweitzer). This is followed by a discussion of those who protest that Paul's views on the law and justification have been presented by perpetrating a distorted view of Judaism. Two scholars represent those who lay the blame for this at Paul's own feet (C. G. Montefiore, H. J. Schoeps), and another represents those who blame his later interpreters (E. P. Sanders). Next, Westerholm describes the work of two scholars (W. G. Kümmel, K. Stendahl) who reject the view that Paul, like Augustine and Luther after him, came to his understanding of law and justification through the experience of a conscience tortured by its inability to

---

[66]*Ibid.*, p. 25.

[67]*Ibid.*, p. 29.

[68]*Ibid.*, p. 33.

[69]Stephen Westerholm, *Israel's Law and the Church's Faith: Paul and his Recent Interpreters* (Grand Rapids: Eerdmans, 1988).

meet the standards of God's law. Rather, they assert, Paul had a robust conscience, and statements in Romans 7 about his inability to keep the law are rhetorical, not autobiographical. This is followed up by a discussion of the work of three scholars, all of whom seek to explain Paul's attitude to the 'righteousness of the law'. While each recognizes that the apostle taught that no-one was justified by means of the works of the law, their assessments of Paul's attitude to the 'righteousness of the law' vary. U. Wilkens believes that Paul saw it as something good, R. Bultmann as something bad, and E. P. Sanders as something indifferent. Westerholm completes his survey with a treatment of three scholars who attempt to explain the apparent inconsistencies in Paul's thought about the law. Two of these (J. Drane, H. Hübner) account for it by suggesting development in Paul's thought, and the third by saying that contradictions and inconsistencies have to be accepted as a constant tension in Paul's thought (Räisänen).

The second part of the book Westerholm devotes to a statement of his own understanding of Paul and the law. This is done in dialogue with a wide range of Pauline scholars, but particularly with Sanders and Dunn, and above all, it seems, with Räisänen. Westerholm begins with matters of definition ('law', 'the law and works', 'the law and faith', 'the law and legalism', and 'the law and the Torah'). He then turns his attention to justification by faith.

Westerholm notes that scholars of the 'new perspective', such as Sanders, Dunn and Räisänen, are all convinced that first-century Judaism did not see salvation as something based on works. He argues that while it is misleading to characterize Judaism as a religion of 'works-salvation', nevertheless obser- vance of the law may be regarded as Israel's path to life. Further, Westerholm stresses that Paul not only implied that his opponents believed that the law serves a soteriological function, but that Paul himself believed that it was given for that purpose. The difference between Paul and his opponents (and Judaism) was not that the apostle argued for salvation by grace whereas his opponents argued for salvation by works. Rather, Paul understood (as his opponents failed to do) that 'the gospel implies the inadequacy of the law to convey life; since, however, divine purposes cannot fail, God's design from the very beginning must have been to grant life by means of faith in Christ, not the law'.[70] Human transgression of the law is the reason the law cannot deliver its promise of life.[71]

If the law cannot deliver its promise of life, then the question of the role of the law in God's scheme of things arises. One way of answering this question is

---

[70]*Ibid.*, p. 150.
[71]*Ibid.*, p. 156.

to say with Schweitzer and others that in Galatians 3:19 Paul implies that law originated with evil angels, and not with God at all. Westerholm maintains that this difficult verse must be interpreted in the wider context of Galatians and other letters of Paul where it is clear that the apostle acknowledges the divine origin of the law.[72] Therefore the question of God's purpose in giving the law must still be explained. Westerholm argues that for Paul God's purpose in giving the law was to transform sins into acts of defiance, to increase the number of sins committed, and to bring about a greater awareness of sin.[73] All this created a deeper bondage of humanity to sin, a necessary prelude to the revelation of God's grace in Christ.

If Paul denies the law any role in soteriology, then it remains to ask whether it has any role in Christian behaviour. Westerholm believes that Paul is consistent in asserting that Christians are no longer under the law. Life in the Spirit replaces obligations to the precepts of the law. Against Räisänen he contends that the facts that Paul's ethical expectations correspond to the moral demands of the law, and that he expects the righteous demand of the law to be fulfilled in them ('fulfilling the law' and 'doing the law' mean different things), do not prove that the Mosaic law is the basis of Paul's ethics.[74]

Frank Thielman

Thielman, in his book *From Plight to Solution*,[75] suggests that, in the light of new information about Judaism, 'It is appropriate to re-examine the possibility that Paul's view of the law owes its origin to an eschatological pattern common within some expressions of Judaism at the time he wrote',[76] rather than to his Christology alone. In particular, he argues that there is evidence in both canonical and non-canonical Jewish literature from the period in which Paul lived which reveals a trend in Jewish thinking about God's dealings with Israel which runs from plight to solution. In some cases at least, this plight was conceived in terms of Israel's inability to keep the law, and the solution in terms of an eschatological future in which Israel, freed from the dominion of sin, will obey the commandants of God.[77] Thielman further argues that a

---

[72]*Ibid.*, pp. 176–179.

[73]*Ibid.*, pp. 179–189.

[74]*Ibid.*, pp. 198–209.

[75]Frank Thielman, *From Plight to Solution: A Jewish Framework for Understanding Paul's View of the Law in Galatians and Romans* (Leiden: Brill, 1989).

[76]*Ibid.*, pp. 26–27.

[77]*Ibid.*, p. 45.

similar pattern underlies Paul's approach to the law in both Galatians and Romans.

Even Galatians does not need to be read as if Paul taught an abrogation of the law in every respect. When he speaks negatively of the law, it is only its function of shutting people up under sin and pronouncing upon them the punishment elicited by their disobedience that he has in mind. When Paul teaches that the Gentiles need not be circumcised or observe calendrical or dietary laws his reasoning is reminiscent of the emphasis upon the superiority of the ethical demands to the ceremonial demands found in the literature of Hellenistic Judaism. On the positive side, Galatians teaches the necessity of fulfilling the law through the love command.[78]

Romans, like Galatians, Thielman argues, is consistent with the 'plight to solution' pattern which he finds in the literature of Judaism of the time. In Romans too, those outside of Christ are in bondage to sin and consequently are unable to fulfil the demands of the law. But in Christ people find forgiveness and are empowered by the Spirit so that they can keep (with the exception of circumcision, dietary and calendrical rules) the commandments of God in a way that was formerly impossible for them.[79]

Accordingly, Thielman concludes, 'Paul's view of the law was neither a new breakthrough which few could understand or accept nor an idea developed *ad hoc* under the pressures of the moment, but was based on familiar ideas and echoed a familiar theme: the period of disobedience would end with the arrival of the eschatological age.'[80]

In a later book,[81] Thielman takes his work on Paul and the law a step further. He believes it is possible to show that Paul's views on the law do form 'a coherent, reasonable and profound theological insight', especially if, in the investigation of the matter, three methodological procedures are followed: (i) Paul's statements should be examined within the context of each letter; (ii) attention should be given also to those letters in which the law is not a bone of contention; and (iii) present-day interpreters of Paul should give attention to the wider cultural contexts in which Paul's own understanding took shape and to their own theological context.[82] In his first chapter Thielman provides a survey of some of the important approaches that have been adopted historically

---

[78]*Ibid.*, p. 86.

[79]*Ibid.*, p. 116.

[80]*Ibid.*, p. 122.

[81]Frank Thielman, *Paul and the Law: A Contextual Approach* (Downers Grove, IL: IVP, 1994).

[82]*Ibid.*, pp. 10–11.

in the interpretation of Paul's understanding of the law, and in the second a discussion of first-century Jewish beliefs about the Mosaic covenant and the law. It is worth citing Thielman's summary of the latter:

> Most Jews believed that the Mosaic covenant distinguished Israel from the surrounding nations, and virtually all Jews believed that it was a gracious sign of God's election. Many believed that Israel lived in a period of punishment for disobedience to the law and awaited a time when God would intervene powerfully to remake the rebellious hearts of his people, live among his people by his Holy Spirit and restore his people's fortunes. Some felt that acquittal before God on the final day would come to those who freely chose to obey God's laws; others believed humanity to be so sinful that true obedience would come only as a result of God's prior work in the human heart.[83]

In successive chapters Thielman makes a detailed examination of all the letters of the Pauline corpus, seeking to allow each letter to speak for itself on the subject of the law. He concludes that Paul was aware that some Jews did believe that cooperation between human effort and God's grace was necessary if one was to be acquitted on the last day. The apostle did not regard all his fellow Jews as legalists, however, nor did he regard Judaism as legalistic in principle. Thielman concludes that Paul believes that most Jews understood that works of the law did not justify. The apostle hoped that, once reminded of the plight of Israel, the Jews would realize that the age of restoration had dawned and the Mosaic covenant had come to an end, and that they would embrace the gospel.[84] Further, Thielman argues, the pattern of Christianity which emerges in the pages of the Pauline letters parallels the pattern of Judaism in the Mosaic law: the experience of grace leads to obedience. More than that, specific demands placed upon the people of God are similar in both cases, especially where Paul appeals to the Mosaic law to settle matters. The puzzle is then why many Jews rejected Paul's gospel if it was so much like Judaism. Thielman believes the reason was that Paul taught that certain of the law's demands need not be observed by Gentiles, in particular circumcision, sabbath-keeping and food laws. Paul continued to read the Mosaic law as scripture, but he interpreted it in unforeseen ways in the light of the gospel.[85] The main difference between Pauline Christianity and first-century Judaism was not found in their respective attitudes to the relationship between God's

---

[83]*Ibid.*, p. 68.
[84]*Ibid.*, pp. 238–239.
[85]*Ibid.*, pp. 240–243.

grace and human effort, but rather in the position of each within salvation history.[86]

Brice L. Martin

Martin's work *Christ and the Law in Paul*[87] begins with a survey of the relevant Pauline data (Galatians; 1 and 2 Corinthians; Romans; Philippians) and of the issues thrown up by the data (the usage of *nomos*; the moral law *versus* the ceremonial law; the origin of the law; the purpose of the law; contradictions in Paul's view of the law; development in Paul's view of the law; the ongoing validity of the law). Martin then treats Paul's understanding of the human problem (involving sin, death, law and flesh) before going on to discuss Paul's solution to the problem (the death and resurrection of Christ). Martin argues that the various emphases (what some call inconsistencies) in Paul's statements about the law are best explained by the differing situations which he addresses. Paul does not change his basic approach with the passage of time, nor do his later statements contradict his earlier ones. Martin says: 'In writing to the Galatians he tends to down play the law because of their attempt to be saved by means of it. In 1 Corinthians he stresses the law and moral values since he is facing an antinomian front. In Romans he gives a carefully balanced statement and assures his readers that he is not an antinomian.'[88] While Paul agrees with the Jewish view that the law originated with God, he rejects the Jewish notion that God gave it in order that salvation might be attained by means of it. On the contrary, the law was given to become part of the human dilemma.[89] Paul's essential difference with Judaism stems from his Christology. To attempt to attain righteousness through the law is to deny the necessity of the death and resurrection of Christ. Through Christ's death, those who belong to him die to sin and the law, so that sin need no longer enslave them and the law no longer condemn them. Paul's view of the law is coherent: 'The negative and positive statements on the law stem from the distinction between the law as a means of salvation and as a way of life for the Christian. To those in Christ the law remains God's law; consequently, they look to the law for instruction (*cf.* 1 Cor. 9:8, 9; 14:21, 34), and empowered by the Spirit they obey it (Rom. 8:4–9). They obey the law not to get saved, or to stay saved, but because they have been saved.'[90]

---

[86]*Ibid.*, p. 245.

[87]Brice L. Martin, *Christ and the Law in Paul* (Leiden: Brill, 1989).

[88]*Ibid.*, p. 155.

[89]*Ibid.*

[90]*Ibid.*, p. 156.

Peter J. Tomson

The argument of Tomson's book, *Paul and the Jewish Law*,[91] is that halakha (the tradition of formulated rules of conduct regulating life in Judaism) is basic to Paul's ethical teaching for *Gentile* Christians. He rejects the three traditional assumptions which have influenced much Pauline scholarship (the centre of Paul's thought is a polemic against the law; the law for Paul no longer had any practical meaning; Jewish literature is not a useful source for explaining Paul's letters). Instead Tomson argues that both the law and Jewish traditions play a significant role in the apostle's ethical instruction for Gentile believers. He identifies Paul as a Hellenistic Pharisee,[92] and one in whose thought halakha is pervasive. While the primary source of Paul's halakha was apostolic tradition, this was supplemented by material from the law and from general Jewish tradition. Halakhic elements abound in 1 Corinthians, in which formal appeal is made by the apostle to Scripture, apostolic tradition and his own apostolic teaching, and in which three informal sources of authority can be identified: Jewish tradition, popular Hellenistic wisdom and informal elements of Christian tradition.[93]

All this has implications for our understanding of Paul's theology of the law and justification. Essentially this theology is related only to the question of the admission of Gentiles to the people of God, and not to commandments for practical living.[94] Paul taught that Gentile Christians were obliged to keep commandments, albeit different ones from those incumbent upon Jewish Christians. The Jews were required to keep the Jewish Law, and the Gentiles the Noachian code (the version of it propagated by Paul).[95]

N. T. Wright

In what appears to be a significant book,[96] Wright argues that Paul, in the light of his understanding of Jesus of Nazareth, has engaged in a major redefinition of the twin Jewish doctrines of monotheism and election, of God and Israel. All this is closely tied up with the story of God and his people which, Paul

---

[91]Peter J. Tomson, *Paul and the Jewish Law: Halakha in the Letters of the Apostle to the Gentiles* (Assen and Maastricht: Van Gorcum; Minneapolis: Fortress, 1990).

[92]*Ibid.*, p. 53.

[93]*Ibid.*, p. 81.

[94]*Ibid.*, p. 269.

[95]*Ibid.*, pp. 271–272.

[96]N. T. Wright, *The Climax of the Covenant: Christ and the Law in Pauline Theology* (Edinburgh: T. and T. Clark, 1991).

believed, reached its climax in the death and resurrection of Christ.

In the first part of his book, which deals with Christology, Wright argues that the idea of Jesus as *the messiah* is fundamental to Paul's thought (the title 'Christ' in the apostle's writings retains the meaning 'messiah', and is not reduced to a mere proper name, as many scholars assume). The messiah is to be understood as an incorporative figure, one in whom the people of God are summed up. Also fundamental to Paul's thought is the belief that Jesus ranks alongside Israel's God, something Wright argues is implicit in three passages in particular (1 Cor. 8; Phil. 2:5–11; Col. 1:15–20).

In the second part of the book, Wright turns his attention to the subject of Paul and the law. He argues that Paul was concerned about the sorry state of Israel. As long as Herod and Pilate ruled over Israel she was still under the curse of the exile, and this was difficult to reconcile with the covenant faithfulness of the God who had chosen her to be his people. Paul believed that the curse of exile reached its climax on the cross when Jesus the Christ, as an incorporative figure, received in full the curse pronounced by the law over a covenant-breaking people. This meant that the restoration could follow, a restoration in which Gentiles too would be invited to share. Justification then is to be understood as the inclusion among the covenant people of God of all those who have faith in Jesus, both Jews and Gentiles.[97]

It had always been God's intention, being one God, to create one family made up of Gentiles as well as Jews. Moses could not be the mediator between God and this family, nor could observance of his law be the mark of that family, because Moses and his law separated the Jews from the Gentiles. Moses and the law had their place, but now with the coming of Christ their time had come to an end; they had fulfilled their purpose.[98] The glory of the old Mosaic covenant has passed away, not because it was bad, but because its temporary purpose has now been accomplished.[99]

In the light of his study, Wright asserts that it has become clear that the actual questions to which Paul sought answers differ from those which his modern interpreters bring to his writings. Paul was concerned

> . . . with the Creator God, with his world, with his people, with his purposes for his world and his people, with his dramatic action in history in bringing those purposes to completion, and so on . . . They are, *mutatis mutandis*, the questions that Paul's

---

[97] *Ibid.*, pp. 2, 156, 214, 255. *Cf. idem*, *The New Testament and the People of God* (Minneapolis: Fortress, 1992), pp. 268–279.

[98] *The Climax of the Covenant*, pp. 162–172.

[99] *Ibid.*, p. 181.

Jewish contemporaries were asking as well: how is God fulfilling the covenant? What is happening to Israel? How is evil being defeated? Why has God apparently done the opposite to what one would have expected? And granted Paul's belief about Jesus and the Spirit as the inauguration of the renewed covenant, further questions were bound to arise, concerning the constitution and maintenance of the new covenant community itself: should Christians keep Torah, and why? What happens when different races come together in the people of God? What has happened to the Jewish dream of the ingathering of the nations? What happens when Christians sin? And so on.[100]

In response to these questions the apostle came to the conclusion that the plight of Israel in the first century (ruled over by Herod and Pilate) was to be explained in terms of Israel's still being under the curse of exile. The solution to this plight Paul came to understand on the road to Damascus, and it radically challenged the normal Jewish way of looking at things. In raising Jesus from the dead the Creator had done for Jesus what he was supposed to do for Israel. This means that the solution to Israel's plight had arrived, but not in the form Israel expected. This in turn led to a more radical understanding of Israel's original plight. By rebelling against the covenant purposes of God she was acting out the primeval sin of Adam, something which came 'to its full flowering in "national righteousness", the meta-sin against which the gospel of the cross struck with its scandalous force', and which resulted in Israel's rejection of that gospel.[101]

Thomas R. Schreiner

In a very recent addition[102] to the monographs on Paul and the law, Schreiner addresses the major issues which are thrown up by the topic. First, he deals with why the works of the law cannot save. He rejects such suggestions as those proposed by Bultmann (human effort to achieve salvation by keeping the law only leads to sin, because that effort itself is already sinful), Sanders (because the solution to the human predicament was found in Christ, then life under the law obviously could not have been the solution) and Dunn (the Jewish notion of national privilege restricted the promises of God to Israel, and the curse of God rests upon those who restrict the promises of God in that

---

[100]*Ibid.*, p. 259.

[101]*Ibid.*, p. 261.

[102]Thomas R. Schreiner, *The Law and Its Fulfilment: A Pauline Theology of Law* (Grand Rapids: Baker, 1993).

way). Instead, Schreiner argues that Paul believed that the works of the law could not save, because the law demands perfect obedience and no-one can obey the law perfectly.[103]

If Paul argued that the law was never intended to provide salvation, what then was the purpose of the law? Schreiner maintains that the apostle believed that God's purpose in giving the law was to increase sin by the multiplication of transgressions to show that no-one could be made righteous by obeying the law.[104]

Schreiner then turns his attention to whether Paul opposes Jewish legalism. While endorsing Sanders' work in so far as it destroys the caricature of Judaism as a religion which had no theology of grace, being rather obsessed with earning merit, Schreiner argues that the apostle did detect legalism in Judaism. It was legalistic because its soteriology was synergistic, *i.e.*, salvation was by God's grace and human works.[105] There was nothing wrong with legalism if the required works could be performed. The problem with legalism is that it rests upon the mistaken view that human beings are good and that their works can be sufficient.[106] Schreiner acknowledges the service done for scholarship by Sanders' refutation of a simplistic view of Judaism which portrayed it as a religion concerned to weigh merits against demerits. He also acknowledges that not every Jew was legalistic (*cf.* Lk. 1:6), but says that all we need to affirm to make sense of Paul's writings is that some Jews lived legalistically, and that some of these became the opponents of Paul (and Jesus!).[107]

In chapters 5 and 6 Schreiner tackles the problem presented by the fact that some Pauline texts appear to claim that some of the commands of the law are normative for Christian behaviour, while others teach that the Mosaic law has been abolished. Schreiner is of the view that one cannot give an unqualified 'yes' or 'no' to the question of the cessation of the law in Paul. The Mosaic law has come to an end in the sense that the promises made to Abraham have begun to be fulfilled with the coming of Christ. This means that laws concerning circumcision, sacrifices and food laws are no longer to be observed literally, because they have found their fulfilment in Christ. The moral demands of the law, however, while also finding fulfilment in Christ, continue to apply.

---

[103]*Ibid.*, p. 44.

[104]*Ibid.*, p. 91.

[105]*Ibid.*, p. 94.

[106]*Ibid.*, p. 98.

[107]*Ibid.*, p. 115.

What is new is that the power to carry out these moral demands is made available through the Spirit.[108]

In chapter 7 Schreiner asks whether, in Romans 2, Paul readmits by the back door the notion of justification by works, which he strongly rejects elsewhere. The key texts are 2:6 (God 'will repay according to each one's deeds') and 2:13 ('For it is not the hearers of the law who are righteous in God's sight, but the doers of the law who will be justified'). Schreiner overcomes the apparent contradiction by saying that 'even though Paul asserts that no one can attain salvation by good works, he also insists that no one can be saved without them'. The saving work of Christ transforms people so that they can now obey the law; something they were previously unable to do. He emphasizes that 'the works that are necessary for salvation, therefore, *do not constitute an earning of salvation but are evidence of a salvation already given*'.[109]

This survey of selected monographs is intended to provide a sample of the more significant studies that have been undertaken on the subject of Paul and the law, and to provide the backdrop to the study of the letters of the Pauline corpus which follows. The many different viewpoints that have been documented in the survey testify to the difficulty involved in describing Paul's understanding of law and justification. This, in turn, should prepare us to expect the apostle's thought on the subject to be both multi-faceted and complex.

---

[108]*Ibid.*, pp. 177–178.
[109]*Ibid.*, pp. 203–204.

2

Galatians

The charter of freedom

Introduction

Galatians is a crucial document for any endeavour to understand Paul's views about the law and justification. In it he combats some form of legalism, but it is not immediately clear what particular form that legalism took. Was it a reliance upon 'works of the law' to be justified in God's sight (instead of reliance upon his free grace)?[1] Or was it observance of certain Jewish national identity markers (circumcision, food laws and sabbath) deemed a minimal requirement to be met by Gentiles who wished to be accepted as members of the true people of God?[2] This, and a number of other key issues related to Paul's understanding of law and justification, are raised by this letter. But, like the rest of Paul's letters, Galatians is not simply an abstract discussion of particular theological themes. Rather, it deals with a concrete pastoral emergency which arose in churches which the apostle had founded. Therefore, any attempt to understand what he says about the law and justification in this letter must be carried out with an appreciation of the nature of that pastoral emergency and Paul's response to it.

---

[1]This was the approach of Luther, and one that has been the predominant Protestant approach until relatively recently, represented, *e.g.*, by such scholars as Weber, Schürer, Bousset and Bultmann.

[2]So, *e.g.*, Dunn, 'The New Perspective on Paul', pp. 95–122; Roman Heiligenthal, 'Soziologische Implikationen der paulinischen Rechtfertigungslehre im Galaterbrief am Beispiel der "Werke des Gesetzes". Beobachtungen zur Identitätsfindung einer frühchristlichen Gemeinde', *Kairos* 26 (1984), pp. 38–53.

The situation in Galatia

Paul's readers

Paul's readers[3] were people who had heard with faith his preaching of the gospel, and as a result had received the Spirit and witnessed miracles performed among them (3:1–5). But more recently they had come to believe that, if they wanted to be true children of Abraham, to be inheritors of his promises, in short to be really the children of God, then they must be circumcised (5:3) and observe days and months and seasons and years (4:11). It is probably fair to sum up by saying that Paul believed that his Gentile Christian readers had accepted the view that to be truly numbered among the people of God, they needed to be circumcised according to the law (5:2–4), and that the law was to have an ongoing role in their lives as believers (3:1–6).

It is important to note that, in summing up the Galatians' position in this way, no particular assumptions have been made concerning what it means to be justified by the law, or what constituted the 'works of the law' by which a person was thought to be justified. It is wrong to assume that the Galatians themselves thought in terms of the observance of all that the law of Moses prescribed, and it is probably wrong also to assume that such observance was being urged upon them.[4] This would seem to be the clear implication of Paul's warning to the Galatians that if they submitted to demands that they be

---

[3]This is not the place to enter upon a detailed discussion of the identity of the Galatian readership of this letter – whether they were members of the churches founded by Paul in the southern part of the Roman province of Galatia on his first missionary journey (South Galatian theory), or members of churches founded in the northern part of the province on his second missionary journey (North Galatian theory). Strong arguments have been made in support of and against both theories, it is therefore wise to hold one's preferred view lightly. The present writer prefers the South Galatian theory, and the arguments in favour of this theory have been ably presented by F. F. Bruce, *The Epistle of Paul to the Galatians: A Commentary on the Greek Text* (NIGTC; Exeter: Paternoster, 1980), pp. 3–19.

[4]Recognizing this fact, Dunn, 'The New Perspective on Paul', pp. 117–118, argues that what was at issue between Paul and his opponents was not whether justification was by faith in Christ or based upon (meritorious) works of the law (the Lutheran view). Rather, it was whether faith in Jesus as the Christ was the all-sufficient mark of a member of the true people of God, or whether this had to be accompanied by the marks of circumcision, and the keeping of the sabbath and food laws. It is true that the expression 'works of the law' seems to have circumcision and observance of days and seasons as its primary reference in Galatians. These were the things the Galatians were being asked to add to their faith in Christ. It does not necessarily follow that Paul's critique of the law in Galatians was restricted to its use to support these identity markers, and there seem to be good grounds for believing it was not. *Cf.* Heikki Räisänen, 'Galatians 2.16 and Paul's Break with Judaism', *NTS* 31 (1985), p. 548.

circumcised, *then* they would be under obligation to fulfil the whole law (5:3). This implication of submitting to circumcision, Paul believed, would have been news to the Galatians. It was apparently not something which they felt obliged to do (at least, not at the time of writing).

The 'troublers' of the Galatians

The Galatian believers did not come unaided to the conclusion that their inclusion among the people of God depended upon 'works of the law', or that the law was to have an ongoing role in their lives as believers. There were in Galatia those whom Paul calls 'troublers' (*hoi tarassontes*, 1:7; *ho tarassōn*, 5:10), who had persuaded the Galatians to accept another gospel (1:6). We have no other evidence apart from Paul's letter to the Galatians upon which to draw in order to build up a picture of their activities and teaching in Galatia. As Paul presents it, their gospel was one which added to the call to faith in Christ the extra demands of submission to circumcision (6:12–13) and the observance of certain other aspects of the law (4:11). Their message appears to have been both legalistic (salvation depends upon works of the law) and nomistic (observance of the law is an indispensable part of Christian living).[5] Hereafter,

---

[5]It is generally accepted that Paul's opponents were 'Judaizers', *i.e.* Jewish Christians who demanded observance of (certain parts of) the law on the part of Gentile believers. Several other viewpoints have, however, been put forward. (i) Paul was waging war on two fronts in Galatians: Judaizers on the one side, and spiritual enthusiasts on the other (a view first propounded by W. Lütgert, *Gesetz und Geist: Eine Untersuchung zur Vorgeschichte des Galaterbriefes* (Gütersloh: Bertelsmann, 1919). This approach offers one way (but not the only way) of explaining why the apostle, having warned against legalism in the first part of his letter, concludes it with a warning about libertinism. (ii) Walter Schmithals, *Paul and the Gnostics* (ET, Nashville: Abingdon, 1972), pp. 13–64 (*cf.* also his 'Judaisten in Galatien?', *ZNW* 74, 1983, pp. 27–58), argues that Paul's opponents were Jewish Christian Gnostics, but Schmithals' arguments have failed to convince. (iii) G. Wagner, 'Les motifs de la rédaction de l'Épître aux Galates', *ETR* 65 (1990), pp. 321–332, argues that Paul's opponents were pagans recently converted to Christianity, who thought that circumcision was a means of attaching themselves to Judaism, the advantage of this being that they would enjoy the security of membership within a *religio licita*. (Wagner's article was not available to me at time of writing. The summary of his view above is based on the entry in *NTA* 35/1, 1991, p. 48.) (iv) Bernard Hungerford Brinsmead, *Galatians – Dialogical Response to Opponents* (SBLDS 65; Chico, CA: Scholars Press, 1982), argues that the diverse elements of Galatians can best be explained if we identify the theology of Paul's opponents as having been drawn from apocalyptic and sectarian Judaism (especially Qumran) which drew upon the methods of 'apologetic' Judaism, and, of course, which was indebted to the early Christian tradition. Brinsmead's methodology, involving extensive 'mirror-reading' of Galatians, has come under criticism (*cf.* John M. G. Barclay, 'Mirror-reading a Polemical Letter: Galatians as a Test Case',

the 'troublers' will be referred to as 'Judaizers', the term by which they are most commonly designated today.

To convince the Galatians to desert Paul and his gospel and accept their gospel, the Judaizers appear to have undermined Paul's apostleship in a number of ways.[6] They said that it was of human origin (*cf.* 1:1), as was his gospel (*cf.* 1:11–12). He had received both from Jerusalem, but had not been faithful to his instructors, because, when he preached the gospel in Galatia, he did not include the demand for circumcision as he did elsewhere (5:11).[7] He omitted the demand for circumcision because he was more interested in pleasing his hearers than in being a faithful servant of Christ (1:10), meaning, presumably, that by watering down the gospel he would make it more palatable for the Galatians, and they would be more likely to accept it.[8]

Paul's response: personal

Independence and authenticity

To win back his converts, Paul had to show that both his apostleship and his gospel had been received independently of the Jerusalem apostles, and therefore any charges that he had not faithfully preached the gospel entrusted to him by them were meaningless. Further, he had to show that his apostleship and gospel were not only received independently of the Jerusalem leaders, but also that they nevertheless recognized both as authentic.

Paul begins his letter to the Galatians by simply denying any dependency upon others as far as his apostleship was concerned: 'Paul an apostle – sent neither by human commission nor from human authorities, but through Jesus

---

JSNT 31, 1987, pp. 82–83) and has therefore not carried the day. It is still best to work with the view that Paul's opponents in Galatians were Judaizers.

[6]These can be inferred from what Paul says in response, as long as caution is exercised so as not to regard everything Paul says as a response to the Judaizers' teaching.

[7]*Cf.* Daniel Hayden King, 'Paul and the Tannaim: A Study in Galatians', *WTJ* 45 (1983), pp. 351–355.

[8]Peder Borgen, 'Paul Preaches Circumcision and Pleases Men', *Paul and Paulinism: Essays in Honour of C. K. Barrett* ed. M. D. Hooker and S. G. Wilson (London: SPCK, 1982), p. 41, rejects as problematic the view that Paul's opponents believed he sought to please men by omitting any demand for circumcision from his preaching, because, according to 5:11, they believed he *still* included it. Borgen suggests that they believed that Paul wished to please the leaders of the Jerusalem church by preaching circumcision, not to please potential converts by omitting it from his preaching. Borgen's objection to the usual view is an important one, but not decisive, because it is possible that Paul's opponents believed that he still normally preached circumcision, but had not done so in Galatia.

Christ and God the Father, who raised him from the dead . . .' (1:1). He makes the same sort of denial of dependency in respect of his gospel: 'The gospel that was proclaimed by me is not of human origin; for I did not receive it from a human source, nor was I taught it, but I received it through a revelation of Jesus Christ' (1:11–12).[9] To support the truth of these denials Paul offers certain evidences.

No immediate visit to Jerusalem after conversion

Paul says in 1:15–17 that when (on the Damascus road) he encountered Christ and was called by God to preach him among the Gentiles, he did not straight away consult with (*prosanethemēn*)[10] other people, nor did he go up to Jerusalem (to consult with) those who were apostles before him, but rather he went into Arabia and then returned to Damascus. By so saying Paul emphasizes that his commission to preach Christ among the Gentiles had come direct from God; he had not received it from others, and he had not needed to have it explained to him by others, especially not by those in Jerusalem.

The purpose of the visit after three years

Paul goes on to say (1:18–24) that it was only after three years that he went up to Jerusalem to 'visit (*historēsai*) Cephas', and that he remained with him for only fifteen days, and did not see (*ouk eidon*) any of the other apostles except James the brother of the Lord (1:18–20). The meaning of *historeō* is 'to visit

---

[9]Paul himself traced both his commissioning as an apostle and the revelation of the gospel back to his Damascus road experience – to the time when, he says, 'God, who had set me apart before I was born and called me through his grace, was pleased to reveal his Son to me, so that I might proclaim him among the Gentiles' (Gal. 1:15–16). This does not mean that all the implications of the gospel were fully apparent to Paul at that time. We must allow for development in his understanding of the gospel's implications as he wrestled with successive problems encountered during his apostolic ministry. *Cf.* Seyoon Kim, *The Origin of Paul's Gospel* (Tübingen: Mohr, 1981), pp. 51–99; J. D. G. Dunn, '"A Light to the Gentiles", or "The End of the Law?"? The Significance of the Damascus Road Christophany for Paul', in *Jesus, Paul and the Law*, pp. 89–107.

[10]BAG gives for *prosanatithēmi* the meaning 'to consult with', and cites parallels in Chrysippus and Diodorus which, as James D. G. Dunn, 'The Relationship between Paul and Jerusalem according to Galatians 1 and 2', *NTS* 28 (1982), pp. 462–463, points out, indicate that it bore a technical sense (of consulting with someone who was a qualified interpreter of a particular matter). Thus, it would appear that Paul denied that he made any attempt, at the time of his call and commission, to consult with any experts about the commission he had received.

for the purpose of coming to know someone'.[11] Such a meaning accords well with Paul's purpose in this passage, *i.e.* to acknowledge that he had made this visit to get to know Cephas, but to deny that the visit should be interpreted to mean that he was dependent upon Jerusalem for his commission and gospel.

The purpose of the visit after fourteen years

Paul relates in 2:1–10 that it was only after fourteen years that he went again to Jerusalem, accompanied by Barnabas and Titus (2:1–2). He went up, he says, 'in response to a revelation' (*kata apokalypsin*), probably stressing that he went because he had been instructed to do so by a revelation from God, and not because he had been called upon by the Jerusalem leaders to do so.[12] Paul acknowledged that the purpose of this visit was very different from that of his

---

[11]See BAG, *ad loc*. There has recently been renewed discussion whether *historeō* can here carry the more precise meaning 'to get information from'. Dunn, 'Paul and Jerusalem', pp. 463–466, argues that this is the case, saying that in 1:18 Paul did not need to maintain his independence of Cephas as far as obtaining information was concerned, seeing that he had already established in 1:16–17 the most important thing, his independence in respect of his commission to preach the gospel to the Gentiles. Otfried Hofius, 'Gal 1:18: *historēsai Kēphan*', *ZNW* 75 (1984), pp. 73–85, rejects this view, however, arguing that the verb means only 'to get to know personally' (*persönlich kennenzulernen*). James D. G. Dunn, 'Once More – Gal 1:18: *historēsai Kēphan*. In Reply to Otfried Hofius', *ZNW*, 76 (1985), pp. 138–139, concedes that '"to get information from Cephas" does push the sense rather hard, and I would accept that the better translation is "to get to know Cephas"', but then argues that '"getting to know Cephas" must, by force of the word and the circumstances of the occasion, have included gaining information about (and indeed from) Peter'.

[12]It has been argued that *kata apokalypsin* here means 'because of the revelation' with the sense 'in defence of the revelation'. *Kata* with the accusative was used with many different nuances in *koinē* Greek, and it did sometimes mean 'because of' (see BAG, '*kata*', II.5.a.d). The only two other uses of *kata apokalypsin* in the New Testament (Rom. 16:25; Eph. 3:3) could be construed in more than one way, and thus provide no clear-cut guide to the way the expression in Gal. 2:2 should be interpreted. Neither of these other uses, however, can be construed as 'because of' with the sense 'in defence of'. This makes it very doubtful that Gal. 2:2 should be interpreted in this way. This option is, nevertheless, adopted in two recent studies: George Howard, *Paul: Crisis in Galatia: A Study in Early Christian Theology* (SNTSMS 35; Cambridge: Cambridge University Press, 1979), pp. 37–39; James Hester, 'The Use and Influence of Rhetoric in Galatians 2:1–14', *TZ*, 42 (1986), pp. 397–398. For the reasons given above, however, it is better to stay with the view that *kata apokalypsin* signifies that Paul went up to Jerusalem on account of another revelation which he had received (so, too Dunn, 'Paul and Jerusalem', p. 467). William O. Walker, Jr, 'Why Paul Went to Jerusalem: The Interpretation of Galatians 2:1–5', *CBQ* 54 (1992), pp. 505–506, argues that the *kata apokalypsin* (v. 2) and *dia de tous pareisaktous pseudadelphous* (v. 4) are syntactically parallel and are both linked to the verb *anabēn* (v. 2), indicating that there were *two* reasons Paul went up to Jerusalem: 'in accordance with a revelation . . . *and* because of the false brothers'.

first visit. He went to Jerusalem this time, not to get to know someone, but to lay before (*anethemēn*)[13] the pillars of the Jerusalem church (James, Cephas and John) the gospel which he preached among the Gentiles (2:2, 6, 9) in order to hear their opinion of it.

Paul had refrained from doing this at the time of his conversion (1:16), but now after many years of missionary service he did so, he says, 'in order to make sure that I was not running, or had not run, in vain' (2:2). This should not be taken to mean that Paul had developed doubts about the validity of his gospel, and therefore needed to be reassured by the Jerusalem leaders. That would fly in the face of the overall thrust of Paul's argument in Galatians 1 – 2. Rather, it is best seen to have a strategic meaning, *i.e.* that without their recognition of his gospel, Paul now realized, his mission would be hampered.

Paul insists, however, that 'those leaders contributed (*prosanethento*)[14] nothing to me' (2:6), presumably meaning that they added nothing to his gospel, neither the demand for circumcision nor the requirement that certain other elements of the law be observed. Furthermore, they recognized that Paul's apostleship to the Gentiles was as authentic as that of Cephas to the Jews, because the same grace of God was at work through both men (2:7–9). The only thing they asked of Paul was that he remember the poor, but he said this was something that he had already been eager to do (2:10).[15] Thus, on the basis of this visit, Paul could inform his readers that his apostleship and his gospel were recognized as authentic by the leaders of the Jerusalem church, even though neither originated with them.[16]

---

[13]The verb *anatithēmi* in the middle voice (as here) has the meaning of laying something before someone for his or her consideration (BAG, *ad loc*). Paul was not merely making known to the Jerusalem leaders the gospel he preached, he wanted to hear their opinion of it as well.

[14]It is difficult to determine the precise nuance of *prosanatithēmi* due to lack of close parallels, but the overall context of Galatians suggests it means to add the extra demands of circumcision and calendrical rules to the gospel (*cf.* discussion in Dunn, 'Paul and Jerusalem', p. 469).

[15]Indicated by his use of the aorist *espoudasa*.

[16]It may be asked why Paul, who was so convinced of the truth of his gospel and the validity of his apostleship, and who stressed his independence of Jerusalem in both these matters, felt it necessary to inform the Galatians about the recognition given by the leaders of the Jerusalem church. Given the situation in Galatia at the time, it would seem that Paul did so because it was something which would 'cut ice' with his readers, even though it was not something he himself regarded as essential (2:6).

The significance of the Antioch incident

In 2:11–14 Paul related an incident that took place at Antioch.[17] Cephas, along with Barnabas, Paul and a number of other Jewish believers, were sharing food with Gentile believers before certain men of the circumcision party arrived from James. When they arrived, Cephas separated himself from the Gentile believers, being afraid of those of the circumcision party. The other Jewish believers, and even Barnabas, were carried along with Cephas' action.[18] Paul's response to all this was to take Cephas to task publicly for such behaviour, which he believed was not consistent with the gospel. The effect of Cephas' action, Paul says, was to 'compel the Gentiles to live like Jews' (*ioudaizein*) (2:14).[19]

---

[17]In recent years a lot of study has been devoted to this incident. *Cf. e.g.* Karlfried Froelich, 'Fallibility Instead of Infallibility? A Brief History of the Interpretation of Gal. 2:11–14', *Teaching Authority and Infallibility in the Church*, ed. Paul C. Empie, T. Austin Murphy, and Joseph A, Burgess (Minneapolis: Augsburg, *c.* 1980), pp. 259–269; Dieter Lührmann, 'Abendmahlsgemeinschaft? Gal. 2:11ff', *Kirche* (Festschrift for Gunther Bornkamm), ed. Dieter Lührmann and Georg Strecker (Tübingen: Mohr, 1980), pp. 271–286; J. D. G. Dunn, 'The Incident at Antioch (Gal.2:11–18)', *JSNT* 18 (1983), pp. 3–57; J. L. Houlden, 'A Response to James D. G. Dunn', *JSNT* 18 (1983), pp. 58–67; Rabbi Dan Cohn-Sherbok, 'Some Reflections on James Dunn's "The Incident at Antioch (Gal. 2:11–18)"', *JSNT* 18 (1983), pp. 68–74; Traugott Holtz, 'Der antiochenische Zwischenfall (Galater 2.11–14)', *NTS* 32 (1986), pp. 344–361; Willi Marxsen, 'Sündige Tapfer. Wer hat sich beim Streit in Antiochen richtig verhalten?', *EvK* 20/2 (1987), pp. 81–84; André Méhat, '"Quand Képhas vint à Antioche . . ." Que s'est-il passé entre Pierre et Paul?', *LumVie* 192 (1989), pp. 29–43.

[18]It is not clear what this table fellowship (before the men from James arrived) would have involved for Cephas and the other Jewish believers. Did it involve a total neglect of restraints as far as clean and unclean foods were concerned? And so did the men from James bring with them the Jerusalem decrees (*cf.* Acts 15:28–29) and demand that they be observed? This is the view argued by David R. Catchpole, 'Paul, James and the Apostolic Decree', *NTS* 23 (1977), pp. 428–444. Or had it involved some compromise on the part of both Gentile and Jewish believers? Had the Gentiles agreed to observe certain basic food laws, and on this basis had the Jewish believers agreed to share table fellowship with them? And so did the men from James then demand a far more scrupulous observance of dietary rules out of fear of reprisals from unbelieving Jews in turbulent times? This is the position argued by Dunn, 'The Incident at Antioch', pp. 31–34. Cohn-Sherbok, 'Some Reflections', pp. 69–70, argues that despite the evidence put forward by Dunn, there is no certainty that such a fear motivated Jews generally or those of the new Jewish sect (Christianity) to insist on the observance of the food laws. They would have done this simply because that is what Judaism demands.

[19]The verb *ioudaizein* is found only here in the New Testament, but was used elsewhere (*e.g.* Est. 8:17 [LXX], Josephus, *Wars* 2.454) to mean 'live like a Jew' or 'adopt Jewish customs'; *cf.* BAG, *ad loc.*; Hans Dieter Betz, *Galatians: A Commentary on Paul's Letter to the Churches in Galatia* (Hermeneia; Philadelphia: Fortress, 1979), p. 112, n. 487.

This passage contains much that is germane to our overall investigation, and we shall return to it again. At this point it is sufficient to observe that it functions as a dramatic illustration of the fact that Paul was in no way dependent upon the Jerusalem pillars, least of all Cephas.[20]

Integrity

Paul's insistence that his apostleship and gospel were received independently of the Jerusalem church was intended to undermine any charge that he was unfaithful to a Jerusalem commission in his preaching of the gospel. But two other accusations related to that charge still needed refutation if the Galatians were to be won back to Paul's gospel.

Not a watered-down gospel

Paul had to refute the accusation that the gospel he preached to the Galatians was but a watered-down version of what he preached elsewhere. In other places, the Judaizers asserted, Paul did preach the need for circumcision as well as faith in Christ, but not in Galatia. The apostle's response to this charge was to ask his readers why, if he still preached circumcision,[21] he was still being persecuted. If his gospel included the demand for circumcision, then its offence to the Jews would be removed, and he would no longer be suffering persecution

---

[20]Nicholas Taylor, *Paul, Antioch and Jerusalem: A Study in Relationships and Authority in Earliest Christianity* (JSNTSup 66; Sheffield: JSOT, 1992), pp. 135–139, goes even further, arguing that, as a result of Paul's confrontation with Peter in Antioch and his rejection of the authority of the Jerusalem church, Paul was actually isolated from the Jerusalem leaders.

[21]This question raises a number of issues. First, it seems to imply that there was a time when he did preach circumcision, even though he did so no longer. If this were the case, it must be asked when had he preached circumcision. Did he do so in a pre-conversion proselytizing mission (so, *e.g.* Bruce, *Galatians*, p. 236), or in an earlier phase of his mission as a Christian apostle (so, *e.g.* Francis Watson, *Paul, Judaism and the Gentiles: A Sociological Approach*, SNTSMS; Cambridge: Cambridge University Press, 1986, p. 30)? Second, the text implies that Paul's opponents said that he was still preaching circumcision. Does this reflect a misunderstanding about his missionary preaching on the part of his opponents? Were they labouring under a genuine misapprehension about Paul's preaching? Did they believe that it was his normal practice to include a demand for circumcision in his message, but for certain practical reasons he had not done so in Galatia? So, *e.g.* Howard, *Crisis in Galatia*, pp. 8–10. Or had they misinterpreted reports of Paul's ethical preaching, understanding it along the lines of Philo's teaching about the circumcision of the heart which had to be accompanied by physical circumcision? So, Catchpole, 'Paul, James and the Apostolic Decree', pp. 428–444.

at their hands (5:11). The clear assumption behind Paul's question is that he was still suffering, which meant that he was not preaching circumcision elsewhere, and therefore the Galatians had not been given a watered-down version of the gospel.

Not seeking human approval

Second, he had to respond to the closely related charge that he was seeking human approval. Thus, Paul asks his readers: 'Am I now seeking human approval, or God's approval? Or am I trying to please people?' and adds, 'If I were still pleasing people, I would not be a servant of Christ' (1:10). This response follows on immediately after Paul's anathematizing of anyone who preaches another gospel (1:8–9). This suggests that those who made the charge were the preachers of another gospel. If this was the case, then it is probable that Paul's 'seeking human approval' was seen by them to be reflected in this watering-down of the gospel by omitting from it any demand for circumcision. This, they probably said, he did to make the gospel more palatable in the hope of securing more converts.

Paul's response was basically to ask how he could possibly be doing what he was accused of, for, if he were, he would not be a true servant of Christ. Taken at face value, it is difficult to see how Paul's response does any more than repeat, in question form, the charge made, and then state the conclusion which the Judaizers themselves had reached. If it is taken as an ironic question, however, then it was clearly expected to elicit an emphatic denial, and therefore would function as a strong refutation of the charge. This is the way it should probably be read.[22] Paul was not giving a reasoned response, but rather making an ironic retort, to the charge.

The ulterior motives of the Judaizers

Paul not only defends his own integrity, he also attacks the integrity of his opponents. He exposes what he believes are their ulterior motives.

---

[22]Betz, *Galatians*, pp. 54–55, points out the ironic nature of the question, and documents the rhetorical background in Greek literature. But *cf.* George A. Kennedy, *New Testament Interpretation through Rhetorical Criticism* (Chapel Hill: University of Carolina Press, 1984), p. 148, who sees in v. 10 Paul's 'calling attention to the fact that his proem does not seek favor with the audience. The verse is a written aside which contributes to his ethos by its candor.'

They wanted to end Paul's friendship with the Galatians

Paul says the Judaizers had ulterior motives in seeking to establish friendship with the Galatians (4:17–18). In previous verses (13–15) he reminds the Galatians of the depth of the friendship they had enjoyed with him in former days, and then, continuing the use of friendship language in verses 17–18, goes on to expose the ulterior motives of the Judaizers in courting the friendship of the Galatians. He concedes that it is a good thing to have one's friendship sought, as long as it is 'for a good purpose' (*en kalō* 4:18), but he accuses the Judaizers of acting 'for no good purpose' (*ou kalōs*) in seeking their friendship. They wanted to shut the Galatians out from their friendship with Paul, in order that they (the Judaizers) might then establish friendship with them instead (4:17).[23]

They wanted to escape persecution

Paul also asserted that the Judaizers had ulterior motives in wanting the Galatians to be circumcised. They wanted this, he says, only so that they themselves might boast in the Galatians' flesh and so escape persecution on account of the cross of Christ (6:12). What this meant is that the Judaizers themselves would escape persecution from their unbelieving compatriots if they could show that the Gentile believers with whom they were associating were actually proselytes, because they had submitted to circumcision.

Paul's response: theological evaluations

It was not enough for Paul to assert the independence and authenticity of his gospel, and to expose the ulterior motives of the Judaizers. He had to convince his readers that justification was independent of works of the law, and that the law had no regulatory role to play in the life of believers. In doing so, the apostle sets before his readers his theological evaluation of two incidents.

Titus' experience in Jerusalem

In the company of Barnabas and Titus, Paul made a visit to Jerusalem in order to lay his gospel before the leaders of the church there (2:2). During this visit certain 'false believers' brought pressure to bear to have Titus, who was a

---

[23]*Cf.* Betz, *Galatians*, pp. 229–233; Bruce, *Galatians*, pp. 211–212; Richard N. Longenecker, *Galatians* (WBC 41; Dallas: Word, 1990), pp. 193–195.

Greek believer, circumcised (2:4).[24] But Paul and his companions did not give in to this pressure (2:5), and Titus 'was not compelled to be circumcised' (2:3).[25] Paul seems to have inserted the description of this incident (rather awkwardly) into the account of the visit to Jerusalem in order to present it as a precedent with important theological implications. If circumcision of Gentile believers was not required even in the mother church at Jerusalem, then it could not be argued that circumcision was a necessary prerequisite for justification, or a necessary part of Christian obedience elsewhere. Accordingly, circumcision should certainly not be required of Gentile believers in the churches of Galatia.

The Antioch incident

The incident itself (2:11–14) was described above, where Paul's claims to independence of Jerusalem (and Cephas) were discussed. It is Paul's theological evaluation of that incident (its implications for justification and the role of the law in Christian living) which now needs to be explored. Paul sets this out in a very compact way in 2:15–21.

> We ourselves are Jews by birth and not Gentile sinners; yet we know that a person is justified not by the works of the law but through faith in Jesus Christ. And we have come to believe in Christ Jesus, so that we might be justified by faith in Christ, and not by doing the works of the law, because no one will be justified by the works of the law. But if, in our effort to be justified in Christ, we ourselves have been found to be sinners, is Christ then a servant of sin? Certainly not! But if I build up again the very things that I once tore down, then I demonstrate that I am a transgressor. For through the law I died to the law, so that I might live to God. I have been crucified with Christ; and it is no longer I who live, but it is Christ who lives in me. And the life I now live in the flesh I live by faith in the Son of God, who loved me and gave himself for me. I

---

[24]Martin Hengel, *The Zealots. Investigation into the Jewish Freedom Movement in the Period from Herod I until 70 A.D.* (ET, Edinburgh: T. and T. Clark, 1989), pp. 197–200, shows how compulsory circumcision was part of the zeal for the law and the sanctuary manifested by the Zealot movement in the period. Robert Jewett, 'The Agitators and the Galatian Congregation', *NTS* 17 (1970–71), pp. 204–206, builds on Hengel's work by suggesting that it was fear of the Zealot movement that motivated the agitators in Galatia to demand that Paul's converts be circumcised.

[25]It has often been noted that this expression is ambiguous. It could mean (i) that Titus was not circumcised, or (ii) that Titus, while not being compelled to submit to circumcision, did so voluntarily. The context clearly seems to demand the former alternative, because the thrust of Paul's argument would be undercut if Titus were circumcised (albeit voluntarily) to appease the false brothers, and if that became known in Galatia.

do not nullify the grace of God; for if justification comes through the law, then Christ died for nothing.

This passage, the subject of keen debate in recent years,[26] can be seen as a continuation of what Paul said to Cephas, or at least the gist of it,[27] and as such can be divided into three parts: (i) verses 15–16, the matters upon which Paul and Cephas agreed, (ii) verses 17–20, the matters about which they disagreed, and (iii) verse 21, a concluding denial by Paul.[28] Each of these parts will be discussed in turn.

Matters upon which Paul and Cephas agreed

Grouping himself with Cephas,[29] Paul said they both knew that 'a person is

---

[26]*Cf.*, *e.g.*, Jan Lambrecht, 'The Line of Thought in Gal 2.14b–21', *NTS* 24 (1978), pp. 484–495; Arland J. Hultgren, 'The *Pistis Christou* Formulation in Paul', *NovT* 22 (1980), pp. 248–263; René Kieffer, *Foi et Justification à Antioche; Interprétation d'un conflit (Ga 2, 14–21)*, LD 111 (Paris: Cerf, 1982); Dunn, 'The New Perspective on Paul', pp. 95–122; Räisänen, 'Paul's Break with Judaism', pp. 543–553; Charles H. Cosgrove, 'Justification in Paul: A Linguistic and Theological Reflection', *JBL* 106 (1987), pp. 653–670; R. G. Hammerton-Kelly, 'Sacred Violence and "Works of Law". "Is Christ Then an Agent of Sin?" (Galatians 2:17)', *CBQ* 52 (1990), pp. 55–75.

[27]Hammerton-Kelly, 'Sacred Violence', p. 61, assumes that it is a continuation of what Paul said to Cephus in Antioch. Dunn, 'The New Perspective on Paul', p. 104, believes that 2:15–16 reflects the line of argument Paul used in Antioch, though probably not a repetition of the precise words. So too John M. G. Barclay, *Obeying the Truth: A Study of Paul's Ethics in Galatians* (Edinburgh: T. and T. Clark, 1988), p. 76. Bruce, *Galatians*, p. 136, appears to adopt essentially the same approach when he says that Paul 'summarizes his rebuke to Peter and then develops its implications, thus passing smoothly from the personal occasion to the universal principle, from *Individualgeschichte* to *Weltgeschichte*'. But *cf.* Franz Mussner, *Der Galaterbrief* (HTKNT 9; Freiburg: Herder, 1974), p. 167, who appears to regard 2:15–21 as a general theological statement expressing Paul's view about the true situation of Jewish believers *vis-à-vis* the law and justification.

[28]This helpful analysis is suggested by Longenecker, *Galatians*, pp. 82–83, following substantially Betz, *Galatians*, p. 114. But *cf.* Lambrecht, 'The Line of Thought in Gal 2.14b–21', pp. 494–495, who argues that v. 17 belongs with vv. 15–16, as it extends the reasoning of those verses, and that vv. 18–21 form a unit in which we find, not an explanation of what was said in v. 17, but a relatively new train of thought. *Cf.* also the later article by Lambrecht, 'Once Again Gal 2, 17–18 and 3, 21,' *ETL* 63 (1987), p. 149, where he argues again for a break between v. 17 and v. 18.

[29]If it is not with Cephas that Paul grouped himself here, then it must have been with other Christian Jews (*cf.* William J. Dalton, 'The Meaning of "We" in Galatians', *AusBR* 38, 1990, pp. 42–44). Paul was not grouping himself generally with those who were Jews by birth, implying that they too knew that justification was not by works of law but by faith. While there may have been such a Jewish belief, it is not what Paul was talking about here. He had in mind a very specific form of faith, faith *in Jesus Christ*, and that was not something shared by first-century Jews in general (a fact noted also by Räisänen, 'Paul's Break with Judaism', p. 546).

justified not by the works of the law but through faith in Jesus Christ' (2:16).[30] Thus Paul could appeal to this agreement against the teaching of the Judaizers in Galatia, who were insisting that only those who were circumcised could be accepted as children of God.

Excursus: 'the works of the law' in Galatians

In the context of Galatians it would seem, on first reading at least, that the expression 'the works of the law' denotes primarily circumcision (and possibly the observance of calendrical rules). But not everyone believes this is really the case.[31]

Traditionally, Protestant exegesis since the Reformation has understood 'the works of the law' in Paul to denote works by which Jews sought to amass merit before God, and so be justified. In the twentieth century it has even been suggested that it was the very attitude behind such an attempt that was sinful. Even if people could carry out all that the law demanded, they would not be justified because the underlying attitude itself was sinful.[32]

In the twentieth century there has also been a long tradition of protest (which went unheeded for a long time) against this portrayal of Jewish belief,[33] but more recently New Testament scholars have recognized that first-century Judaism was not, in principle, a religion in which salvation was based upon works of the law. Now efforts are being made to exegete Paul's references to 'works of the law' in new ways.

Dunn draws attention to the social function of the law for the Jewish people. Their observance of the law was the primary thing which distinguished them from the Gentiles, and in particular those observances which were more overt: circumcision, sabbath and dietary rules. These functioned as observable identity markers, and had become the ground of Jewish boasting. Paul attacks their misplaced emphasis on the 'outward and physical'; he does not attack the law as such, or the observance of the law by Jewish Christians. What he did

---

[30]Taking the genitive of *pisteōs* as objective. *Cf.* Hultgren, 'The *Pistis Christou* Formulation', pp. 248–263.

[31]Thomas Schreiner, '"Works of Law" in Paul', *NovT* 33 (1991), pp. 217–244, discusses in detail the ways in which the phrase 'works of law' has been interpreted in recent years.

[32]So, *e.g.*, Rudolph Bultmann, *Theology of the New Testament* 1 (ET, London: SCM, 1952), p. 264. Schreiner, '"Works of Law" in Paul', pp. 219–220, documents the many scholars who have followed Bultmann in this respect.

[33]Outstanding among the earlier protesters were Montefiore, Moore, Schoeps, Davies, Stendahl and Sandmel.

attack was their understanding of the works of the law which meant that righteousness was defined in exclusively Jewish terms, and so excluded Gentiles, unless they carried out the works of the law (understood in this way).[34]

The strength of Dunn's approach is that it takes note of the fact that the works of the law in view in Galatians involved at least circumcision, calendrical rules (including sabbaths) and possibly dietary rules as well. It was these things, the Judaizers said, that must be observed if people wished to be true children of Abraham and inheritors of the promises made to him. What is open to question, however, is whether Paul's critique of the Judaizers' teaching begins and ends with an attack on this sort of understanding of the works of the law.

The evidence of Galatians seems to indicate that Paul's critique of the law was far more thoroughgoing than this. It was not restricted to a mere misunderstanding of the law.[35] He believes that the coming of Christ had put an end to the role of the law as a restraining force as far as believers were concerned. In 3:23–25 Paul speaks about the time before faith came, when 'we' were under the law's guardianship, but when faith came 'we' were no longer under it. The guardianship of the law involved restraint of the Jewish people in a wide range of religious, moral and ethical matters, as well as requiring circumcision and the observance of sabbaths and food laws. When Paul referred to the works of the law, then, he had something more than Jewish identity markers in mind. The works of the law are the carrying out of all those things which the law requires.[36] This would seem to be the implication of Paul's words in 3:10: 'For all who rely on the works of the law are under a curse; for it is written, "Cursed is everyone who does not observe and obey all the things written in the book of the law."'

We seem, then, to be on the horns of a dilemma. The view that Paul regarded the works of the law as sociological identity markers is not completely

---

[34]'The New Perspective on Paul', pp. 107–111; see his further development of the idea in 'Works of the Law', pp. 219–225. A similar approach is adopted by Heiligenthal, 'Soziologische Implikationen', pp. 38–53.

[35]Räisänen, 'Paul's Break with Judaism', pp. 543–553, argues that 'Paul's critique of the law is far more radical than Dunn allows' (p. 544). He points out that just a few verses later Paul spoke of dying to the law that he might live to God (2:19), a statement whose meaning can hardly be exhausted in the notion of a change of attitude to the law as identity marker (p. 548).

[36]David Flusser, ' "Durch das Gesetz dem Gesetz gestorben" (Gal 2, 19)', *Judaica* 43 (1987), p. 34, says that in Judaism the works of the law belong organically and inseparably with the law itself, and the law is actualized only when its demands are carried out. In other words, the 'works of the law' are the carrying out of the demands of the law. So also Heikki Räisänen, *Paul and the Law* (Philadelphia: Fortress, 1986), p. 177; Schreiner, ' "Works of Law" in Paul', pp. 232–244.

satisfying. To say that Paul regarded the works of the law as good works done to amass merit is to have him misrepresent Judaism, for in principle Judaism was not a religion in which the law was observed for this reason, but simply because it was required under the terms of the Mosaic covenant.[37] To escape the horns of this dilemma, it is probably best to say that Paul's argument was not with Judaism in principle, and certainly not with the religion of the Old Testament, but with those who, by the demands they were placing upon his Galatian converts, were insisting that salvation did depend upon the observance of certain demands of the law.

Matters about which Paul and Cephas disagreed

Paul and Cephas agreed about rejecting legalism (*i.e.* that fulfilling the demands of the law was not necessary for justification), but they disagreed on the matter of nomism (*i.e.* that those who had been justified by faith were required to observe the demands of the law as part of their ongoing Christian obedience).[38] Paul expresses this disagreement in the question: 'But if, in our effort to be justified in Christ, we ourselves have been found to be sinners, is Christ then a servant of sin? Certainly not!' (2:17). This question has been interpreted in a number of ways.

First, it has been interpreted to mean that when Jewish Christians, depending upon Christ for justification, ceased to observe all that the law demanded (*e.g.* by eating with Gentile believers), they found themselves branded as sinners by the law, and thus no better than Gentiles (*cf.* 2:15). Thus it could be said that Christ was a servant of sin in so far as it was faith in him which turned them into transgressors. To such a preposterous suggestion Paul responds, 'Certainly not!' He then goes on to explain that it is only when Jewish believers re-erect for themselves the jurisdiction of the law that they become transgressors of it (2:18). But in fact Jewish believers need not fear being branded sinners by the law, because in Christ they have died to any relationship to the law (2:19).[39]

---

[37]*Cf.* Cohn-Sherbok, 'Some Reflections', p. 70.

[38]Longenecker, *Galatians*, pp. 88, 95–96, makes this helpful distinction between legalism and nomism and I am indebted to him for much of what follows in the treatment of vv. 17–20. This approach assumes that, at this point, Paul has in mind, not primarily his opponents, the Judaizers, but Cephas who agrees with him about legalism but disagrees about nomism. *Cf.*, however, Gijs Bouwman, '"Christus Diener der Sünde". Auslegung von Galater 2,14b–18', *Bijdr* 40 (1979), p. 54, who argues that literary analysis of the passage suggests that v. 15 reflects the objections of Paul's imaginary opponents.

[39]*Cf.* Barclay, *Obeying the Truth*, pp. 79–81.

Second, the passage has been interpreted in the light of the supposed libertine tendencies of the Galatians themselves (*cf.* 5:13–26). In this case verses 17–20 would be Paul's response to assertions that it was his law-free gospel which had allowed the Galatian believers to indulge in a licentious lifestyle, and so his Christ was a servant of sin. Paul's response would then be to acknowledge that while we (a rhetorical softening by identifying himself with those whom he seeks to correct) were seeking to be justified in Christ, we were found (sadly) to be guilty of a sinful lifestyle. But does this mean that Christ is a servant of sin? God forbid! Longenecker, who espouses this view, expresses it as follows: 'For, Paul insists, to go back to the law (as a Christian) after having finished with the law (for both acceptance before God and living a life pleasing to him) is what really makes one a law breaker – which, of course, sounds paradoxical, but is what happens if one rejects legalism but still espouses nomism.'[40]

Third, the passage has been interpreted by Hammerton-Kelly in yet another way. His interpretation is presented in the paraphrase which he offers:

> Now if we Jews, you and I, Peter, who are seeking to be justified in Christ discover that we are living like 'Gentile sinners,' does that not make Christ the servant of sin? Of course it does, and because that is an absurd notion, you must see firstly, that the Gentiles are not sinners *en masse* and secondly, that your own action in withdrawing from them is wrong. By erecting again the wall of separation between Jew and Gentile (*oikodomein*) you have, on the Jewish premise that the Gentiles are sinners, made Christ the servant of sin who, in turn, made us transgressors, because it is at his behest we live as Gentiles.[41]

Hammerton-Kelly detects palpable irony in Paul's reference to 'Gentile sinners' in 2:15, and this irony carries over into 2:17–18, so that it represents the *reductio ad absurdum* of the position reflected there. It is absurd to say that Gentiles in Christ are sinners (in the sense of those who have no place among God's people). It is just as absurd to say that Jewish Christians who share table fellowship with them are sinners. Therefore it is equally absurd to say that Christ is the servant of sin because it is at his behest that Jewish Christians share table fellowship with Gentile believers.

---

[40]*Galatians*, p. 90. This interpretation involves penetrating insight into human psychology, and enables Longenecker to take into consideration both the nomistic and libertine tendencies of the Galatians. The weakness of this approach is that it does not tie the argument of 2:15–21 in with the Antioch incident described in 2:11–14, but it must be admitted that Longenecker is not concerned to do this, because he treats 2:15–21, not as a continuation of Paul's account of the Antioch incident, but as his *propositio*.

[41]'Sacred Violence', p. 61.

While Hammerton-Kelly's approach makes sense of the passage, it is nevertheless doubtful whether Paul was actually using irony here to effect a *reductio ad absurdum*. If so, it would involve a unique use of the characteristic Pauline expression, 'Certainly not!' (*mē genoito*), which is otherwise reserved for straightforward indignant responses to the unthinkable.[42] And as the passage yields good sense when *mē genoito* is read in the normal way, there would seem to be insufficient reason to posit a unique ironic use here.

The first of these interpretations appears preferable, as it presents the fewest problems and relates the text firmly to the historical situation. No matter which of these interpretations is adopted, however, the area of disagreement between Paul and Cephas is highlighted. It was not a disagreement over legalism (whether the observance of the law was necessary for justification). This was the issue between Paul and the Judaizers, and he could appeal to Cephas in support of his position on this issue. Rather, the disagreement was over nomism (whether those who had been justified by faith had then to fulfil all the demands of the law). Paul argued that the law was not the regulatory norm for Christian living, for Christians had died to the law (ending their relationship with it) so that they might live to God (v. 19).

Concluding denial

Paul concludes 2:15–21 with a denial: 'I do not nullify the grace of God; for if justification comes through the law, then Christ died for nothing' (v. 21). There are a number of ways in which this verse has been understood. First, Paul is denying a charge made by his Judaizing opponents to the effect that his law-free gospel had set at nought the covenant grace of God to Israel involving the giving of the law. In this case v. 21b functions as a *reductio ad absurdum* of the charge, based upon the foundational truth of Christianity, for if the charge were correct, then Christ's death would have been pointless.[43]

Second, Paul is levelling a charge against his opponents, saying in effect: 'Far from nullifying the grace of God revealed in the death of Christ for me (*cf.* v. 20), my gospel highlights it. It is the preaching of justification through

---

[42]So, Longenecker, *Galatians*, p. 94. Following Betz, *Galatians* p. 126, he points out that the *propositio* of an apologetic speech often concludes with a spirited denial of the charge against which the speaker is defending himself.

[43]So Heinrich Schlier, *Der Brief an die Galater* (KEK; Göttingen: Vandenhoeck und Ruprecht, 1962), pp. 103–104. Bruce, *Galatians*, p. 146, also adopts essentially this view, only he says that Paul is not primarily contrasting himself with his opponents, but with anyone who pleads the validity of the law after the coming of Christ.

(works of) the law which nullifies the grace of God, for on that preaching Christ's death was for nought (*cf.* v. 21).'

Sanders regards verse 21 as a key text for understanding Paul's rejection of the law. It is precisely because it would make Christ's death unnecessary that Paul rejects the possibility of justification by works of the law.[44] While it is debatable whether it was his understanding of the death of Christ that led Paul to reject justification by works of the law, it was at least an important corollary of his understanding of it. And this corollary he brings forward to show that the Judaizers' argument (that justification was dependent upon the works of law) is unacceptable.

In concluding this section on the Antioch incident, it is important to ask why Paul was so hard on Cephas. After all, Cephas was only behaving in Antioch in the same way as the Jewish believers in Jerusalem behaved. It would seem that Paul was so hard on him because what was merely nomistic behaviour on Cephas' part was putting pressure on the Gentile believers to think legalistically about the basis of their inclusion among the people of God.

Paul's response: theological arguments

In the passage 3:1 – 4:31 Paul brings forward a number of arguments to refute the view that justification depends upon works of law and that law observance is an integral part of Christian living.

It has been suggested that 3:1 – 4:31 functions rhetorically as a *probatio* or proof supporting a preceding *propositio* or thesis (2:15–21).[45] Even so, 3:1 – 4:31 is not easy to analyse, and recent interpreters have done their analyses in different ways.[46] Irrespective of the way this section is analysed, it contains a

---

[44]*Paul and Palestinian Judaism*, p. 482.

[45]So Betz, *Galatians*, pp. 19–22; François Vouga, 'La construction de l'histoire en Galates 3 – 4', *ZNW* 75 (1984), pp. 261–262. Longenecker, *Galatians*, pp. 97–98, and Joop Smit, 'Naar een nieuwe benadering van Paulus' brieven. De historische bewijsvoering in Gal 3, 1–4, 11', *TijdT* 24 (1984), pp. 231–232, see the *probatio* ending at 4:11.

[46]E.g., Betz, *Galatians*, p. viii, identifies seven elements in the section: A. The First Argument: The Galatians' Experience of the Spirit (3:1–5); B. The Second Argument: God's Promise to Abraham (3:6–14); C. The Third Argument: Common Human Practice of Law (3:15–18); D. A Digression about the (Jewish) Torah (3:19–25); E. The Fourth Argument: Christian Tradition (3:26 – 4:11); F. The Fifth Argument: Friendship (4:12–20); G. The Sixth Argument: The Allegory of Sarah and Hagar (4:21–31). Vouga, 'La construction', p. 261, adopts virtually the same analysis. Longenecker, *Galatians*, pp. 97, 186–187, while recognizing, for the most part, similar literary units in this section, nevertheless puts forward a different overall analysis in accordance with his view that 3:1 – 4:11 provides proofs of the *two* parts of the thesis set out in 2:15–21, *i.e.*, 3:1–18

number of theological arguments which are crucial for our understanding of Paul's teaching about the law and justification. These are taken up in turn.

The Galatians' own experience

In 3:1–5 Paul seeks to show the Galatians that both justification and progress in the Christian life are independent of works of the law. This he does by making them face up to the implications of their own conversion and ongoing experience as believers before the arrival of the Judaizers. To do this Paul asks a series of questions, five in five verses:

1. You foolish Galatians! Who has bewitched (*ebaskanen*) you? It was before your eyes that Jesus Christ was publicly exhibited as crucified!
2. The only thing I want to learn from you is this: Did you receive (*elabete*) the Spirit by doing the works of law or by believing what you heard?
3. Are you so foolish? Having started (*enarxamenoi*) with the Spirit, are you now ending (*epiteleisthe*) with the flesh?
4. Did you experience (*epathete*) so much for nothing? – if it really was for nothing.
5. Well then, does God supply (*epichorēgōn*) you with the Spirit and work miracles among you by your doing the works of law, or by your believing what you heard?

The second, third and fifth questions are vital for the study of Paul's views about the law and justification. Before these are discussed, however, brief comments will be made about the first and fourth questions.

In his first question Paul asks, 'Who has bewitched (*ebaskanen*) you?' Recent studies[47] have drawn attention to the use of the verb *baskanein* in the first century in relation to magic and witchcraft. It has been pointed out that Paul and his contemporaries accepted, much more than western theologians do today, the reality and influence of the devil. Thus, where we might identify the dispute between Paul and his opponents as purely theological, he would have recognized it as a battle with the devil. In other words, Paul's question, 'Who

---

supports the thesis that the law plays no positive role in a person becoming a Christian (*contra* 'legalism'), and 3:19 – 4:7 supports the thesis that the law plays no positive role in Christian living (*contra* 'nomism'). And 4:8–11 expresses Paul's concern for his readers, while 4:12–31 forms part of Paul's exhortations against the Judaizing threat. G. Walter Hansen, *Abraham in Galatians: Epistolary and Rhetorical Contexts* (JSNT Sup 29; Sheffield: JSOT, 1989), p. 109, detects a chiastic structure in 3:1 – 4:11.

[47] Jerome H. Neyrey, SJ, 'Bewitched in Galatia: Paul and Cultural Anthropology', *CBQ* 50 (1988), pp. 72–100; John H. Elliott, 'Paul, Galatians, and the Evil Eye', *CTM* 17 (1990), pp. 262–273.

has bewitched you?', reflects a belief that his opponents are functioning as agents of the devil to turn the Galatians away from the true gospel.[48]

In addition to its use in relation to magic and witchcraft generally, *baskanein* was also used particularly in reference to the 'evil eye'. Certain individuals were thought to have power to bewitch or cast an evil spell upon others by a glance or look. It has been suggested that in Galatians 3:1 Paul was turning the tables upon his opponents (who said that he had put the 'evil eye' upon the Galatians when he influenced them to accept his deficient gospel) by implying that it was they who had put the 'evil eye' upon them. The expression 'evil eye' was often associated with envy, and if it is right to interpret 3:1 in the light of this background, then Paul could be implying that it was out of envy that his opponents had sought to turn the Galatians away from Paul and his gospel to their own 'other gospel'.[49]

The fourth question is, 'Did you experience (*epathete*) so much for nothing? – if it really was for nothing' (v. 4). The verb *pathein* can refer to either good or bad experiences which befall a person, and it is the context which provides the clue to which of these is intended.[50] Some translations do construe Paul's question as, 'Have you suffered so many things in vain?' (implying that the Galatians had experienced persecution for their faith), but it is better construed as, 'Did you experience so much [good] for nothing?' This positive rendering of *pathein* here is supported by the fact that all the other experiences to which Paul calls his readers' attention in 3:1–5 are positive, and by the fact that there is no hint elsewhere in the letter that the Galatians had suffered persecution on account of their faith. Paul's purpose in asking the question was to appeal to the significance of the Galatians' experience before the coming of the Judaizers in order to encourage them to adhere to the gospel by which they had experienced so many good things.

It is now time to turn to those questions which are vital for our understanding of Paul's views about the law and justification. In his second question Paul asks: 'The only thing I want to learn from you is this: Did you receive the Spirit by doing the works of the law or by believing what you heard (*ex akoēs pisteōs*)' (v. 2).[51] This question on first reading appears to move the

---

[48]Neyrey, 'Bewitched in Galatia', pp. 98–100.

[49]Elliott, 'Paul, Galatians, and the Evil Eye', pp. 264–270.

[50]*Cf.* BAG, *ad. loc.*

[51]*Ex akoēs pisteōs* has been usually construed by commentators to mean 'by faith in what was heard', *i.e.* the gospel: so, *e.g.*, Schlier, *Galater*, p. 122; Sanders, *Paul and Palestinian Judaism*, pp. 482–483; Betz, *Galatians*, p. 133; Bruce, *Galatians*, p. 149; Longenecker, *Galatians*, pp. 102–103. Richard B. Hays, *The Faith of Jesus Christ. An Interpretation of the Narrative Substructure of*

debate away from the matter of the law and justification to that of the law and the Spirit. This, however, is not really the case.[52] While Paul could speak of justification and the reception of the Spirit separately, he did not believe they could be experienced separately. Thus to ask whether they had received the Spirit by works of law or by the hearing of faith was tantamount to asking whether they had been justified by works of law or by the hearing of faith. The expected answer was, of course, 'By believing what was heard.' By asking this question Paul seeks to show that the legalistic demands of the Judaizers are unnecessary. Just as one's initial reception of the Spirit is independent of works of the law, so too is one's initial acceptance by God, *i.e.* one's justification. It is the hearing of faith that matters.

The third question also relates to the Galatians' experience of the Spirit. This question, however, relates not to the initial reception of the Spirit but rather to the Spirit's role in the ongoing life of believers: 'Are you so foolish? Having started with the Spirit, are you now ending with the flesh' (v. 3). In the context of 3:1–5, 'ending with the flesh' functions as synonym for 'ending with the works of the law'. The purpose of this question was to stimulate the Galatians to recognize that, having begun the Christian life with the Spirit, they should not be seeking its completion with the flesh. They must recognize that just as they began their new life as believers with the Spirit (and independently of the works of the law), so they must seek its completion in the same way. The question implies, of course, that the nomistic thrust of the Judaizers' teaching was erroneous. As the Christian life is begun, so it is to be completed. There is no more place for 'the works of the law' in the ongoing Christian life than there was at its beginning. They must not follow the example of Jewish believers, for what is nomistic for Jewish believers (*i.e.* what those *already* included among God's people must do) becomes legalistic when applied to Gentile believers

---

Galatians 3:1 – 4:11 (SBLDS 56; Chico, CA: Scholars Press, 1983), pp. 143–149; 197–198, prefers to interpret *akoē pisteōs* as the proclaimed message which evokes faith. Sam K. Williams, 'The Hearing of Faith: *AKOĒ PISTEŌS* in Galatians 3', *NTS* 35 (1989), pp. 82–93, however, has made a good case for rendering the expression as 'the hearing of faith'. He points out that *akoē* in its various uses never loses the force of a passive noun; it never means primarily the 'thing heard'. He suggests that 'the hearing of faith' means 'the hearing which Christians call faith'. This was essentially how J. B. Lightfoot, *Saint Paul's Epistle to the Galatians* (London: Macmillan, 1902), p. 135, preferred to read it as well. Hansen, *Abraham in Galatians*, pp. 110–111, argues for 'hearing with faith', by which he means the human activity of believing. This, he argues, is supported by the inferences Paul draws in 3:7 from his citation of Gn. 15:6 in 3:6.

[52]Some interpreters regard the section 3:1ff. as a digression, as Longenecker, *Galatians*, pp. 101–102, notes, but Longenecker is right in recognizing that the section is integral to Paul's argument.

(*i.e.* what people must do *in order to* be included among God's people).

The fifth question appeals to the Galatians' experience of the Spirit to show that it is faith, not works of the law, that is important in the ongoing Christian life: 'Well then, does God supply you with the Spirit and work miracles among you by your doing the works of the law, or by your believing what you heard?' (v. 5). The reference to the supplying of the Spirit (by God) is probably an allusion to the Galatians' conversion when they received the Spirit initially, and the reference to the working of miracles (by God) is probably a reference to the ongoing work of the Spirit among them. If this is the case, this last question picks up the two different aspects of the Galatians' experience of the Spirit (the initial and the ongoing) referred to in the second and third questions respectively. The fifth question then is intended to reinforce the implications of the second and third questions, *i.e.* that both the legalistic and nomistic implications of the Judaizers' teaching were wrong. The works of the law make possible neither the initial experience of the Spirit nor his ongoing activity among believers; believing what was heard is all that is needed.[53] And so, contrary to the Judaizers' teaching, it is those of faith who are Abraham's children (3:7).

Before proceeding, it is necessary to take note of Räisänen's criticism of Paul's argument in these verses. He has drawn attention to what he regards as question-begging and empirical problems in 3:1–6. Paul begs the question when he asks whether the Galatians received the Spirit 'by works of the law or by hearing with faith'. It is begging the question because it does not involve real alternatives. Räisänen says:

> Obviously, the reason for their experiencing great things had not been their love of their neighbours or avoidance of fornication, so why bother about such things. One would never come to the idea that observance of the law ought to be the *source* of spiritual gifts, as long as the law is properly viewed as the imperative resulting from the indicative of God's covenant.[54]

Paul's argument is beset with empirical problems, Räisänen says, because those communities which did stress the importance of law observance were not lacking in the experience of the Spirit's activity among them (Acts 2), and because even Galatians 3:1–6 implies that, despite their regression into law observance, Paul's readers continued to experience the Spirit's activity (this is the force of the present participles *epichorēgōn* and *energōn* in v. 5).

---

[53]*Cf.* Longenecker, *Galatians*, pp. 105–106.
[54]*Paul and the Law*, p. 189.

Räisänen's criticism seems to miss the mark in three ways. First, Paul is not arguing against the view that observance of the law is the source of spiritual gifts. Rather, he is arguing from the Galatians' experience of the Spirit (without works of the law) that justification also is received independently of works of the law. Second, the empirical evidence of the activity of the Spirit in law-observant communities is beside the point. Paul does not deny this. He denies that it is because of their observance of the law that they experience it. Third, the works of the law in Paul's mind here are not primarily such things as the love of neighbour and the avoidance of fornication but circumcision and the observance of special days and months and seasons and years, which the Judaizers did insist were necessary for inclusion among the true children of Abraham.

At this point it is possible to provide further support for the view that the experience of the Spirit and justification were inseparable as far as Paul was concerned. This can be done if 3:6 ('Just as Abraham "believed God and it was reckoned to him as righteousness"') is seen as a reference back to 3:5 (with its reference to God supplying the Spirit to those who believed what they heard) thus implying a parallel between the Galatians' experience of the Spirit and Abraham's justification.[55] The close link between justification and the experience of the Spirit is also implied by 3:14, where Paul says that the purpose of redemption was 'in order that in Christ Jesus the blessing of Abraham [*i.e.* justification, *cf.* 3:8] might come to the Gentiles, so that we might receive the promise of the Spirit through faith'.

Thus the primary thrust of Paul's argument in 3:1–5 is that the Galatians should recognize that justification is received without the works of the law. The argument has a secondary thrust as well, *i.e.* that they should recognize that there is no necessity for the works of the law in their ongoing Christian lives either.

---

[55]This approach has been argued cogently by S. K. Williams, 'Justification and the Spirit in Galatians. *JSNT* 29 (1987), pp. 92–93, and involves seeing 3:6 as a reference back to 3:5, and not the beginning of a new section (so also Bruce, *Galatians*, p. 152). Those who argue that 3:6 begins a new section either read *kathōs* as equivalent to or an abbreviated form of *kathōs gegraptai* (so, *e.g.* Schlier, *Galater*, p. 127; Betz, *Galatians*, p. 137), or see it as introducing an example (so, *e.g.*, Lightfoot, *Galatians*, p. 136; Longenecker, *Galatians*, p. 112, *cf.* NIV, REB, NRSV). This latter alternative is essentially little different from the approach argued by Williams. In both cases the parallel between the Galatians' experience of the Spirit and Abraham's justification is highlighted. It may be better to see 3:6 as a transitional verse which both draws out the implications of 3:1–5 and paves the way for the scriptural argument in 3:7–14.

The argument from Scripture

Paul's argument from Scripture in 3:6–14 draws upon the experience of Abraham, the great patriarch of Israel. Abraham is portrayed variously in Jewish literature,[56] but here Paul gives his own interpretation of the significance of the patriarch's experience of God. His argument has three parts. (i) Verses 6–9: it is those of faith who are Abraham's true children, who are justified along with him and share his blessing. (ii) Verses 10–12: it is not those of the works of the law who are justified, because the law brings a curse, and is not of faith. (iii) Verses 13–14: Christ has redeemed us from the curse of the law, so that the blessing of Abraham might flow to the Gentiles.

While it is possible to identify these three parts, and even to discern a logical connection between them, that does not mean that the interpretation of Paul's argument here is a simple task. In fact it is fraught with exegetical problems, and the literature on this passage is vast. The problems include the following. (i) What is the precise meaning of those of faith and those of the works of the law? (ii) How is 'the curse of the law' to be understood? (iii) Is it possible or necessary to keep the whole law? (iv) Why is the law not of faith? (v) How did Deuteronomy 21:23 ever come to be applied to Christ, and what is its significance? (vi) Who are the 'us' redeemed from the curse of the law by Christ – Jews only, or Jews and Gentiles? Because it is in the resolution of these problems that the meaning of the passage is to a very large extent determined, they will be discussed in turn below.

Those of faith and those of the works of the law

In the excursus above it was noted that in recent years there has been an increasing reluctance to accept the traditional Reformation view of 'the works of the law', which involved identifying those of the works of the law as persons who performed good works in order to amass merit before God, upon which they could rely for salvation.

Dunn's view that 'the works of the law' refers to the identity markers of Israel was also noted. These identity markers served to distinguish Israel sociologically as well as theologically from the Gentiles. Those of the works of the law are those who believed that justification was limited to Israel and those who joined themselves to her, adopting her exclusionist Jewish way of life. Dunn argues that 'to be *ex ergōn nomou* is something which *falls short* of abiding by everything written in the law'. This is indicated by the fact that Paul

---

[56] *Cf.* Hansen, *Abraham in Galatians*, Appendix 2: 'Abraham in Jewish Literature', pp. 173–199.

says that those who are of the works of the law are under a curse, *i.e.* the curse which applies to those who do *not* fulfil all that the law demands. Thus, while acknowledging that the Judaizers would take for granted that to be *ex ergōn nomou* involved an obligation to observe all the demands of the law, Paul denies this equation. Instead, Dunn claims, for Paul 'those who are *ex ergōn nomou* are those who have understood the scope of God's covenant people as Israel *per se*, as that people who are defined by the law and marked out by its distinctive requirements'.[57]

It is the last step in this argument which is problematical. If Paul (as Dunn allows) thought that the Judaizers taught that being of the works of the law involved an obligation to observe *all* that the law requires, then it is unlikely that, in seeking to counter their influence, he would point out that it was not those who believed that all these demands were to be fulfilled (but failed to do so) who were under the curse, but only those who taught that God's covenant people are defined by the law and marked out by its distinctive requirements.

Seeing that neither the traditional Reformation view nor Dunn's view is without problems, a third option was seen to be preferable. The works of the law are best understood as the fulfilment of all that the law requires, not in any sense of amassing merit before God, but simply because that was what was required under the terms of the Mosaic covenant. In 3:6–14, then, those of the works of the law would be those who believed that fulfilment of the demands of the law was necessary for justification, without realizing that those who adopt such a stance come under the curse of the law itself, if they do not succeed in doing all that the law requires.[58]

Can this third view be defended against the background of the provenance of Galatians? Does it fit with what the Judaizers were teaching and what the Galatians themselves were adopting? One problem with this view is that the Galatians did not think that all that was written in the law had to be obeyed. The indications are that they thought only in terms of circumcision, calendrical rules and possibly food taboos, and that this was what the Judaizers had been teaching them. That submitting to circumcision might involve them in taking upon themselves the full yoke of the law was something Paul felt he had to point out to them (5:3). If this was the case, it can be asked (in respect of

---

[57]'Works of the Law', pp. 225–230.

[58]Hong In-Gyu, 'Does Paul Misrepresent the Jewish Law? Law and Covenant in Gal. 3:1–14', *NovT* 36 (1994), pp. 180–181, noting that obedience to the law by Jewish people was necessary for remaining in the covenant, argues that Paul believed they had broken the covenant by disobedience and that therefore the curse of the law rested upon them.

Galatians at least) whether those of the works of the law does not refer, after all, to those who insist on the observance of those elements of the law which clearly function as identity markers.

But there is another way of approaching this matter. While the Judaizers may have been demanding (initially?) that the Galatians submit to circumcision, observe calendrical rules, and (perhaps) dietary regulations, and the Galatians' understanding of being people of the law involved little more than that, Paul pointed out to them that much more was involved.[59] In submitting to circumcision they would be obliged to obey *all* that was written in the book of the law, and if they did not do so they would come under its curse: 'For all who rely on the works of the law are under a curse; for it is written, "Cursed is everyone who does not observe and obey all the things written in the book of the law"' (v. 10). Paul, then, warns his readers of the dangers of legalism. What he warns them against is probably not a 'bad' legalism which requires the doing of good works *to amass merit* (it is questionable whether first-century Jews themselves operated in this way). Rather, he warns them against what might be called a 'good' legalism which involves doing the works of the law, simply because this is what the law itself demands, and believing that this will bring justification. Even this so-called 'good' legalism must be avoided because 'all who rely on the works of the law are under a curse'.

The curse of the law

In Galatians 3:10b Paul cites Deuteronomy 27:26: 'Cursed is everyone who does not observe and obey all that is written in the book of the law'. There is an emphasis in this text upon the need for *everyone* to abide by *all* that is written in the law.[60] Paul cites it to support his point that it is the people of faith who are the true children of Abraham, not those who rely upon the works of the law. It cannot be those who rely on the works of the law, because the law itself pronounces a curse on everyone who fails to keep all its demands.

This does not mean that Paul had forgotten that there was provision for forgiveness of transgressions under the law. Paul's point is simply that those who rely on their performance of what the law requires, instead of trusting in God's grace, come under the curse of the law.

---

[59]*Cf.* Sanders, *Paul, the Law and the Jewish People*, p. 29.

[60]It is noteworthy that the LXX text cited by Paul differs from the Hebrew text in that the LXX speaks of 'everyone' (*cf.* Heb. 'he who') and 'all that is written in the book of the law' (*cf.* Heb. 'the words of this law').

A number of scholars have suggested that here in 3:10 Paul is saying the exact opposite to what the Mosaic law says. The law says people are under a curse if they do not abide by all that is written in the law, whereas Paul says they are under a curse if they do. This rests on a wrong reading of *hosoi ex ergōn nomou eisin* (those who are of the works of the law) in 3:10a, taking it to indicate that 'those who perform the works of the law', instead of 'those who are of (or belong to) the works of the law', are under a curse.[61] Those who are under the curse of the law are those who rely on their performance of the works of the law for acceptance by God.

Dunn, in line with his thesis that 'the works of the law' refer primarily to the sociological identity markers which distinguished Israel from the Gentiles, argues that 'the curse of the law has here to do primarily with that attitude which confines the covenant promise to Jews as Jews: it falls on those who live within the law in such a way as to exclude the Gentile as Gentile from the promise'.[62] Such an approach is less than convincing, because it depends upon a problematic interpretation of 'the works of the law', and because it takes insufficient account of 3:10b where Paul says that the curse rests upon those who do not *abide by* all that is written in the book of the law, and not, as Dunn suggests, upon those who *have a wrong attitude to* the law by which the covenant promises are confined to Jews as Jews.[63]

N. T. Wright argues that the curse of the law is to be understood in terms of Israel's ongoing exile. 'Deuteronomy 27 – 30', he says, 'is all about exile and restoration, *understood as* covenant judgment and covenant renewal.' On the basis of 'many sources' in the Qumran documents (*e.g.* CD 1:5–8), he argues that some first-century Jews, at least, believed that the exile still continued, and 'as long as Pilate and Herod were in charge of Palestine, Israel was still under the curse of Deuteronomy 29'.[64] While it may be true that some first-century Jews believed that they still languished under the curse of exile in a Roman-

---

[61]*Cf.* Ardel Caneday, '"Redeemed from the Curse of the Law": The Use of Deut 21:22–23 in Gal. 3:13', *TrinJ* 10 (1989), pp. 193–194, who cites BAG which notes that *eimi* with *ek* denotes belonging to someone or something. Thus *hosoi ex ergōn nomou eisin* means 'those who belong to the works of the law'. Thus when Paul speaks of those who are of the works of the law, he is referring to those who believe that all the demands of the law must be fulfilled (not implying that they do fulfil them all) and are nevertheless under a curse.

[62]Dunn, 'Works of the Law', pp. 228–229.

[63]*Ibid.*, pp. 226–227, raises certain problems with the 'usual' interpretation of 3:10b, but his own interpretation leaves one feeling that he has not really dealt with Paul's assertion that the curse is upon those who do not abide by all that is written in the book of the law.

[64]Wright, *The Climax of the Covenant*, pp. 140–141, asserts that Gal. 1:4 (Paul's reference to 'the present evil age') is enough to show that Paul thought in this way.

occupied Palestine,[65] there seems to be little in this context to suggest that Paul was thinking of the curse primarily in these terms.

Thus we come back once again to the view that in Paul's mind the curse involved loss of acceptance by God, and applied, not merely because people had wrong attitudes to the law, but also because they failed to keep all its demands.[66] To be under the curse, in Galatians 3, was to miss out on being justified by God (v. 11), on sharing the blessing promised to Abraham (vv. 9, 14) and on receiving the promise of the Spirit (v. 14). The curse involves the decision of God against his people, and the consequent loss of his blessings.

Keeping the whole law

Paul's claim that those of the works of the law are under a curse because they do not abide by all that is written in the book of the law has given rise to a couple of interrelated questions. Was perfect obedience of the law possible? Did not the law itself make provision through the cultus for forgiveness in case of failure to do so?

Bruce seems to imply that Paul did think that perfect obedience of the law was possible. In Philippians 3 Paul refers to himself in pre-conversion days as 'blameless' in respect of the righteousness of the law (v. 6), and tells of his desire, nevertheless, to be found in Christ not having his own righteousness based on the observance of the law, but that which comes through faith in Christ, the righteousness of God based on faith (v. 9). It was as a result of his Damascus road experience that Paul came to the conclusion that, even though one might be blameless according to the law, justification was not to be found by that means. For the cross of Christ stood as a barrier carrying a notice: 'No road this way.'[67]

It is very doubtful, however, whether Philippians 3:6 will bear the weight

---

[65]Mark A. Seifrid, 'Blind Alleys in the Controversy over the Paul of History', *TynBul* 45 (1994), pp. 86–89, draws attention to several Jewish texts which indicate that there was a range of views concerning the status of Israel, and not all of these reflect the view that all Israel was still in exile.

[66]So, too, recently, Hong In-Gyu, *The Law in Galatians* (JSNT Sup 81; Sheffield: JSOT, 1993), p. 141; *contra* Daniel P. Fuller, 'Paul and "The Works of the Law"', *WTJ* 38 (1975), pp. 31–33, who regards 'the works of the law' as the sin of bribing God, and the curse applies to those who do so on account of this heinous sin. So also Charles H. Cosgrove, "The Mosaic Law Preaches Faith: A Study in Galatians 3' *WTJ* 41 (1978), pp. 146–164. See the critique of Fuller's view in Thomas R. Schreiner, 'Is Perfect Obedience to the Law Possible? A Re-examination of Galatians 3:10', *JETS* 27 (1984), pp. 151–152, 155–156.

[67]*Galatians*, p. 160.

that such an interpretation places upon it. This verse is found in a context (3:4–6) in which Paul deals with externals, the evidences of his Jewish pedigree and piety. As it will be argued in a later chapter, he is not claiming perfect obedience to all that the law demanded.[68] It is better then to understand Philippians 3:6 in terms of the misplaced pride in which the apostle indulged in pre-Christian days. It does not reflect his views about the possibility of perfect obedience to all that the law requires.

One of the criticisms of Paul's attitude to the law is that he seems to ignore the fact that it makes provision for repentance and forgiveness. As Howard says, 'To keep the law then was, among other things, to find cultic forgiveness for breaking the law.'[69] Paul's insistence in Galatians 3:10 that those who do not obey the law perfectly are under a curse therefore seems to overlook this fundamental aspect of the law, and of Judaism. It reflects a rigour of interpretation which from a Jewish point of view would appear grossly overstrained. This criticism seems to miss the significance of Paul's point. When he says that those who are of the law are under a curse, he is not necessarily overlooking the fact that the law makes provision for repentance and forgiveness for those who trust in the covenant grace of God. What he is saying is that those who trust, not in that covenant grace, but in their fulfilment of the law's demands, will come under the curse of that law.

The law is not of faith

In 3:11–12 Paul says that one of the reasons those of faith are justified, and not those of the works of the law, is that the law is not of faith:

> Now it is evident that no one is justified before God by the law; for 'The one who is righteous will live by faith.' But the law does not rest on faith; on the contrary, 'Whoever does the works of the law will live by them.'

This passage raises two issues. The first is what is meant by 'the law' in this context. Fuller argues that 'law' in 3:12 means the same as 'works of the law' in 3:10, *i.e.* a legalistic misunderstanding of the revelatory law.[70] But this is

---

[68]Schreiner, 'Perfect Obedience', p. 158, reaches similar conclusions about Phil. 3:6, on the grounds that 'it is even doubtful that in his Pharisaic days Paul thought that he kept the law entirely, for Paul's blamelessness in Phil. 3:6 probably included the notion that he went up to the temple and offered the required sacrifices.'

[69]*Crisis in Galatia*, p. 53.

[70]'The Works of the Law', p. 40. Fuller is supported by Cosgrove, 'The Mosaic Law Preaches Faith', pp. 146–164.

very difficult to maintain. It is true that those of the works of the law in 3:10 are those who think that their justification depends upon the performance of what the law requires. But in what follows Paul shows that this is a false notion, because the law itself pronounces a curse on those who do not obey it all.[71] Here the law must be understood as God's law, not as a legalistic misunderstanding of it. And this meaning of law carries over into 3:12 where a further explanation is given why those of the works of the law are not justified, *i.e.* because the law operates, not on the principle of faith, but on the principle of performance; it is those who do them (what the law requires) that will live by them. Once again, 'law' here is best understood to denote the requirements of God's law, not legalism.[72]

The second issue raised by the quotation is how we are to deal with Paul's statement that 'the law does not rest on faith' (lit. 'the law is not of faith'). If Fuller's line were to be followed, it could be said that the law (understood as legalism) is not of faith because it involves dependence upon one's own achievements, not faith in Christ. But, as noted above, there are problems with Fuller's view, and therefore another explanation must be sought. If the law is, in this context, to be understood as the requirements of the law of God, why did Paul say that it is not of faith? It is not of faith, he says, because those who *do* them will live by them. In other words the law operates on the principle of performance, calling for obedience to its requirements, and promising life to those who do obey.[73] This is not the principle of faith which calls people to trust in God's promise of justification, even when they find themselves under the curse of the law for having failed to do what it demands.

The application of Deuteronomy 21:23 to Christ

In the third element of his argument from Scripture, Paul, drawing on Deuteronomy 21:23, says: 'Christ redeemed us from the curse of the law by

---

[71]*Contra* Fuller, 'The Works of the Law', pp. 31–33, there does appear to be an implied proposition here, *i.e.* that no one obeys it all. *Cf.* Schreiner, 'Perfect Obedience', p. 156.

[72]So too Schreiner, 'Perfect Obedience', p. 156; Westerholm, *Israel's Law and the Church's Faith*, p. 111.

[73]*Cf.* Mussner, *Galaterbrief*, pp. 230–231; Räisänen, *Paul and the Law*, p. 163; Westerholm, *Israel's Law and the Church's Faith*, pp. 113–114; Schlier, *Galater*, p. 134. So too Longenecker, *Galatians*, p. 120, who also provides documentation in targumic tradition and rabbinic thought illustrating that, in Judaism, life in the age to come was thought to be dependent upon obedience to the Torah. This does not mean that a notion of amassing merit was involved; rather, it was the fulfilment of covenant obligations that determined one's participation in the life to come. It was this that Paul opposed.

becoming a curse for us – for it is written, "Cursed is everyone who hangs on a tree"' (3:13).

Deuteronomy 21:23 is used often in the New Testament in reference to Christ's death (*cf.* Acts 5:30; 10:39; 13:29; 1 Pet. 2:24), suggesting that early Christians had to come to terms with this text. On first reading it seems to undermine all claims they might make about Jesus being God's messiah. How could it be said that he was both chosen by God and cursed by God? Early Christians probably had to respond to Jewish attacks along this line, as well as resolving the apparent contradiction for their own sakes. The resolution of this problem reflected in Galatians 3:13 was achieved by recognizing that Christ was hung on the tree, not because he himself deserved to be accursed by God, but because he took the place of those who did.[74] This he did in order to redeem people from the curse of the law (which is God's curse, seeing that it is God's law), so that the redeemed might experience the blessing of Abraham and receive the promise of the Spirit.

Not all scholars see the removal of the curse through Christ's death in these terms. For example, Dunn argues:

> Christ in his death had put himself under the curse and outside the covenant blessing (*cf.* Deut. 11.26; 30.19–20) – that is, put himself in the place of the Gentile! Yet God vindicated him! Therefore, God is *for* the Gentiles; and consequently the law could no longer serve as a boundary dividing Jew from Gentile. In short, Christ in his death had effectively abolished this disqualification, by himself being disqualified.[75]

It is true that one of the effects of the death of Christ was to enable Gentiles to share in the blessing of Abraham (this is implied in 3:14, as we shall see below). But to narrow the notion of redemption here to this alone, as Dunn

---

[74]*Cf.* F. F. Bruce. 'The Curse of the Law', *Paul and Paulinism: Essays in Honour of C. K. Barrett*, ed. M. D. Hooker and S. G. Wilson (London: SPCK, 1982), p. 32. Caneday, 'Redeemed from the Curse', pp. 199–202, points out that in terms of the Old Testament a person was not cursed because his corpse was hung upon a tree, but rather he was cursed because of a covenant violation and his corpse was hung upon a tree because of the curse, and to propitiate God's wrath on the land. Accordingly, we should not conclude that Christ came under God's curse *because* he hung 'on a tree', but rather that he hung upon a tree to propitiate God's wrath towards those who were under the curse of the law. Brendan Byrne, *'Sons of God' – 'Seed of Abraham': A Study of the Idea of the Sonship of God of All Christians in Paul against the Jewish Background* (Analecta Biblica 89; Rome: Biblical Institute, 1979), pp. 154–155, says that speaking 'of Christ as satisfying the Law's demand by concentrating its wrath wholly upon himself is not sufficient'. He argues that 'Christ has redeemed us from the curse of the Law in that he has provided the opportunity of dying proleptically with him and so of being free from it from now on.'

[75]'Works of the Law', p. 230.

does, involves a failure to take account of the fact that, in 3:6–14, Paul has in mind also the Jews' need for justification (v. 11). Therefore, in the case of some Jews at least (those who rely upon their obedience to the law), there is a need for deliverance from the curse of the law (understood as the judgment it pronounces on those who fail to keep all its demands). They needed redemption just as much as the Gentiles did.

Other scholars have speculated that it was Paul's realization on the Damascus road that the law wrongly pronounced a curse upon the one whom God had exalted that led him to reject the law, and to replace it with Christ in his theology.[76] It is better, however, to follow the clues that Paul himself provides, which indicate, not that he rejected the law (even though he certainly believed that its time had been brought to an end with the coming of Christ), but that he believed that Christ suffered God's 'rejection' under the terms of the law, so that we might be justified before him (*cf.* Gal. 3:13; Rom. 3:23–26; 2 Cor. 5:21).

N. T. Wright, in line with his thesis that some first-century Jews (including Paul) believed that Israel was still in exile suffering the curse of Deuteronomy 29, argues that in Christ's death 'the curse of exile reached its height, and was dealt with once for all, so that the blessing of covenant renewal might flow out the other side, as God always intended'.[77] While it is debatable whether the context supports the view that Paul thought of the curse in terms of a Roman-occupied Palestine, it is clear that the redemption of Jews from the curse (however understood) was necessary if the blessing of Abraham was to flow to the Gentiles.

Summing up, Paul applied Deuteronomy 21:23 to Christ because he believed that Christ was hung on the tree, not because he himself was accursed of God, but because he took the place of those who were (*i.e.* Jews who by their disobedience to the law had come under its curse), so that they might enjoy the blessings of God (especially the promised Holy Spirit), and so that these blessings might flow out to the Gentiles.

To whom does 'us' refer in 3:13?

In 3:13–14 Paul says: 'Christ redeemed *us* from the curse of the law, having becomes a curse for *us* . . . in order that in Christ Jesus the blessing of Abraham might come to the Gentiles, so that we might receive the promise of

---

[76] *Cf.*, e.g., Kim, *The Origin of Paul's Gospel*, pp. 274–275.

[77] *The Climax of the Covenant*, p. 141.

the Spirit.' In the preceding sub-section it was assumed that the 'us' referred to Paul and his fellow Jews. There is, however, another view. The word can be understood inclusively, meaning Jews and Gentiles, as well as exclusively, meaning Jews alone.[78]

Bruce is one who understands it inclusively, arguing that even though the Gentiles might not be under the law in the same way as the Jews are, nevertheless they 'show that what the law requires is written on their hearts' (Rom. 2:14). Thus both Jews and Gentiles are under the curse of the law, because they have not persevered in everything, 'whether specifically "written in the book of the law" or more generally "written on their hearts"'.[79] Räisänen also argues for the inclusivist view, on the grounds (i) that the 'we' of verse 14b must include the Galatian Gentile Christians, as the mention of the Spirit here ties in with verses 2–3 (where the Galatian believers' experience of the Spirit is in view), and (ii) that there is no indication of any contrast between the 'us' of verse 13 and the Gentiles of verse 14.[80]

The case for the exclusivist view has been made strongly by Donaldson.[81] He points out that three passages in Galatians (3:13–14; 3:23–29; 4:3–7) confront the interpreter with the same problem, but he argues that in each case

---

[78]There is a third option, that it refers only to believing Gentiles, a view espoused by Lloyd Gaston, 'Paul and the Torah', *Antisemitism and the Foundations of Christianity*, ed. Alan Davies (New York: Paulist, 1979), pp. 62–63. He argues that in Paul's writings 'under the law' refers to the Gentile situation, and accordingly the 'us' who are redeemed from the curse of the law are Gentile believers. A check of Paul's uses of the expression 'under the law', however, reveals that while in many cases it refers explicitly to Jews, in none does it refer explicitly to Gentiles (Rom. 6:14, 15; 1 Cor. 9:20; Gal. 3:23; 4:4, 5, 21; 5:18). Gaston's view then is problematic.

[79]Bruce, *Galatians*, pp. 166–167. Longenecker, *Galatians*, p. 121, adopts a similar view, saying that 'the first person plural pronoun *hēmas*, which in Galatians often refers to Jewish Christians (see esp. 2:15; 3:23–25; 4:5) and here certainly has in mind those "under the law", yet refers to Gentiles who as yet had not submitted to circumcision.' Longenecker, however, offers no reasons for his view. Westerholm, *Israel's Law and the Church's Faith*, pp. 192–195, says that Paul does not systematically maintain a distinction between Jews who are under the law and Gentiles who are not. *Cf.* also Hansen, *Abraham in Galatians*, pp. 122–123.

[80]*Paul and the Law*, pp. 19–20. See also Westerholm, *Israel's Law and the Church's Faith*, pp. 194–195.

[81]T. L. Donaldson, 'The "Curse of the Law" and the Inclusion of the Gentiles: Galatians 3.13–14', *NTS* 32 (1986), pp. 94–112. So too Caneday, 'Redeemed from the Curse', pp. 203–204. Betz, *Galatians*, p. 148, agrees but adds that if the Galatians decided to accept circumcision they too would come under the curse. So too David Hill, 'Salvation Proclaimed IV. Galatians 3:10–14: Freedom and Acceptance', *ExpT* 93 (1981), p. 198, who says that the 'us' refers to 'both Jewish Christians and Gentile Christians, should the latter confirm their state of bondage by accepting circumcision and thereby lapsing into the domain of the law'.

there appears to be an identifiable progression: (i) the 'we' group and its plight, (ii) identification of Christ with the plight, (iii) the redemption of the 'we' group, and (iv) saving blessings for all believers. This suggests that Paul thought that the redemption of Israel was a necessary step on the way to the inclusion of the Gentiles.[82] Next, Donaldson draws attention to the Jewish notion of the eschatological inclusion of the Gentiles, according to which God would act first for the redemption of Israel, and then Gentiles would share in Israel's blessing. He argues that 3:13–14 makes good sense when understood against this background.[83] This then raises a further question: how does Israel's redemption from its plight under the law make possible blessings for the Gentiles? The answer, Donaldson suggests, is to be found by recognizing that Israel's bondage under the law is but a special form of the universal bondage of humanity under the *stoicheia tou kosmou* ('the elemental spirits of the universe'). The way Israel is redeemed from the curse of the law is the way in which the Gentiles also will be redeemed. Christ has identified himself not only with humanity's universal plight but also with Israel's particular form of it, so that Israel's redemption may function as a representative sample of the universal redemption.[84]

There is a lot to commend this view. It goes a long way towards resolving the problems which those such as Bruce have with the exclusivist view, *i.e.* that it fails to recognize that the Gentiles need redemption just as much as the Jews. Donaldson's approach also offers help in seeing why Paul moves from the redemption of Israel to the participation of the Gentiles in the blessing of Abraham. Paul does so because he recognizes Israel's priority in salvation, albeit in modified form, seeing its redemption as a representative sample of universal redemption. It is possible to add to this the suggestion that Jewish redemption and Gentile blessing are connected in that Jewish believers, having been redeemed from the curse of the law themselves, carried the message of redemption to the Gentiles.

Wright also adopts an exclusivist approach to the interpretation of the 'us' of this passage. In line with his own overall approach, he suggests that Paul has in mind a scenario something like this: God had promised to Abraham a blessing intended for the whole world. But the covenant people, Israel, had come under the curse of the covenant because, as a nation, they had failed to keep the Torah. Their exile, which continued down to the time of Jesus, was the

---

[82]'The "Curse of the Law"', pp. 95–99.

[83]'The "Curse of the Law"', pp. 99–102.

[84]'The "Curse of the Law"', pp. 102–106.

outworking of that curse. In the death of Christ the curse reached its climax and the covenant was renewed, so that the promised blessing might come to Israel and then pass on to the Gentiles.[85] While, as has been noted previously, Wright's interpretation of the nature of the curse in terms of the Roman occupation of Palestine is debatable, it would, if correct, provide further support for the exclusivist view.

Now that the major exegetical issues related to 3:6–14 have been reviewed, Paul's theological argument in this passage may be summarized. Against his Judaizing opponents Paul argues that it is those of faith who are Abraham's true children, not those of the works of the law. Those of the works of the law will not be justified because the Scripture promises justification to those of faith, and the law is not of faith. The law does not make its offer of life on the basis of faith but on the basis of obedience to its demands. Those who rely on their obedience to the law for acceptance before God come under the curse of the law, because they do not fulfil all its demands. Christ has redeemed Jewish believers from the curse of the law by becoming a curse for them. This he did by accepting in himself the curse the law had pronounced upon them, and this was reflected even in the manner of his death (hanging on the tree). The purpose of Christ's redemption of Jewish believers was that the blessing of Abraham might then overflow to the Gentiles, so that both Jews and Gentiles might receive the promise of the Spirit. And Jewish believers, having been redeemed from the curse of the law which hung over them, brought this good news to the Gentiles.

The argument from human legal practice

In 3:15–18 Paul gives an example drawn from human legal practice to show that the Mosaic law, given 430 years after the promise of an inheritance made by God to Abraham, cannot nullify or add to the terms under which that inheritance is to be received.

Paul begins by stating what pertains in human legal practice. Once a will (*diathēkē*) is ratified by the testator, no-one else can nullify it or add codicils to it. There are problems for the modern reader who wishes to know to which particular system of human law Paul is referring,[86] but the direction of Paul's

---

[85] *The Climax of the Covenant*, pp. 141–156.

[86] These are discussed fully by Longenecker, *Galatians*, pp. 128–130, who also provides excellent documentation for the relevant Graeco–Roman, Graeco–Egyptian and Jewish jurisprudence. *Cf.* also Betz, *Galatians*, pp. 155–156.

argument is clear enough: a testament once ratified by the testator can neither be nullified nor have codicils added to it (by anyone else).

Next, the apostle says: 'Now the promises were made to Abraham and to his offspring; it does not say, "And to offsprings," as of many; but it says, "And to your offspring," that is, to one person, who is Christ' (3:16). The text has proved very difficult for commentators. Wright, however, has proposed a very satisfying interpretation. He suggests that Paul's argument in 3:15–18 runs as follows: 'It is impossible to annul a covenant; the covenant with Abraham always envisaged a single family, not a plurality of families; therefore the Torah, which creates a plurality by dividing Gentiles from Jews, stands in the way of the fulfilment of the covenant with Abraham; and this cannot be allowed.' The one family to whom the promise applies are the family of Christ, in whom there is no longer Jew or Greek, slave or free, male or female, for all are one [family] in Christ.[87] And, it may be added, the promise made to this one family was conditional only upon faith, and the giving of the Mosaic law could not change that.

Thus, Paul says, the covenant (*diathēkē*) with Abraham and his seed, made and ratified by God, could not be made void by the coming of the Mosaic law 430 years later,[88] nor could the promises involved be nullified. Paul concludes by saying that, if sharing in the inheritance promised to Abraham depended on the observance of the law, then it would no longer be by promise. Although it is not Paul's point, it has been suggested that, if the promise was either annulled or added to, God himself would be guilty of acting illegally, for he it was who gave the law.[89]

The function of the law

If the law can neither annul the promise made to Abraham nor be added to it as an extra condition for receiving the inheritance, then one might ask why it was necessary for the law to be given at all. This problem is addressed in 3:19–25. There is a difference of opinion among scholars concerning the function of this passage in Galatians. Some regard it as a digression on the

---

[87] *The Climax of the Covenant*, pp. 163–168.

[88] Most commentators say that Paul's figure of 430 years is taken from Ex. 12:40, but *cf.* Dieter Lührmann, 'Die 430 Jahre zwischen den Verheissungen und dem Gesetz (Gal 3, 17)', *ZAW* 100 (1988), pp. 420–423, who argues that Paul is not alluding to Ex. 12:40–41, but has taken over a historical schema known to the third-century BC exegete, Demetrius.

[89] *Cf.* Charles H. Cosgrove, 'Arguing Like a Mere Human Being: Galatians 3.15–18 in Rhetorical Perspective', *NTS* 34 (1988), pp. 537–538.

role of the law,[90] others as the crux of what Paul wanted to say to the Galatians.[91] There is some truth in both opinions. On the one hand, the passage is a digression in so far as it turns aside from the main flow of argument running in the previous section. There Paul argued that the law cannot annul the promise made to Abraham, or be added as a supplementary condition to it. Here he turns aside to ask, if that is the case, for what purpose the law was introduced. On the other hand, the passage is not a digression in so far as it is central to Paul's main concerns in the letter as a whole, *i.e.* to combat not only legalism but also nomism. The present passage is crucial in achieving this, for in it Paul shows what the true function of the law was in salvation history. To do this he raises, and then answers, two questions.

Why then the law?

The first question, 'Why then the law?' (v. 19a) paves the way for Paul's comments in verses 19b–20, where he makes four points about the nature and function of the law. First, he says, 'it was added because of transgressions' (v. 19b). In saying that the law was 'added', Paul recognizes a supplementary role for the law. It was added to the promise, which had been given 430 years previously (*cf.* v. 17), 'because of transgressions' (*tōn parabaseōn charin*). This is best understood in the light of Paul's *paidagōgos* image introduced in verses 24–25 to describe the function of the law, which, as will be seen below, was to restrain moral decline in Israel.[92]

Second, Paul says that the law was added 'until the offspring would come to whom the promise had been made' (v. 19c). By so saying he stresses the temporary nature of the role of the law. It has as its *terminus ad quem* the arrival of the 'offspring', whom Paul has already identified as Christ [and those in him] (v. 16).

Third, he says that the law was 'ordained through angels' (v. 19d). There is no reference to the presence of angels in the Exodus account of the giving of

---

[90]So, *e.g.*, Betz, *Galatians*, p. 161.

[91]So, *e.g.*, Longenecker, *Galatians*, p. 137.

[92]The preposition *charin* in the expression *tōn parabaseōn charin* can mean either 'for what reason' (the option adopted here), or 'for what purpose'. If the latter option is chosen, the text would be rendered 'it was added for the purpose of transgressions', *i.e.*, to produce transgressions, an idea Paul expresses in Rom. 5:20, but not found elsewhere in the present context. Therefore it is better to adopt the former option, which yields the translation, 'it was added because of transgressions'. This is in line with Paul's use of the *paidagōgos* image just a few verses later (vv. 24–25). *Contra* Hübner, *Law in Paul's Thought*, p. 26; Räisänen, *Paul and the Law*, pp. 144–145.

the law on Sinai. But the presence of angels at the giving of the law at Sinai is assumed in Deuteronomy 33:2–4 LXX, and this tradition is widespread in later Jewish tradition, where their presence serves to enhance the importance of the law.[93] The reference to angels in the present context, where the law is being downgraded in its importance relative to the promise, however, is intended to underscore its inferiority in this respect. To be ordained by angels is inferior to being ordained directly by God. But although Paul downgrades the law in comparison with the promise, he is not thereby denigrating the law – just as the writer to the Hebrews (2:2–3) does not denigrate it when he says the message spoken through the Son (the gospel) is superior to that spoken through angels (the law).

Fourth, Paul says that the law was ordained through angels 'by a mediator' (v. 19e). This is followed by the cryptic comment, 'Now a mediator involves more than one party; but God is one' (v. 20). Together, these two statements have defied interpretive efforts for centuries. (As has been often noted, one commentator said that there are 430 interpretations, as many as there were years between the promise made to Abraham and the giving of the law on Sinai!)[94] A recent proposal by Wright, however, makes a lot of sense. In keeping with his suggestion that 3:15–18 must be understood along the lines that God's promises were for one seed (one family of God made up of people from all nations) and not two seeds (two families, one made up of Jews and the other of Gentiles), he says that Paul's point here is this:

> Moses is not the mediator through whom this promised 'one seed' is brought into existence. He cannot be, since he (Moses) is the mediator of a revelation to Israel only, *hoi ek nomou*. This offers a quite satisfactory reading of *henos*, understanding only a typically Pauline ellipse: 'the mediator is not [the mediator] of one'. We can simply cut out the manifold theories about mediatorship implying a plurality of parties on one side or the other. That is not the point. Paul is saying that Moses, to whom the Galatians are being tempted to look for membership in the true people of God, is not the one through whom that single family is brought about.[95]

The points Paul makes about the law in 3:19–20 may be summarized as follows. The function assigned to the law was to restrain moral decline in Israel

---

[93]This is documented by Terrence Callan, 'Pauline Midrash: The Exegetical Background of Gal 3:19b', *JBL*, 99 (1980), pp. 550–554. See also Betz, *Galatians*, pp. 168–169; Longenecker, *Galatians*, pp. 139–140.

[94]*Cf.* Schoeps, *Paul*, p. 182.

[95]*The Climax of the Covenant*, p. 169.

until the coming of [the family of] Christ to whom the promises applied. Though it had this important function it was nevertheless inferior to the promise because, unlike the promise made directly by God to Abraham, the law was ordained indirectly through angels and with the help of Moses as mediator. And Moses was not the mediator of the one family to which the promises applied (a family made up of people from all nations), but God is one and wants that one family, not two (consisting of Jews and Gentiles). The Galatians, therefore, should not be looking to Moses and obedience to his law for their incorporation into the people of God, but rather looking to Christ and placing their faith in him.

Is the law contrary to the promises?

The second question which Paul raises is whether the law is contrary to the promises (v. 21a). This question paves the way for him to explain that the law is not contrary to the promise (vv. 21b–22), but rather functioned to provide moral restraint for Israel until the time for the fulfilment of the promise arrived (vv. 23–25).

In 3:21b–22 Paul rejects the suggestion that the law is contrary to the promise by saying that if the law could do what the promise does (*i.e.* make alive), then certainly righteousness would come through the law (v. 21b). But this is clearly not the case, for Scripture itself (in spite of the giving of the law) declares that everything is shut up under the power of sin (v. 22a), with the result that what was promised is given to those who believe, and not to those who depend upon observance of the law (v. 22b).

In 3:23–24 the apostle moves on from the denial that the law is contrary to the promise, to show exactly what the function of the law was. He now makes explicit what was only implicit in 3:19: the law was 'added because of transgressions until the offspring [Christ] would come to whom the promise had been made'. Before the coming of faith (with the coming of Christ), Paul says, we were shut up under the law's restraint (v. 23). What this means is clarified with an illustration based on the role of the *paidagōgos* (NRSV, 'disciplinarian').

The law as paidagōgos

Quite a lot of research has been undertaken in recent years on the significance of the role of the *paidagōgos*. This has confirmed the view that the *paidagōgos* was not a teacher (the duties of the *paidagōgos* differed from that of the *didaskalos*), but rather a guardian. The *paidagōgos* was charged with responsibility for the moral and behavioural restraint as well as the protection of minors until such time as they attained their majority.[96]

Using the *paidagōgos* illustration, then, Paul informs his readers that the law's function was to restrain Israel morally until the coming of Christ. Thus the law was not against the promise, rather it had a restraining role to play until the time for the fulfilment of the promise should come. The corollary, as Paul does not hesitate to point out, is that once the promise is fulfilled, and faith has come, then believing Israel is no longer under the law (v. 25). And if Jewish believers are no longer under the law, then neither are Gentile believers.[97]

The law as guardian or trustee

In 4:1–5 Paul uses an analogy concerning an heir who was a minor to explain how believers have been released from bondage to the *stoicheia tou kosmou*, and in particular from the form of that bondage experienced under the law.

The analogy itself is contained in 4:1–2: 'My point is this: heirs, as long as they are minors, are no better than slaves, though they are the owners of all the property; but they remain under guardians and trustees until the date set by the father.' While there is discussion about the precise first-century legal background to Paul's analogy[98] and the hyperbolic nature of one aspect of

---

[96] *Cf. e.g.* Norman H. Young, *'Paidagōgos:* The Social Setting of a Pauline Metaphor', *NovT* 29, (1987) pp. 157–169; *idem*, 'The Figure of the *Paidagōgos* in Art and Literature', *BA* 53 (1990), pp. 80–86; David J. Lull, ' "The Law was our Pedagogue": A Study in Galatians 3:19, 25', *JBL* 105 (1986), pp. 489–495; Richard N. Longenecker, 'The Pedagogical Nature of the Law in Galatians 3:19 – 4:7', *JETS* 25 (1982), pp. 53–56; T. David Gordon, 'A Note on *PAIDAGŌGOS* in Gal 3.24-25', *NTS* 35 (1989), pp. 150–154, who all find the predominant background of Paul's *paidagōgos* illustration in the Graeco–Roman world.' A. T. Hanson, 'The Origin of Paul's Use of *PAIDAGŌGOS* for the Law', *JSNT* 34 (1988), pp. 71–76, on the other hand, argues that when Paul spoke of the law as *paidagōgos* he had in mind the reference to Moses as 'nurse' in Nu. 11:11–12, which in the Targums is rendered 'guardian'. By this allusion Paul is able to stress even more aptly the temporary nature of the Mosaic law.

[97] *Cf.* Betz, *Galatians*, p. 179.

[98] According to Roman law, the age of maturity was fixed, not by the father, but by the government. W. M. Ramsey, *A Historical Commentary on St Paul's Epistle to the Galatians* (London: Hodder and Stoughton, 1900), pp. 391–393, however, argues that there were differences between Roman law and the provincial law which operated in the Phrygian cities of Asia Minor, and that it was the latter (which did make provision for the father to set the time when his son would be deemed to have reached maturity) which forms the background to Paul's analogy here. But there

it,[99] nevertheless the picture presented is quite clear. The child designated by his father as the one to inherit the estate was, during the period of his minority, very little different from a slave in so far as neither was an independent agent; both were under the authority of others.

In 4:3 Paul applies this analogy to believers: 'So with us; while we were minors, we were enslaved to the elemental spirits of the world (*stoicheia tou kosmou*).' It is not immediately clear precisely which believers Paul had in mind as those who were previously enslaved (believers generally, or Jewish believers in particular), or what exactly he meant here by the *stoicheia tou kosmou* (the powers that held men and women of the ancient world in bondage, or the law as a particular expression of those powers operating in respect of the Jewish people).[100] What follows in 4:4–5, however, supports the view that it was Jewish believers and their bondage under the law that Paul intended to depict here.[101]

Most modern commentators recognize in 4:4–5 traditional pre-Pauline Christological statements which the apostle has taken up and used for his own purposes. Be that as it may, Paul is here making an important point about the effect of Christ's redemptive work upon the relationship of Jewish believers to the law:

> But when the fullness of time had come, God sent his Son, born of a woman, born under the law, in order to redeem those who were under the law, so that we might receive adoption as children (4:4–5).

When Paul says that God's Son was born under the law, he means he was born under the Jewish law, and if he was born under the law to redeem those who were under the law, then it follows that Jewish people also need redemption. In this way 4:4–5 throws light back upon 4:3, indicating, as noted above, that it was Jewish believers and their bondage under the law whom Paul had in mind there also.

In 4:6–7, however, Paul applies all this to the Galatians: 'And because *you*

---

are some dating problems with Ramsay's sources, as Longenecker, *Galatians*, pp. 163–164, points out. *Cf.* also Betz, *Galatians*, p. 204.

[99]There was, of course, a huge difference of status between the heir who was a minor and the slave. But in one respect they were the same; they were both under the authority of others.

[100]Howard, *Crisis in Galatia*, pp. 67–71, provides a useful discussion of the history of interpretation of Gal. 4:1–10.

[101]While many modern commentators take the 'we' to be inclusive, there are a number who argue, rightly in my view, for the exclusive option; so, *e.g.*, Bruce, *Galatians*, p. 193; Longenecker, *Galatians*, p. 164; Donaldson, 'The "Curse of the Law"', pp. 95–99.

are children, God has sent the Spirit of his Son into our[102] hearts, crying, "Abba! Father!" So *you* are no longer a slave but a child, and if a child then also an heir, through God.' Having shown how the Jewish believers had been redeemed and received their adoption, Paul now reminds his (predominantly) Gentile Christian readers that because they (too) are God's children, God has sent the Spirit of his Son into their hearts (v. 6). Then Paul draws the conclusion for which the analogy and its application have prepared the way: you Gentile believers, being children, are also heirs of God (v. 7).

The significance of such a conclusion in the context of the situation in Galatia is obvious. Paul is saying that the Galatian Gentile believers, just as much as Jewish believers, are heirs of the promises of God. By so saying he seeks to counteract the teaching of the Judaizers, who were insisting that observance of the law is an indispensable requirement for obtaining the inheritance. And this provides a basis upon which he can make his appeal to them (4:8–11) not to become enslaved again by feeling obliged to observe days and months and seasons and years.[103]

Argument from allegory: Sarah and Hagar

Paul's use of allegory in 4:21–31 raises a number of general issues which call for brief comment before the discussion of the text itself. First, there is the nature of the passage and whether it can rightly be called allegory. It is certainly not allegory in the Alexandrian sense, in which there was virtually no account taken of the historical context of the passage being allegorized. For this reason some scholars regard Paul's use of the Sarah–Hagar story as typological rather than allegorical. Hanson has shown that a typological form

---

[102]There is a variant reading, 'your' instead of 'our', preserved in a number of later uncial manuscripts, and this represents early scribal efforts to overcome a certain awkwardness in the text. The earlier and better witnesses, however, support the harder reading 'our'. *Cf.* Bruce M. Metzger, *A Textual Commentary on the Greek New Testament* (London and New York: United Bible Societies, 1971), p. 595.

[103]Such observance can be regarded either as typical behaviour of the religious person, Jew or Gentile (so Betz, *Galatians*, pp. 217–218), or more particularly as that which the Jewish law requires: so Longenecker, *Galatians*, p. 182, following Ernest De Witt Burton, *The Epistle to the Galatians* (ICC; Edinburgh: T. and T. Clark, 1921), p. 234. For other recent discussions of this matter see Dieter Lührmann, 'Tage, Monate, Jahreszeiten, Jahre (Gal. 4, 10)', *Werden und Wirken des Alten Testaments* (Festschrift for Claus Westermann), ed. Rainer Albertz, Hans-Peter Müller, Hans Walther Wolff und Walther Zimmerli (Göttingen: Vandenhoeck und Ruprecht; Neukirchen-Vluyn: Neukirchener, 1980), pp. 428–445; T. C. G. Thornton, "Jewish New Moon Festivals, Galatians 4:3–11 and Colossians 2:16', *JTS* 40 (1989), pp. 97–100.

of allegorizing was practised among the rabbis of Palestine,[104] and it seems likely that Paul's allegorizing[105] reflects this sort of approach to the application of Scripture.[106]

Second, there is the question of the function of the allegory. Is it to be seen as part of Paul's exhortations and appeals to the Galatians,[107] or as a continuation of the arguments which Paul offers in refutation of the Judaizers' position?[108] For our purposes it does not make a lot of difference which of these approaches is adopted. In either case Paul would be encouraging his readers not to be influenced by the Judaizers' teaching. But either way a further question is raised. Just how effective is this allegorical passage either as argument or exhortation? Is not allegory a rather weak form of both? This depends upon how the use of allegory is viewed. There is some evidence that it can in fact be the strongest weapon in a speaker's armoury, not because it adds new reasons in support of a position, but because it better secures the agreement of those who listen. For by using allegory a speaker shows his respect for the intelligence of his hearers, and so does not spell everything out. This means that the hearers actively discover for themselves at least part of

---

[104]R. P. C. Hanson, *Allegory and Event: A Study of the Sources and Significance of Origen's Interpretation of Scripture* (London: SCM, 1959), pp. 11–36, esp. pp. 13–14.

[105]Paul's allegorizing is not restricted to Gal. 3:21–31. Other examples may be found in 1 Cor. 5:6–8; 9:8–10 and possibly 1 Cor. 10:1–11 and 2 Cor. 3:13 – 4:6.

[106]Hanson, *Allegory and Event*, pp. 80–83. See also Longenecker's 'Excursus: The Hagar–Sarah story in Jewish writings and in Paul', in *Galatians*, pp. 200–206, in which he concludes: 'With respect to the specific Hagar–Sarah story, though there is enough interest in the contrasts and conflicts of the story in Jewish writings to suggest that Paul's use of it was not entirely unique, there is no evidence that his particular allegorical treatment of it was following any Jewish prototype, particularly in the identification he makes between Hagar, Ishmael, Mt. Sinai, and the present city of Jerusalem, and in the contrast he sets out between "the Jerusalem that is above" *vis-à-vis* Mt. Sinai and the present city of Jerusalem. To understand Paul's Hagar–Sarah allegory, therefore, it seems that at least four factors must be taken into account: (1) Paul's Jewish heritage, which was not averse to highlighting the contrasts and conflicts of the story; (2) tendencies within the various streams of Judaism generally to contemporize the persons and places of the biblical narrative for their own purposes, whether such contemporizations be understood as allegorical or typological treatments; (3) the Judaizers' contemporization of the story with the polemics of their usage probably directed against Paul; and (4) Paul's own ad hominem use, with his polemics directed against the Judaizers' (p. 206).

[107]So Longenecker, *Galatians*, p. 199. *Cf.* Hansen, *Abraham in Galatians*, pp. 145–154, who argues that epistolary and rhetorical analyses show that 'the Hagar–Sarah allegory was carefully crafted by Paul to add biblical weight to his request that the Galatians protect their freedom in Christ by expelling the troublemakers.'

[108]So Betz, *Galatians*, p. 238.

what the allegory is getting at, and are therefore prepared to defend what they have discovered.[109]

Third, there is the question of the introduction of the Sarah–Hagar story into the debate. Normally it has been assumed that Paul himself introduced the story to illustrate his position and convince his readers of it. But it is possible that it was the Judaizers who first made use of the story, employing it polemically against Paul. Then he responded with an *ad hominem* argument in which he turned the story around and used it polemically against them. Presenting this view, Longenecker explains the Judaizers' use of the story as follows:

> In explicating their position, the Judaizers undoubtedly claimed that Paul's preaching represented an 'Ishmaelian' form of the truth. Their argument probably was that while Ishmael was, indeed, the first son of Abraham, it was only Isaac who was considered the true son of Abraham, with the conclusion being that only as Paul's converts are related to Isaac and so the Jewish nation, and not Ishmael the non-Jewish representative, can they legitimately be called 'sons of Abraham'.[110]

Paul's response, then, would have been to show that it was the Judaizers' position that was 'Ishmaelian', and that it was those who stood for the believers' freedom from the law who were like Isaac, the true children of Abraham (and Sarah).

Turning now from preliminary matters to the text itself, we see that Paul begins by saying, 'Tell me, you who desire to be subject to the law, will you not listen to the law?' (v. 21). The allegory is addressed to those who 'desire to be [but were not yet] subject to the law', which to them meant primarily submitting to circumcision.[111]

The allegory concerns the two sons of Abraham: Ishmael, the one born of a slave woman (Hagar), and Isaac, the one born of the free woman (Sarah). The former was born 'according to the flesh', while the latter was born through the promise (vv. 22–23). Being interpreted allegorically, says Paul, these women (*autai*)[112] represent two covenants, the one from Mount Sinai giving birth to slavery, which is represented by Hagar and corresponds to the present

---

[109]*Cf.* Betz, *Galatians*, pp. 239–240.

[110]*Galatians*, p. 199.

[111]*Cf.* 5:2; 6:12.

[112]*Autai* in v. 24b is feminine plural and can only refer to the two women.

Jerusalem,[113] the other (it would seem to be implied)[114] from Mount Zion offering freedom, which is represented by Sarah and corresponds to the Jerusalem above (vv. 24–26).[115] Paul then cites Isaiah 54:1 (which calls upon the barren woman to rejoice because her children will be more than those of the woman who has a husband), and, taking his cue from the use of the word 'barren' both here and in the Genesis account of Sarah's condition before the promise of Isaac, he illustrates that the blessing of God is with those of the promise, not those of the flesh.

The first explicit point which Paul makes from all this is that it is his believing Gentile readers who are, like Isaac, children of the promise (v. 28) and therefore the true children of Abraham. By so saying he turns the tables on the Judaizers, who were apparently implying that unless Gentile believers were circumcised they could not be numbered among Abraham's true children.

The apostle then takes his allegory one step further by saying: 'But just as at that time the child who was born according to the flesh persecuted the child who was born according to the Spirit, so it is now also' (v. 29).[116] Thus Paul implies that there is a correspondence between the persecution of Isaac by Ishmael[117] and the 'confusing' (*cf.* 1:7; 5:10) of believing Gentiles by the Judaizers. This then leads on to a further allegorical application of the

---

[113]This does imply a negative assessment of contemporary Judaism on Paul's part, but it is not the main point which he seeks to make. Paul's explicit applications of the allegory, as we shall see, are aimed at countering the teaching of the Judaizers, not criticizing Judaism. *Cf.* Lloyd Gaston, 'Israel's Enemies in Pauline Theology', *NTS* 28 (1982), pp. 407–411; Hansen, *Abraham in Galatians*, pp. 148–149.

[114]Paul does not fill out this side of the comparison with the same detail as the other. This is left for the reader to do.

[115]In v. 25a there is a parenthetical statement ('Now Hagar is Mount Sinai in Arabia') which raises many questions, not least because of the textual variants involved. The problems related to this text are discussed by M. McNamara, '*To de (Hagar) Sina estin en tē Arabia* (Gal 4,25a): Paul and Petra', *MS* 2 (1978), pp. 24–41, which unfortunately was not available to me at the time of writing. For the most recent discussion see Longenecker, *Galatians*, pp. 211–213. While the problems of this text are important, they do not obscure the overall thrust of 4:21–31 and in particular what Paul says there about what is and is not necessary for one to be a true child of Abraham, a true child of the promise.

[116]Paul now contrasts the one born 'according to the flesh' with the one born (not through the promise, as previously, but) 'according to the Spirit'. While the terminology is different, those contrasted are the same, those who rely on the flesh on the one hand and those relying on the promise (who also received the Spirit, *cf.* 3:2) on the other.

[117]Gn. 16:4, 6 mention Hagar's contempt for Sarah (and Sarah's harsh treatment of Hagar) but make no mention of Ishmael persecuting Isaac. The Targums, however (esp. Targum Pseudo-

Sarah–Hagar story: 'But what does the scripture say? "Drive out the slave and her child; for the child of the slave will not share the inheritance with the child of the free woman"' (v. 30). It would seem that the readers were meant to recognize in this piece of allegorizing a mandate to reject the Judaizers and their demands.[118] And if they were to do so, Paul would have succeeded in turning the tables upon his opponents, for their purpose in agitating in Galatia was to pressurize the believers there to reject Paul and his gospel.

Paul concludes his allegorizing with another explicit statement: 'So then, friends, we are children, not of the slave but of the free woman' (v. 31). This is the main point to be made in the whole passage. This is indicated by the fact that the only other explicit piece of application to the situation in hand which Paul offers in this passage makes the same point: 'Now you, my friends, are children of the promise, like Isaac' (v. 28). It is therefore reasonable to draw the conclusion that the major point at issue in Galatia was whether law-free believing Gentiles were or were not true children of Abraham. By a series of theological arguments Paul had defended the case for regarding believing Gentiles as true children of Abraham, and concluded it with a piece of allegorizing in which this main point was made explicitly and other matters were left for the readers to infer.

Throughout the long section of Galatians 3:1 – 4:31 Paul consistently argues that believing Gentiles have become, and continue to be, true children of Abraham without the necessity of law observance. Both the legalistic and the nomistic implications of the Judaizers' demands are to be rejected.

Paul's response: warnings and exhortations

Paul's response to the crisis in Galatia consisted not only of theological arguments but also of strong warnings and exhortations. These are included in the so-called paraenetic section in the latter part of the letter (5:1 –

Jonathan at Gn. 22), speak of tension between Ismael and Isaac. *Cf.* Michael G. Steinhauser, 'Gal 4, 25a: Evidence of Targumic Tradition in Gal. 4, 21–31?', *Bib* 70 (1989), pp. 234–240; Gaston, 'Israel's Enemies', pp. 406–407; Betz, *Galatians*, pp. 248–249. If Paul is using *ad hominem* argument, picking up his opponents' own exegetical assumptions in order to turn those against them, then we should not necessarily assume that Paul accepted the truth of the Targumic tradition he used.

[118]Andrew C. Perriman. 'The Rhetorical Strategy of Galatians 4:21 – 5:1', *EvQ* 65 (1993), pp. 41–42, argues that the real purpose of Paul's 'allegorization' is to show the applicability of the scripture 'Drive out the slave and her child' to the situation in Galatia.

6:10).[119] While the presence of paraenesis in 5:1 – 6:10 cannot be disputed, there are a number of points which can be made in favour of the view that it is not merely a piece of paraenesis tacked on to the end of the theological part of the letter. For example, there is a clear link between Paul's use of the Hagar–Sarah allegory in 4:21–31 (to urge his readers to protect their freedom by resisting the pressure of the Judaizers) and his exhortations in 5:1–12 (that they should stand fast in their freedom and not submit to the yoke of bondage again). Also, it should be noted that the main issue of the letter (whether or not the Galatian believers should submit to circumcision) is mentioned explicitly only in this part of the letter (5:2–3; 6:12–13), and that in this part of the letter Paul gives further explanations why they should not do so.[120]

The dire consequences of submission to circumcision

In 5:2–4 Paul outlines two dire consequences for his readers should they submit to circumcision:

> Listen! I, Paul, am telling you that if you let yourselves be circumcised, Christ will be of no benefit to you. Once again I testify to every man who lets himself be circumcised that he is obliged to obey the entire law. You who want to be justified by the law have cut yourselves off from Christ; you have fallen away from grace.

Being circumcised obliges people to observe the whole law

Paul warns the Gentile believers that if they are circumcised they will be obliged to keep the whole law (5:3). Two points may be inferred from this warning. First, that while the Galatians were intending to be circumcised, they

---

[119]There has been debate over the extent of the paraenetic section. Betz, *Galatians*, pp. 22–23, speaks of an *exhortatio* running from 5:1 to 6:10, and Longenecker, *Galatians*, pp. vii–viii, of a 'Request Section' running from 4:12 to 6:10.

[120]Frank J. Matera. 'The Culmination of Paul's Argument to the Galatians: Gal. 5.1 – 6.17', *JSNT* 32 (1988), pp. 79–91, argues fairly persuasively that it is wrong to view 5:1 – 6:17 as the paraenetic section added on at the end of the theological section (1:6 – 4:31). He too notes that it is only in 5:1ff. that explicit mention is made of the fact that the Galatians were being asked to be circumcised. He also points out that 5:1 – 6:17 itself falls into three parts: a piece of paraenesis (5:13 – 6:10) bracketed by two shorter sections, both of which give reasons for the Galatians not to submit to circumcision (5:1–12 and 6:11–17). On these grounds, among others, he argues that 5:1 – 6:17 is actually the culmination of the letter. So also essentially, Hansen, *Abraham in Galatians*, pp. 150–154. *Contra* Longenecker, *Galatians*, p. 237, who asserts that at 5:13ff. Paul redirects his attention to libertinism which was indigenous to the churches.

had not yet done so (*cf.* 6:12–13). Second, that they were not intending to observe all the requirements of the law. The indications from the letter to the Galatians are that it was only circumcision, and perhaps certain other specified elements of the law, which were being laid upon them. These elements included the observance of days, months, seasons and years (4:10), and possibly also food taboos (if it be allowed that a subsidiary purpose of 2:11–14 was to counteract the demand for the observance of food laws). Paul's warning, then, that those who are circumcised are obliged to keep the whole law,[121] would have come as a shock to the Galatians, and especially so if they remembered their apostle's words in 3:10: 'For all who rely on the works of the law are under a curse; for it is written, "Cursed is everyone who does not observe and obey all the things written in the book of the law."'

Circumcision means abandonment of the faith

Paul further warns Gentile believers that if they submit to circumcision Christ will be of no benefit to them (5:2); they will be cut off from Christ and fall from grace (5:4). For the apostle, wanting to be justified by the law is the opposite of eagerly awaiting the hope of righteousness through the Spirit and by faith (5:5). People cannot 'through the Spirit, by faith' await the hope of righteousness, while at the same time seeking to be justified by the law. The two are mutually exclusive experientially. A legalistic attitude cannot be combined with faith in Christ.[122] It is difficult to be sure whether Paul is here implying that his readers (and his opponents and the Jews) believed the fulfilment of the law can

---

[121]Paul certainly taught that being circumcised obliged one to keep the whole law (*cf.* also Rom. 2:25), but there is debate over how widespread this view was in Judaism. While some Jewish rabbis might have advocated a more lenient approach, there is evidence for the more rigorous view in the Mishnah, the Gemara, the Tosephta, the Apocrypha, the Qumran literature and even in the New Testament. For documentation, see Longenecker, *Galatians*, p. 227, who concludes his discussion of the evidence with a quotation from David Daube: 'The interdependence of all precepts, their fundamental equality, the importance of even the minor ones, or apparently minor ones, because of their association with the weightiest – these were common themes among the Tannaites' (*The New Testament and Rabbinic Judaism*, London: University of London, Athlone, 1956, p. 251). For Paul, however, the important point would not have been whether what he said about the implications of submitting to circumcision corresponded to the views held by Jewish teachers of the day, or even to what the Judaizers taught. What mattered to him was that the Law itself would countenance no deliberate neglect of its requirements. To choose to be circumcised without observing all the other directives of the law was not an option, and the Galatians needed to realize that.

[122]*Cf.* Longenecker, *Galatians*, p. 228.

justify,[123] or simply indicating that the Galatians had not seen the implications of their contemplated action. They were regarding it more like 'changing denominations' than abandoning their faith.[124] But Paul saw more clearly what the implications were. For Gentile believers, such a 'change of denomination' would be tantamount to abandoning Christianity because it involved a change in the basis of their belief.[125]

The law summed up in a single commandment

Paul, having defended the freedom of the Gentile believers from the law, makes a point of warning them, in 5:13–14, not to use this freedom as an opportunity for self-indulgence. Instead, they should 'through love become slaves to one another' because 'the whole law is summed up [fulfilled] in a single commandment, "You shall love your neighbor as yourself."'

The command 'You shall love your neighbor as yourself' is quoted from Leviticus 19:18, a passage to which, in the synoptic gospels, Jesus appeals several times.[126] The question sometimes raised in connection with Paul's reference to the command in which the whole law is summed up is whether, having thrown legalism out of the front door, he is not re-admitting it by the back door. Having laboured so hard in his theological arguments to show that the law has no place as a regulatory code in the lives of believers, has he not reinstated it as just that in his exhortation?[127] Even though, on first reading, there may appear to be grounds for such a criticism of Paul, there are three reasons this should not be seen to be the case.

First, in this passage believers' freedom from the law is assumed, and on that basis Paul urges his readers to serve one another through love, adding that the whole law is summed up in the command to love one's neighbour. Paul is defining love in terms of the law,[128] not reinstating the Mosaic law as a

---

[123]So, *e.g.*, Räisänen, *Paul and the Law*, p. 162; Westerholm, *Israel's Law and the Church's Faith*, p. 144.

[124]*Cf.* Betz, *Galatians*, p. 261.

[125]This does not apply to Jewish believers in the same way. They were already circumcised when they realized that neither circumcision nor observance of the law brought them justification, and so they trusted in Christ (2:15–16). But when things are reversed, as they were in the case of Gentiles being urged to be circumcised, everything changes. They already trusted in Christ, but then came to think that this was not enough, and so to believe that they must undergo circumcision to be justified. This is a denial of the faith.

[126]Mt. 5:43–44; Mt. 19:18–19 par.; Mt. 22:37–39 par.

[127]So, *e.g.*, Räisänen, *Paul and the Law*, pp. 82, 199.

[128]*Cf. ibid.*, p. 63.

regulatory norm, every part of which believers must obey.

Second, even though Paul does sometimes speak of believers fulfilling the law, a closer examination of Paul's statements to this effect suggests that he distinguished between 'fulfilling the law' and 'doing the law'.[129] 'Doing the law' denotes the observance of all that the law prescribes (*cf.* 3:10–12), whereas 'fulfilling the law' means living a life in which the great moral concerns of the law are exemplified, even though many of the actual regulations of the law (including circumcision, dietary laws and calendrical rules) are not observed.[130]

Third, Westerholm has shown that in the three places where Paul speaks about believers fulfilling the law (Rom. 8:4; 13:8–10; Gal. 5:14), he is *describing*, not prescribing, Christian behaviour.[131] Paul's prescriptive statements are based on the new life in the Spirit which those in Christ enjoy. His references to fulfilling the law in these contexts are made to describe the results of new life in the Spirit. He is not re-introducing the law as a regulatory norm for those who are in Christ.

When Paul says, that 'the whole law is summed up in a single commandment, "You shall love your neighbor as yourself"' (5:14), the words 'the whole law' signify all one's obligations to one's neighbour, as the context indicates ('through love serve one another'). Paul was not here thinking of all one's obligations to God, or of the fulfilling of the many legal and ritual demands of the law. By serving one another by love, people do not carry out all these.

Exhortation to walk by the Spirit

In Galatians 5:16–26, a passage which seems to foreshadow Romans 8:1–14, Paul speaks of the tension between the flesh and the Spirit in the life of believers, and then urged his readers to walk by the Spirit:

> Live by the Spirit, I say, and do not gratify the desires of the flesh. For what the flesh desires is opposed to the Spirit, and what the Spirit desires is opposed to the flesh; for these are opposed to each other, to prevent you from doing what you want. But if you are led by the Spirit, you are not subject to the law (5:16–18).

---

[129]*Cf*, Betz, *Galatians*, p. 275.

[130]*Cf.* Karl Kertelge, 'Gesetz und Freiheit im Galaterbrief', *NTS* 30 (1984), p. 390.

[131]See *Israel's Law and the Church's Faith*, pp. 201–205, where Westerholm summarizes his article, 'On Fulfilling the Whole Law (Gal. 5:14)', *SEÅ* 51–52 (1986–87), pp. 229–237.

These verses are a part of the larger section, 5:13–18, where Paul urges his readers not to use their freedom from the law as an opportunity for self-indulgence (5:13). They are to live by the Spirit and not gratify the desires of the flesh. What is involved in these two different lifestyles Paul himself spells out in the section which follows (5:19–24), where he contrasts the 'works of the flesh' (vv. 19–21) with the 'fruit of the Spirit' (vv. 22–24).

In 5:16–18 Paul reminds his readers of the conflict between the Spirit and the flesh: 'For what the flesh desires is opposed to the Spirit, and what the Spirit desires is opposed to the flesh; for these are opposed to each other, to prevent you from doing what you want' (5:17). The next verse comes as something of a surprise. We might have expected Paul to say that if people are led by the Spirit they will not fulfil the desires of the flesh. What he says is not that, however, but rather, 'If you are led by the Spirit, you are not subject to the law' (5:18). The implication of this surprising statement is that being free from the law is intimately connected with overcoming the desires of the flesh.

This is contrary to the fears which probably haunted many Jewish believers (including the Judaizers) when they heard about the influx of Gentiles into the church as a result of Paul's mission. They feared that the Gentile believers who were not under the law would quickly succumb to the desires of the flesh. But Paul implies that not being under the law had the opposite effect. It enabled people to resist the desires of the flesh. Longenecker sums up the matter well:

> The Judaizers had undoubtedly argued that only two options existed for Galatian Christians: either (1) a lifestyle governed by Torah, or (2) a lifestyle giving way to license, such as formerly characterized their lives as Gentiles apart from God. The Christian gospel, however, as Paul proclaimed it, has to do with a third way of life that is distinct from both nomism and libertinism – not one that takes a middle course between the two, as many try to do in working out a Christian lifestyle on their own, but that is 'a highway above them both' (Burton, *Galatians*, 302). The antidote to license in the Christian life is not laws, as the Judaizers argued, but openness to the Spirit and being guided by the Spirit. For being 'in Christ' means neither nomism nor libertinism, but a new quality of life based in and directed by the Spirit.[132]

---

[132]*Galatians*, p. 246. It may be asked whether there is evidence to justify the confidence with which Longenecker says that the Judaizers saw things as he describes them here. But this aside, Longenecker's comments seem to be right on target.

Bear one another's burdens and fulfil the law of Christ

In 6:2 Paul urges his readers: 'Bear one another's burdens, and in this way you will fulfill the law of Christ (*ton nomou tou Christou*).' The expression 'the law of Christ', and exactly what Paul meant by it, have been the subject of much debate.[133] The most important step in seeking to determine its meaning, however, is the examination of the immediate context in which it is found (6:1–10).

It is difficult to know whether the injunction to 'bear one another's burdens, and in this way you will fulfil the law of Christ' was meant to be simply one of a series of independent exhortations beginning at 6:1 and running through to 6:10, or whether it was intended to be read with the first of those exhortations: 'My friends, if anyone is detected in a transgression, you who have received the Spirit should restore such a one in a spirit of gentleness' (6:1).

In the latter case, the bearing of one another's burdens would mean taking upon one's own shoulders the care for another's spiritual state, and doing what one could to restore that person. In this case the law of Christ would be fulfilled in the exercise of love to care for and restore a fellow believer who had been overtaken in some transgression. In the former case, we would have simply a general exhortation to assist fellow believers who were burdened in some way or another by sharing their burdens with them. The law of Christ would be fulfilled in the exercise of love to share the burdens.

It would appear that 'the law of Christ' that was in Paul's mind was the command to love one's neighbour as one's self.[134] It is not a matter, as some have suggested, of Paul, having fought to deliver Gentile believers from the yoke of the Mosaic law, immediately placing upon them the heavier yoke of Christ's law (understood as a collection of the many injunctions such as those found in, *e.g.*, Mt. 5 – 7). The law of Christ is the law of love. For Paul, love was the fruit of the Spirit (Gal. 5:22), fruit which those under the law could never produce on their own. It is only in the lives of those freed from the law, and walking by the Spirit, that the law of Christ is fulfilled.

---

[133]The various approaches to the matter, and those who support them, are helpfully documented by Longenecker, *Galatians*, pp. 275–276. *Cf.* also Betz, *Galatians*, pp. 299–301.

[134]Alternative suggestions have been made by Hong, *The Law in Galatians*, p. 176, who argues that the law of Christ is another way of speaking of the Mosaic law and that to fulfil the law of Christ is to satisfy the true intention of the law without carrying out all its particular details, and Richard B. Hays, 'Christology and Ethics in Galatians: The Law of Christ', *CBQ* 49 (1987) pp. 276–283, who argues that conformity to the law of Christ means conformity to the figure of Christ (*i.e.* following Christ's example).

Summary

The nature and function of the law

In the course of his response to the Galatian crisis Paul made many statements which reflect his understanding of the nature and function of the law, and these were discussed above. In what follows, a summary is given of what these statements reveal of this important aspect of Paul's theology. The summary includes three negative statements about the nature and function of the law, and one positive statement.

The law is not of faith

In 3:12 Paul says: 'But the law does not rest on faith; on the contrary, "Whoever does the works of the law will live by them."' In the discussion of this passage above it was argued that the law 'does not rest on faith' because it operates on the principle of performance (those who *do* them shall live by them) and not on the principle of faith (trusting in Christ for justification without dependence upon performance).

The law does not annul the promise

Paul apparently believed that the Judaizers, in their teaching, were implying that the promise given to Abraham was nullified by the giving of the law 430 years later. To demand observance of the law as well as faith in Christ implied that God had reneged on his promise to Abraham. To support his view, Paul cited legal practice in his day, whereby, once a testamentary document had been ratified, it could not be added to or altered (by someone else). On this analogy, the law, coming 430 years after God made the promise to Abraham, can neither annul nor add extra conditions to that promise.

The law cannot make alive

Paul's statement implying that the law cannot make alive is part of his answer to the rhetorical question, 'Is the law then opposed to the promises of God?' (3:21a). To this question he replies, 'Certainly not! For if a law had been given that could make alive, then righteousness would indeed come through the law' (3:21b). For Paul it was impossible to say that the law could 'make alive', because Scripture itself shuts up everything under the power of sin (3:22).

On first reading this seems to contradict a statement earlier in chapter three where Paul, citing Leviticus 18:5, says, 'Whoever does the works of the law will live by them' (3:12). Paul there (and also in Rom. 10:5) seems to acknowledge that the law does offer life to those who observe its demands. This is in line with statements in the law itself where blessings are promised to those who obey, while those who do not are threatened with curses (*cf.* Dt. 27 – 28). The apparent contradiction in Paul's thought is resolved, however, when we take account of his understanding of the power of sin. It is his recognition of the power of sin which leads Paul to the conclusion that a law could not be given which could make alive. There is no problem on the side of the law; its promise of life is genuine. The problem is on the side of those who hear its promise. They are shut up under the power of sin, and therefore cannot meet the conditions of life set down by the law. Paul makes this very point in 3:22, and it is also the implied condition of 3:10: 'For all who rely on the works of the law are under a curse; for it is written, "Cursed is everyone who does not observe and obey all the things written in the book of the law."'

The law as paidagōgos

In 3:19 Paul says that the law 'was added because of transgressions, until the offspring would come to whom the promise had been made'. The question needing to be answered now is: in just what way did the law function in the period before the coming of Christ? The crucial passage for answering this question is 3:23–26:

> Now before faith came, we were imprisoned and guarded under the law until faith would be revealed. Therefore the law was our disciplinarian until Christ came, so that we might be justified by faith. But now that faith has come, we are no longer subject to a disciplinarian, for in Christ Jesus you are all children of God through faith.

It appears that the law, added because of transgressions (3:19), had the function of keeping people under restraint until the new order of things should come – until faith should be revealed. It is implied that under the new order of faith, people would not need the law as disciplinarian (*paidagōgos*) to prevent them breaking out in transgression.

The function of a *paidagōgos* in the ancient world was not that of the teacher (*didaskalos*), though inevitably some informal instruction about behaviour and morals was involved. The primary function of the *paidagōgos* was to exercise custody over minors on behalf of their father. He was charged with the responsibility for the moral and behavioural restraint as well as the protection of the minors until they achieved their majority. On this analogy, the law's function was not to teach people beforehand about Christ, but rather to keep them from moral danger until Christ should appear, and when that time came the law's custodial role would come to an end.

In 4:1–7, Paul painted a similar picture of people's existence under the law prior to the coming of Christ, and the change that took place afterwards. A son who was to inherit everything from his father differed very little from a slave until he came of age, in so far as both were in the custody of guardians and trustees. So too, those who were to receive adoption as children of God were held in custody under the law like slaves, until the coming of Christ. Then they would be no longer like children in custody, but like adults in no further need of the custodianship of the law.

Thus, in Galatians, Paul portrays a custodial and disciplinarian role for the law. It kept people from danger until the coming of faith. It could not itself provide people who were under the power of sin with a means of justification. But its role was positive in the sense that it was intended to keep people from danger until the coming of Christ and faith in him.

Justification

A number of points concerning justification emerged in the discussion of Paul's response to the crisis in Galatia, and the main ones are summarized under six headings below.

Justification by faith in Christ

Paul appealed to two incidents, in which he and his companions had been involved, to demonstrate that justification was by faith in Christ and not by works of the law. The first took place in Jerusalem and involved Titus, whom 'false believers' demanded be circumcised. Paul and his companions strongly resisted this demand, and then the rest of the members of the Jerusalem church did not require it. They recognized that Titus' faith in Christ was enough for him to be numbered among the true people of God and to be justified in God's sight.

The second incident was the dispute over table fellowship between believing Jews and Gentiles in Antioch. In describing the common theological ground between himself and Cephas Paul says they both believed in Jesus Christ in order to be justified by faith because no-one is justified by the works of the law (2:15–16). This clearly implies that justification by faith was an important doctrine held to by Paul and Cephas alike. It was not merely a 'fighting doctrine' introduced by Paul in order to get the better of the Judaizers.

Justification and the hearing of faith

The distinction between faith and works of the law as means by which a person is justified was further clarified by Paul when he appealed to his readers to consider their own experience of the Spirit. While justification and the reception of the Spirit can be distinguished theologically, for Paul they were inseparable experientially. Thus he could ask the Galatians to consider their conversion experience, and then say whether they had received the Spirit by works of law or by the hearing of faith. They would have to reply that they had received the Spirit without having done anything other than responding to the gospel in faith. When the Judaizers came on the scene the Galatians contemplated adding works of law to this faith, but Paul reminded them that the performance of works of the law had not been necessary for them to receive the Spirit. And because the reception of the Spirit and justification cannot be separated experientially, it follows that nothing but faith is necessary for justification.

No changes to the means of justification

Paul believed that the means by which people are justified in God's sight had always been, and would always be, by faith. He argued that it had been so in Abraham's case, and that the giving of the law 430 years later did not change that. In this respect, the promise God made to Abraham was like a human will. Once made, it could be neither added to nor altered (by someone else). Thus, no matter what the Judaizers might say to the contrary, the giving of the law 430 years after God made his promise to Abraham could neither nullify nor add extra conditions to that promise. As in Abraham's time, so now, justification is by faith.

Justification rests upon redemption

The promise of justification by faith rests upon the redemption effected through Christ. Paul says that Jewish people, himself included, were under the curse of the law for failure to fulfil all its demands. Christ became a curse for them particularly, in order to redeem them from the curse of the law so that they might be justified by faith, and so that justification might come to the

Gentiles also. For while the Gentiles were not under the law in the same way as the Jews were, they experienced an analogous bondage – under the *stoicheia tou kosmou* – and from this bondage they needed to be redeemed in order to be justified. Justification by faith as far as Paul was concerned was intimately related to the death of Christ, so much so that if there were another means of justification, then Christ would have died in vain. This also indicates that justification by faith was no mere fighting doctrine introduced by Paul for polemic purposes in his struggle with the Judaizers. It was of crucial importance, stemming as it did from the central event of redemptive history, the cross of Christ.

Faith in Christ is incompatible with reliance on works

Paul warned the Galatians that if they were circumcised they would fall from grace and be cut off from Christ. Circumcision was not a problem for Jewish believers. They had been circumcised before they believed in Christ, and they put their trust in him because they knew that neither circumcision nor other works of the law were effective means of justification for them. Circumcision was, however, a problem for Gentile believers. They had already put their faith in Christ for justification, but were now tempted to think that this was insufficient. They needed to add circumcision and other works of the law to this faith if they wanted to be truly justified. This was not only futile (by works of law no-one is justified), but it is incompatible with faith in Christ. One cannot at the same time trust in Christ for justification and rely upon one's own performance. It is experientially impossible.

Justification by faith is incompatible with covenantal nomism

In his reflections on the Antioch incident, Paul makes plain that both he and Cephas agreed that 'a person is justified not by the works of the law but through faith in Jesus Christ'. Their disagreement was related to the role of the law in the life of believers. In the case of the Gentile believers in particular, Paul insists that they must be free from the law as a regulatory norm, *i.e.* they were not to become covenantal nomists, people justified by grace through faith but then required to live under the law. Jewish believers might live like nomists if they wished, because they were used to living under the law and for them it meant no change in lifestyle; it entailed no extra conditions for justification apart from faith in Jesus Christ. But in the case of the Gentiles it would mean a change in lifestyle; it would involve extra conditions for justification. So then, what was covenantal nomism for the Jewish believers became legalism when applied to the Gentiles.

The law and the believer

In the course of the treatment of Paul's response to the Galatian crisis above, several statements concerning the place of the law in the life of the believer were discussed. The contribution of those statements to an understanding of Paul's beliefs about this matter is summarized under the several headings which follow.

Freedom from the law

At several places in Galatians the freedom of believers from the law is defended, assumed or argued. It is defended in 2:3–5 where Paul tells how he resisted pressure in Jerusalem to have Titus circumcised, and in 2:11–14 where he recounts how he rebuked Peter for his failure to act in accordance with the gospel when in Antioch. It is assumed in 3:1–5, where Paul quizzes the Galatians on what it was that brought them the experience of the Spirit, hearing the gospel with faith or obedience to the law. It is argued in 3:6–18 by appeal to what the Scriptures say about Abraham, and in 3:23 – 4:5 by the use of the analogies of the law as *paidagōgos* and as guardian or trustee. Finally, freedom from the law is assumed in 4:21–31, where Paul uses the allegory of Sarah and Hagar to urge his readers to reject the Judaizers and their demands, and in 5:1, where he exhorts them to stand fast in their liberty in Christ, refusing to submit to bondage again.

No rebuilding what was torn down

In 2:15–21 Paul sets out the essential theological agreements and disagreements which existed between himself and Cephas at the time of the Antioch incident. In the course of highlighting the disagreements he writes:

> But if, in our effort to be justified in Christ, we ourselves have been found to be sinners, is Christ then a servant of sin? Certainly not! But if I build up again the very things that I once tore down, then I demonstrate that I am a transgressor (vv. 17–18).

The historical context of the exchange between Paul and Cephas provides the clue to the meaning of this difficult passage. Prior to the arrival in Antioch of those of the circumcision party from James, Cephas and other Jewish believers apparently felt that their being justified in Christ released them from the demands of the law so that they could eat with Gentile believers. But when those from James arrived, their weak conscience placed them back under the law, and so they felt forced to withdraw from table fellowship with the Gentile believers.

In this situation they had re-erected for themselves the jurisdiction of the law, which in the freedom of the gospel they had previously torn down. Once they had done so they immediately appeared as transgressors of the law. It was as if their faith in Christ had turned them into wrongdoers, or, to use Paul's words, it seemed as though Christ was 'a servant of sin'. This is clearly a repugnant idea and this in itself shows how untenable was the position in which Cephas and the other Jewish believers had placed themselves. Furthermore, it was a position they need never have occupied, because as believers they had died to the law in order to live for God (2:19). There was no need to fear being branded as transgressors.

Thus whatever might be the function of the law in the life of the believer, as far as Paul was concerned it was never to be rebuilt to function as a standard by which believers (whether Jews or Gentiles) *must* live.

Learning from the law

While believers were not to reinstate the law as a compulsory standard for life, it nevertheless continued to be a source of valuable instruction. That Paul expected his converts to learn from the law is clearly implied by his introduction to the allegory of Hagar and Sarah: 'Tell me, you who desire to be subject to the law, will you not listen to the law?' (4:21).

It was not only allegorical lessons that Paul believed were to be learnt from the law. This is evident from his repeated appeals to the law to support his doctrine of justification by faith, and in particular from his appeal to the Abrahamic narratives in Genesis (*cf. e.g.*, 3:6 [Gn. 15:6]; 3:8 [Gn. 12:3]; 3:16 [Gn. 12:7]; 4:30 [Gn. 21:10]). What is also evident from these appeals is that Paul used the word 'law' (*nomos*) in more ways than one in Galatians. It could refer to the whole Pentateuch (including the narrative sections) as well as the legal requirements which were contained in it.

The law fulfilled in one word

It was argued that when, in 5:14, Paul says, 'For the whole law is summed up in a single commandment, "You shall love your neighbor as yourself"', he was *not* implying that *all* the demands of the law were fulfilled in that way. For example, the apostle clearly did not expect the laws of circumcision and clean and unclean foods to be fulfilled in this way. The context (*cf.* v. 13: 'through love become slaves to one another') suggests that Paul's thinking here was more restricted. Serving one another through love fulfils the obligations the law places upon people in respect of their neighbours.

Those led by the Spirit are not under the law

It is not surprising that Paul, in 5:16–17, warned the Galatians not to 'gratify the desires of the flesh', reminding them that 'what the flesh desires is opposed to the Spirit, and what the Spirit desires is opposed to the flesh; for these are opposed to each other, to prevent you from doing what you want'. But the next verse does come as something of a surprise. We might have expected Paul to say that if people are led by the Spirit they will not fulfil the desires of the flesh. What he says is not this, however, but rather: 'If you are led by the Spirit, you are not subject to the law' (5:18). The implication of this is that not being under the law is intimately connected with overcoming the desires of the flesh. Paul implies that the Gentiles' not being under the law, contrary to expectations, actually contributes to their being able to resist the desires of the flesh.

Fulfilling the law of Christ

In 6:2 Paul urged his readers: 'Bear one another's burdens, and in this way you will fulfil the law of Christ (*ton nomon tou Christou*).' This could mean either the exercise of love to care for and restore a fellow believer who has been overtaken in some transgression, or, more generally, showing love by assisting fellow believers by sharing their burdens with them. In both cases the law of Christ would be fulfilled in loving service to fellow believers in need. Thus it would appear that 'the law of Christ' that was in Paul's mind was the command to love one's neighbour as one's self. It was not a matter of Paul, having fought to deliver Gentile believers from the yoke of the Mosaic law, immediately placing upon them the heavier yoke of Christ's law (understood as a collection of the many injunctions such as those found in *e.g.* Mt. 5 – 7).

From the letter to the Galatians, with its radical stance in regard to the law, we turn now to 1 Corinthians, which, on first reading, might appear to adopt quite a different stance.

3

1 Corinthians

The regulation of freedom

Introduction

Moving from Galatians to 1 Corinthians, the reader is conscious of a marked change in subject matter as well as tone. In Galatians the role of the law and the means of justification are matters of great importance and are addressed directly by Paul, but these matters are not discussed at any length in 1 Corinthians. Here Paul makes repeated appeals to the law in ethical instructions to his readers, and this has led some scholars to argue that Paul threw out the law in Galatians only to reintroduce it in 1 Corinthians. This, and other contentious matters in relation to Paul's understanding of the law and justification, will be addressed once all the letters of the Pauline corpus have been reviewed. Such matters must not be allowed to determine our approach to this study of 1 Corinthians. Instead, we will first seek to understand the way in which Paul used the law in dealing with the issues which confronted him as he wrote, and if and how he brought the doctrine of justification into play. The first step is to sketch in something of the background to this letter in the relationship between Paul and the Corinthians.

The background to 1 Corinthians

Because of the number, nature and size of Paul's letters to the Corinthians, we know more about the relationship existing between the apostle and that church than we do about his relationship with any other church. It was complex, involving three visits by the apostle to Corinth, two delegations from Corinth to Paul while he was in Ephesus, the sending of two emissaries from Paul to Corinth, four (or five) letters from Paul to the Corinthians, and one letter from the Corinthians to Paul. What is offered below is one reconstruction of the progress of this relationship up to the writing of 1 Corinthians.[1]

The relationship began with Paul's pioneer missionary visit to Corinth (1 Cor. 2:1–5; Acts 18:1–18). This was followed by the earliest of Paul's letters, often referred to as the 'previous letter' (no longer extant), in which he urged the Corinthians not to associate with immoral believers (1 Cor. 5:9). Next, Paul received a letter from the Corinthians, written perhaps in response to his 'previous letter', and in which they raised matters about which they had disagreements with him (1 Cor. 7:1). Paul then wrote the next of his letters (our 1 Corinthians), in which he sought to correct the Corinthians' misunderstanding of his 'previous letter' (they thought he wanted them to have no contact with any immoral person, not just with immoral believers, *cf.* 5:10–11). In 1 Corinthians he also sought to clarify his position on a number of other contentious issues. One of thxese issues (whether a man should 'touch a woman', 7:1) and possibly several of the others (food offered to idols, 8:1; spirituality, 12:1; the collection, 16:1; and Apollos' movements, 16:12) had been raised in the letter he had received from the Corinthians themselves.[2] In addition to these matters, there were other contentious issues with which Paul had to deal in 1 Corinthians. One of

---

[1]Like any other reconstruction, this one depends upon certain decisions made about literary and historical problems which are interrelated and very complex. For further discussion see Colin G. Kruse, *The Second Epistle of Paul to the Corinthians* (TNTC; Leicester: IVP; Grand Rapids: Eerdmans, 1987), pp. 17–21.

[2]All these other issues are introduced in 1 Corinthians with the formula, *peri de* ('now concerning'). The first occurrence reads, 'Now concerning the things about which you wrote . . .' (7:1), and this has led numerous commentators to assume that the subsequent uses of the formula also introduce responses to issues raised in the Corinthians' letter to Paul; so, most recently, Gordon D. Fee, *The First Epistle to the Corinthians* NICNT; Grand Rapids: Eerdmans, 1987, p. 267. This assumption has been questioned by Margaret M. Mitchell, 'Concerning *peri de* in 1 Corinthians, *NovT* 31 (1989), pp. 233–234, who argues from the usage of the formula in a wide variety of ancient Greek texts (especially letters) that *peri de* is simply a topic marker, a shorthand way of introducing the next subject of discussion. It can be used to refer to information received in a letter, but is not restricted to such, even in letters which refer to a previous letter. The only requirement for its use is that the topic be one about which both the writer and the reader have knowledge.

these, the issue of party spirit, had been reported to him by 'Chloe's people' (1:11), and they and/or Stephanus, Fortunatus and Achaicus (16:17) were also possibly responsible for informing him of other contentious issues (pride in wisdom, 1:17 – 4:13; criticism of Paul himself, 4:1–21; *cf.* 9:1–14; litigation among believers, 6:1; and sexual immorality, 6:12–20). Concerning these matters also, Paul felt he had to clarify his position when writing 1 Corinthians.

It is clear, then, that in 1 Corinthians Paul was not merely dealing with problems experienced by the Christian community at Corinth. Rather, he was dealing with issues of contention between himself and the believers there, and underlying these was a criticism of Paul's gospel, style of speaking, spirituality, and integrity (*cf.* 4:1–21; 9:1–6, 12).

While it is possible that those called 'false apostles' by Paul in 2 Corinthians 11:13 were already present and aggravating the situation in Corinth when 1 Corinthians was written, they were not the 'opponents' reflected in this letter. Those whom Paul took to task in 1 Corinthians were members of the Corinthian church. Clearly, some of them believed that they had already arrived spiritually, and that Paul had not (1 Cor. 4:8–10). It was, in part, because they believed they had arrived, or, in other words, because of their over-spiritualized eschatology, that they found themselves at loggerheads with their founding apostle over a number of issues.

In what follows, Paul's responses to some of these contentious issues will be explored, in particular those responses which reflect something of his understanding of the law and justification.

A case of incest

It had become known to Paul that one of the members of the church was living with his father's wife, a form of behaviour condoned not even by Gentiles (5:1). Even worse, however, was the attitude of the Corinthian believers to this incestuous relationship: they were puffed up with pride instead of being filled with grief (5:2–3). Paul's response to this situation is found in 5:3–13, and it contains three elements.

Judgment pronounced

Being absent from Corinth, Paul passed judgment upon the man in the name of the Lord Jesus. This judgment, he said, was to be implemented in his (physical) absence by the Corinthians when they were gathered together with Paul's spirit and the power of the Lord Jesus.[3] They were then to hand the man over to Satan for the destruction of the flesh,[4] in the hope that his spirit might be saved in the day of the Lord (5:3–5).

The law provides a paradigm for purity of life

Paul rebuked the Corinthians for boasting in the face of such scandalous behaviour. Using the analogy of the effects of one small piece of leavened bread upon a whole batch of new dough (it caused the whole lot to be leavened), Paul drove home the fact that the presence of the unrepentant incestuous man in the Corinthian Christian community would have deleterious effects upon all its members. They were to rid themselves of that person so that they might truly be a new community. And then, perhaps to avoid any suggestion that genuine purity could be achieved merely by their own actions, he reminded them that they were already a new community in Christ; already they were like a new batch of unleavened dough. Therefore, they must act to maintain the purity of their community. What was involved in this is teased out in verses 7b–8 with an allusion to the law:

> For our paschal lamb, Christ, has been sacrificed. Therefore, let us celebrate the festival, not with the old yeast, the yeast of malice and evil, but with the unleavened bread of sincerity and truth.

It was because Christ had been sacrificed for them that they were now in a position to celebrate God's grace in purity of life. Just as the Jewish passover was followed by the feast of unleavened bread in houses free from leaven, so those for whom Christ the passover lamb had been sacrificed should celebrate

---

[3]It is very difficult to determine exactly what Paul meant by saying his spirit and the power of the Lord Jesus were present while he (Paul) was physically absent. There is sometimes some overlap in Paul's thinking about his human spirit and his participation in the Holy Spirit, as, *e.g.*, when he says of tongues-speaking that his spirit (or Spirit) prays (1 Cor. 14:14). Perhaps he thought of his spirit and the power of Christ being present because of the Holy Spirit's presence in the gathered Christian community in Corinth. *Cf.* Fee, *The First Epistle to the Corinthians*, pp. 203–205.

[4]At a minimum, handing the offender over to Satan meant expelling him from the Christian community, and so relegating him to the sphere of the world where Satan held sway. This much is demanded by 5:2. It may have involved physical suffering inflicted by Satan (*cf.* 2 Cor. 12:7), or even possibly death, as the words 'the destruction of the flesh' seem to imply. In any case, the purpose of the disciplinary action for which Paul called was remedial: 'that his spirit may be saved in the day of the Lord.'

that event in a Christian community free from the leaven of evil and wickedness.[5]

The law provides a paradigm for excommunication

In 5:9–13 Paul mentions his earlier instructions to the Corinthians in the 'previous letter' (that they should not associate with evil people), explaining that these instructions were intended to apply only in the case of those who called themselves believers and were guilty of blatant sins. While the judgment of outsiders was to be left to God, the judgment of blatantly sinful insiders was the responsibility of the church. Paul repeated his call to the Corinthians to implement the judgment he had passed upon the offender, this time using words found repeatedly in Deuteronomy: *exarate ton ponēron ex hymōn autōn* ('Drive out the wicked person from among you', v. 13).[6]

Thus in two of the three elements of his response to news of incestuous behaviour in the church, Paul made use of the law. It is significant, however, that the law was not reintroduced as a set of demands to be observed as a regulatory norm; rather it provided believers with a paradigm for Christian behaviour.[7] So, for example, the church did not have to excommunicate blatantly unrepentant offenders in obedience either to the law which called for the removal of leaven in connection with the passover, or to the law which called upon Israel to purge out certain offenders from their midst. Rather, these passages from the law served as paradigms of purity which could be applied in an instructive, analogous way in certain situations in which the Christian community found itself.

The matter of litigation

In 1 Corinthians 6:1–11 Paul responds to news that one believer was involved

---

[5] *Cf.* J. K. Howard, '"Christ our Passover": A Study of the Passover–Exodus Theme in I Corinthians', *EvQ* 41 (1969), pp. 100–102; C. Leslie Mitton, 'New Wine in Old Wine Skins: IV. Leaven', *ExpT* 84 (1972–73), pp. 339–343.

[6] *Cf.* Dt. 17:7; 19:19; 22:21, 22, 24; 24:7. In each case except one, the evil is purged by the death of the offender. The exception (19:19) relates to the false witness, and in this case the evil is purged by the false witness suffering whatever it was he intended the victim of his lies to suffer – eye for eye, tooth for tooth, hand for hand, foot for foot.

[7] I am indebted to Christopher J. H. Wright, *Living as the People of God: The Relevance of Old Testament Ethics* (Leicester: IVP, 1983), for this insight into the way the Old Testament functions in Christian ethics.

in legal proceedings against another. These proceedings were being carried out in civil lawcourts, instead of within the Christian community (v. 1). The apostle reminds members of the church that (in association with Christ) they are to judge the world and angels. It was, then, incredible that they should have to resort to the world's lawcourts to resolve trivial disputes arising within their own community (vv. 2–5a). He asks the Corinthians (who prided themselves on their wisdom) whether there was not *one* wise person among them able to settle a dispute between believers, so that they had to resort to pagan magistrates instead (vv. 5b–6).

You were . . . justified

Chiding the Corinthians for their failure in this matter, and with the plaintiff primarily in mind, Paul asks, 'Why not rather be wronged (*adikeisthe*)? Why not rather be defrauded (*apostereisthe*)?' (v. 7b). And then with the offender primarily in mind he adds, 'You yourselves wrong (*adikeite*) and defraud (*apostereite*) – and believers at that' (v. 8). To drive home the seriousness of such wrongdoing, Paul issues a stern warning:

> Do you not know that wrongdoers (*adikoi*) will not inherit the kingdom of God? Do not be deceived! Fornicators, idolaters, adulterers, male prostitutes, sodomites, thieves, the greedy, drunkards, revilers, robbers – none of these will inherit the kingdom of God (vv. 9–10).

The thrust of this statement is to remind Corinthian believers that there is no place in the kingdom of God for the unrighteous, and therefore those who persist in defrauding others should heed this warning. Paul cannot leave the matter there, however, for he knows that the purpose of God is to save people from their sins. So, recalling the pre-Christian days of his converts, he adds: 'And this is what some of you used to be. But you were washed, you were sanctified, you were justified in the name of the Lord Jesus Christ and in the Spirit of our God' (v. 11). Thus he reminds them that while they had been evil-doers in the past, they had been transformed by God's action[8] in the name of Christ[9] and through the Spirit.

---

[8]God is the implied active agent of the three passive verbs, 'washed', 'sanctified' and 'justified'.

[9]It is difficult to determine what is the exact nuance of being washed, sanctified and justified 'in the name of the Lord Jesus Christ (*en tō onomati tou kyriou Iēsou Christou*)'. The expression *en tō onomati* combined with the name of Jesus is found in only two other places in the Pauline corpus: 1 Cor. 5:3–4 (' I have already pronounced judgment in the name of the Lord Jesus') and Phil. 2:10 ('at [in] the name of Jesus every knee should bend'). These uses do not provide much positive help,

Verse 11 is an important text for our understanding of the place of justification in Paul's thought. It is important precisely because in this context Paul is not defending his gospel against any overt attack. So here the idea of justification is not used as a polemic doctrine. Rather, justification is mentioned as a central part of the experience of God's grace in conversion as Paul understood it (*cf.* 1 Cor. 1:30). It is also noteworthy that justification and the experience of the Spirit are very closely associated, implying again, it would seem, that they were inseparable as far as Paul was concerned. These factors were crucial to Paul's argument in Galatians, as we saw in the previous chapter, and their recurrence in 1 Corinthians indicates that the case for inconsistencies between Galatians and 1 Corinthians is not as strong as it might at first seem.

Questions about marriage

In 1 Corinthians 7 Paul responds to questions about his view of marriage and singleness raised in the letter sent to him by the Corinthians. Basically Paul argues that people should remain in the marital status in which they were called, while affirming all along the preferability of the single life if that is still a legitimate option. The chapter begins with a section conceding the preferability of the single life, but nevertheless urging each man to have [sexual relations with][10] his own wife and each woman [with] her own husband because of [temptations to] immorality (vv. 1–2). Within the marriage relationship, normally each partner was to give conjugal rights to the other in order to avoid the temptations of Satan. The only exception was abstinence by mutual consent for a limited period for prayer (vv. 3–5). But Paul's approval of such abstinence constituted a concession, not a command (v. 6). He concluded this first section of the chapter by conceding again the preferability of the single life, but by also adding that each person has his or her own particular gift from God, one of one sort (marriage), and one of another (singleness) (vv. 6–7).

---

but they do suggest that the formula did not mean 'by faith in Jesus Christ' (Paul customarily used the preposition *eis* with some form of the name of Jesus to denote that). It is probably best to adopt some such meaning as 'in the person and work of Christ', *i.e.* the Corinthian believers were washed, sanctified and justified by God's action in the person and work of Christ and through the Spirit.

[10]Following Fee, *The First Epistle to the Corinthians*, pp. 277–279, who argues persuasively for this view, and against the traditional view which takes v. 2 as advice for each person to 'take' a spouse, meaning to get married.

There then follow responses to questions about people of differing marital status: the unmarried (vv. 8–9), the married (vv. 10–11) and those in mixed marriages (vv. 12–16). In each case, Paul's response is that people should remain in the marital status in which they found themselves when they first became believers, and this he argues explicitly in verses 17–24. The following sections contain Paul's answers to questions about the betrothed (vv. 25–38), and his response to the question about widows (vv. 39–40). At three points in this chapter there is material which is relevant for our investigation of Paul's understanding of the role of the law in the life of the believer.

Obedience to the command of the Lord

In verses 10–11 Paul commands women not to separate themselves from their husbands, but if they did, to remain unmarried, or else be reconciled to their husbands.[11] Husbands are told they should not divorce their wives. In a chapter full of advice and concessions, the command in these verses stands out, the more so because dominical authority is invoked to reinforce it:

> To the married I give this command – not I but the Lord – that the wife should not separate (*mē chōristhēnai*) from her husband (but if she does separate, let her remain unmarried or else be reconciled to her husband), and that the husband should not divorce his wife.[12]

Paul rarely, if ever, cites the law of Moses simply as a command to be obeyed by believers, but here he refers to Jesus' prohibition on divorce, known

---

[11]Peter Richardson, '"I Say, Not the Lord": Personal Opinion, Apostolic Authority and the Development of Early Christian Halakah', *TynBul* 31 (1980), pp. 79–84, interprets 1 Corinthians 7 as Pauline halakha, and sees in vv. 10–11 Paul's attempt to develop his own halakha to meet a situation which neither Scripture nor the Jesus-tradition addresses adequately (Paul appealed to a command of the Lord, 'a wife must not separate from her husband,' v. 10, and gave instructions to apply when it was contravened: 'but if she does separate, let her remain unmarried or else be reconciled to her husband', v. 11).

[12]Jerome Murphy-O'Connor, 'The Divorced Woman in 1 Cor 7:10–11', *JBL* 100 (1981), pp. 601–602, citing J. A. Fitzmyer, 'The Matthean Divorce Texts and Some New Palestinian Evidence', *TS* 37 (1976), p. 200, argues that the aorist passive infinitive *chōristhēnai* in 7:10 should be taken at face value and translated, 'the wife should not *be separated* from her husband, meaning that she should not accept a bill of divorce, as willing acceptance would be cooperation in disobedience. Fee, *The First Epistle to the Corinthians*, p. 293, n. 14, disagrees, saying that 'the passive of this verb functions as middle when used of "divorce" ("be separated from" = "separate oneself from") and does not imply that the other person is the initiator of the action.' So too most modern translations and commentators.

to us through the synoptic tradition,[13] implying that believers were definitely under obligation to obey the commands of the Lord Jesus. Yet Paul was realistic enough to recognize that even so, some believers would divorce their spouses, in which case, he said, they should remain unmarried or be reconciled to their spouses.

Obeying the commandments of God

In 7:17–24 Paul argues that believers should normally remain in the state of life in which they found themselves when they were called. Verses 17–19 are of particular relevance.:

> However that may be, let each of you lead the life that the Lord has assigned, to which God called you. This is my rule in all the churches. Was anyone at the time of his call already circumcised? Let him not seek to remove the marks of circumcision. Was anyone at the time of his call uncircumcised? Let him not seek circumcision. Circumcision is nothing, and uncircumcision is nothing; but obeying the commandments of God is everything.

The purpose of this passage was not to teach the Corinthians about circumcision, but rather to illustrate and underline the advice being given, *i.e.* that people should maintain the marital status (married, single, widowed and even betrothed) they had when converted. Being married or single is presented as analogous to being circumcised or uncircumcised. Paul argues that just as the uncircumcised were not to seek circumcision, and the circumcised uncircumcision, when they believed, so the unmarried should not seek marriage, or the married seek singleness.[14]

It would appear that the saying, 'Circumcision is nothing, and uncircumcision is nothing, but obeying the commandments of God is everything' (v. 19), was something not in dispute between Paul and the Corinthians. It could, therefore, function as a useful analogy to support Paul's views about the

---

[13]*Cf.* Mt. 5:32; Mk. 10:11–12; Lk. 16:18. In the synoptics Jesus directed the prohibition to the husband, whereas here Paul directed it primarily to the wife. This possibly reflects a situation in Corinth in which 'eschatological women' were, for 'spiritual' reasons, wanting to opt out of their conjugal responsibilities (7:1–7), and even in some cases seeking divorce (7:10–11).

[14]Gregory W. Dawes, ' "But If You Can Gain your Freedom" (1 Corinthians 7:17–24)', *CBQ* 52 (1990), pp. 681–697, argues rightly that 7:17–24 is not a digression in the modern sense of turning away from the matter in hand. Rather, it is an example of *digressio* in the ancient rhetorical sense of an illustration drawing upon matters different from that being discussed, but which nevertheless throw light upon it.

ultimate indifference of either marriage or singleness. Paul wanted to assert (perhaps against those who, for super-spiritual reasons, wanted to dissolve their marriages) that what was important was not one's marital status, but rather one's Christian obedience – keeping God's commandments.

This text raises important questions about Paul's understanding of the role of the law in the lives of believers. The most important is whether Paul, by saying that 'obeying the commandments of God is everything', places believers back under the law from which, in Galatians, he insisted they were free.[15]

The answer emerges once we give attention to the fact that the text itself includes the statement, 'Circumcision is nothing'. Whatever else this text means, it cannot mean that Paul placed believers back under the law, because circumcision, one of the primary demands of the law, it says, is nothing! Clearly, 'obeying the commandments of God' cannot mean carrying out all that the law requires.[16] It is worth noting at this point just how different Paul's view of keeping the commandments of God was from that of his Jewish contemporaries. For them there could be no keeping of God's commandments if one neglected the fundamental command to be circumcised.[17]

While the text itself makes clear what 'obeying the commandments of God' here does not mean, unfortunately it gives no clues concerning what it does mean. This can only be inferred from hints we find elsewhere. One such hint is found in Paul's references in 1 Corinthians to commands of the Lord Jesus (*cf.* 7:10; 9:14; 14:37). Beyond that, we should probably be guided by the apostle's teaching concerning the ethical imperatives of the gospel being summed up in the command to love one's neighbour. And love, the apostle taught, is the fruit of the Spirit's work in those who believe in Christ (*cf.* Gal. 5:13–15, 22–26; 6:2).

---

[15]Drane, *Paul, Libertine or Legalist?*, pp. 62–64, regards the general approach of 1 Corinthians as legalistic, and Räisänen, *Paul and the Law*, p. 68, believes Paul's favourable reference to the commandments here must be taken at face value and allowed to stand in tension with his other statements about the law.

[16]Frank Thielman, 'The Coherence of Paul's View of the Law: Evidence of First Corinthians,' *NTS* 38 (1992), pp. 237–240, argues that 'the commandments of God' does refer to the Mosaic law, but that Paul makes a distinction between those parts of the law which Christians must obey and those they need not obey.

[17]The great importance of circumcision is reflected in *Nedarim* 3:11: 'R. Jose says: Great is circumcision which overrides even the rigour of the sabbath': Herbert Danby, *The Mishnah* (London: Oxford University Press, 1933), p. 268.

Observing the rule laid down in all the churches

Paul reinforced his teaching that his converts are to lead the life that the Lord has assigned, to which God has called them (7:17a), by adding: 'This is my rule in all the churches' (7:17b). There are two other places in 1 Corinthians where Paul appeals to the practice followed in (all) the churches (*cf.* 11:16; 14:33b). In both of those, it is the behaviour of liberated Christian women that the apostle is seeking to regulate. And it may well be that here also he has in mind primarily such women, who, in the name of Christian liberty, were intent upon abandoning their marriages.[18] The other appeals, and the significance of universal ecclesiastical practice as an authority in the lives of believers, will be discussed below. Here it is enough to note that, whereas Paul gave the Mosaic law no place as a regulatory norm in the life of believers, he did regard the universal practice of the churches, as well as the demands of the Lord, as norms to be observed.

Things offered to idols

Paul's response to questions raised about his attitude to things offered to idols, and about his own practice in this matter, is found in 1 Corinthians 8 – 10. Certain elements of both chapters 9 and 10 are relevant to the present enquiry. In chapter 9 Paul asserts that he was a true apostle, something which had been called into question in Corinth. As an apostle he has the right to financial support like any other apostle, even though he has not made use of that right. Reminding his readers of the apostolic right to financial support, Paul appeals *inter alia* to the law and to the command of Christ. Also in chapter 9 he mentions his practice of accommodating his behaviour to different sorts of people, and this involved living under the law when among Jews, and outside the law when among Gentiles. In chapter 10 Paul issues a stern warning to his readers by drawing their attention to the law's depiction of Israel's experience in the wilderness. All of these things throw some light upon Paul's understanding of the law, and are dealt with in turn below.

The law provides a paradigm for financial support

Paul appeals twice to the law in arguing for the right of apostles (including himself) to receive financial support from those to whom they ministered the gospel. The first is an appeal to Deuteronomy 25:4. Having made use of

---

[18]*Cf.* Fee, *The First Epistle to the Corinthians*, p. 270.

analogies drawn from military life, agriculture and animal husbandry to support this right Paul asks:

> Do I say this on human authority? Does not the law also say the same? For it is written in the law of Moses, 'You shall not muzzle an ox while it is treading out the grain.' Is it for oxen that God is concerned? Or does he not speak entirely for our sake? It was indeed written for our sake, for whoever plows should plow in hope and whoever threshes should thresh in hope of a share in the crop. If we have sown spiritual good among you, is it too much if we reap your material benefits? If others share this rightful claim on you, do not we still more? (9:8–12a)

Paul's use of the quotation from Deuteronomy 25:4 in this passage raises a number of questions. Is he saying that God has no concern for oxen? Is he interpreting Scripture allegorically,[19] or is he seeing in the law here a paradigm of God's provision for human labourers?[20] Can it be said that Paul preserved both the literal and theological significance of the Old Testament Scripture?[21] And was Paul reintroducing the law as a regulatory norm, having rejected it as such in Galatians?

When Paul asks, 'Is it for oxen that God is concerned? Or does he not speak entirely for our sake?' (vv. 9b–10a), is he denying the obvious meaning of Deuteronomy 25:4? The answer hangs on the meaning of *pantōs*, which may be construed as either 'entirely' (NRSV) or 'surely' (NIV). If it is construed as 'entirely' ('Does he not speak entirely for our sake?') then Paul appears guilty of blatant allegorizing which shows little respect for the primary meaning of the text. If, however, it is construed as 'surely' ('Surely he says this for us, doesn't he?', NIV) then Paul can be seen to be recognizing the primary reference of the text (a command about the treatment of oxen) while perceiving

---

[19]So, *e.g.*, Hans Conzelmann, *1 Corinthians* (ET, Hermeneia; Philadelphia: Fortress, 1975), pp. 154–155. Richard N. Longenecker, *Biblical Exegesis in the Apostolic Period* (Grand Rapids: Eerdmans, 1975), pp. 126–127, argues that Paul definitely interpreted Dt. 25:4 allegorically, but adds that he did not reject the literal meaning, but rather, using the rabbinic *qal wahomer* (light to heavy) method of exegesis, he subordinated the literal meaning. Anthony Tyrell Hanson, *Studies in Paul's Technique and Theology* (London: SPCK, 1974), pp. 161–166, says that formally 1 Cor. 9:9 is an example of allegory, but adds that it was not a deliberately designed allegorical use of Scripture. Paul was referring to a well-known text without reflecting very much on the exegetical implications of doing so.

[20]Fee, *The First Epistle to the Corinthians*, p. 408, points out that there was an analogical and paradigmatic character to law. Because laws are limited in number, they can never cover every situation, and therefore they regularly function as paradigms in all sorts of human situations.

[21]So, *e.g.* Walter C. Kaiser, Jr, 'The Current Crisis in Exegesis and the Apostolic Use of Deuteronomy 25:4 in 1 Corinthians 9:8–10', *JETS* 21 (1978), pp. 11–18.

in it also a paradigm of God's provision for human workers as well. This is in line with contemporary rabbinic exegesis, which taught that 'ox' in Scripture implied all labourers of any sort, human as well as animal.[22] Such an application of Deuteronomy 25:4 is in keeping with its original context, in which fair and compassionate treatment of labourers and the poor is emphasized (Dt. 24 – 25). So Paul may be said to have taken note of the literal sense (proper provision for all workers, both human and animal), and then applied that to apostles who labour in the cause of the gospel.[23]

Paul's second appeal to the law to support the right of apostles (including himself) to financial support does not involve a citation, but appeals generally to the law relating to priests who served in the temple: 'Do you not know that those who are employed in the temple service get their food from the temple, and those who serve at the altar share in what is sacrificed on the altar?' (9:13). That Paul interprets this analogically is made plain by his saying that '*in the same way*, the Lord commanded that those who proclaim the gospel should get their living by the gospel' (v. 14). Paul's analogical use of the law here is both clear and non-controversial. There is respect for the original intent of the Old Testament text, and the analogy between those in view there (priests) and those in view in 1 Corinthians (apostles) is obvious and legitimate.

The command of the Lord and financial support

As noted above, Paul clinched the point of the analogy by an appeal to the command of the Lord: 'In the same way, the Lord commanded that those who proclaim the gospel should get their living by the gospel' (9:14). It is worth remarking that, for Paul, while the law no longer has the regulatory force of a command to be obeyed (it functions now as a paradigm for Christian behaviour), the commands of Christ certainly do.

It may be objected that this cannot be so because, in the very next verse (9:15), Paul says that he refused to receive his living from the gospel.[24] In response, a number of points can be made. (i) The saying of the Lord to which

---

[22]*Cf.* D. Instone Brewer, '1 Corinthians 9.9–11: A Literal Interpretation of "Do Not Muzzle the Ox"', *NTS* 38 (1992), pp. 555–560.

[23]*Cf.* Kaiser, 'The Current Crisis in Exegesis', pp. 13–15.

[24]David L. Dungan, *The Sayings of Jesus in the Churches of Paul: The Use of the Synoptic Tradition in the Regulation of Early Church Life* (Oxford: Blackwell, 1971), pp. 16–24, argues that Paul set aside a dominical command when he refused to accept financial support. Gerd Theissen, *The Social Setting of Pauline Christianity: Essays on Corinth* (Philadelphia: Fortress, 1982), pp. 40–54, argues that the conflict between Paul and the Corinthians was due in part to disagreement

Paul referred, at least as it is known to us from Matthew 10:10 and Luke 10:7, is in the form of a proverb ('laborers deserve their food'; 'the laborer deserves to be paid') and it implies that those who preach the gospel *deserve* to be supported by those who benefit from it, not that they *must* receive such support. (ii) The instructions given by Jesus for a brief Galilean mission (*i.e.* to take no gold or silver in their belts, and to accept hospitality) do not necessarily have to be applied to all subsequent missions. (iii) When Paul said that the Lord commanded that those who preach the gospel should live by the gospel he was alluding to the Corinthians' obligation to support him (as they did other apostles). In other words Paul's reference to the command of the Lord was made to underline their obligation to provide support and his right to receive it, not their right to provide it and his obligation to receive it.

The law and Paul's accommodation to Jews and Gentiles

In 1 Corinthians 9:1 Paul asks: 'Am I not free? Am I not an apostle?' He responds to the criticism reflected in the second of these questions ('Am I not an apostle?') by asserting, in 9:2–18, that while he may not be an apostle to others, he certainly is to the Corinthians. Therefore he has just as much right to receive financial support as any other apostle, even though he had decided not to make use of that right.

After dealing with the matter of his rights as an apostle in 9:3–18, Paul, in 9:19–23, seeks to answer the criticism which prompted him to ask in 9:1: 'Am I not free?' Because Paul's response to this criticism is embedded in chapters 8 – 10, which deal with the matter of eating food offered to idols, it would seem that the criticism itself related to the apostle's practice in this matter. Exactly what the nature of the criticism was can only be surmised, as Paul himself does not spell it out. Perhaps the Corinthians had heard that Paul adopted different practices in different places, and regarded him as inconsistent and hypocritical. If this was the case, Paul's statements in 9:19–23 were not primarily an example of the sort of self-denial that he wanted the Corinthians themselves to adopt in the matter of *eidōlothyta* (for the sake of believers whose consciences were weak).[25] Rather, they were intended primarily to explain the underlying motive for his own behaviour in this respect, and so to defend his integrity as an apostle.

---

on the matter of financial support. They felt that he was disobedient to the command of Christ in being unwilling to receive support, insisting instead on paying his own way.

[25]*Contra* C. H. Dodd, 'ENNOMOS CHRISTOU', *Studia Paulina in honorem Johannis de Zwaan*, ed. J. N. Sevenster and W. C. Unnik (Haarlem: De Erven F. Bohn N. V., 1953), p. 96. 1 Cor. 9:19–23, however, probably has the *secondary* function of providing a model of self-denial.

Accordingly, in 9:19–23 Paul explains that, while he was free from all, he made himself slave of all to win as many as possible. Becoming a slave to all in this context involved accommodating his behaviour so as to be identified as closely as possible with different groups: those under the law, those outside the law, and the weak. In doing so, Paul insists, he did not compromise his Christian beliefs. When he became as one under the law, he did not place himself under the law in principle. When he became as one outside the law, he did become lawless towards God, he remained under the law of Christ. All of this he did for the sake of the [progress of the] gospel.[26]

The passage raises a number of questions important for the study of Paul's understanding of the role of the law. First, what did Paul mean by saying that he is not free from God's law but under Christ's law (*mē ōn anomos theou all' ennomos Christou*) (9:21)? Second, did Paul expect others to emulate his own practice in respect of the law? Third, was Paul inconsistent in that he advocated a flexible approach in 9:19–23, but rebuked Cephas for practising the same sort of flexibility in Antioch (Gal. 2:11–14)? These matters are taken up in turn below.

Under the law of Christ

When Paul said, 'I am not free from God's law (*mē ōn anomos theou*)' (v. 21), he meant something other than that he was obliged to carry out all the requirements of the Mosaic law. For the whole point of his remarks in 9:19–23 was to defend his policy of accommodation, which included living like those who do not have the law (v. 21), *i.e.* adapting himself to the lifestyle of the Gentiles by not observing all that the law required.[27] To explain what 'I am not free from God's law' means in practice, Paul adds, 'but [I] am under Christ's law (*all' ennomos Christou*)'.

Unfortunately, however, the apostle does not explain what he means by the expression *ennomos Christou*. There are, nevertheless, some hints as to what

---

[26]For recent discussion of Paul's practice of accommodation see Peter Richardson and Paul W. Gooch, 'Accommodation Ethics', *TynBul* 29 (1978), pp. 89–142; Peter Richardson, 'Pauline Inconsistency: I Corinthians 9:19–23 and Galatians 2:11–14', *NTS* 26 (1980), pp. 347–362; David Carson, 'Pauline Inconsistency: Reflections on I Corinthians 9.19–23 and Galatians 2.11–14', *Churchman* 100 (1986), pp. 6–45.

[27]Thielman, 'Paul's View of the Law', pp. 243–246, argues that this practice involved only a setting aside of those parts of the law which distinguished Jews from Gentiles, and did not imply a radical rejection of the law. It is true that this text probably refers only to Paul's *practice* of setting aside certain *parts* of the law. But his earlier statement that, although he behaved as one under the law to win those under the law, he himself was not subject to the law (v. 20) does seem to imply a radical rejection of the law as a regulatory norm for believers.

this might mean. On two occasions in 1 Corinthians, Paul refers to the commands of the historical Jesus (7:10; 9:14) and once to a command of the exalted Christ through his apostle (14:37), all of which Paul expects his readers to heed. In Galatians Paul speaks of the law summed up in one word, 'You shall love your neighbor as yourself' (5:14), and of those who bear one another's burdens as fulfilling the law of Christ (*ton nomou tou Christou*, 6:2). It is feasible to assume, then, that to live *ennomos Christou* involved at least the obligation to keep the commands of Christ and to live by the law of love (in the power of the Spirit).[28] But it probably meant much more than this for the apostle Paul. He spoke of Christ as the one who 'died for all, so that those who live might live no longer for themselves, but for him who died and was raised for them' (2 Cor. 5:15). For Paul, to live *ennomos Christou* would not have been a new legalism based on the commands of the historical Jesus and the exalted Christ, but probably a life lived in the service of Christ out of gratitude for his amazing love, in which the commands of Christ were gladly obeyed.[29]

Emulating Paul's practice of accommodation

One question which has been raised in relation to Paul's practice of accommodation is whether he expected others to emulate it. Paul states that his motive in making the accommodations referred to in 9:19–23 was to 'win more of them' (v. 19), which included winning Jews (v. 20a), those under the

---

[28]Dodd, 'ENNOMOS CHRISTOU', pp. 99–110, says: 'Certainly it would be a mistake to attempt to confine the connotation of *ho nomos tou Christou* to the comparatively restricted body of traditional sayings of Jesus, but it appears that even for Paul, with his strong sense of the immediate governance of Christ through the Spirit in the Church, that which the Lord "commanded" and "ordained" remains the solid, historical and creative nucleus of the whole.' Conzelmann, *1 Corinthians*, p. 161, rejects Dodd's interpretation as one which is 'at variance with the whole Pauline use of *nomos*', preferring rather Kümmel's view that *ennomos Christou* means only 'obliged to be obedient' to Christ (by which presumably he means obedient to the promptings of Christ through the Spirit). Conzelmann fails to make any mention in this connection of the fact that Paul in 1 Corinthians actually cites commands of Jesus with the expectation that they will be obeyed, preferring, it seems, to allow his understanding of Paul's use of *nomos* to decide the matter. Fee, *The First Epistle to the Corinthians*, p. 430, follows Conzelmann. Räisänen, *Paul and the Law*, p. 82, argues that 'the "law of Christ" refers simply to the way of life characteristic of the church of Christ'.

[29]Carson, 'Pauline Inconsistency', p. 12, agrees with Dodd that *ennomos Christou* is related to *ho nomos tou Christou* in Gal. 6:2, and that being *ennomos Christou* involves obedience to a corpus of demands given by Jesus himself as well as obedience to the promptings of the Spirit. Carson rightly widens the notion of *ennomos Christou*, however, to include being bound by 'all that Christ accomplished and represents'.

law (v. 20b), those not having the law (v. 21) and the weak (v. 22). All this he summed up with the words, 'I have become all things to all people, that I might by all means save some' (v. 22). Thus it is clear that the background to this description of accommodation is the missionary situation. This raises the question whether Paul expected others to apply the principles of accommodation in non-missionary situations. The answer to this would seem clearly to be in the affirmative, on two grounds. First, Paul's discussion of accommodation is embedded within the broader context of a problem (the matter of *eidōlothyta*) which had arisen in the Christian community. Second, in the concluding remarks of this section of the letter he explicitly urges his readers to apply his principle of accommodation in their own Christian community:

> So, whether you eat or drink, or whatever you do, do everything for the glory of God. Give no offense to Jews or to Greeks or to the church of God, just as I try to please everyone in everything I do, not seeking my own advantage, but that of many, so that they may be saved. Be imitators of me, as I am of Christ (10:31 – 11:1).

Paul wanted the Corinthians to emulate his practice of seeking to please everybody in every way (in this context his practice of accommodating himself to each different group of people). He wanted them to emulate him as he emulated Christ (*cf.* Rom. 15:1–8), and so cause none to stumble in the matter of eating (*eidōlothyta*) or drinking, whether Jews, Greeks or *the church of God*. By including 'the church of God' among those who must not be caused to stumble, Paul indicates that accommodation was to be practised also in the Christian community; it was not only for the missionary situation.[30]

Was Paul inconsistent?

In Galatians 2:11–14 Paul recalled how in Antioch he rebuked Cephas for accommodating his behaviour to the demands of the Jews who came from James. Previously Cephas had accommodated himself to the Gentile believers by sharing table fellowship with them. But when those from James arrived he withdrew from that fellowship, thus accommodating himself to the Jews from James instead. This earned him a stern rebuke from Paul in front of all. On the surface of things it appears that Paul rebuked Cephas for doing exactly what he

---

[30]Richardson, 'Pauline Inconsistency', pp. 350–351, gives two other reasons for not restricting Paul's accommodation to the missionary situation: (i) a purely missionary situation cannot be assumed for any length of time in any place; (ii) one could not adopt practices in the missionary situation which would need to be jettisoned when the church grew and developed.

himself practised in the missionary situation. Is this a clear instance of inconsistency on Paul's part?

Richardson argues that Paul failed to allow Cephas to adopt the same principle of accommodation which he himself followed. Cephas, he suggests, was not guilty of wavering or hypocrisy as Paul asserted. On the contrary, he had simply accommodated himself, at first to the Gentile believers because he was then operating in Paul's area of responsibility, but when the Jews arrived from James he accommodated himself to them for the sake of his own ministry in his own area of responsibility. 'As an apostle of the circumcision, the demands that circumcision laid on him could not be denied.'[31]

This view is not without its problems, for, as Carson rightly points out, it exonerates Cephas at the expense of Paul.[32] But the real question is not that, but whether this view accounts best for the evidence in the relevant texts. This is not the place for a detailed critique of Richardson's argument,[33] but two points may be made.

First, Richardson suggests that Paul's anger at Cephas was related to the implied affront to Paul in his own territory. Cephas should have continued to accommodate himself to the Gentile believers while in Antioch even after the Jews from James had arrived, because he was operating in Paul's territory. Richardson recognizes that this notion is not mentioned in Paul's rebuke to Cephas in Galatians 2:11–14. Nevertheless, claiming that it is implied in Galatians 2:7–9, he imports it into his exegesis of Galatians 2:11–14.[34] This is a dubious procedure on several counts. (i) It is not at all clear that Paul thought of 'territorial' areas of responsibility. Galatians 2:7–9 speaks of a division of labour in respect of (primary) responsibilities for the circumcised (Cephas) and uncircumcised (Paul). On this basis Cephas would have had just as much right to minister among the circumcised in Antioch as Paul had to minister among the uncircumcised. (ii) If Paul had any sense of territorial rights, it was probably in respect of those areas in which he had carried out the primary evangelism, *i.e.* in the churches he had founded (*cf.* 2 Cor. 10:13–16). Neither he nor Cephas had founder's rights in Antioch, and therefore it is unlikely that Paul would have been angry with Cephas because of an implied affront in his own territory. (iii) The indications are that, while Paul had an ambition not to work in churches founded by others (Rom. 15:20), he did not mind others

---

[31]*Ibid.*, pp. 360–361.

[32]*Ibid.*, p. 33.

[33]This has been ably carried out by Carson, *ibid.*, pp. 7–33.

[34]*Ibid.*, p. 361.

working in those he had founded, so long as they did not undermine his work there (1 Cor. 3:5–11). Therefore, even if a case could be made for Paul having greater territorial rights than Cephas in Antioch,[35] it is unlikely that this would be the basis of his rebuke to him.

Second, while emphasizing something (territorial rights) which Paul did not stress, Richardson fails to take sufficient account of what Paul did stress (the theological implications of Cephas' behaviour). These theological implications are spelt out in Galatians 2:15–21. Paul argued that Cephas, by withdrawing from table fellowship, had implied that Gentile believers were still 'sinners', and that Jewish believers who shared table fellowship with them became sinners too; and that if this was the case then Christ was a servant of sin, because it was as a result of their freedom in Christ that they shared with Gentiles believers in this way. It was then for theological reasons that Paul took Cephas to task in Antioch, not because Cephas had affronted him in his own territory.

When he rebuked Cephas in Antioch, Paul was not guilty of inconsistency because he failed to allow Cephas to practise the accommodation which he himself advocated in 1 Corinthians 9:19–23. It is one thing to accommodate oneself to Jews and Gentiles when such accommodation promotes closer identification with the groups concerned. This is the sort of accommodation Paul practised, and he would no doubt have approved of Cephas practising it also. It is quite a different thing to refuse to accommodate oneself to a particular group, as Cephas did, when such refusal implies that those who have accepted the gospel are still 'Gentile sinners'. The inconsistency lay with Cephas, not Paul, and Cephas' inconsistency called into question the very gospel itself.

The law and Israel's experience in the wilderness

Paul's recitation of certain events that occurred during Israel's wilderness experience, and his application of these to his readers in 1 Corinthians 10:1–3, come as a surprise. On first reading the passage appears to digress from the main subject (questions raised about his attitude to *eidōlothyta*) of chapters 8 – 10. But a more attentive reading reveals that this is not a digression but an integral part of Paul's response. (This is confirmed, not only by the fact that the theme of idolatry and idolatrous feasting is found in both 10:1–13 and 10:14–

---

[35]Acts 11:25–26 tells of a whole year's ministry in Antioch by Paul and Barnabas before they set off on the first missionary journey (Acts 13:1–3). Paul himself, as far as we know, made no claims to territorial rights on this basis.

22, but also by the fact that the warning theme so prevalent in 10:1–13 is picked up again in 10:22.)

Recent studies of 10:1–13 have drawn attention to the midrashic character of Paul's handling of material from the law (notably Exodus, Numbers and Deuteronomy) here.[36] These studies throw some light upon Paul's understanding of the law, and in particular upon his understanding of the role of the law in the lives of believers. The passage falls into two parts. (i) In verses 1–5 Paul points out how the people of Israel, despite participation in events analogous to the Christian sacraments of baptism (being under the cloud and passing through the sea) and the Lord's Supper (eating the 'spiritual' food and drinking the 'spiritual' drink), fell under the judgment of God because of their sins. (ii) In verses 6–13 Paul shows which specific failures on Israel's part brought down God's judgment upon them.

The second part of the passage begins with an exhortation to the Corinthians not to desire evil as Israel did (v. 6), and this is followed by a list of Israel's failures (vv. 7–10). This list could be regarded as non-specific as far as its application to the Corinthians is concerned (except perhaps for the sin of idolatry). In this case, the function of the list would have been simply to show that the Lord judges sinners, and so to act as a warning to the Corinthians lest they sin and come under judgment also.[37] An alternative approach is to regard the sin of desiring evil as a general description of sin, which Paul then fills out by listing the specific sins of idolatry, sexual immorality, testing Christ and grumbling – sins of which the Corinthians were also guilty.[38]

Another approach is to take particular note of the fact that the warning not to desire evil as the Israelites did (v. 6) is an allusion to Numbers 11 (in particular vv. 4, 34) where the Israelites craved food other than that which the Lord had provided. Paul may have mentioned this sin first, as Perrot suggests, because it was analogous to the fundamental sin of the Corinthians to which Paul was responding in 1 Corinthians 8 – 10,[39] *i.e.* the craving to eat *eidōlothyta* in idol temples even though their apostle had taught that it was not right for them to do

---

[36]*Cf.*, *e.g.*, Charles Perrot, 'Les examples du desert (1 Co. 10.6–11)', *NTS* 29 (1983), pp. 437–443; A. McEwan, 'Paul's Use of the Old Testament in 1 Corinthians 10:1–4', *VoxRef* 47 (1986), pp. 3–10.

[37]Conzelmann, *1 Corinthians*, p. 165, describes 10:1–10 as a 'piece of teaching that was already established before the composing of this epistle'. From this it may be inferred that he regarded the list of sins as non-specific to the Corinthians.

[38]So, *e.g.*, C. K. Barrett, *A Commentary on the First Epistle to the Corinthians* (London: A. and C. Black, 1968), p. 224; Fee, *The First Epistle to the Corinthians*, p. 453.

[39]'Les examples du desert', p. 438.

so. It is perhaps better, however, to describe the craving for *eidōlothyta* as the initial sin of the Corinthians, rather than as their fundamental sin. If it is recognized as their initial sin, it is possible to explain how it might have led on to the other sins of idolatry, sexual immorality, testing Christ and grumbling. It could have led to idolatry because it was carried out in idol temples, to sexual immorality because that was often associated with idolatry, to testing Christ because it 'tempted' him to bring judgment upon them, and to grumbling because they murmured against their apostle's teaching about having nothing to do with idolatrous worship.[40]

Paul's use of the law in this passage raises important questions concerning his understanding of the role of the law in the lives of believers. He made two explicit statements which call for comment. (i) 'Now these things occurred as examples (*typoi*) for us, so that we might not desire evil as they did' (10:6). (ii) 'These things happened to them to serve as an example (*typikōs*), and they were written down to instruct (*pros nouthesian*) us, on whom the ends of the ages have come' (10:11). The question raised by these statements is whether *typos* and *typikōs* are used by Paul in a technical sense indicating a typological connection between things or events described in the Old Testament and the experience of the Corinthians. Goppelt, in his famous monograph, argues for a full typological connection between the two. Paul, the first to use *typos* and *typikōs* as terms for the prefiguring of the future in prior history, believed that God dealt with Israel in previous days in a manner that was a pattern for his dealing with the church in the last day. Put another way, God's action in the Mosaic period prefigured his action in the new age.[41]

---

[40]When Paul applied the experiences of Israel to his readers he generally did so using the first person plural: 'these things occurred as examples for *us*, so that *we* might not desire evil', v. 6; '*we* must not indulge in sexual immorality,' v. 8; '*we* must not put Christ to the test', v. 9. But on two occasions he switched to the second person plural: 'Do not become idolators' (*mēde eidōlolatrai ginesthe*), v. 7; 'do not complain' (*mēde gongyzete*), v. 10. (While there is an alternative reading for the latter – 'let us not complain', *mēde gongyzōmen* – it has less external support, and can be explained by assimilation to the predominant use of the first plural in the passage, and especially to *ekpeirazōmen* in v. 9.) If the adoption of the second plural on these two occasions was not merely a stylistic variation on Paul's part, it might reflect what had become for Paul the key areas of dispute between himself and the Corinthians in the whole matter of *eidōlothyta*, *i.e.* the possibility of falling into idolatry and grumbling against their apostle.

[41]Leonhard Goppelt, *Typos: The Typological Interpretation of the Old Testament in the New* (ET, Grand Rapids: Eerdmans, 1982), pp. 4, 144–146, 218–220. *Cf.* the treatment of 1 Cor. 10:1–13 by Richard M. Davidson, *Typology in Scripture: A Study of Hermeneutical Tupos Structures* (Andrews University Seminary Doctoral Dissertation Series 2; Michigan: Andrews University, 1981), pp. 193–297, who also argues for the presence of typology in this passage.

Not all scholars are prepared to follow Goppelt (and Davidson) in recognizing the presence of typology in 1 Corinthians 10:1–13. Barrett prefers to speak of 'warning examples', and denies the presence of typological exegesis.[42] Conzelmann similarly denies a technical, hermeneutical use of the term *typos*, preferring to speak of a paraenetic sense.[43] Fee recognizes technical typology in respect of the Old Testament 'sacraments', but prefers to speak of the warning events as analogies.[44]

Whether Paul used typological exegesis, or simply cited examples from Israel's wilderness experiences which were analogous to the Corinthians' situation, will continue to be debated. Either way, it is clear, once again, that Paul found in the law paradigms for Christian behaviour (and paradigms of God's response) on which he could draw in his ethical exhortations without reinstating the demands of the law as a regulatory norm for believers.

Women praying and prophesying

When discussing Paul's response to questions about marriage above, it was noted that objections to his views on this matter may have emanated from 'eschatological women', who did not want their new spiritual status to be restricted by the obligations of the marital state in which they found themselves. It is possible that such women may also have been those whom Paul had in mind when he insisted that certain dress codes be followed in the worship service (11:2–16). This passage has been the subject of intense study over recent years in connection with debate about women's ordination. It is not necessary, for the purpose of this present study, to enter or describe that important debate. What is necessary, however, is to note the way in which the apostle appeals to the law and ecclesiastical practice in his response to the presenting problem, and to glean from this what we can about his understanding of the role of the law and tradition in the lives of believers.

While there has been some suggestion that 11:2–16 is a non-Pauline interpolation into the text of 1 Corinthians,[45] most recent commentators accept

---

[42]*The First Epistle to the Corinthians* p. 227.

[43]*1 Corinthians*, pp. 167–168.

[44]*The First Epistle to the Corinthians*, p. 452.

[45]So, *e.g.*, Wm. O. Walker, Jr, '1 Corinthians 11:2–16 and Paul's Views Regarding Women', *JBL* 94 (1975), pp. 97–110; Lamar Cope, '1 Cor 11:2–16: One Step Further', *JBL* 97 (1978), pp. 435–436.

it as an integral part of Paul's letter.[46] The majority view is adopted here and so the passage is used as a source of evidence for Paul's understanding of the law.

The law provides a paradigm for human relationships

In 11:2–16 Paul assumes that women will pray and prophesy in the worship service. The bone of contention was the use or otherwise of a head-covering while doing so. The women had dispensed with their head-coverings in this setting, and Paul argues that they should reinstate them. In the central section of his argument (11:7–12) Paul alludes to the law, in particular to the Genesis creation accounts:

> For a man ought not to have his head veiled, since he is the image and reflection of God; but woman is the reflection of man. Indeed, man was not made from woman, but woman from man. Neither was man created for the sake of woman, but woman for the sake of man (vv. 7–9).

This text presents exegetes with several problems, and these are discussed at length in the major commentaries and in articles and monographs on women's ministry. The overall thrust of the passage, however, is clear enough. Paul argued from the man's creation in the image of God, and the woman's creation from man, that the woman ought to have a sign of authority on her head. The law was used here to support an ethical imperative. Once again it is worth noting that Paul was not reinstating the demands of the Mosaic law as a regulatory norm for believers, but finding in the narrative section of the law a paradigm for the way in which God intended males and females to relate.

Appeal to the universal practice of the churches

In 11:13–16 Paul appeals to standards of propriety and, on that basis, asks his readers to judge for themselves whether it is proper for women to pray and prophesy with their heads uncovered. Anticipating that his arguments so far might not convince the contentious, he concludes with an appeal to the universal practice in the churches: 'But if anyone is disposed to be contentious – we have no such custom, nor do the churches of God' (v. 16).

---

[46]Jerome Murphy-O'Connor, 'The Non-Pauline Character of 1 Corinthians 11:2–16?', *JBL* 95 (1976), pp. 615–620, discusses in detail Walker's hypothesis that 11:2–16 is a non-Pauline interpolation, before rejecting it in favour of the majority opinion.

Speaking in tongues

In 14:20–25 Paul urges his readers not to be childish in their thinking about tongues-speaking in the congregation. The passage presents the exegete with some thorny problems, but its overall thrust is clear enough. As far as outsiders (*idiōtai*) or unbelievers (*apistoi*) who might come to the meeting of the Christian community are concerned, tongues-speaking is not a sign of God's presence among his people but rather of their madness (v. 23). Thus tongues-speaking would function negatively as far as they were concerned, confirming them in their unbelief. Prophecy, on the other hand, is of far more value to the unbeliever (*apistos*) or outsider (*idiōtes*), because through it unbelievers hear an intelligible word of God which convicts them of their sin. As a result they 'bow down before God and worship him, declaring, "God is really among you"' (vv. 24–25).

The 'law' as a paradigm for the effect of tongues

The problematic part of the passage is found in verses 21–22, where Paul cites from the 'law':

> In the law it is written,
>
> > 'By people of strange tongues
> >   and by the lips of foreigners
> > I will speak to this people;
> >   yet even then they will not listen to me,'
>
> says the Lord. Tongues, then, are a sign not for believers (*pisteuousin*) but for unbelievers (*apistois*), while prophecy is not for unbelievers (*apistois*) but for believers (*pisteuousin*).

The citation is from Isaiah 28:11–12. The problem is that the inference which Paul draws from this citation of the 'law' is couched in terms which seem to run contrary to the overall thrust of 14:20–25 as described above. While we might wish Paul had expressed himself more clearly, nevertheless it is possible to see how the inference he draws from the citation might have been intended to reinforce the essential point he was making.

In its original context, Isaiah 28:11–12 speaks of Israel's stubborn unbelief which was not overcome even when God brought foreign armies (made up of 'people of strange tongues') against them. Still they would not listen to God. The 'tongues' in this instance were a sign (of God's judgment) for unbelievers, *i.e.* unbelieving Israel.

Accordingly we can say that Paul's application of the 'law' to his readers' situation runs, perhaps, like this. Tongues-speaking was a sign, not for believers, but for unbelievers, because it functioned as a sign of judgment for any outsiders who might join the worship service, confirming them in their unbelief. On the other hand, prophecy was a sign, not for unbelievers, but for believers in so far as any outsiders who joined the worship service would be convicted of their sin and worship God, so becoming believers.[47]

Paul's use of the 'law' in this passage is relevant for the present enquiry in two ways. First, it is an example of just how wide the meaning of the term 'law' can be in Paul's writings. It can range from the law as Mosaic legislation, through the law as the five books of Moses, to the law as the whole Old Testament (which includes the prophets). It is the last of these meanings which the term 'law' bears in 14:21. Second, it is another example of Paul finding in the 'law' a paradigm for the way God deals with his people. In this case the paradigm is applied not so much as a direct warning (as in 10:1–13), but rather to correct a misunderstanding about the usefulness of uninterpreted tongues-speaking in the congregational meeting. This paradigmatic use of the 'law' is, of course, quite different from a reinstatement of the 'law' as a regulatory norm. Paul's use of the law here smacks of neither legalism nor nomism.

Appeal to the command of the Lord

To make sure that his readers did not regard what he said about the regulation of tongues-speaking in the congregation as advice which they could accept or reject as they thought fit, Paul concludes with the words:

> Anyone who claims to be a prophet, or to have spiritual powers, must acknowledge that what I am writing to you is a command of the Lord. Anyone who does not recognize this is not to be recognized (vv. 37–38).

The command of the Lord to which Paul refers here is of a different order from those to which he referred previously. In this case Paul does not refer to teaching of Jesus known through the synoptic tradition. Rather, he refers to his

---

[47]This reading of the passage assumes that *apistoi* has a different meaning in v. 22 from what it has in vv. 23–24. In the former, *apistoi* means rebellious Israelites, and in the latter it has a synonym for *idiōtai*, *i.e.* outsiders. Thus on the one hand Paul can say that tongues are a sign (of God's judgment) for *apistois* (meaning rebellious Israelites), and then on the other he can say that tongues are not a sign (which is in any way helpful) for *apistoi* (meaning outsiders attracted to the congregational meeting of the Christians).

own teaching about church order,[48] and claims that any truly spiritual person will recognize in it the command of the Lord. We can only speculate whether the apostle might have received this command as a special word from the Lord (*cf.* 1 Thes. 4:15) or in some other way.

What is significant for our present purposes is that because Paul (on whatever basis) believed that his instructions were based on such a command of the Lord, they were authoritative, and therefore must be obeyed: 'Anyone who does not recognize this is not to be recognized' (14:38). This underlines once more, that, while the demands of the Mosaic law were not binding upon believers, the commands of Christ were.

Women keeping silence

The statement in 14:33b–36 about women keeping silence in the churches has, like Paul's words in 11:2–16, been the subject of intense study in recent years in relation to women's ordination. Again, however, it is not necessary for our present purposes to enter that debate. We are interested primarily in the way Paul appeals to the law and to the universal practice of the churches in dealing with this matter. Before we explore the way Paul does this, some issues of a preliminary nature need comment.

It has been argued that 14:34–35 is a (non-Pauline) interpolation, and it must be admitted that a case can be made for this view. Reasons advanced in favour of the interpolation theory include the following. (i) The textual tradition reveals that verses 34–35 were found following 14:40 in several witnesses, and (ii) if verses 34–35 are removed from their context following 14:33, the text flows fairly smoothly from 14:33 to 14:36 without them. Recent commentators are divided on this matter, some arguing for the view that 14:34–35 is a non-Pauline interpolation,[49] others that it is authentic Pauline material which has been integral to the letter from the beginning.[50] It is hard to see how this matter

---

[48]Fee, *The First Epistle to the Corinthians*, pp. 711–712, agrees that 'the command of the Lord' refers to all that Paul had written on the present matter. He argues that because Paul was an apostle, and so also a prophet, what he wrote had the status of a command of the Lord.

[49]Fee, *The First Epistle of the Corinthians*, pp. 699–705 and Conzelmann, *1 Corinthians*, p. 246, regard 14:33b–36 as an interpolation. Barrett, *The First Epistle to the Corinthians*, pp. 332–333, also prefers to see vv. 34–35 as an interpolation, but allows the matter is not certain.

[50]Christian Wolff, *Der erste Brief des Paulus an die Korinther, Zweiter Teil: Auslegung der Kapitel 8 – 16* (THKNT; Berlin: Evangelische Verlagsanstalt, 1982), pp. 140–143, puts the case for authenticity and integrity; and this is assumed by F. W. Groesheide, *Commentary on the First Epistle to the Corinthians* (NICNT, Grand Rapids: Eerdmans, 1953), pp. 341–343.

could be decided convincingly one way or the other. For our present purposes it will be assumed that verses 34–35 are an authentic part of the letter,[51] and so constitute a further source of evidence for Paul's understanding of the law. Proceeding on this basis, two factors relevant to the present study may be noted.

The law provides a paradigm for submission

Instructing the women to be silent in the assemblies, Paul explains that they 'should be subordinate, as the law also says' (v. 34). There is in the Mosaic law no explicit command that women should be subordinate to men. Various attempts have been made to identify the part of the law to which Paul is alluding. The most common suggestion is that he is alluding to Genesis 3:16, where the woman, following the fall, was told that her desire would be for her husband and that he would rule over her.[52] This solution is not without its problems. It is not a command to the woman, but a statement of fact. Alternatively, it has been suggested that Paul was alluding to the creation narratives (Gn. 1:26ff.; 2:21ff.), texts to which he has already alluded in 11:7–9.[53] Another suggestion is that Paul probably had in mind the fact that women took part in temple and synagogue worship only as hearers, and this notion derived from the law.[54] None of these suggestions is self-evident or compelling. As none of the Mosaic laws demands subordination of women to men, however, it may be said that Paul was certainly not re-establishing these laws as a regulatory norm for believers. It is possible that he had in mind the narrative sections of the law which reflect the subordination of godly women to their husbands (*cf.* Gn. 18:12, quoted in 1 Pet. 3:5–6). If this were the case, then once again we see that Paul looked to the law for a paradigm for the way in which believers should behave.

---

[51]It seems to me that the variations in the textual tradition can be best accounted for by saying that scribes, faced with the awkward aside about women keeping silence in the midst of Paul's treatment of tongues, resolved the problem by shifting vv. 34–35 from their original position to the end of the chapter. The inclusion of vv. 34–35 after v. 33 has the strongest support in the textual tradition.

[52]So, *e.g.*, Barrett, *The First Epistle to the Corinthians*, p. 330; Groesheide, *The First Epistle to the Corinthians*, p. 343.

[53]F. F. Bruce, *1 and 2 Corinthians* (NCB; London: Oliphants, 1971), p. 136.

[54]So Wolff, *Der erster Brief des Paulus an die Korinther, Zweiter Teil*, p. 144.

Appeal to the universal practice of the churches

Alongside his appeal to the law as a paradigm for Christian behaviour, Paul appeals to the universal practice in the churches to support his call for women to 'keep silence' in the churches (vv. 33b–34a: 'As in all the churches of the saints, women should be silent in the churches'), and rebukes the Corinthians for acting as if they were independent of all other churches (v. 36: 'Or did the word of God originate with you? Or are you the only ones it has reached?').

The resurrection

The defeat of death

In 1 Corinthians 15:50–58 Paul brings to a climactic conclusion his response to questions raised by the Corinthians concerning his teaching about the resurrection. In this passage he says that 'flesh and blood', *i.e.* human beings in their natural state, 'cannot inherit the kingdom of God' (v. 50). There must be a transformation. In the case of those who have died before the last trumpet is sounded there must be a resurrection to immortality, and in the case of those who remain alive until that time there must be a transformation by which what is subject to mortality puts on immortality. In both cases death will have been thwarted, and the prophetic word will have come true: 'Death has been swallowed up in victory' (v. 54; *cf.* Is. 25:8). Thus the believer can taunt death for its failure: 'Where, O death, is your victory? Where, O death, is your sting?' (v. 55; *cf.* Ho. 13:14).

The power of sin is the law

Before completing the section 15:50–58 with a doxology (v. 57) and an exhortation to his readers to stand firm and give themselves fully to the work of the Lord (v. 58), Paul interposes an explanatory comment concerning death: 'The sting of death is sin, and the power of sin is the law' (v. 56). Because this statement connecting death, sin and the law is so unexpected, and its relevance in the context is not immediately obvious, some scholars have argued that it is an interpolation. Such an approach is always a last resort. Recently, Hollander and Holleman have argued that the verse can be explained in relation to its context if 'law' here is not taken to mean the Torah, and if the connections between death and sin, and sin and law, are understood against the background of Hellenistic popular philosophy.[55] Thus Paul is reminding his readers of the deplorable state of humanity, of which not only sin and death but also the necessity of laws was symptomatic. This, Hollander and Holleman argue, the Corinthians would have understood, and was therefore used by Paul to underline the power of death in the present age, something they were in danger of forgetting.[56] The advantage of this approach is that it makes possible an interpretation of 1 Corinthians 15:56 without recourse to Paul's statements in Galatians and Romans, of which the Corinthians were ignorant. But it is very debatable whether recourse to Hellenistic popular philosophy to interpret this text is better than recourse to Paul's letters to the Galatians and the Romans.

If we do allow that Galatians and Romans are better sources for gaining an understanding of 1 Corinthians 15:56, then this text could still function in the way that Hollander and Holleman suggest. It could still be highlighting the deplorable state of humanity in the present age, from which believers will be rescued by their resurrection to immortality at the sound of the last trumpet. And if the verse picks up themes from Galatians and foreshadows Paul's development of them in Romans, it has an importance for our study of Paul's understanding of the law out of all proportion to its brevity. It reveals that Paul's statements about the role of the law were not merely part of the polemic he employed in his battle with the Judaizers, or with Jewish objectors to his gospel, and therefore something which could be jettisoned once that campaign was over. Instead, these statements were integral to Paul's whole understanding of salvation, in particular his understanding of what it was from which people needed to be saved.[57]

Summary

The nature and function of the law

Unlike Galatians, Paul's first letter to the Corinthians does not address directly either the nature of the law or its role in justification and Christian living. Nevertheless, it does reflect something of the apostle's understanding of the law, and this is summarized briefly below.

---

[55]H. W. Hollander and J. Holleman, 'The Relationship of Death, Sin, and Law in 1 Cor 15:56', *NovT* 35 (1993), pp. 272–273.

[56]'The Relationship of Death, Sin, and Law in 1 Cor 15:56', pp. 290–291.

[57]*Cf.* Thomas Söding, '"Die Kraft der Sünde ist das Gesetz" (1 Kor 15, 56). Anmerkungen zum Hintergrund und zur Pointe einer Gesetzkritischen Sentenz des Apostels Paulus', *ZNW* 83 (1992), pp. 77–84.

The law as the power of sin

Paul brings his response to the Corinthians' questions about his understanding of resurrection to a climactic conclusion in 1 Corinthians 15:50–58 by showing how death had been overcome, even taunting death in the light of its ultimate defeat: 'Where, O death, is your victory? Where, O death, is your sting?' (v. 55). Then he adds: 'The sting of death is sin, and the power of sin is the law (v. 56), indicating that sin derives its power from the law. In this passage he only states *that* 'the power of sin is the law', not *how* or *why* that is so. There are, however, some clues about these matters in 2 Corinthians, as we shall see in the next chapter.

Justification

There is very little in 1 Corinthians about justification, but what there is reflects important aspects of Paul's understanding of the subject.

A central part of the experience of grace

In 1 Corinthians 6:1–11 Paul takes his readers to task for engaging in litigation against one another in pagan courts. He concludes with a warning that evil-doers (he lists various types) will not inherit the kingdom of God (vv. 9–10). He could not leave it at that, however, because he was aware of the grace of God at work in the lives of his troublesome readers, so he adds: 'And this is what some of you used to be. But you were washed, you were sanctified, you were justified in the name of the Lord Jesus Christ and in the Spirit of our God' (v. 11). Here, where he is not defending his gospel against Jewish or Judaizing objections, Paul refers to justification as a central part of the experience of grace, and one that was closely associated with the experience of the Spirit. In both respects this reflects what Paul said about justification in Galatians.

The law and the believer

It is not surprising that in 1 Corinthians, a letter dealing with disputes between the apostle and his readers concerning various behavioural matters, we should find repeated appeal to the law as a paradigm for Christian behaviour. 1 Corinthians also reflects something of Paul's belief in believers' freedom from the law on the one hand, and their obligation to keep the 'commandments of God', to observe the commands of Christ and to follow the universal practices of the churches, on the other.

The law as a paradigm for Christian behaviour

As noted above, Paul's predominant appeal to the law in 1 Corinthians is as a paradigm for Christian behaviour. By appealing to the law in this way, Paul was not reinstating its demands as a regulatory norm, but rather finding in the law (predominantly, but not exclusively, its narrative sections) instructive examples of the way in which God dealt with his people, and of the ways in which they were to relate to one another.

The many examples of this paradigmatic use of the law can be mentioned briefly. As the Israelite passover led into the feast of unleavened bread, so believers, for whom Christ the passover lamb had been sacrificed, should celebrate the feast with the unleavened bread of sincerity and truth (1 Cor. 5:6–8). As the ancient Israelites were to purge from their midst those who defiled their land, so too the Corinthian church was to remove from their midst the person guilty of, yet unrepentant about, his blatant sin of incest (5:13). As Israelites were not to muzzle the oxen which trod out the grain, so believers were to provide for preachers of the gospel (9:8–12). In similar vein, as the priests who served in the temple ate of the sacrifices the people brought, so too those who preached the gospel were to obtain their living from those to whom they ministered the gospel (9:13–14). God's dealings with Israel in the wilderness were written down as warning examples of the way he will deal with believers should they be guilty of similar offences (10:1–11). The Genesis creation accounts, and (probably) the accounts in the law of the way ancient women of God related to their husbands, are paradigms to be applied to the way women should behave in Christian congregational meetings (11:7–10; 14:34–35). As in the 'law' (in this case Is. 28:11–12) strange tongues were a sign of God's judgment upon unbelieving Israel, so tongues-speaking in the Corinthian congregation would only confirm in unbelief any outsider who might attend their meeting (14:20–25).

It is noteworthy that in none of these examples is there a direct, literal application of the law to the situation addressed by Paul; rather, an analogical or paradigmatic approach to application is adopted. There is, of course, in all this no attempt to reinstate all the demands of the law as a regulatory norm binding upon believers.

Freedom from the law

Nowhere in 1 Corinthians did Paul have to defend the freedom of believers from the law. His allusions to, and assumptions about, such freedom in this letter are, then, all the more significant. They reveal that freedom from the law was an essential part of Paul's understanding of the gospel, not merely something introduced as a fighting doctrine used in the battle against Jewish or Judaizing objectors to his gospel, to be jettisoned once that battle was over.

As part of the defence of his apostleship in 1 Corinthians 9, Paul explains to his readers that his practice of living like a Jew in some situations and like a Gentile in others was motivated by the desire to win as many as possible to faith in Christ (vv. 19–23). In pursuing this aim, he says, 'To those under the law I became as one under the law . . . To those outside the law I became as one outside the law' (vv. 20–21). This statement reveals two important aspects of Paul's understanding of freedom from the law. On the one hand, it shows that he was at liberty to ignore many of the demands of the law and so live like a (Christian) Gentile, and on the other, that he was also at liberty to continue observing all the demands of the law and so live like a Jew (who believed in messiah Jesus). Paul's defence of his practice of accommodation was part of his overall response to questions raised about eating *eidōlothyta*. He urged his readers to follow his example so that whether they ate or drank or whatever they did, they should do it all for the glory of God. This makes it clear that accommodation based upon freedom from the law was not something which was appropriate only as an evangelistic strategy for an apostle, but that Paul believed that it was appropriate behaviour for all believers in analogous circumstances.

Obeying the commandments of God

In his response to questions raised by the Corinthians about marriage and singleness, Paul makes the statement: 'Circumcision is nothing and uncircumcision is nothing; but obeying the commandments of God is everything' (7:19). While the context of this statement makes it clear that keeping the commandments of God does not mean observing all that the law demands, unfortunately it gives no clues concerning what it does mean. This can only be deduced from hints we find elsewhere. One such hint is found in those references in 1 Corinthians to commands of the Lord which Paul expected his readers to obey (*cf.* 7:10; 9:14; 14:37). Beyond that we should probably be guided by the apostle's teaching concerning the ethical imperatives of the gospel, which would include both living for the one who died for us (*cf.* 2 Cor. 5:15), and fulfilling the command to love one's neighbour, in which the entire law is summed up (Gal. 5:13–15).

Observing the commands of Christ

While Paul did not reinstate the demands of the Mosaic law as a regulatory norm for believers, there is little doubt that he expected them to obey the commands of Christ. On three occasions in 1 Corinthians the apostle appealed to a command of the Lord, and each time it was clear that believers were expected to obey it.

The first of these was the command that the married should not separate from or divorce their spouses (7:10), and the second that those who preach the gospel have the right to receive their living from the gospel (9:14). Both of these can be traced back to the synoptic tradition, but this is not the case with the third. In this case the command of the Lord has for its content Paul's teaching about the regulation of tongues-speaking in the congregation, suggesting that Paul either received these instructions as a special word from the Lord, or that, being an apostle, he also had prophetic gifts and could so utter a word from the Lord addressed to a specific situation.

Besides these explicit references to the commands of the Lord, there is also in 1 Corinthians reference to the law of Christ. In defending his practice of accommodation to those outside the law Paul says: 'To those outside the law I became as one outside the law (though I am not free from God's law but am under Christ's law [*ennomos Christou*]), so that I might win those outside the law' (9:21). By saying that he is *ennomos Christou*, Paul is seeking to explain what he meant by asserting that he was 'not free from God's law'. In the context of his claim to live as those outside the law, saying that he was 'not free from God's law' cannot mean that he felt obliged to observe all the demands of the Mosaic law. Accordingly, to be *ennomos Christou* cannot mean this either.

As noted earlier in the chapter, it is easier to say what *ennomos Christou* does not mean than to determine what it does mean. In the discussion there it was concluded that to live *ennomos Christou* involved at least the obligation to keep the commands of Christ and to live by the law of love (in the power of the Spirit), and that it probably also involved living for the Christ who died for us.

Following the universal practices of the churches

In three places in 1 Corinthians Paul appeals to the universal practice of the churches as something which must be respected and observed by his readers. In the first of these he refers to the rule laid down in all the churches that people should retain the status in life which they had when they were called (7:17), in the second he refers to the universal practice in the churches that women wear head-coverings when praying or prophesying in the congregation (11:16), and in the third he refers to the universal practice that women keep silence in the churches (14:33b–34). Each of these passages presents its own particular problems to the exegete. It may be that the rules laid down in every case were intended primarily as guidance for Christian women concerning the way they were to live in the new freedom that Christ had brought them, while the old age was still running its course. One thing is clear: Paul expected believers to abide by the universal practices of the churches, something which he did not say about the demands of the Mosaic law.

In the next chapter the relevant material in 2 Corinthians is examined to discover in what ways that might present a different picture of Paul's understanding of law and justification.

4

2 Corinthians

Authentic ministry, the law and justification

Introduction

It has been suggested that, if Galatians teaches a radical freedom from the law and 1 Corinthians reverses this by reintroducing the law as an ethical norm, then 2 Corinthians represents a step on the way towards a synthesis of these two opposing viewpoints. (The full synthesization, it is suggested, is found in Romans.) How much truth there is in these suggestions will be evaluated in the general conclusions at the end of this book. Before this can be done, a clear understanding of the significance of Paul's statements about the law and justification in 2 Corinthians is needed. And this can be achieved only as the relevant statements are studied against the background of Paul's response to the crises reflected in 2 Corinthians.

The background to 2 Corinthians

The course of events

The course of Paul's relationship with the Corinthians up to the writing of 1 Corinthians was described at the beginning of the previous chapter. After 1 Corinthians was written, much happened to complicate the relationship further, and in fact to bring it into successive crises. What is offered below is one reconstruction of the progress of the relationship from the time 1 Corinthians was written up to and including the writing of 2 Corinthians.[1]

When 1 Corinthians had been written, Timothy was sent to Corinth (1 Cor. 4:17; 16:10–11), either as the bearer of 1 Corinthians, or as a follow-up to it. He then returned to Paul in Ephesus (*cf.* 2 Cor. 1:1) with a report on the situation he had found in Corinth. It was not good. So Paul made his second visit to the city (2 Cor. 13:2) to deal with the situation. Upon arrival, he found himself the object of a personal attack, emanating from an individual whom Paul referred to as the one who 'caused pain' (2 Cor. 2:5) and the 'one who did the wrong' (2 Cor. 7:12). This individual received tacit support from false apostles already exercising some influence in the congregation.[2] During this attack, Paul received no support from the Corinthian church as a whole (*cf.* 2 Cor. 2:1–2), and so he felt forced to withdraw.

Paul returned to Ephesus and sent his next letter (no longer extant), known as the 'tearful' or 'severe' letter (2 Cor. 2:4; 7:8), in which he called upon the church to discipline the offender (*cf.* 2 Cor. 7:8–12). Titus was sent to Corinth, either as the bearer of this letter, or as a follow-up to it, Paul having arranged to meet him in Troas to learn how he had been received in Corinth. Paul travelled to Troas, but not finding Titus there he crossed over to Macedonia to intercept him on the way (2 Cor. 2:12–13).

When the two men met in Macedonia Paul received the good news that the Corinthians had responded positively to his severe letter, and that Titus had been well received (2 Cor. 7:5–7, 13–16). The offender had been disciplined, and the Corinthians themselves had come out in strong support of Paul and with a clear demonstration of their affection for him (2 Cor. 7:9–13). Paul then wrote once more (our 2 Cor. 1 – 9), this time to express his joy and relief, to clear up residual misunderstandings, to deal with certain objections to his apostolate that had emerged in Corinth during the crisis, and to reopen with the Corinthians the matter of the collection mentioned in earlier correspondence.

Once again Titus was sent to Corinth (2 Cor. 8:16–17), whether as bearer of this latest letter or as a follow-up to it, we do not know. What we do know is that the situation had drastically deteriorated. Once the offender had been disciplined and restored, those whom Paul was later to call 'false apostles' (2 Cor. 11:13) had brought the Corinthian believers under their influence, and

---

[1]This reconstruction, like any other, depends upon certain decisions made about literary and historical problems which are interrelated and very complex. For further discussion see Kruse, *The Second Epistle of Paul to the Corinthians*, pp. 21–25; Victor Paul Furnish, *II Corinthians* (AB 32a, New York: Doubleday, 1984), pp. 41–55.

[2]*Cf.* Colin G. Kruse, 'The Offender and the Offence in 2 Corinthians 2:5 and 7:12', *EvQ* 60 (1988), pp. 129–139.

persuaded them to accept another gospel (2 Cor. 11:4). They questioned the validity of Paul's apostolate on a number of counts: his failure to carry letters of recommendation (*cf.* 2 Cor. 3:1–3); his not having the proper Jewish connections (2 Cor. 11:21–22); the lack of visions and revelations (2 Cor. 12:1) as the basis of his claims to be an apostle; and his failure to perform signs and wonders (2 Cor. 12:11–13).[3]

Paul now faced the most decisive crisis in his relationship with the Corinthians, and he wrote what was (as far as we know) his final letter (our 2 Cor. 10 – 13) to them. In this letter he defended his apostolate and strongly attacked the false apostles, in an effort to win back the Corinthians. It would appear that this effort was successful, for when Paul wrote Romans shortly afterwards from Corinth, he indicated that the Corinthians had contributed to the collection for the poor saints in Jerusalem (Rom. 15:25–26), something they would not have done if they were still at loggerheads with their apostle.

Paul's opponents in 2 Corinthians

The crises to which Paul responds in 2 Corinthians had two phases, that reflected in chapter 1 – 7 being the first phase, and that in chapters 10 – 13 being the second. These two phases may be distinguished from each other on at least two grounds. (i) The crisis reflected in chapters 1 – 7 was precipitated by one individual offender to whom Paul refers as the one who 'caused pain' (2:5) and 'the one who did wrong' (7:12), whereas the crisis reflected in chapters 10 – 13 was brought on by a group of people to whom Paul refers (sarcastically) as 'super-apostles' (11:5;12:11) or 'false apostles' (11:13). (ii) The crisis reflected in chapters 1 – 7 had been resolved by the time those chapters were written, but that reflected in chapters 10 – 13 was far from resolution at the time of writing. (It is arguable that the false apostles of chapters 10 – 13 were present in Corinth at the time of the earlier crisis reflected in chapters 1 – 7, though not primarily responsible for it.)[4]

In responding to these two crises Paul had occasion to compare and contrast the glory of apostolic ministry with that of Moses (3:7–18), to warn the Corinthians again to have nothing to do with idolatry (6:14 – 7:1), to urge his readers to carry through their original intention to contribute to the collection for the saints in Jerusalem (8:1 – 9:15) and to speak of his sufferings at the

---

[3]*Cf.* Colin G. Kruse, 'The Relationship between the Opposition to Paul Reflected in 2 Corinthians 1–7 and 10–13', *EvQ* 61 (1989), pp. 195–202.

[4]*Cf. Ibid.*, pp. 195–202.

hands of the Jews (11:24, 26). In each case Paul made statements which are relevant to our study of his understanding of the law and justification. We will now look at these in turn.

Two ministries compared and contrasted

The most important passage in 2 Corinthians as far as this study is concerned is 3:7–18. Here Paul compares and contrasts the ministries of the old and new covenants, and in so doing he reveals something of his view of the law (its negative and positive functions) and justification.

Before these matters are explored, brief comment is needed concerning the function and purpose of 3:7–18 within the first major part of 2 Corinthians. It can be argued that 2:14 – 7:4 is an extended defence of Paul's ministry which he provided to correct the rather depressing account of it given earlier in the letter. The purpose of this corrective would then be to neutralize any residual doubts about his ministry that his readers may have been harbouring, following the resolution of the crisis precipitated by the 'offender'. In this case, 3:7–18, in which Paul compares and contrasts the glory of ministry under the new covenant with the glory of ministry under the old covenant, functions to elevate in the minds of his readers the significance of the ministry entrusted to Paul, and so helps to neutralize any doubts they continued to have about him. This comparison and contrast inevitably involves some critique of the Mosaic covenant and the law.

It is possible that Paul's purpose was not only to neutralize any residual doubts on the part of his readers, but also to carry the attack to the 'false apostles' already present and voicing their criticisms of him in Corinth during the period of the crisis reflected in chapters 1 – 7.[5] The view that 3:7–18 does have such a polemic purpose has been supported by several modern commentators,[6] but it is not necessary to go as far as Dalton does and say that 'it is the adversaries of Paul (not the Jews) who need to turn to the Lord (3.16)',[7] with the implication that there is very little critique of the old covenant and the law to be found in 3:7–18.

---

[5] *Cf. Ibid.*, pp. 199–202.

[6] So, *e.g.*, Dieter Georgi, *The Opponents of Paul in Second Corinthians* (Philadelphia: Fortress, 1986), pp. 254, 260–261; William J. Dalton, 'Is the Old Covenant Abrogated (2 Cor 3.14)?, *AusBR* 35 (1987), pp. 90–91. Furnish, *II Corinthians*, p. 225, recognizes that polemic concerns surface in 2:17; 3:1; 4:1–2 and 3:7–18, but argues that 3:7–18 is not *fundamentally* polemic. Ralph P. Martin, *2 Corinthians* (WBC 40; Waco, TX: Word, 1986), p. 66, speaks of a polemic undertone.

[7] Dalton, 'Is the Old Covenant Abrogated?', p. 91.

In 3:6 Paul describes the ministry of the new covenant as one which was 'not of letter but of spirit; for the letter kills, but the Spirit gives life'. The implied contrast is with the old covenant, as the reference to the 'tablets of stone' three verses earlier (v. 3) and the explicit reference to the 'old covenant' a little later (v. 14) indicate. The ministry of the old covenant was one of the law, the ministry of the new covenant was one of the gospel.

Negative functions of the law

In 3:7–11, while contrasting the lesser splendour of the ministry of the law to the greater splendour of the ministry of the gospel, Paul makes statements which reveal three negative aspects of his understanding of the law. (i) In contrast to the ministry of the new covenant which makes alive (v. 6), the ministry of the old covenant brings death (v. 7). Understood in the light of his statement that 'the letter kills' (v. 6), this implies that the law brought death to the transgressors. (ii) In contrast to the ministry of the new covenant which brings justification, the ministry of the old covenant condemns (v. 9), implying that the law condemns those who transgress its demands. (iii) In contrast to the new covenant which is permanent, the old covenant, though attended by glory, has been set aside (vv. 10–11, *cf.* v. 13).[8]

While Paul affirmed the splendour of the old covenant, and thereby

---

[8]Sanders, *Paul, the Law, and the Jewish People*, p. 139, says that the neuter participle *katargoumenon* ('set aside') here refers to the law itself, not to the glory with which it came (which would require a feminine participle). The temporary nature of the law has been the subject of some discussion in recent periodical literature. Peter von der Osten-Sacken, 'Geist im Buchstaben: vom Glanz des Mose und des Paulus', *EvT* 41 (1981), p. 231, claims: 'Nicht nur wohnt dem Dienst des Mose Doxa inne, es ist mit dieser Doxa auch nach Paulus noch keineswegs vorbei; "sie *wird* beseitigt" – viermal verwendet Paulus präsentische Formen, kein einziges Mal solche des Prätertium (vv. 7, 11, 13, 14) – nicht etwa, dass sie beseitigt *worden* wäre' ('Not only is glory inherent in the ministry of Moses, this glory is, according to Paul, by no means [already] finished; "it *is being* set aside" – four times Paul uses the present tense, not once the past tense – [he does] not [say], for example, that it *has been* set aside'). While Osten-Sacken's observations about the use of the present tense are correct, he appears to overlook the fact that Paul could have been speaking of a glory which had not yet faded only because he was presenting the situation as it appeared in Moses' day, not as it had become following the Christ event. Dalton, 'Is the Old Covenant Abrogated?', pp. 90–91, says that the old covenant is still in force, arguing that Paul believed that 'the transitory nature of Moses' glory is a sign of the passing relationship of the Law *with Gentiles*' (italics added). He appeals to Romans 9 – 11 (esp. 11:25–32) as evidence that the old covenant is still in force for Israel. Rom. 11:25–32 does not say that the old covenant is still in force, however, but that God's gift and calling in respect of Israel are irrevocable. This means that God's promises to them will be honoured if they do not persist in their unbelief (11:23). Unbelief in this context

acknowledged the importance of the law, it is clear from this passage that he saw its effect upon a sinful humanity in largely negative terms, and its function as temporary. This is not the whole story, however, as 3:12–18 reveals.

A positive function of the law

In 3:12–13 Paul draws upon Exodus 34:33–35 in which Moses veiled his face when he spoke to the Israelites and unveiled it when he spoke to the Lord. Paul uses this text to contrast the lack of boldness on the part of Moses as a minister of the old covenant with the boldness which he himself had as a minister of the new covenant. Paul uses the veil on Moses' face also as an analogy for the 'veil' which continued to cover the minds of unbelieving Israelites when they read the law (referred to as 'the old covenant' in v. 14 and 'Moses[' writings]' in v. 15. It is here implied that this 'veil' prevented the Israelites from perceiving the true meaning of what they heard read from the law. From this it may be inferred that Paul believed that the law had a *positive* function for those who were not blinded to its true meaning.

What this positive function is may be deduced from what Paul says in verses 16–18. Taking the analogy a little further there, he says that when people turn to the Lord, the veil on their minds is removed (v. 16), so that with 'unveiled' faces they behold the Lord's glory (v. 18). Then in 4:3–6, still using the analogy of the veil, Paul speaks of his gospel being veiled to the perishing, of whom he says: 'In their case the god of this world has blinded the minds of the unbelievers, to keep them from seeing the light of the gospel of the glory of Christ, who is the image of God' (v. 4). Taking all this together, it would seem that Paul believed that if the veil over the minds of the Israelites were to be removed, they would recognize that the law bears witness to the glory of God revealed in the face of Jesus Christ. Thus the positive function of the law was to bear witness to Christ.[9]

---

must be understood to mean rejection of the gospel, which indicates that even the Jews must now relate to God under the terms of the new covenant. Morna D. Hooker, 'Beyond the Things that are Written? St Paul's Use of Scripture', *NTS* 27 (1981), p. 304, argues that the law was temporary in so far as its offer of life to those who fulfil its demands has been superseded with the coming of Christ. The law is abiding, however, in so far as it is a witness to Christ. This seems to be the most satisfactory approach, giving due weight to the various nuances of the text itself.

[9]*Cf.* Martin, *2 Corinthians*, p. 69; Wright, *The Climax of the Covenant*, p.181.

Justification

While contrasting the ministry of the old covenant with that of the new, Paul described the former as a ministry of condemnation (*diakonia tēs katakriseōs*) and the latter as a ministry of justification (*diakonia tēs dikaiosynēs*) (3:9). Without importing into the exegesis of this text what Paul says elsewhere about justification, we can nevertheless recognize here a reflection of Paul's understanding of justification. For here the ministry of justification is the opposite of the ministry of condemnation. If condemnation (*katakrisis*) involves adjudication against a person, then in this context justification (*dikaiosynē*) must involve adjudication in favour of the person, and this is a crucial aspect of justification as Paul expounds it elsewhere.

It has been claimed that justification was a polemic doctrine which Paul introduced to combat the teaching of the Judaizers and the objections of Jews, and which he was content to jettison once those campaigns were over. But 3:9 makes it clear that this was not the case. Here the apostle introduced the theme of justification as a fundamental aspect of the new covenant of which he was a minister.[10]

Abstention from idolatrous worship

Paul's exhortation to his readers in 2 Corinthians 6:14 – 7:1 to have nothing to do with idolatry comes as something of a surprise. It is not a theme which the apostle takes up elsewhere in this letter, and this has led some scholars to conclude that it is an interpolation. The interpolation theory, however, presents the reader with as many problems as it solves, if not more.[11] For the purposes of this study it will be assumed that the passage is an integral part of the letter. Such an assumption still leaves the reader with a significant problem, namely, how to understand the function of the passage in its context.[12]

---

[10]*Cf.* Furnish, *II Corinthians*, pp. 228–229.

[11]In particular the problem of explaining *why* anyone would wish to insert the material at this point in the letter, and so break up what would have been a more obvious transition from 6:13 to 7:1. It is even more difficult to solve this problem than it is to suggest possible functions for 6:14 – 7:1 as an original part of the letter.

[12]For a succinct discussion of the place and function of 6:14 – 7:1, see Kruse, *The Second Epistle to the Corinthians*, pp. 37–40. J. Duncan M. Derrett, '2 Cor. 6:14ff. a Midrash on Dt 22, 10', *Bib* 59 (1978), pp. 231–250, believes that 6:14 – 7:1 is an integral part of the letter, and argues that its function was to impress upon the Corinthians that in a partnership (Paul was thinking of his own partnership with them) the quality of purity was essential (p. 247).

The law provides a paradigm for the experience of God

If it is assumed that 6:14 – 7:1 is an integral part of the letter, then it provides one more example of how the apostle used the law as an instructive paradigm for Christian behaviour, without reinstating all its demands as a regulatory norm which must be observed. In this passage Paul cites from the law (6:16; *cf.* Lv. 26:12: 'I will live in them and walk among them, and I will be their God, and they shall be my people') to remind his readers of the promise of God to dwell among his people Israel. But because the Corinthian believers had become a community of God's people by faith in Christ, this promise was being fulfilled among them also. Therefore, if God dwelt among them and God walked with them, it is implied, they, like Israel before them, must have nothing to do with idolatry.

The collection

In 8:10–15 Paul urges the Corinthians to follow through on their earlier desire to participate in the collection for the saints in Jerusalem (vv. 10–11a). He explains that it is acceptable for them to do so according to what they possessed (vv. 11b–12), and that he does not expect them to relieve others if they themselves are hard pressed (v. 13a). What he wants to see is a measure of equality emerging from a situation in which they were experiencing abundance while others were experiencing need (vv. 13b–14).

The law provides a paradigm for equality

To underline the fact that he was not asking them to assist others by reducing themselves to a state of need, Paul draws attention to a passage from the law (Ex. 16:18) which provides a paradigm for the sort of equality he has in mind: 'As it is written, "The one who had much did not have too much, and the one who had little did not have too little"' (8:15). The significance of Paul's appeal to this passage for our present study is that it constitutes another instance of the apostle's use of the law as a paradigm for Christian living without reinstating its legal demands as a regulatory norm.

Suffering, the mark of a true apostle

In chapters 10 – 13 Paul responds to a fresh crisis which had broken out in Corinth, a crisis which was far from resolution at the time of writing. Those whom he describes as 'false apostles' had infiltrated the Christian community and called into question Paul's status as an apostle of Christ. In the course of his response to their criticisms, Paul asserts ('talking like a madman') that he was a better servant of Christ than any of the false apostles, because he had suffered more in the fulfilment of his apostolic commission. He sets out, in 11:23–33, a catalogue of sufferings and hardships to substantiate this claim, and to pave the way for showing that the true power of apostleship was God's power revealed through human weakness.

This catalogue of sufferings includes two references to persecution which Paul suffered at the hand of his fellow Jews: (i) 'Five times I have received from the Jews the forty lashes minus one' (v. 24); and (ii) '[I was in] danger from my own people' (v. 26). The second of these references is very general and offers little to the exegete in terms of understanding why Paul was persecuted, or what form the persecution took. The first is more specific, referring to five occasions on which Paul received the official synagogue flogging at the hands of the Jews, and thus offers a little more to the exegete.

The Mishnah lists the offences which were punishable by flogging. These include various sexual offences, violating the holiness laws, violating the laws regarding humane treatment of birds and animals, making oneself bald or cutting the edges of the beard for the dead, tattooing the skin, violating the Nazarite laws, and deliberately violating the laws of cleanliness.[13] The list should probably not be regarded as comprehensive, especially in light of the 207 offences listed later by Maimonides, which, as Gallas notes, include twenty-one cases of transgression against the negative commands (*e.g.* of the moral law), eighteen cases of offences against the cultic laws, and 168 other cases (including disregarding the law against the manufacture of images of God, levitical laws and priestly instructions, food laws, and marriage laws, as well as cases of slander, perjury, and breaking of vows).[14]

Despite the information provided by these lists of offences that attracted official Jewish floggings, it is still impossible to determine from 2 Corinthians 11:24 or its context just what 'offence(s)' on Paul's part led to his floggings. Numerous suggestions have been made by scholars, including disregard for or slander of the law, denial of the law's salvific efficacy, the offering of messianic salvation to the Gentiles, social intercourse with Gentiles (and in that connection the eating of unclean food and encouraging others to do the

---

[13]Tractate *Makkot* 3.1–8; see Danby, *The Mishnah*, pp. 405–407.

[14]Sven Gallas, '"Fünfmal vierzig weniger einen . . ." Die an Paulus vollzogenen Synagogal-strafen nach 2 Kor 11, 24', *ZNW* 81 (1990), p. 183.

same), bringing the Jewish religion into disrepute, and slandering God. Others suggest it was antipathy towards Paul's missionary success among (financially strong) potential proselytes.[15]

Observance of the law not incumbent upon believers

In Galatians 5:11 Paul indicated that he was still suffering persecution because he refused to preach circumcision to the Gentiles. Acts mentions rumours that Paul was teaching the Jews who lived among the Gentiles to turn away from Moses, telling them not to circumcise their children or live according to the customs (21:21). Acts also provides a text of the letter of Claudius Lysias to Felix which speaks of the Jewish accusations made against Paul in Jerusalem as having to do with 'questions about their law' (23:29), and says that the actual charge made against Paul before Felix was that he was 'a ringleader of the sect of the Nazarenes' who 'even tried to profane the temple' (24:5–6). None of these 'offences' are associated with floggings in the contexts in which they are mentioned. While it is, therefore, impossible to be certain that one or more of these 'offences' resulted in the floggings Paul mentions in 2 Corinthians 11:24, it is very likely that such was the case.[16]

If that conclusion be allowed, then 2 Corinthians 11:24 provides further indirect evidence concerning Paul's view of the law, namely, that its observance was not incumbent upon either Jewish or Gentile believers.

Summary

The nature and function of the law

The nature of the law and its role in justification or Christian living are not addressed directly in 2 Corinthians. Nevertheless, 2 Corinthians does reflect some aspects of the apostle's understanding of the law, and these are summarized briefly under three sub-headings below.

---

[15]*Cf.* documentation provided by Gallas, 'Fünfmal vierzig weniger einen', pp. 183–184, who concludes that the offence which most likely led to Paul's floggings was his eating of unclean food.

[16]*Cf.* Colin G. Kruse. 'The Price Paid for a Ministry Among the Gentiles: Paul's Persecution at the Hands of the Jews', *Worship, Theology and Ministry in the Early Church: Essays in Honour of Ralph P. Martin*, ed. Michael J. Wilkins and Terence Paige (JSNTSup 87; Sheffield: JSOT, 1992), pp. 260–272.

The law brings condemnation and death

In 2 Corinthians 3:7–11 Paul contrasts the lesser splendour of the ministry of the law with the greater splendour of the ministry of the gospel. In doing so he implies that, in contrast to the gospel which brings justification, the law condemns (v. 9), and in contrast to the Spirit who makes alive (v. 6), the law brings death (v. 7). This provides us with some clues to why elsewhere (1 Cor. 15:56) the law can be said to be the power of sin. The law condemns sinners for the violation of its demands, and so brings death upon them. This is one way in which sin gains power over humanity.

The temporary function of the law

By contrasting the new covenant which is permanent with the old covenant which was set aside (v. 11), Paul implies that the law had only a temporary function. Again Paul does not spell out his meaning here, but, as we have seen in an earlier chapter, the temporary function of the law was an important part of Paul's argument in Galatians: for those in Christ their custodianship under the law has come to an end.

The law as witness to Christ

In 2 Corinthians 3:14–15, having spoken of the way Moses veiled his face, Paul uses the idea of the veil analogically to depict the blindness of his Jewish contemporaries. When they heard the law read, a veil lay over their minds preventing them from understanding its true meaning. Then, speaking of those from whose minds the veil has been lifted, Paul says they are now able to see the glory of God in the face of Jesus Christ. Bringing these things together, we may infer that, for Paul, one positive function of the law is to bear witness to Christ.

Justification

There is very little in 2 Corinthians about justification, but what there is reflects important aspects of Paul's understanding of the matter.

A fundamental aspect of the ministry of the new covenant

When contrasting the ministry of the old covenant with that of the new in 2 Corinthians 3:9, Paul describes the former as a ministry of condemnation (*katakriseōs*) and the latter as a ministry of justification (*dikaiosynēs*). If condemnation (*katakrisis*) involved adjudication against a person, then in this context justification (*dikaiosynē*) must involve adjudication in favour of the person. Such an understanding of justification is consistent with what we find elsewhere in Paul's writings, notably in Romans.

The law and the believer

In 2 Corinthians Paul appeals to the law as a paradigm for Christian behaviour, and writes of his persecutions in a way that reflects his belief in the Christian's freedom from the law.

The law as a paradigm for Christian behaviour

Two examples of this paradigmatic use of the law can be found in 2 Corinthians. First, there is Paul's reference to the great promise of God to Israel found in the law ('I will live in them and walk among them, and I will be their God, and they shall be my people'), which is used to remind the Corinthians (as it originally served to remind the Israelites) that God will dwell among them if they have nothing to do with idolatry (6:14 – 7:1). Second, there is the reference to the story in the law of how ancient Israelites, gathering manna according to the needs of their families, found that those who gathered much had none left over, while those who gathered little suffered no lack. In this Paul sees a paradigm for the sort of equality he wanted to bring about among the churches through the collection (8:13–15).

Freedom from the law

In 11:22–33 Paul claims that he was a better servant of Christ than any of the false apostles because he has suffered more persecution for the sake of Christ than they have. Included among these persecutions were the forty lashes less one which he had received five times at the hands of the Jews (v. 24). While Paul does not say why he received these five floggings, other references in his letters and the Acts of the Apostles indicate that he suffered persecution from the Jews because he did not preach circumcision, and was believed to have taught Jews to neglect the law. Paul was certainly 'guilty' on both counts, and it is quite likely that his five floggings at the hands of the Jews were punishments for breaking the law himself and encouraging others to do the same. If so, then 11:24 reflects indirectly Paul's belief that observance of the law was not incumbent on either Jewish or Gentile believers.

It is now time to turn to Paul's letter to the Romans, which contributes more to our understanding of the apostle's views concerning law and justification than any other letter of the Pauline corpus.

5

Romans 1 – 5

Justification apart from the law

Introduction

Turning to Romans from both 1 and 2 Corinthians, the reader is once again conscious of a marked change in subject matter and tone. In 1 Corinthians Paul dealt with issues of contention between himself and the believers in Corinth, underlying which was criticism of his gospel, style of speaking, spirituality and integrity. In 2 Corinthians Paul responded to two crises in his relationship with the Corinthians: one which had already been resolved (chs. 1 – 7) and one which was far from resolution (chs. 10 – 13) at the time of writing. Thus in 1 and 2 Corinthians Paul was dealing with particular contentious issues between himself and a church which he had founded. In Romans, however, Paul addresses a Christian community which he did not found and which he has not yet visited. He expounds his gospel and defends it against various objections. In doing so the apostle speaks explicitly and at length about the law and justification as he seeks to show God's righteousness in making no distinctions between Jews and Gentiles in the matters of sin, judgment and salvation. Therefore this letter is the most important of all Paul's writings as far as the subject matter of this study is concerned.

Because of the large amount of relevant material in Romans, the study of this letter is spread over two chapters. In this chapter introductory issues and Romans 1 – 5 are examined, and in the next chapter Romans 6 – 15 is studied and a summary of all the findings is provided.

As may be expected with such a complex letter as Romans, there are many contentious issues related to its interpretation. These will need to be borne in mind as the significance of Paul's statements about law and justification in Romans is explored. But once again these issues must not be allowed to determine our approach to this letter. It is the way in which Paul speaks of the law and justification to achieve his own purpose(s) that must be explored first. The prior task, then, is to seek to understand the purpose(s) for which the apostle wrote Romans.

The purpose of Romans

The purpose of Romans has been the subject of much debate in recent years,[1] and this debate has not yet fully run its course. Part of the problem presented by the letter to those who would discern its purpose is that in 1:1–15 and 15:14 – 16:27 Paul implies that he was writing to prepare the way for his visit to Rome and a subsequent mission to Spain, while seeking prayer support for his impending 'collection visit' to Jerusalem. Such a purpose does not seem sufficient, however, to explain the long theological and paraenetic sections of the letter (1:16 – 11:36; 12:1 – 15:13). Any satisfying solution to the problem, therefore, must show how these sections relate to the purpose implied in Paul's statements at the beginning and end of the letter. Put another way, the argument running through 1:16 – 15:13 has to be first understood, and then related to the implied purpose found in 1:1–15 and 15:14 – 16:27. It is important to attempt first of all, then, a brief statement of the argument of 1:16 – 15:13.

A statement of the argument in 1:16 – 15:13

Paul states his basic thesis in 1:16–17:

> For I am not ashamed of the gospel; it is the power of God for salvation to everyone who has faith, to the Jew first and also to the Greek. For in it the righteousness of God is revealed through faith for faith; as it is written, 'The one who is righteous will live by faith.'

Essentially, then, Paul's thesis is that the power of God is revealed through

---

[1] L. Ann Jervis, *The Purpose of Romans: A Comparative Letter Structure Investigation* (JSNTSup 55; Sheffield: JSOT, 1991), pp. 11–28, provides one of the most up-to-date surveys of the debate. Many of the major contributions to this debate are conveniently collected in Karl P. Donfried, *The Romans Debate* (Peabody, Massachusetts: Hendrikson, revised and expanded edn., 1991).

the gospel for all who have faith. In succeeding sections of the letter he argues the case for this thesis, defends it against possible objections, and spells out some of its ethical implications.

He begins by arguing in 1:18 – 3:20 that God acts righteously in making no distinctions between Jews and Gentiles in the matter of sin, and therefore none in the matter of judgment either. In 3:21 – 5:21 he goes on to argue that, just as God reveals his righteousness in making no distinctions in the matter of sin and judgment, so too he reveals his righteousness in making no distinctions in the matter of salvation either. Jews and Gentiles alike are to be justified by the grace of God through faith in Jesus Christ, and that apart from works of the law.

Such a thesis was open to a number of objections, in particular objections in respect of the moral standards required of the people of God, the nature and purpose of the law, and the election and privileges of Israel as God's chosen people. Paul responds to some of these objections as he goes along, but in chapters 6 – 8 he deals specifically and at some length with objections concerning moral standards and the nature and role of the law. In chapters 9 – 11 he deals with objections concerning the place of Israel in the saving purposes of God, maintaining that God has been righteous in his dealings with Israel and will not fail to act in faithfulness to his covenant with her.

Having argued the case for his thesis, and having dealt with some of the objections that could be raised against it, Paul, in 12:1 – 15:13, proceeds to draw out the ethical implications of all this in respect of such matters as ministry in the church, submission to rulers, love of fellow believers, life in the light of an imminent end, and toleration towards other believers.

Relating the argument to the implied purpose

If the brief description of the overall argument of Romans outlined above is accepted, it must then be asked what Paul's purpose was in arguing along those lines. We could answer, at one level, that his purpose was to explain and defend his gospel of justification through grace by faith for Jews and Gentiles without distinction. That is probably true. If so, we must then ask: why did he feel he had to give this explanation and make this defence when writing Romans, and how is it all to be related to the implied purpose for writing found in the opening and closing sections of the letter? In other words, what was Paul's overall purpose in writing Romans? Numerous suggestions have been made in response to this question. Basically they fall into three categories.

Response to a situation in the Roman church

Various attempts have been made to identify a particular situation in the Roman church which might have called forth this letter. These include the following. (i) The Roman church lacked apostolic foundation, so Paul wrote Romans to provide the church with an apostolic presentation of the kerygma, something he says he intends to do in person when he makes his visit to Rome.[2] (ii) When the Christian Jews who had been expelled from Rome by Claudius were allowed to return, they found that the Christian house churches in Rome had developed a form of organization quite different from the synagogal form they had when they left. They also found themselves as a small Jewish Christian minority within a Gentile Christian majority. Paul wrote Romans to urge the Gentile Christian majority to live harmoniously with the Jewish Christian minority.[3] (iii) There was conflict in the Roman church between law-observant Christian Jews and law-free Gentile Christians,[4] between the *peritomē* (the circumcision) and the *akrobystia* (the 'foreskins') as the opponents labelled one another. It was in response to this situation that Paul wrote Romans. (iv) There was conflict between strong and weak Gentile believers over the matter of law observance. Paul dealt with this problem by applying the conclusions he had reached in his debate with the synagogue concerning what had become a central issue in the Christian church.[5]

Related to Paul's apostolic career

In this case the overall purpose is to be understood in terms of Paul's missionary career. This approach has led scholars to suggest a number of reconstructions, including the following. (i) Paul wrote his letter to the Romans (and others) at the close of a period of bitter controversy over matters affecting the churches of Galatia, Corinth and possibly Macedonia. The letter sums up

---

[2]Günter Klein, 'Paul's Purpose in Writing the Epistle to the Romans', *The Romans Debate*, pp. 29–43.

[3]Wolfgang Wiefel, 'The Jewish Community in Ancient Rome and the Origins of Roman Christianity', *The Romans Debate* pp. 85–101. *Cf.* also W. S. Campbell, 'Romans III as a Key to the Structure and Thought of the Letter', *NovT* 23 (1981), pp. 37–39, who also identifies anti-Judaism on the part of Gentile Christians as a cause of division in the Christian community in Rome.

[4]*Cf.* A. J. M. Wedderburn, *The Reasons for Romans* (Edinburgh: T. & T. Clark, 1988), pp. 64–65.

[5]Ulrich Wilkens, *Der Brief an die Römer*, 1. Teilband (EKKNT 6/1; Zurich: Benzinger; Neukirchen–Vluyn: Neukirchener, 1978), pp. 39–42.

the positions reached by Paul in these various controversies, and it constitutes a 'manifesto' setting forth the apostle's deepest convictions on central issues; a manifesto to which he sought to give the widest publicity.[6] (ii) Paul wrote his letter to the Romans on the eve of his departure for Jerusalem with the collection. In the core of the letter (1:18 – 11:36) he sets out for his Roman readers the content of the 'collection speech' he intended to give in Jerusalem so as to elicit their support and intercession for him when he went to Jerusalem.[7] (iii) Paul wrote in order to let the Roman Christians know about the collection being taken up among the Gentiles for the saints in Jerusalem. He wanted their moral support and prayer for this gift, even though it was too late for them to be involved financially. Yet it was by no means certain that the different factions in the Roman church would feel they could support this initiative of Paul's. Hence the apostle wrote Romans to overcome any misgivings they might have had about his gospel and mission so that they would then give the moral support he sought.[8] (iv) Paul wished to involve the Roman believers in all aspects of his mission, including the trip to Jerusalem and the subsequent Spanish mission. Thus in Romans he sought to instruct and exhort them, and share with them his concerns and ambitions so that they might make these their own, and so help in the accomplishing of the unfinished task.[9] (v) Paul, on the eve of his collection visit to Jerusalem, wrote Romans as a last testament of his teaching, and to explain the basis for his mission, and to explain the basis upon which the Jerusalem church could accept the gift of the Gentiles.[10] (vi) Paul wrote Romans as an 'ambassadorial' letter to advocate a cooperative mission to evangelize Spain. The theological section of the letter expounds the gospel to be proclaimed in the mission, and the paraenetic section shows how the gospel had to be lived out by believers to ensure its success.[11] (vii) Paul had a number of interrelated purposes in writing Romans, but these were all associated with his own plans rather than with the situation in

---

[6]T. W. Manson, 'St Paul's Letter to the Romans – and Others', *The Romans Debate*, pp. 3–15. Gunther Bornkamm, 'The Letter to the Romans as Paul's Last Will and Testament', *The Romans Debate*, pp. 16–28, takes up and extends Manson's approach by seeing in Romans a statement of Paul's 'realizations' about the gospel, which he now wanted to defend in Jerusalem. Bornkamm believes that Romans is the last of the authentic letters of Paul, and as such it has become in fact the historical 'testament of Paul'.

[7]Jacob Jervell, 'The Letter to Jerusalem', *The Romans Debate*, pp. 53–64.

[8]A. J. M. Wedderburn, 'The Purpose and Occasion of Romans Again', *ExpT* 90 (1979), pp. 140–141.

[9]F. F. Bruce, 'The Romans Debate – Continued', *BJRL* 64 (1982), p. 358.

[10]Klaus Haacker, 'Exegetische Probleme des Romerbriefs', *NovT* 20 (1978), pp. 1–6.

[11]Robert Jewett, 'Romans as An Ambassadorial Letter', *Int* 36 (1982), pp. 9–10.

the Roman Christian community. He wrote to prepare the way for his visit to Rome and subsequent mission to Spain, and to seek the prayers of the Roman Christians for his impending collection visit to Jerusalem. To facilitate all this he introduced himself by setting out for the Roman Christians an orderly account of the gospel as he had come to understand it.[12] (viii) Paul wrote Romans as an attempt to 'evangelize' by letter those whom he had so far been unable to 'evangelize' in person in order to elicit a proper response to the gospel on the part of his Roman readers (15:15–16).[13] (ix) The main function of Romans was to allow the Christians at Rome to hear the gospel from Paul so that they might be drawn into his apostolic orbit, and so that they too might become part of that offering of the Gentiles which, by Paul's priestly ministry of the gospel, would become acceptable to God.[14]

Emerging from both the above

The overall purpose of Romans has been understood in terms of both the situation of the Roman church and the stage of his missionary career in which Paul found himself. This general approach has several particular expressions. (i) Paul wrote to confront the Roman churches on the matter of their Jew–Gentile relationships, and to challenge them to participate fully in the universal mission of God in which Paul was engaged. He showed that their ethnocentrism opposed God's eternal plan to justify all people by faith and include them in his redemptive plan.[15] (ii) When Paul wrote Romans he did so with two areas of concern. The first was to prepare for his visit to Rome and subsequent Spanish mission, while seeking prayer support for his visit to Jerusalem. The second was to respond to certain problems in the Roman church with which he had been acquainted.[16] (iii) 'The "Jewish question", which Paul had to deal with in his former missionary territories, which had become a living issue again because of his forthcoming visit to Jerusalem and the threat of disunity in the church of Rome, compelled him to reflect on the

---

[12]C. E. B. Cranfield, *A Critical and Exegetical Commentary on the Epistle to the Romans*, 2 (ICC; Edinburgh: T. & T. Clark, 1979), pp. 814–818.

[13]Neil Elliott, *The Rhetoric of Romans: Argumentative Constraint and Strategy and Paul's Dialogue with Judaism* (JSNTSup 45; Sheffield: JSOT, 1990), pp. 69–104.

[14]Jervis, *The Purpose of Romans*, pp. 163–164.

[15]Walter B. Russell, 'An Alternative Suggestion for the Purpose of Romans', *BSac* 145 (1988), p. 180.

[16]John Ziesler, *Paul's Letter to the Romans* (London: SCM: Philadelphia: Trinity, 1989), pp. 15–16.

relationship of Judaism to Christianity, on its continuous and discontinuous dimensions.[17] (iv) Among the Jews returning to Rome after the expulsion by Claudius were Jewish Christians who had heard about the conflicts Paul had in Galatia, Philippi and Corinth. They opposed Paul and his gospel, and their criticisms are reflected in the rhetorical questions of 3:7; 4:1; 6:1, 15; 7:7, 12, 14. Paul wrote Romans to overcome these criticisms so as to prepare the way for his planned visit to Rome and so that he might secure the help of the church there for his Spanish mission.[18] (v) A significant section of the Roman church was still clinging to the law as the means of obtaining justification at the coming judgment. Paul writes to get them to let go of the law for the sake of unity, for the sake of his grand vision – one eschatological people made up of Jews and Gentiles (15:6) – and to bring the church within the scope of his own authority as apostle to the Gentiles.[19]

In trying to achieve some working hypothesis about the purpose(s) of Romans for this study, it is worth noting that the only *explicit* statement the apostle makes about his purpose for writing is found in 15:15–16:

> Nevertheless on some points I have written to you rather boldly by way of reminder, because of the grace given me by God to be a minister of Christ Jesus to the Gentiles in the priestly service of the gospel of God, so that the offering of the Gentiles may be acceptable, sanctified by the Holy Spirit.

This suggests that Paul's *primary* purpose in writing Romans was to bring the Roman believers within the orbit of his apostolic ministry because he felt responsible for them. He wanted to ensure that their understanding of the gospel was such that they too would be included among those Gentiles who constitute an acceptable sacrifice to God, consecrated by the Holy Spirit. Earlier in the letter he indicates that the Roman believers were included among the Gentiles for whom he felt this responsibility (1:5–6), and that he wanted to exercise a ministry among them, as he had done among other Gentiles (1:13–15).

If this was Paul's primary purpose, we can understand why it was necessary for him to provide such a comprehensive statement and defence of his gospel. We can also understand why he wanted to deal with divisions within the

---

[17]J. C. Beker, 'The Faithfulness of God and the Priority of Israel in Paul's Letter to the Romans', *HTR* 79 (1986), p. 12.

[18]Peter Stuhlmacher. 'Der Abfassungszweck des Römerbriefes', *ZNW* 77 (1986), pp. 186–191.

[19]Brendan Byrne, ' "Rather Boldly"(Rom. 15,15): Paul's Prophetic Bid to Win the Allegiance of the Christians in Rome', *Bib* 74 (1993), pp. 85–86.

Roman Christian community (11:13–32; 14:1 – 15:13), and to answer various objections to his gospel (3:1, 9; 4:1; 6:1, 15; 7:7, 13; 9:6, 14, 30; 11:1, 11) which were being voiced in Rome (16:17–18).

And, if Paul's primary purpose is identified in this way, it does not rule out such *secondary* purposes as preparing the way for his visit to Rome and subsequent mission in Spain, and soliciting the Roman Christians' prayers for his impending 'collection visit' to Jerusalem (15:22–32).

Paul's theme: the gospel and the righteousness of God

It is widely recognized that 1:16–17 functions as a statement of the major theme that Paul works out in the theological and paraenetic sections of Romans. The text of 1:16–17 runs:

> For I am not ashamed of the gospel; it is the power of God for salvation to everyone who has faith, to the Jew first and also to the Greek. For in it the righteousness of God is revealed through faith for faith; as it is written, 'The one who is righteous will live by faith.'

Particularly germane to the present study are the statements that 'in it [the gospel] the righteousness of God is revealed', and that it is a righteousness 'revealed through faith for faith' (something to which the prophet Habakkuk bore witness when he wrote, 'The one who is righteous will live by faith').

The righteousness of God revealed in the gospel

The discussion of the meaning of the righteousness of God in Romans has generated a vast literature which it is beyond the scope of this book to review. Before attempting to explain what Paul means by saying that the righteousness of God is revealed in the gospel, however, it might be helpful to note the different aspects of the righteousness of God as they emerge in the apostle's argument in Romans.

First, God's righteousness as *distributive justice* is implied in 1:18–32 where Paul says that God recompenses humanity in accordance with its response to his revelation, and also in 2:2–11 where he says that God renders to all people according to their works – those who with patience and well-doing seek immortality will be rewarded with eternal life, while those who are factious and do not obey the truth will be rewarded with wrath and fury. It is implied again in 3:1–20 where Paul defends God's righteousness by arguing that God acts justly when he judges unfaithful Jews.

Second, God's righteousness as *covenant faithfulness* is defended in 3:3–9, where Paul argues that when God judges Israel it is evidence not of failure of covenant loyalty on his part, but of sinfulness on Israel's part. In 9:1–29 God's covenant faithfulness is further defended when Paul rejects charges that God's word has failed (v. 6), that there is injustice on God's part (v. 14) and that God has no right to find fault with Israel (v. 19). Paul argues that Israel has failed to obtain the blessing, not because God is unfaithful to his covenant with Israel, but because that blessing always depended upon election and mercy, not on any inherent rights based on being born a Jew. God's covenant faithfulness is further defended in 11:1–10 where Paul argues that God has always maintained a remnant of Israel in whom his covenant promises are being fulfilled.

Third, God's righteousness as *saving action* is expounded in 3:21–26. Here God's righteousness is manifested, apart from the law, by providing redemption through Christ's death, so making possible a righteousness (a right standing before God) to be received by faith.

Fourth, God's righteousness as *the gift of justification and a right relationship* with himself, already foreshadowed in 3:21–26, is expounded in terms of the experience of Abraham in 4:1–25. It is referred to again in 5:17 ('the free gift of righteousness' received by believers as a result of Christ's obedience), and explained further in 9:30 – 10:4, where the apostle speaks of a righteousness not based on law[-observance by Jews], but which comes from God, and is received by all those who believe.

Fifth, the righteousness of God (as a gift] which leads to *righteousness of life* in believers is expounded in 6:1–23 (esp. vv. 16–18) where Paul points out that those who are under [the] grace [of justification] are no longer slaves of sin but slaves of righteousness. This aspect of the righteousness of God is also reflected in 8:4, where the purpose of Christ's death is to condemn sin in the flesh so that the just requirement of the law might be fulfilled in believers.

All these aspects of God's righteousness can be included under the one umbrella idea of *God acting in accordance with his own nature for the sake of his name.*[20] Understood in this way, it can include God's distributive justice, his covenant loyalty, his saving action, and his gift of justification leading to righteousness of life.

The central thrust of Paul's teaching about the righteousness of God in Romans, however, is to explain the way God's righteousness is revealed in the gospel. And what he means by this is that God's power for salvation, by

---

[20]John Piper, 'The Demonstration of the Righteousness of God in Romans 3:25, 26', *JSNT* (1980), pp. 2–32, argues for this meaning of the righteousness of God in these verses.

which Gentiles as well as Jews are justified freely by his grace, is revealed in the gospel. This is done without any compromise of his distributive justice (because he has set forth Christ as an atoning sacrifice for sin), of his covenant faithfulness to Israel, or of his demands for righteousness of life in his people.

A righteousness by faith

By describing the righteousness of God revealed in the gospel as a righteousness by faith, Paul foreshadows something that he will argue in detail later in the letter, *i.e.* that justification is not received from God simply because one belongs to the people of Israel, or because of human works. Justification is to be received through faith in what God has done in Christ.

To reinforce the truth that justification is by faith, in Romans 1:17 Paul cites Habakkuk 2:4. But there is some ambiguity in the Greek text of Romans 1:17b itself. In this connection it is instructive to compare the rendering of Habakkuk 2:4 in the LXX with the three citations of it in the New Testament:

LXX	*ho dikaios*	*ek pisteōs mou zēsetai*	
Rom. 1:17	*ho dikaios*	*ek pisteōs*	*zēsetai*
Gal. 3:11	*ho dikaios*	*ek pisteōs*	*zēsetai*
Heb. 10:38	*ho dikaios mou ek pisteōs*		*zēsetai*

If Paul and the writer of Hebrews were working with a Greek text the same as that preserved in the preferred text of the LXX cited above, then it would appear that both of them modified the text to make it express the theological point they were making.[21] Hebrews 10:38 is unambiguous and may be rendered: 'My righteous one shall live by faith.' But the LXX itself is ambiguous, and may be rendered in one of three ways: (i) 'the righteous shall live by my faithfulness', (ii) 'the righteous shall live by his faith in me', (iii) 'my by-faith-righteous-one shall live'. Romans 1:17 and Galatians 3:11 are also ambiguous, the translation being determined by what *ek pisteōs* is believed to qualify. If it qualifies *dikaios*, then the text should be rendered 'the one who is righteous through faith shall live', but if it qualifies *zēsetai*, then it

---

[21]Dietrich-Alex Koch, 'Der Text von Hab 2 4b in der Septuaginta und im Neuen Testament', *ZNW* 76 (1985), pp. 84–85, argues that the preferred LXX text of Hab 2:4b is the original, all three New Testament readings of the text are secondary, and the variant readings of the LXX are the result of the later influence of the three New Testament readings.

would have to be rendered 'the righteous one shall live by faith'. The translation of Romans 1:17, then, cannot be decided simply upon the word order, but must be decided upon other grounds, *i.e.* the context and comparison with other Pauline usage.

Cavallin argues that Romans 1:17 should be understood in the light of Galatians 3:11. There, in his view, *ek pisteōs*, in the citation of Habakkuk 2:4b, must be taken to qualify *zēsetai*, not *ho dikaios*, because in Galatians 3:11–12 the logic is that 'where there is life there is also righteousness, and vice versa. What gives life – faith or law – also gives righteousness.' Therefore, he argues, the only acceptable translation of Romans 1:17 is 'the righteous shall live by faith'.[22]

Cranfield, on the other hand, argues for the interpretation 'the one made righteous by faith shall live', because the immediate context (which says nothing about living by faith) requires it, because the structure of the letter requires it (for 1:18 – 4:25 expounds the meaning of *ho dikaios ek pisteōs*), and because the connection between righteousness and faith is made explicitly in 5:1.[23]

Moody agrees with Cavallin that 'the just shall live by faith' is the only satisfactory translation, but, following Barrett, he suggests that 'by faith' (*ek pisteōs*) qualifies *both* 'just' (*dikaios*) and 'shall live' (*zēsetai*). He argues for this view on the grounds that 1:16–17 is an introduction to the whole letter, and the letter deals with more than faith in its initial role in respect of justification; it deals with the role of faith in the ongoing Christian life as well.[24] Dunn also suggests a 'both . . . and' approach, arguing that rules of interpretation current in Pharisaic circles in Paul's day were designed to draw out as much meaning as possible from a given text, and that this is probably what the apostle is doing in 1:17. He also takes the very inability of commentators to resolve the 'either . . . or' debate over 1:17 as evidence supporting a 'both . . . and' approach.[25] Davies also opts for a 'both . . . and' approach, arguing that, while the primary reference is to the righteous who live by faith, there is a secondary reference to

---

[22]H. C. C. Cavallin, '"The Righteous shall Live by Faith": A Decisive Argument for the Traditional Interpretation', *ST* 32 (1978), pp. 40–43.

[23]C. E. B. Cranfield, *A Critical and Exegetical Commentary on the Epistle to the Romans*, 1 (ICC; Edinburgh: T. and T. Clark, 1975), p. 102.

[24]R. M. Moody, 'The Habakkuk Quotation in Romans 1:17', *ExpT* 92 (1981), pp. 205–208. He supports his argument with appeal to syntax and to the relationship of 1:17 to the rest of the letter, with a comparison of Paul's use of Hab. 2:4 in 1:17 and Gal. 3:11, and with a consideration of Paul's approach to Hab. 2:4.

[25]James D. G. Dunn, *Romans 1 – 8* (WBC 38a; Dallas, TX: Word, 1988), pp. 45–46.

the fact that they are also made righteous by faith. In his view the citation from Habakkuk 2:4 'bears witness to a justifying faith which produces a life characterized by faith', and this 'establishes a continuity of God's way of salvation before and after Christ. The same principle which was outlined by the prophet in the seventh century (and previously demonstrated in the life of Abraham) is operative now',[26] and, we might add, applies to both Jews and Gentiles.

Even if we adopt the 'both . . . and' approach to Paul's citation of Habakkuk 2:4, we must still seek some explanation of Paul's statement that the righteousness revealed in the gospel is 'from faith to faith'. There are a number of options. (i) It is a righteousness which is received entirely through faith (through faith from beginning to end).[27] (ii) It is a righteousness which justifies sinners through faith and then leads them to live out the obedience of faith. (iii) It is a righteousness which begins with the faithfulness of Christ and leads to the faith[fulness] of the believer.[28] (iv) It is a righteousness which begins with God's faithfulness and leads to faith[fulness] in the believer.[29] The first two options may be designated anthropological interpretations, and the third and fourth options Christological and theological interpretations respectively. There is a lot to commend the theological interpretation, for, as Dunn points out, following a verb like 'reveal', *ek* ('from') is more naturally understood to relate to the source of the revelation than to the recipient of the revelation; to God's faithfulness rather than to the faith(fulness) of the believer.[30]

Paul's argument: no distinctions in sin or judgment

Having stated his theme in 1:17, *i.e.* that the righteousness of God revealed in the gospel is a righteousness through faith for both Jews and Gentiles, Paul sets out to demonstrate in 1:18 – 3:20 that God makes no distinctions between them in the matter of sin or judgment. Recent studies have rightly recognized that the

---

[26]Glen N. Davies, *Faith and Obedience in Romans: A Study In Romans 1 – 4* (JSNTSup 39; Sheffield: JSOT, 1990), pp. 41–42.

[27]So, *e.g.*, C. K. Barrett, *A Commentary on the Epistle to the Romans* (London: A. and C. Black, 1957), pp. 30–31.

[28]Douglas A. Campbell, 'Romans 1:17 – A Crux Interpretum for the *PISTIS CHRISTOU Debate', JBL* 113 (1994), pp. 277–281, argues that this Christological interpretation gains support when Hab. 2.4 is recognized as an early-church messianic proof text.

[29]So, *e.g.*, Dunn, *Romans 1 – 8*, pp. 43–44.

[30]*Romans 1 – 8*, p. 44.

major thrust of 1:18 – 3:20 is to prove not so much that all Jews and all
Gentiles are sinners, and so all need justification, but rather that God shows no
partiality towards the Jews in his dealings with humanity in respect of sin and
judgment.[31]

In 1:18–32 the apostle teaches that the wrath of God is revealed against 'all
ungodliness and wickedness of those who by their wickedness suppress the
truth'. In 2:1–11 he argues that those who have the knowledge to pass
judgment upon others will not escape the judgment of God if their own deeds
are evil. In 2:12–16 Paul reasons that all people will be judged impartially. The
Jews will be judged impartially in accordance with the light they have received
through the law, and the Gentiles will be judged impartially in accordance with
the light given them by having the work of the law written on their hearts. In
2:17–29 Paul acknowledges that the Jews indeed have many privileges
(election, the law and circumcision), but if they break the law they will be no
better off than the Gentiles. God will judge everyone impartially according to
their deeds.[32] Finally, in 3:1–20 Paul quotes from the 'law' to conclude that,
despite the privilege of having the law, those under it stand condemned by it if
they break it, and so every mouth will be silenced and the whole world be held
accountable before God for their sins.

In the process of demonstrating God's impartiality in the matter of sin and
judgment, the apostle makes a number of statements and allusions which
contribute to our understanding of his views concerning the law and
justification, and some which raise difficult questions as well.

Human failure depicted with allusions to the law

In 1:18–32 Paul explains that the wrath of God is being poured out on the
ungodliness of human beings because, even though what may be known of him
is plain to them, they suppressed that knowledge. While Paul does not quote
from the law in this passage, both the language and sequence of events outlined
in it are reminiscent of the story of Adam told in Genesis 1 – 3. It would be
hard to improve on Hooker's presentation of the correspondence between
Romans 1 and Genesis 1 – 3. It is therefore reproduced here:

---

[31]*Cf. e.g.*, Jouette M. Bassler, 'Divine Impartiality in Paul's Letter to the Romans', *NovT* 26
(1984), p. 54.

[32]See Klyne R. Snodgrass, 'Justification by Grace – To the Doers: An Analysis of the Place of
Romans 2 in the Theology of Paul', *NTS* 32 (1986), pp. 79–80, for a succinct description of the
sequence of thought in 1:18 – 2:29.

Of Adam it is supremely true that God manifested to him that which can be known of him (v. 19); that from the creation onwards, God's attributes were clearly discernible to him in the things which had been made, and that he was thus without excuse (v. 20). Adam, above and before all men, knew God, but failed to honour him as God, and grew vain in his thinking and allowed his heart to be darkened (v. 20). Adam's fall was the result of his desire to be as God, to attain knowledge of good and evil (Gen. iii.5), so that claiming to be wise, he in fact became a fool (v. 21). Thus he not only failed to give glory to God but, according to rabbinic tradition, himself lost the glory of God which was reflected in his face (v. 23). In believing the serpent's lie that his action would not lead to death (Gen. iii.4) he turned his back on the truth of God, and he obeyed, and thus gave his allegiance to a creature, the serpent, rather than to the Creator (v. 25). Adam, certainly, knew God's *dikaiōma* (*cf.* Rom. v. 12–14); by eating the forbidden fruit he not only broke that *dikaiōma*, but also consented with the action of Eve, who had already taken the fruit (v. 32).[33]

This is a striking list of echoes from Genesis 3 in Romans 1:18–32, and constitutes compelling evidence for an Adamic background to this passage.[34] It may be going too far to say that Paul was intentionally describing Adam's fall, but clearly the apostle saw in Genesis 1 – 3 something which aptly depicted the state of the unrighteous of his own day. It is further evidence that the apostle, who rejected the law as a regulatory norm for believers, nevertheless consistently looked to it as a source of instruction.

Justification for the doers

Romans 2:1–16 presents a number of difficulties to interpreters. On first reading it seems to contradict the basic thrust of Romans,[35] which is that no-one will be justified by works of the law, but only by grace through faith. In this passage Paul says, for instance, that God 'will repay according to each one's deeds' (v. 6); 'there will be anguish and distress for everyone who does evil' (v. 9), 'but glory and honor and peace for everyone who does good' (v. 10). In addition to these surprising statements, Paul says:

---

[33]M. D. Hooker, 'Adam in Romans I', *NTS* 6 (1960), pp. 300–301. *Cf.* also D. J. W. Milne, 'Genesis 3 in the Letter to the Romans', *RTR* 39 (1980), pp. 10–12.

[34]So also Dunn, *Romans 1 – 8*, p. 53; A. J. M. Wedderburn, 'Adam in Paul's Letter to the Romans', StudBib 1978 III: *Papers on Paul and Other New Testament Authors* (JSNTSup 3; Sheffield: JSOT, 1980), pp. 413–419.

[35]So much so that Sanders, *Paul, the Law, and the Jewish people*, p. 123, believes that in the whole section 1:18 – 2:29 Paul has taken over homiletic material from diaspora Judaism and his treatment of the law here cannot be harmonized with what he says about it elsewhere.

When Gentiles, who do not possess the law, do instinctively what the law requires, these, though not having the law, are a law to themselves. They show that what the law requires is written on their hearts (vv. 14–15).

Snodgrass notes that more often than not scholars who discuss this text spend more time explaining it *away* than explaining it. He lists the following 'common ways of evading the text'.

1. Paul is speaking only hypothetically *as if* the law could be fulfilled and *as if* the gospel had not come. What Paul really believes one finds in 3.9f. and 3.20f.
2. Paul was speaking of Gentile Christians who fulfil the law through faith in Christ and a life in the Spirit.
3. This section (like other texts which speak of judgment) is an unexpurgated and unnecessary fragment from Paul's Jewish past.
4. This chapter is merely a contradiction in Paul's thought which must be allowed to stand.
5. Paul only means to say in 2:14–15 that Gentiles have a law and therefore are responsible and will be judged. There is only one outcome for both Jews and Gentiles on the basis of works and it is negative.[36]

If these are all evasions of what the text really says, how should it be explained properly? Did Paul really teach that God's judgment of human beings is based upon their works? And did he really mean to say that, whereas Jews who have the law did not keep it, the Gentiles who did not have the law practised what the law demanded? These two matters are now taken up in turn.

Is judgment according to works?

It must be recognized that Paul *did* say that God will judge all people according to their works (*cf.* vv. 6–10). It must also be recognized that the point Paul himself wanted to emphasize in saying this was that God's judgment would be entirely impartial. This is in line with his overall purpose in 1:18 – 3:20, which is to show that the Jews have no special immunity where God's judgment is concerned. Modern interpreters have no problem with impartiality in judgment. Their problem is to identify whom Paul refers to when he says, on the basis of God's impartial judgment, there would be 'glory and honour and peace for everyone who does good, the Jew first and

---

[36]*Cf.* Snodgrass, 'Justification by Grace – To the Doers', p. 73. As well as the above, Snodgrass lists also the more radical suggestion made by J. C. O'Neill that Romans 2 was a Hellenistic Jewish tract which was added by a later hand to Paul's letter.

also the Greek'.[37] The difficulty is exacerbated because it is often assumed that the basis of judgment is to be human success or otherwise in fulfilling the demands of the law.[38]

It is evident from Paul's emphasis upon repentance in this passage, however, that he did not have in mind judgment according to human success in fulfilling the demands of the law. Paul says that it is by their hard, impenitent hearts that those who judge others while excusing themselves are storing up wrath for themselves on the day of God's wrath. They do not realize that the goodness of God is intended to lead them to repentance, and so to forgiveness according to his grace (vv. 4–5).[39] God judges people impartially according to their works when out of his kindness and forbearance he gives eternal life to the repentant who seek glory and immortality by persistence in well-doing (vv. 7, 10). He also judges people impartially according to their works when he repays with wrath and anger the unrepentant who reject the truth and follow evil (vv. 8–9).

The residual problem of this approach is that it still seems to leave justification dependent upon persistence in well-doing.[40] But the problem is more apparent than real. No-one would want to say, for instance, that Paul thought that there was justification for those who persist in evil-doing. The fact of the matter is that, while Paul believed that justification was received by faith, independently of works of the law, he strenuously resisted the blasphemous suggestion that those who were so justified would persist in evil-doing (*cf.* 3:8).

---

[37]Douglas J. Moo, *Romans 1 – 8* (The Wycliffe Exegetical Commentary, Chicago: Moody Press, 1991), pp. 139–141, provides a succinct summary of the various suggested identifications of those Paul had in mind.

[38]This problem arises when interpreters import into ch. 2 the notion of justification by works of the law which Paul mentions in 3:20. *Cf.* Snodgrass, 'Justification by Grace – To the Doers', pp. 82–84.

[39]Nigel M. Watson, 'Justified by Faith: Judged by Works – An Antinomy', *NTS* 29 (1983), pp. 217, 220, correctly observes that Paul's warnings of judgment are directed primarily to those who are puffed up, whereas his assurances of justification are for the penitent. He concludes: 'The message of judgment is the valid word of God, not for those whose sins have found them out, but for those who are presuming on God's grace.'

[40]Bassler, 'Divine Impartiality', p. 58, recognizes that 'the simultaneous affirmation of the two doctrines, judgment according to works and justification by grace, does give rise to a certain degree of logical tension, especially if one seeks in Paul a perfectly consistent and coherent system. Paul himself, however, does not seem to recognize this tension. The reason for this is probably that in both cases the point Paul stresses is the same. Whether justifying on the basis of faith or judging on the basis of performance, God makes no distinction between Jew and Gentile. In both cases he shows no partiality.'

On the contrary, they would persist in doing good (yielding their members as instruments of righteousness, *cf.* 6:11–14).[41]

Did the Gentiles keep what the law requires?

The pivotal point in Romans 2 comes in verse 11: 'For God shows no partiality.' This sums up what has gone before (that God judges all people impartially in accordance with their works, vv. 1–10), and sets the stage for what follows (that this impartiality means that the Jews will have no advantage in the judgment just because they have the law, vv. 12–16).[42] So Paul writes:

> All who have sinned apart from the law will also perish apart from the law, and all who have sinned under the law will be judged by the law. For it is not the hearers of the law who are righteous in God's sight, but the doers of the law who will be justified (vv. 12–13).

This is straightforward enough. It is what follows that has caused such difficulties for interpreters.

> When Gentiles, who do not possess the law, do instinctively what the law requires, these, though not having the law, are a law to themselves. They show that what the law requires is written on their hearts, to which their own conscience also bears witness; and their conflicting thoughts will accuse or perhaps excuse them on the day when, according to my gospel, God, through Jesus Christ, will judge the secret thoughts of all (vv. 14–16).

Crucial to the understanding of this passage is the translation of *ta mē nomon echonta physei ta tou nomou poiōsin* in verse 14b. The question is whether the dative noun *physei* is to be rendered adverbially and regarded as qualifying what follows (*ta tou nomou poiōsin*), thus yielding a translation like that of the NRSV cited above: 'Gentiles, who do not possess the law, do instinctively what the law requires', or whether *physei* should be taken as adjectival and regarded as qualifying what precedes (*ethnē ta mē nomon echonta*), thus yielding a translation like: 'The Gentiles who by virtue of their birth do not have the law, do the things required by the law.' While the majority

---

[41]*Cf.* Snodgrass, 'Justification by Grace – For the Doers', p. 86. *Cf.* Davies, *Faith and Obedience in Romans*, pp. 53–71, esp. p. 70, where he says, for Paul: 'Where there is no obedience, there is no faith; where there is true faith, there is also obedience.'

[42]*Cf.* Bassler, 'Divine Impartiality', p. 45.

of modern translations adopt the former option,[43] some scholars argue that the way the dative of *physis* is used elsewhere in the Pauline corpus suggests that the latter is to be preferred,[44] *i.e.* verse 14b should be construed: 'The Gentiles, who by nature do not have the law, do the things required by the law.' As Dunn points out, however, where the dative of *physis* is used elsewhere in the Pauline corpus, it is used within the phrase it qualifies, not after it as here.[45] It is therefore best to stay with the first option.

Once this translation has been decided upon, interpreters face much greater difficulties. How are the Gentiles, who do by nature the things required by the law, to be identified? Does not such a notion contradict the whole thrust of Paul's argument that no-one is justified by works of the law?

Yates lists the three possible ways of understanding the statement about Gentiles who do the things required by the law. (i) Paul is able to view the morality of at least some Gentiles in a positive light. (ii) Paul applies a thoroughgoing principle of judgment to both Jew and Gentile. (iii) The Gentiles in this passage are Christian Gentiles.[46] He rejects (i) and (iii) as reflecting pre-exegetical considerations, and argues that all Paul was saying in this passage is that, as a matter of fact, we find pagans conforming formally and externally to the moral precepts of the law about which they are unaware.[47] Achtemeier adopts a similar approach, arguing that the passage in no way indicates that the Gentiles, who had the 'natural law', have achieved what the Jews, who had the written law, could not achieve. Davies, however, argues that Paul does view the status of some Gentiles in a positive light, and that here the apostle is seeking to show that God's impartiality has always extended to the Gentiles, and that God saves those upon whose hearts has been written the work of the law (he points to such Old Testament figures as the citizens of Nineveh, Job, Melchizedek, Rahab, Ruth and Naaman as examples). Davies' conclusion is that 2:12–16 refers to 'pre-Christian Gentiles, who are not only doers of the law but who are also justified before

---

[43]So, *e.g.*, NIV, NRSV, REB.

[44]*Cf.* Gal. 2:15 (*hēmeis physei Ioudaioi kai ouk ex ethnōn hamartōloi*); 4:8 (*edouleusate tois physei mē ousin theois*); Eph. 2:3 (*hēmetha tekna physei orgēs hōs kai hoi loipoi*). *Cf.* discussion in Cranfield, *Romans*, 1, pp. 156–157; Paul J. Achtemeier, '"Some Things in them Hard to Understand": Reflections on an Approach to Paul', *Int* 38 (1984), pp. 257–258.

[45]*Romans 1 – 8*, p. 98.

[46]J. C. Yates, 'The Judgement of the Heathen: The Interpretation of Article XVIII and Romans 2:12–16', *Churchman* 100 (1986), p. 222.

[47]'The Judgement of the Heathen', p. 225. Similarly, Dunn, *Romans 1 – 8*, pp. 98–99; Moo, *Romans 1 – 8*, pp. 144–147.

God'.[48] A different approach is adopted by Martens. He argues that when Paul spoke of 'doing the law by nature' he was dependent upon the Stoic theory of the law of nature, according to which only sages could understand it and so be in a position to perform it. He also argues that both Paul and his readers would have known that the Stoics believed that there were only a few sages, if any, who had ever managed to do so. Thus, Martens concludes, Paul adopts the Stoic view, according to which it is theoretically possible to keep the law of nature, but practically it is out of the question.[49]

For Paul's argument to stand, he must have believed that some Gentiles at least did observe something of what the law demanded, therefore the hypothetical approach is unsatisfactory. The view that Paul adopts the Stoic view is also unsatisfactory, for to enable Paul's argument to stand it is not enough to say that he implies that, while it is theoretically possible to obey the law, it is practically impossible. The view that the Gentiles who do the things required by the law were Gentile Christians in whose hearts the law had been written (in accordance with the promise of Je. 31:33) runs into difficulty because Paul does not speak of the *law*, but the *work of the law*, written on the Gentiles' hearts. Thus we come to the conclusion that Paul was saying, either that some pagans conform formally and externally to the moral precepts of the law about which they are unaware (Yates), or that he has in mind 'pre-Christian Gentiles, who are not only doers of the law but who are also justified before God' (Davies).

The main point of 2:14 is not to praise the Gentiles but to remind the Jews of God's impartiality. The Jews cannot boast simply because they possess the law, for it can be shown that, in some cases at least, the Gentiles who do not possess the law often have, in fact, such good behaviour that they put the Jews to shame.[50]

Summing up, it can be said that 2:1–16 does indeed speak of impartial judgment according to people's works, but that this must not be equated with judgment based upon works of the law. The works upon which people are judged are to be understood as the way they respond to the goodness of God which they have experienced.[51] In all cases this is meant to lead people to repentance and so to the experience of forgiveness and justification. Failure to

---

[48]*Faith and Obedience in Romans*, pp. 60–67.

[49]John W. Martens, 'Romans 2.14–16: A Stoic Reading', *NTS* 40 (1994), pp. 66–67.

[50]*Cf.* Thomas Schreiner, 'Did Paul Believe in Justification by Works? Another Look at Romans 2', *BBR* 3 (1993), pp. 144–147.

[51]Snodgrass, 'Justification by Grace – To the Doers', p. 81, comments: 'Those people who have seen Romans 2 as a description of circumstances prior to the coming of the gospel are correct. They

respond to the goodness of God, no matter what form the experience of his goodness may take, renders people liable to wrath on the day of wrath. In particular the Jews cannot boast in their possession of the law, as if that put them in a better position as far as the judgment of God is concerned, for in some cases Gentiles who do not have the law actually live out some of its precepts in a way that puts those who do have it to shame.

The Jews and the law

In 2:17–29 Paul takes his unbelieving kinspeople to task for boasting about their privileges as God's people while not living up to them. They boast about having the law, yet they dishonour the God who gave it to them by disobeying that law (2:17–24).[52] Similarly, they boast of their circumcision, but it is of value only if it is accompanied by obedience to the law; otherwise it is tantamount to uncircumcision (2:25), and Paul points out, those who are uncircumcised, but nevertheless keep the law, will be regarded as circumcised (2:26). For circumcision is essentially a matter of the heart and spiritual (effected by the Spirit), and not merely a matter of an outward observance of (the letter of) the law (2:28). All this prepares the way for the apostle's

---

are incorrect, however, if they conclude that the coming of the gospel negated or reversed the basic structure of what preceded. The issue after the coming of Christ, as before, is an obedient response to the amount of light received so that God is honoured as God and a relationship with him is established.'

[52]Paul's depiction of Jewish disobedience to the law with rhetorical questions ('Do you steal? . . . do you commit adultery? . . . do you rob temples?', 2:21–23) presents interpreters with difficulties. Are these questions to be taken literally or metaphorically (Do you rob God of his honour? Do you consort with other gods? Do you commit sacrilege?)? If taken literally, the idea of Jews robbing temples is very puzzling. Edgar Krentz, 'The Name of God in Disrepute: Romans 2:17–29 (22–23)', *CTM* 17 (1990), p. 433, n. 22, draws attention to the extensive use of *hierosylein* in vice lists of Greek authors prior to AD 200. There it always carries the literal sense of robbing temples, and Krentz argues that its use in Rom. 2:22 should be understood in the same way. J. Duncan M. Derrett, 'You Abominate False Gods; but do you Rob Shrines?' *NTS* 40 (1994), p. 570, argues that ' "temple robbery" includes profiting in any way from a heathen religious endowment's assets, whether directly or indirectly'. Opportunities for such profiting occurred, he says, when, due to negligence, dishonesty, mishaps or war, stolen items from pagan shrines entered the market, and then Jewish businessmen took the commercial opportunities this presented to them (pp. 564–565). D. B. Garlington, '*HIEROSYLEIN* and the Idolatry of Israel (Romans 2.22)', *NTS* 36 (1990), pp. 148–149, argues for a metaphorical rendering of *hierosylein* maintaining that Paul was referring to '*Israel's idolatrous attachment to the law itself*'. Another way of interpreting it metaphorically is to see it referring to the withholding of the temple tax which Jews were obliged to send to the Jerusalem temple (*cf.* Moo, *Romans 1 – 8*, p. 161).

conclusion a little later (3:9), where he says that Jews are no better off than Gentiles, because both are under the power of sin.[53]

It is important to note that Paul, while chiding the Jews for disobeying the law, acknowledges the positive benefits of having the law. Being instructed out of the law, the Jews know the will (of God) (2:18), and in the law they have the form of knowledge and the truth so that they are able to be guides to the blind, a light to those in darkness, correctors of the foolish and teachers of children (2:19–20). This reflects Paul's positive attitude to the law as far as its revelatory and ethical role in the life of Israel was concerned (and, we might add, his positive attitude to its revelatory and paradigmatic function in the lives of believers).

In defence of the righteousness of God

As noted above, Paul shows in Romans 2 that all people will be judged impartially according to their works, by which he meant that they would be judged on the basis of whether or not they have responded with repentance and obedience to the light God had given them (not whether or not they have perfectly fulfilled the demands of the Mosaic law). Thus even though the Jews had the immense privilege of knowing the will of God, and had in the law the embodiment of knowledge and truth, that would profit them nothing if they did not respond with repentance and obedience. Even their circumcision would be tantamount to uncircumcision if they failed to do so, just as the uncircumcision of the Gentiles would be counted as circumcision if they did.

All this raises the question of the righteousness of God. Is God acting with faithfulness to his covenant promises to Israel if Jews are judged as sinners in the same way as the Gentiles? Romans 3:1–20 is written in response to this question, and its overall thrust is to defend the righteousness of God, *i.e.* to show that God acts in complete faithfulness to his promises even when he judges Jews.[54]

---

[53]To say this, we do not have to assume that in 2:17–24 Paul is trying to elicit a confession of *culpability* on the part of the hypothetical Jewish dialogical partner, only a confession of *accountability*. If Jews have all the privileges that possession of the law bestows upon them, that does not mean that they escape accountability if they break the law. So ultimately they are no better off than Gentiles. *Cf.* Elliott, *The Rhetoric of Romans*, pp. 196–198.

[54]Assuming that the 'some [who] were unfaithful' (3:3) could only have been understood as a reference to unbelieving Jews by members of the house churches of Rome who heard Paul's letter read out to them. This is confirmed by the fact that Paul's other uses of *apistia* always denote failure to believe. It is used in this way in, *e.g.*, Rom. 4:20 (of Abraham who did not waver through

Romans 3:1–20, when understood as a defence of the righteousness of God, can be seen as a coherent whole, and not as series of disjointed or unrelated arguments.[55] Thus in 3:1–9 Paul asks if God has abandoned his faithfulness to promises made to Israel and if he acts righteously in visiting judgment upon those Jews who do not believe in Jesus. In 3:10–20 he defends the righteousness of God by showing from the 'law' that all unbelievers are under the power of sin. What the 'law' says, it says particularly to those under the law, *i.e.* the Jews. Therefore, if God condemns unbelieving Jews along with unbelieving Gentiles, it is not because he is unfaithful to his promises, but because they too are under the power of sin and refuse to repent.

Has God abandoned his faithfulness to Israel?

Using the diatribe format,[56] Paul is able, in 3:1–9, to deal with two important Jewish objections to his gospel: that it implied (i) that there was no benefit in being a Jew, and (ii) that God is unfaithful to his promises to Israel, Jews being judged in the same way as the Gentiles. The way Paul deals with the first of these objections is clear enough: there is indeed great benefit in being a Jew, for to them were entrusted the promises of God. The way he deals with the second objection is more difficult to follow. It involves response to three questions.

Paul responds to the first question (v. 3: 'What if some were unfaithful? Will their faithlessness nullify the faithfulness of God?') by showing that it cannot be said that God would be untrue to his promises (in judging unbelieving Israelites). God must be seen as true to his promises, even if that means that

---

unbelief regarding the promise) and Rom. 11:20, 23 (of Israel broken off because of unbelief, and restored if she does not persist in unbelief). *Cf.* Charles H. Cosgrove, 'What If Some Have Not Believed? The Occasion and Thrust of Romans 3 1–8', *ZNW* 78 (1987), pp. 91–92; David R. Hall, 'Romans 3.1–8 Reconsidered', *NTS* 29 (1983), p. 185.

[55]*Cf.* Richard B. Hays, 'Psalm 143 and the Logic of Romans 3', *JBL* 99 (1980), p. 113.

[56]Most modern interpreters of Romans agree that 3:1–9 is in the form of a diatribe. So, *e.g.*, Stanley Kent Stowers, 'Paul's Dialogue with a Fellow Jew in Romans 3:1–9', *CBQ* 46 (1984), pp. 710–715, who points to the formal correspondences between ancient Greek diatribes (esp. Epictetus) and Rom. 3:1–9. Hall, 'Romans 3.1–8 Reconsidered', p. 183, however, prefers to speak of the passage as internal debate rather than diatribe, arguing that elsewhere in his letters where Paul adopts the diatribe form he introduces the objections of the opponent with formulae more typical of the diatribe, *e.g. all' erei tis* (1 Cor. 15:35), *ereis oun* (Rom. 9:19; 11:19) and *phēsin* (2 Cor. 10:10), whereas in Rom. 3:5 Paul uses the formula *ti eroumen*, which is indicative of internal debate, not diatribe. Hall does not, however, take into account the various parallels with the diatribe noted by Stowers, *e.g.* esp. *ti oun* and *mē genoito*.

every human person is seen to be a liar (3:4a). A citation from Psalm 51:4 (LXX 50:6) in 3:4b ('Although everyone is a liar, let God be proved true, as it is written, "So that you may be justified in your words, and prevail in your judging"') underlines the fact that God's judgment of the unrighteous cannot abrogate his faithfulness to his promises. On the contrary he is fully justified in judging them. This citation from Psalm 51:4 is singularly appropriate for the purpose, for in that psalm the writer acknowledges that he has sinned against God and done evil in his sight, so that God would be righteous in passing judgment upon him. The citation then serves to refute the charge that God's judgment of unbelieving Jews abrogates his faithfulness to Israel. Like the psalmist, they had sinned, and therefore God would be acting righteously in passing judgment upon them.[57]

In response to the second question (v. 5: 'But if our injustice serves to confirm the justice of God, what should we say? That God is unjust to inflict wrath on us?'), Paul reveals the intolerable moral assumptions of such a question. If God was unable to judge the wicked, he would not be able to judge the world, and all moral accountability would disappear (3:6). And, in any case, Psalm 51:4 (cited in 3:4b) affirms that God is just when he judges the unbelieving among his own people. Because they have sinned he will be proved right when he judges them.[58]

Finally, Paul turns to the third question (vv. 7–8: 'But if through my falsehood God's truthfulness abounds to his glory, why am I still being condemned as a sinner? And why not say [as some people slander us by saying that we say], "Let us do evil so that good may come"?'). But he does not dignify it with a reasoned reply. Instead, it is summarily dismissed with the retort, 'Their condemnation is deserved!' (3:8), directed against those who suggest such a thing.

Scriptural proof of universal sinfulness

In 3:10–18 the apostle uses a catena of scriptural quotations from the Psalms and Isaiah to underline the fact that (unbelieving) Jews as well as (unbelieving) Gentiles are under the power of sin.[59] These quotations apply to the Jews as

---

[57]Cf. Hall, 'Romans 3:1–8 Reconsidered', pp. 186–188.

[58]Elliott, *The Rhetoric of Romans*, p. 151, observes correctly that in 2:17 – 3:9 'it is the integrity of God that remains the paramount issue for Paul. Not soteriology but theodicy is at stake here.'

[59]Cf. Moo, *Romans 1 – 8*, p. 207. Davies, *Faith and Obedience in Romans*, pp. 88–96, argues that Paul does not charge *all* Jews and *all* Gentiles without distinction as being under the power of sin, any more than do the passages which he cites.

well, Paul argues, because what the 'law' (here referring to the passages just quoted from Psalms and Isaiah) says, it says to those under the law, *i.e.* Jews (3:19a). The law says this about those under it, so that every mouth may be silenced and the whole world held accountable to God (3:19b). Paul's train of thought appears to be that if the Jews, who so often took the high moral ground over against the Gentiles, are declared to be under the power of sin by their own 'law', then clearly all peoples stand guilty before God, Jews as well as Gentiles. This leads to the statement which brings the passage 3:10–20 (and in fact the whole section 1:18 – 3:20) to a conclusion:

> For 'no human being will be justified in his sight' by deeds prescribed by the law, for through the law comes the knowledge of sin (3:20).

Here Paul alludes to Psalm 143, in which the psalmist asks God, in his faithfulness and righteousness, to come to his relief (v. 1), and not to bring him into judgment, for no-one living is righteous in his sight (v. 2), to which the apostle adds, 'by deeds prescribed by the law'. Paul's allusion to Psalm 143 is most appropriate. It underlines what he has just demonstrated by his catena of scriptural quotations (3:10–19), *i.e.* that no-one living will be declared righteous by God on the basis of his or her own moral achievements. It also foreshadows what Paul will go on to demonstrate, *i.e.* that the faithfulness and righteousness of God come to the relief of sinners (3:21–26).[60]

If Paul intended his allusion to Psalm 143 to function in the way suggested, two further points may be made. First, Romans 3 is not just a collection of disparate ideas, but rather a coherent whole. Second, Paul's use of Psalm 143 here is further support for the view that the underlying sense of the righteousness of God with which Paul works in Romans is that of God acting in accordance with his own righteous nature. In 3:1–19 God acts righteously in judging unbelievers (Jews as well as Gentiles), and this is balanced in 3:21–26 where Paul shows that God also acts righteously when justifying believers (both Jews and Gentiles) freely by his grace.[61]

The whole passage, 3:1–20, is significant for the present study in three ways. First, it reflects again the positive side of Paul's attitude to the law: the law contains the promises of God to Israel and thus constitutes the primary

---

[60]*Cf.* Hays, 'Psalm 143 and the Logic of Romans 3', pp. 113–114.

[61]Hays, *ibid.*, p. 115, notes that the righteousness of God in Ps. 143 is unambiguously God's own righteousness – his power of deliverance. Thus the psalm supports Käsemann's view of the righteousness of God as salvation-creating power. This is certainly true as far as it goes, but as we have already seen, it needs to be supplemented with the idea of God's righteousness expressed in judgment.

benefit given to the Jews by God. Second, it provides crucial information concerning the underlying meaning of the term 'the righteousness of God' as it is used in Romans. In 3:1–9 the righteousness of God, like faithfulness and truth, is an aspect of his character which is expressed in his acting with integrity in respect of his covenant promises to Israel, even when he judges unbelieving Jews.[62] But this does not mean that the passage therefore supports the view that the righteousness of God is to be understood exclusively as his saving activity. Such a conclusion fails to recognize that this passage defends the righteousness of God's action when he *judges* unbelieving Jews.[63] It would seem, on the basis of this passage at least, that the righteousness of God needs to be understood in terms of God's action in faithfulness to his promises, not only in saving those who believe (as emphasized later in 3:21–26), but also in bringing judgment upon those who do not (as stressed in 3:2–9).

Third, 3:1–20 reveals again how Paul's use of the term 'law', which normally denotes either the Pentateuch or the demands of the Mosaic law, sometimes denotes the Old Testament as a whole.[64]

Excursus: the meaning of 'the works of the law' in Romans

What does Paul mean by 'the works of the law' in Romans? The expression is found only twice in the letter: (i) as an addition to Paul's allusion to Psalm 143 in 3:20, and (ii) in the statement, 'For we hold that a person is justified by faith apart from works prescribed by the law', in 3:28. But the same expression is found six times in Galatians (2:16, three times; 3:2, 5, 10), where its primary reference is to circumcision and observance of special days and seasons. These were the outward Jewish observances which the Judaizers were insisting the Galatians should take on board.

But in Romans, the expression 'the works of the law' denotes primarily something other than these observances. When Paul concludes that no flesh

---

[62]John Piper, 'The Righteousness of God in Romans 3, 1–8', *TZ* 36 (1980), pp. 9–10, adopts this view and suggests that *dikaiosynē theou* refers to God's 'truthfulness . . . in keeping his promises'.

[63]Piper, 'The Righteousness of God in Romans 3:1–8', pp. 11–15, argues that scholars who fail to recognize this do so because they do not distinguish between Paul's view of the righteousness of God and his opponents' view. His opponents believed that God's righteousness completely excluded any judgment at all upon the covenant people. Paul's view was that God's righteousness embraced both his merciful faithfulness and his punitive judgment.

[64]It is significant that the Psalms, as well as Isaiah, are included under the term 'law' here, seeing that it is still debated whether the Psalms were already recognized as part of the Jewish canon in the first century.

would be justified by works of the law (3:20), it was because even the Jews who had the law failed to observe it. What the apostle has in mind is not their failure to practise circumcision or to observe the special days and seasons laid down in the law. The Jews whom Paul accuses of breaking the law had been circumcised (2:27); their failure in respect of the works of the law was in the moral area:

> You, then, that teach others, will you not teach yourself? While you preach against stealing, do you steal? You that forbid adultery, do you commit adultery? You that abhor idols, do you rob temples? You that boast in the law, do you dishonor God by breaking the law? (2:21–23).

Hence, when Paul says in Romans that no flesh will be justified by works of law, he means that no-one would be justified on account of his or her moral achievements. For even the Jews who were best placed to do this, being instructed by the law so that they knew God's will and could approve what was excellent, nevertheless failed to perform God's will or practise what was morally excellent. Thus we may conclude that 'the works of the law' here, while not excluding those aspects of the law highlighted in Galatians (circumcision and observance of special days and seasons), denotes primarily the moral demands of the law.[65]

Paul's argument: no distinctions in the matter of salvation

In the long section 1:18 – 3:20, Paul argues that God does not show partiality in his dealings with humanity in respect of sin and judgment. Jews and Gentiles alike stand accountable before God, and no-one is justified in his sight by works of the law. But at 3:21 there is a distinct, new turn in Paul's argument. Thus, in 3:21–31 he argues that a righteousness of God has now been revealed apart from the law, *i.e.* God has acted according to his righteousness to make salvation available to all who believe without making distinctions between Jews and Gentiles on the basis of the law. Then in 4:1–25 Paul shows that the example of Abraham, far from disproving his argument, actually supports it. Finally, in 5:12–21 (following a pastoral application of the comforting doctrine of justification by faith in 5:1–11) the apostle further demonstrates that there are

---

[65]Agreeing here with C. E. B. Cranfield, '"The Works of the Law" in the Epistle to the Romans', *JSNT* 43 (1991), pp. 93–95, *contra* Dunn, 'Works of the Law', p. 223, who puts it the other way around: '"works of the law" refer not exclusively but particularly to those requirements which bring to sharp focus the distinctiveness of Israel's identity'.

no distinctions between Jews and Gentiles in the matter of salvation by affirming that the humanity-wide implications of Adam's sin are more than matched by the humanity-wide salvation made available through Christ's obedience.

The heart of Paul's gospel

In 3:21–31 Paul argues that, as the law and the prophets foreshadowed, God has now acted according to his righteousness to justify both Jews and Gentiles without distinctions based upon the law. This had to be so because all people, Jews as well as Gentiles, have sinned and fallen short of the glory of God.[66] Justification is given freely to all who believe, without any compromise of God's righteousness, because of the redemption won through Christ, whom God himself set forth as an atoning sacrifice for the sins of all. Because God's righteousness has been revealed in this way, and because justification is to be received by faith (and is not based upon works of the law), all human boasting, except boasting in God's grace, is excluded.

As has been often noted, this passage is very compressed. This has sometimes been accounted for by saying that Paul is using earlier confessional material,[67] but whether this is the case or not, the passage expresses his own deepest convictions about the salvation God had effected in Christ.

The meaning of the term 'the righteousness of God'

One crucial matter to be decided in interpreting 3:21–31 is what is meant here by the term *dikaiosynē theou* ('the righteousness of God'), which is used four times (vv. 21, 22, 25, 26) in just six verses.[68] In recent years there has been a

---

[66]This is generally taken to refer to the forfeiture, because of the entry of sin, of the glory humanity once bore. Alternatively, it could refer to humanity's failure to give God the glory due to him so that they fall under his judgment, something which the apostle points out in 1:18–23; *cf.* Ziesler, *Romans*, p. 110. Piper, 'Demonstration', pp. 28–29, argues that God had to act in Christ to manifest his righteousness, for to do nothing in face of the dishonouring of his name by sinful humanity would not only be to indicate that sin does not matter, but more importantly to say that his glory does not matter; thus, 'if God is to be righteous he must repair the dishonour done to his name by the sins of those whom he blesses'.

[67]Douglas A. Campbell, *The Rhetoric of Righteousness in Romans 3.21–26* (JSNTSup 65; Sheffield: JSOT, 1992), pp. 37–57, rehearses the various form–critical hypotheses advanced in favour of the view that Rom. 3:24–26 is an interpolation, and concludes that 'the four considerations commonly cited in their support are, without exception, unsound'.

[68]Campbell, *The Rhetoric of Righteousness in Romans 3.21–26*, pp. 139–156, provides a review of the recent debate on the meaning of *dikaiosynē theou* in this passage.

growing tendency among scholars to construe *dikaiosynē theou* as a subjective genitive, and to interpret it as the salvation-creating activity of God. This tendency is correct in respect of 3:21–26, for here the righteousness of God expresses itself in God's action in Christ, on the basis of which he justifies those who believe and passes over their former sins. It needs to be added, however, that Paul stresses that God does this in a way which does not compromise his distributive justice. That is satisfied by his setting forth Christ as an atoning sacrifice.[69]

The manifestation of the righteousness of God

The apostle begins this passage by asserting: 'But *now*, apart from law, the righteousness of God has been disclosed' (v. 21a). The 'now' here seems to be more than an inferential particle. While it does signal that what is to follow will draw out the implications of what has already been said, it also indicates that God has acted in the present time, the great eschatological now, to manifest his righteousness apart from the law.

It is important to note that, by saying that this righteousness has been manifested 'apart from the law', the apostle makes it clear that it is therefore available to 'all who believe', both Gentiles (who do not have the law) and Jews (who have the law but do not keep it).[70] This being the case, there cannot be even the illusion of a human claim of righteousness before God. The sovereign and gracious initiative of God in the matter is preserved.[71]

The witness of the law and the prophets

Although Paul speaks here of the manifestation of a righteousness of God 'apart from law', he hastens to add that it is something to which the law (and the prophets) bear witness (v. 21b). Paul's understanding of the witness of the law has been variously explained. (i) The Old Testament sacrificial cultus, and in particular in the great day of atonement, foreshadowed the atoning sacrifice of Christ in which God's righteousness was shown.[72] (ii) The story of

---

[69]*Cf.* Piper, 'Demonstration', pp. 28–32.

[70]It is insufficient, in my view, to restrict the meaning of 'apart from the law' here to 'apart from the law understood as a badge of Jewishness', as Dunn does (*Romans 1 – 8*, p. 177). The reason righteousness has to be revealed 'apart from the law' is that the law itself shows that all human beings (Jews as well as Gentiles) stand guilty before God, as Paul was at pains to show in 3:1–20, and states again in 3:22–23.

[71]*Cf.* Elliott, *The Rhetoric of Romans*, p. 149.

[72]*Cf.* Campbell, *The Rhetoric of Righteousness in Romans 3.21–26*, pp. 130–133.

Abraham's being accounted righteous by God (Gn. 15) foreshadows God's righteousness justifying sinners without reference to the law (*cf.* Rom. 4). (iii) Paul's understanding of the witness of the prophets to God's righteousness being manifested without the law is best explained in terms of his reference to Habakkuk 2:4 ('the just shall live by faith') in 1:17. The second of these suggestions has most to commend it, because Paul himself goes on to speak of Abraham in the next chapter.

The faithfulness of Christ and the righteousness of God

The righteousness of God is further described as a righteousness of God *dia pisteōs Iēsou Christou* (v. 22). The majority of interpreters construe *Iēsou Christou* here as an objective genitive, so that *dia pisteōs Iēsou Christou* then denotes believers' faith in Jesus Christ. It is, however, possible to read *Iēsou Christou* as a subjective genitive. In this case, v. 22a would yield the translation, 'through the faithfulness [or faith-obedience] of Jesus Christ'.[73] To interpret the expression in this way is not to deny that the *means* of justification is 'by faith' as far as the recipients are concerned (that is made abundantly clear when Paul says in this same verse that the righteousness of God is 'for all who believe', and by the explicit statements of v. 30). Rather, construed in this way, the expression stresses that the ground of our justification is the faith-obedience of Jesus Christ.

The faithfulness of Christ and his atoning sacrifice

In verses 24b–25a Paul elucidates how God's righteousness was manifested through Christ's faith-obedience. Redemption came through Christ, because God set him forth as an atoning sacrifice *dia pisteōs* ('through faith[fulness]') in his blood. Here we find a second use of *dia pisteōs* in this passage. Generally this has also been understood to denote the faith of believers, so that verse 25a then speaks of God setting forth Christ as an atoning sacrifice 'to be received by faith'. But it is possible that *dia pisteōs* here also denotes, not the faith of believers, but the faithfulness of Christ. In this case, verse 25a speaks of Christ whom God set forth as an atoning

---

[73]So Luke Timothy Johnson, 'Rom 3:21–26 and the Faith of Jesus', *CBQ* 44 (1982), pp. 78–80; Bruce W. Longenecker, '*Pistis* in Romans 3.25: Neglected Evidence for the "Faithfulness of Christ"?', *NTS* 39 (1993), pp. 478–480; Davies, *Faith and Obedience in Romans*, pp. 106–108. *Cf.* Stanley K. Stowers, '*EK PISTEŌS* and *DIA TĒS PISTEŌS* in Romans 3:30', *JBL* 108 (1989) p. 667; Campbell, *The Rhetoric of Righteousness in Romans 3:21–26*, pp. 58–69.

sacrifice through his (Christ's) faithfulness in his death (in his blood).[74]

Understood in this way, verse 25a makes possible a very satisfying way of understanding the general thrust of verses 25b–26. By setting forth Christ as an atoning sacrifice, God shows that he acted righteously when formerly he passed over sins without punishing the offenders[75] (he did not pass over sins lightly; an atoning sacrifice was to be made through the faithfulness of Christ), and that he acts righteously when in the present time he justifies those who have faith in Jesus (he is not condoning their sins; an atoning sacrifice has been made through the faithfulness of Christ).

The exclusion of boasting

In 3:27 Paul asks, 'Then what becomes of boasting? (*pou oun hē kauchēsis?*)', and answers his own question by saying, 'It is excluded.' In this way he begins to draw out the implications of all that he has argued for in 2:17 – 3:26,[76] *i.e.* that the Jews have no ground of boasting which establishes them as better off in God's sight. The boast of the Jews which Paul condemned was *not* that they had earned their salvation by observance of the law, but rather a presumption that they are better off in God's sight than the Gentiles because they are Jews, and because they have the law (2:17–20). Paul's argument in 2:17 – 3:20

---

[74]So, Longenecker, '*Pistis* in Romans 3:25', pp. 478–480. This is better than the other view (suggested by Stowers, '*EK PISTEŌS* and *DIA TĒS PISTEŌS*, p. 668) that it is the faithfulness of God that Paul has in mind in v. 25a. The introduction of the idea of God's faithfulness disrupts the flow of thought in v. 25a, for then 'the atoning sacrifice' refers to Christ, 'the faithfulness' refers to God, and 'in his blood' refers to Christ. It is better to regard all three expressions as referring to Christ.

[75]Piper, 'Demonstration', p. 16, interprets the passing over of former sins as the withholding of the full judgment which sins of a former time deserved (agreeing with Leon Morris, *The Apostolic Preaching of the Cross* [Grand Rapids: Eerdmans, 1965], p. 278). Ziesler, *Romans*, p. 116 interprets it as the forgiveness of the former sins of those who now respond to the gospel. Davies, *Faith and Obedience in Romans*, pp. 109–110, argues that it is the sins of the righteous (both Jews and Gentiles) that God passed over formerly, and not the sins of the unrighteous, for upon those the wrath of God had been manifested. Stowers, '*EK PISTEŌS* and *DIA TĒS PISTEŌS*', pp. 668–669, suggests that Paul has in mind primarily, but not exclusively, the sins of the Gentiles who had not been visited with the judgment their sins deserved. It would then appear that God had lightly passed over their sins. The same could not be said of God's attitude to the sins of the Jews, because the whole cultus of the Old Testament emphasized the seriousness of sin and the need for propitiation.

[76]The adverb *oun* is clearly inferential, referring to what precedes. It is best to see the reference going right back to 2:17 where Paul first took up the matter of Jewish boasting, *Cf.* Richard W. Thompson, 'Paul's Double Critique of Jewish Boasting: A Study of Romans 3, 27 in its Context', *Bib* 67 (1986), p. 521.

demonstrates that these privileges made them no better off. Their boasting was misplaced because, having the law, they did not keep it. The 'law' itself condemned them and so silences all Jewish boasting.

Having asked, in 3:27, 'Then what becomes of boasting?' and answered, 'It is excluded', Paul goes on to ask, 'By what law? By that of works?' His answer is, 'No [not by the law of works], but by the law of faith.'[77] This is unexpected because in 2:17 – 3:20 Paul argued on the principle of works that Jewish boasting was excluded, since the Jews did not carry out the works which the law required. Why then does he say here that boasting is excluded by the principle of faith? The answer is given in 3:28. If (as argued in 3:21–26) all people are justified by means of faith without any reference to works of the law,[78] then the principle of faith excludes boasting. Paul further supports the exclusion of Jewish boasting by appealing to the fact that the one God is God of both Jews and Gentiles, and that being one he justifies both Jews and Gentiles in the one way – by means of faith (3:29–30).[79]

Thus it becomes apparent that Paul has a 'double critique' of Jewish boasting, based on their failure to observe the demands of the law on the one hand, and on the levelling effect of the one God's one way of justifying sinners (by faith) on the other.[80]

---

[77]Agreeing with Heikki Räisänen, 'Das "Gesetz des Glaubens" (Röm. 3.27) und das "Gesetz des Geistes" (Röm. 8.2)', *NTS* 26 (1979), pp. 101–117, who argues for an understanding of the 'law of works' and the 'law of faith' as the principles of law and faith respectively, and disagrees with those who argue that 'law of works' is the Torah used wrongly and the 'law of faith' is the Torah used correctly; so, *e.g.*, Hübner, *Law in Paul's Thought*, p. 138; Peter von der Osten-Sacken, *Römer 8 als Beispiel paulinischer Soteriologie* (Göttingen: Vandenhoeck und Ruprecht, 1975), p. 245; Dunn, *Romans 1 – 8*, p. 192.

[78]Taken to mean all that the law demands, agreeing here with Cranfield, 'The Works of the Law', pp. 95–96.

[79]Stowers, '*EK PISTEŌS* and *DIA TĒS PISTEŌS*', pp. 670–672, has a point when he argues: 'Paul consistently applies *dia tēs pisteōs* to the redemption of the Gentiles. The case is different for *ek pisteōs*, which can refer to both Jews and Gentiles'. He is less convincing when he says: 'Paul clearly assumes that Jews also have some sort of relationship to Jesus Christ, but he does not speak as if the Jewish and Gentile relationship is the same.' He is even less convincing when he asserts: 'In my estimation there is no text where Paul could unambiguously be said to indicate that Israel needs or has received the same kind of atonement through Christ as the Gentile nations.' This last statement seems to fly in the face of Rom. 3:21–25b.

[80]*Cf.* Thompson, 'Double Critique', pp. 525–530. *Cf.* J. Lambrecht, 'Why is Boasting Excluded? A Note on Rom. 3,27 and 4,2', *ETL* 61 (1985), p. 368.

Upholding the law

Having excluded, on the principle of faith (as well as the principle of works) all grounds for Jewish boasting based on the law, Paul then asks, 'Do we then overthrow the law by this faith?' (v. 31a). To this question he responds with an emphatic 'By no means! On the contrary, we uphold the law' (v. 31b). In what sense can it be said that Paul's principle of faith upholds the law? There are two possible answers, both of which have some support in the text of Romans. First, in 8:4 Paul says that the purpose of God's action in Christ was 'so that the just requirement of the law might be fulfilled in us, who walk not according to the flesh but according to the Spirit'. Thus, it may be argued, the principle of faith upholds the law in so far as those of faith walk in the Spirit and the just requirement of the law is fulfilled in them. Second, in 3:21 Paul speaks of the law as a witness to the righteousness of God manifested without the law (referring possibly to Gn. 15:6 and the story of Abraham's being declared righteous). Thus it may be said that the principle of faith (justification apart from the works of the law) upholds the law because it fulfils what the law foreshadowed. This second explanation is probably to be preferred because supporting evidence for it is found in the section of Romans in which our text appears, *i.e.* in Paul's discussion of the story of Abraham, which follows immediately.

The case of Abraham

Before highlighting the main points emerging from 4:1–25 in relation to law and justification, a few preliminary comments need to be made.

First, it is important to recognize that this passage really continues what Paul says in 3:29–31. Three considerations support such a view. (i) It is possible to discern a line of argument proceeding from 3:29 through to 4:25. (ii) What Paul emphasizes in 3:29–30 (God justifies both the circumcision [*peritomē*] and the uncircumcision [*akrobystia*] by faith) is also the main thrust of 4:9–12. (iii) 4:2–8 is an exposition of the law (in particular the law's description of Abraham's being accounted righteous) to show that the principle of faith is consistent with what the law says; it upholds the law and does not overturn it, which is what Paul asserts in 3:31.

Second, Paul's discussion of the case of Abraham is certainly not intended simply to provide an example of one who was justified by faith. Paul's primary purpose is to show that God makes no distinctions between Jews and Gentiles as far as salvation is concerned.

Third, 4:1–25 functions as an apology in which the apostle appeals to the

Scriptures to defend his gospel in light of possible Jewish objections.[81] To make this defence, Paul appeals not only to Abraham, but also to David, thus drawing upon the experience of two great Old Testament heroes to support his case. In addition he draws attention to Abraham as a *universal* father figure, an idea often used in Jewish apologetics. Further, he defends his gospel by showing that it is consistent with God's previous acts in history, thereby emphasizing the continuity between the way God acted in the case of Abraham and the way he acts now in accordance with Paul's gospel.[82]

Justified by faith without works

In 4:1 Paul introduces the case of Abraham, asking, 'What then are we to say was gained by Abraham, our ancestor according to the flesh?'[83] He then proceeds with an explicit discussion about justification by faith in verses 2–8,[84] saying that 'if Abraham was justified by works, he has something to boast about, but not before God' (v. 2).[85] He shows that Abraham in fact has no

---

[81] Among Paul's Jewish contemporaries it was believed that Abraham was a clear example of one who was justified by works, in particular because of his obedience to God in being willing to offer up his son Isaac. For his gospel to have credibility for those with a background in the synagogue, Paul had to show that Abraham was in fact justified by faith, not works. Paul does allude to the offering of Isaac (when describing God as the one 'who did not spare his own son but delivered him up for us all', *cf.* 8:32), but when he wants to show that Abraham was accounted righteous by God he chooses an incident earlier in the patriarch's life, his response to the promise of God. *Cf.* Eva Meile, 'Isaaks Opferung: Eine Note an Nils Alstrup Dahl', *ST* 34 (1980), pp. 111–112. In some Jewish exegesis, however, Gn. 15:6 itself is interpreted in terms of the offering of Isaac (1 Macc. 2:52, *cf.* Jas. 2:22–23).

[82] *Cf.* Anthony J. Guerra, 'Romans 4 as Apologetic Theology', *HTR* 81 (1988), pp. 258–265.

[83] While this translation from the NRSV seems quite straightforward, in fact the original Greek is ambiguous at two points. (i) It is possible to punctuate the verse differently so that it yields: 'What shall we say? Have we found [on the basis of Scripture] that Abraham is our forefather according to the flesh?' *Cf.* Richard B. Hays, ' "Have we Found Abraham to be our Forefather According to the Flesh?" A Reconsideration of Rom 4:1', *NovT* 27 (1985), pp. 76–98. (ii) It is possible that *kata sarka* goes not with *propatora* (thus yielding 'Abraham our forefather according to the flesh', which implies that Paul includes the Jewish members among his readers with him in his use of 'our') but with *heurēkenai*, so that the text reads: 'What then shall we say Abraham has found according to the flesh?'

[84] The only place in the whole of ch. 4 where he does so, and even here it is with an eye to the main point he wishes to make, *i.e.* that there are no distinctions between Jews and Gentiles in so far as the way God justifies is concerned.

[85] Even this apparently straightforward statement is based on a puzzling Greek construction. As Lambrecht, 'Why is Boasting Excluded?', p. 366, points out, it is a conditional sentence in which the form of the protasis indicates a condition contrary to fact, and that of the apodosis indicates a

ground of boasting before God because the Scriptures (Gn. 15:6) say that he 'believed God, and it was reckoned to him as righteousness' (v. 3). Paul makes the point that a person who works for justification receives it not as a gift but as a due (v. 4), but the one 'who without works trusts him who justifies the ungodly' has faith reckoned as righteousness (v. 5),[86] and Abraham falls in to this second category. So, far from being justified by his works (*e.g.*, by his obedience in being prepared to offer up Isaac), the great ancestor of Israel had righteousness reckoned to him because he believed God.[87] Thus he is the prototype of *all* those who without works trust him who justifies the ungodly, Gentiles as well as Jews.

Paul then calls another witness from the Scriptures, this time David:

> So also David speaks of the blessedness of those to whom God reckons righteousness apart from works:
> > 'Blessed are those whose iniquities are forgiven,
> > > and whose sins are covered;
> > blessed is the one against whom the Lord will not reckon sin.'
>
> (vv. 6–8; cf. Ps. 32:1–2)

David speaks of God's righteousness being reckoned to people apart from their works. Paul takes it that the works lacked by those here reckoned righteous are moral achievements, for it is their *iniquities* that are forgiven and their *sins* which are covered. Those whom David pronounces blessed are, like Abraham, those who have no grounds for boasting; they are the ungodly to whom God reckons righteousness apart from works.

Justified by faith without circumcision

In 4:9–12 Paul moves back to his main point, *i.e.* whether the blessings of justification are restricted to God's covenant people. He asks: 'Is this blessedness, then, pronounced only on the circumcised, or also on the uncircumcised?' (v. 9). To answer the question he first reminds his readers

---

condition of fact; *i.e.* it reads: 'If Abraham was justified by works (and he was not) he has something to boast about (and he has)'.

[86] Paul clearly does not regard faith as a work, because in this verse the one who exercises faith is described as one who is 'without works'.

[87] Moo, *Romans 1 – 8*, p. 265, points out, correctly, that Paul's intention is not to say that Abraham's faith was reckoned as equivalent to righteousness, but rather that, in the light of Abraham's faith, God reckoned to him a righteousness which was not inherently his (the other uses of the Hebrew verb *hašab* in the Old Testament indicate that this is the case).

that it was Abraham's faith that was reckoned to him as righteousness, and then asks a subsidiary question, 'How then was it reckoned to him? Was it before or after he had been circumcised?' (v. 10a). The answer to this subsidiary question is, 'It was not after, but before he was circumcised' (v. 10b).

Paul bases this answer upon his reading of Genesis, in particular upon the fact that Genesis 15:6 speaks of Abraham's faith being reckoned to him as righteousness before Genesis 17:10 speaks of circumcision being required of him. Circumcision then functioned as a sign of the righteousness Abraham already had by faith, and not as a prerequisite for it (v. 11a).

Paul then comes back to his main point and asserts that God's purpose in all this was that Abraham might be 'the ancestor of all who believe without being circumcised and who thus have righteousness reckoned to them, and likewise the ancestor of the circumcised who are not only circumcised but who also follow the example of the faith that our ancestor Abraham had before he was circumcised' (vv. 11b–12).What Paul does here is to read the law in such a way as to show that, because Abraham himself was justified without circumcision, then the blessing of justification cannot be limited to those who are circumcised. Because the blessing of justification depends upon faith alone, it is available to the uncircumcised (Gentiles) as well as to the circumcised (Jews). Paul can thus claim Abraham as the father of all believers, Gentiles as well as Jews.[88]

The promise realized by faith without the law

Having argued from Abraham's experience to show that justification is by faith and independent of either works or circumcision, Paul proceeds in 4:13–24 to use the case of Abraham further to demonstrate that the realization of God's promises does not come through the law. The promise to Abraham (that he would become the inheritor of the world,[89] Paul points out, had nothing to do with the law, but depended upon the righteousness of faith (v. 13). The law

---

[88]If the article *tois* is retained before *stoichousin* in v. 12, then the verse can be translated so as to mean that Abraham 'is the father of circumcision not only to those who are circumcised but also to those of the uncircumcision who follow the example of the faith of our father Abraham'. This, as James Swetnam, 'The Curious Crux at Romans 4,12', *Bib* 61 (1980), p. 115, points out, would make it appear that Paul is claiming not only Abraham for Gentile Christians, but circumcision (on the level of the spirit) as well.

[89]Among God's promises to Abraham was the promise that he would give the land of Canaan to him and his descendants (Gn. 13:14–15; 17:8) and that they would possess the gate of their enemies (Gn. 22:17). Before Paul's time this had been extended to mean that Abraham would inherit the world; *cf*, Dunn, *Romans 1 – 8*, p. 213, and references there.

could not be involved (quite apart from the fact that Scripture indicates that it had not yet been given) because if it depended upon (obedience to) the law, then faith as Paul understood it would be nullified and the promise (made without reference to the law) would be invalidated (v. 14). This has important implications for Paul's main argument, but before drawing these out, the apostle makes a parenthetical statement about the function of the law which shows further why the inheritance must come through faith: For the law brings wrath; but where there is no law, neither is there violation (v. 15).

Two functions of the law are implied here. First, it pronounces (God's) wrath upon those who transgress, *i.e.* those who fail to fulfil its demands. Second, it makes transgression a possibility, for 'where there is no law, neither is there violation'. What it does is to make people conscious of their sins,[90] which, of course, exist whether or not there is a law to turn those sins into transgressions.[91]

Following this parenthetical statement, Paul, in verses 16–17a, draws out the significance for his main argument of the fact that the promises of God are realized by faith, *i.e.* because they are realized by faith, the fulfilment of the promises may be guaranteed in respect of *all* who believe. It applies not just to possessors of the law (believing Jews) but also to those who share the faith of Abraham (here meaning believing Gentiles). Thus Abraham is 'the father of us all', and so the scriptural promise to Abraham ('I have made you the father of many nations') is fulfilled. Once again Paul shows that there are no distinctions between Jews and Gentiles in the matter of salvation. Both realize the promises by faith.

In verses 17b–22 Paul speaks of the nature of Abraham's faith. It was essentially a belief that God was able to do what he promised, even though Abraham's advanced age (and his wife Sarah's advanced age as well) seemed to make the fulfilment of the promise impossible. Nevertheless, he gave glory to God by not doubting his word, being fully convinced that God was able to do what he promised. Then Paul, citing Genesis 15:6 once again, says, 'Therefore his faith "was reckoned to him as righteousness".'

Verses 23–24 are important, for here Paul draws a lesson from the description of Abraham's faith just given, and in particular from the scriptural citation with which he concluded that description. The lesson is not that his readers should emulate the faith of Abraham (though he would certainly be glad if they did), but rather, that, in the scripture just cited, 'the words, "it was reckoned to him," were

---

[90]Paul refers to this function of the law again in 7:7.

[91]Something Paul makes clear in 5:13.

written not for his sake alone, but for ours also'. For, he says, 'It will be reckoned to us who believed in him who raised Jesus our Lord from the dead.'[92] Thus yet once more the apostle drives home his point that in the matter of salvation God makes no distinctions between Jews and Gentiles. Believing Gentiles, like believing Jews, are included among those for whose benefit it was written that Abraham's faith was reckoned to him for righteousness.

Justification depends upon the Christ event

Paul concludes chapter 4 by describing Jesus as the one 'who was handed over to death [*paradothē*, lit. 'delivered up'] for our trespasses and was raised for our justification' (v. 25). This should not be read to mean that justification is dependent upon Christ's resurrection and not upon his death (Paul makes it plain in 3:24–26 and 5:9, 18 that it is dependent upon Christ's death). The statement should be taken as a rhetorical unit, which states that our trespasses are dealt with and our justification secured through the death and resurrection of Christ thought of as one great event.

The fruits of justification by faith

Before noting what Paul has to say about the fruits of justification by faith in 5:1–11, brief comment is needed concerning the place of chapter 5 in the overall context of Romans. There has been some debate whether chapter 5 belongs with chapters 1 – 4 or with chapters 6 – 8. The position adopted here is that chapter 5 is in fact transitional. Several considerations support this view. (i) 5:1–11 functions as a pastoral application of the doctrine of justification by faith for all

---

[92]There is some ambiguity in this statement. It is not clear whether it is Abraham's faith that is being reckoned to us as righteousness, or whether our faith is being reckoned to us as righteousness, as Abraham's was to him. Hays, 'Have we Found Abraham to be our Forefather?', pp. 94–95, prefers the former. He says: 'However, it was not just reckoned to him as an individual: these words apply also to us (who believe in God who raised Jesus from the dead) to whom righteousness is going to be reckoned (vicariously, because we are Abraham's seed).' Hays adds that 'Paul is explicating his doctrine of justification in terms analogous to the Jewish idea of "the merits of the fathers". This does not imply any meritorious work of Abraham, but rather that, because of his faithfulness to the promise to Abraham, God is granting to Gentiles as well as to Jews the blessing of justification. Hays claims that, while this is the main thrust of Paul's argument, it is not 'antithetical to the customary interpretation,' adding that 'the dichotomy between receiving a blessing vicariously as a result of the archetype's faith/obedience ("in Abraham") and receiving a blessing through re-enacting the faith/obedience of the archetype ("like Abraham") is our dichotomy, not Paul's. Paul sees the two as indissoluble.'

who believe, for which Paul argued in 1:16 – 4:25. (ii) 5:12–19 provides further proof of this universal application of God's justifying grace. (iii) 5:20–21 introduces the subjects of the law, sin and death, and grace, righteousness and life, thus foreshadowing the major elements of the ethical discussion in chapters 6 – 8. Chapter 5, then, looks both backwards and forwards, and so functions as a transition between chapters 1 – 4 and chapters 6 – 8.[93]

Paul assumes in 5:1 what he argues for in 1:16 – 4:25, *ie.* that we have been justified by faith. He then proceeds to draw out in a pastoral fashion (using the first-person plural pronoun) the implications of this assumption, and in so doing lays out the fruits of justification by faith. These fruits are fourfold. (i) We have[94] peace with God.[95] (ii) We have access into this grace in which we stand. (iii) We have confidence in our hope of sharing the glory of God. (iv) We have confidence in the midst of sufferings,[96] because suffering produces endurance [in the sufferer] and endurance produces a tried and tested character;[97] this in turn produces hope [in God], and that hope does not disappoint because already [the sense of] God's love [for us] has been poured into our hearts by the Holy Spirit given to us[98] (and the presence of the Spirit is

---

[93]Dunn, *Romans 1 – 8*, pp. 242–244, believes that ch. 5 as a whole must be seen as a conclusion to the argument of Romans so far, but that it also foreshadows what is to follow. In particular 5:1–11 foreshadows the working out of the implications of justification by faith for the individual (chs. 6 – 8) and 5:12–21 for humanity as a whole (chs. 9 – 11). Ziesler, *Romans*, p. 135, identifies 5:1–11 as transitional, seeing 5:12 as the beginning of a new section in which various aspects of the new life in Christ are dealt with: 5:12–21, freedom from wrath and condemnation; ch. 6, freedom from sin; ch. 7, freedom from the law; ch. 8, freedom from the flesh.

[94]Following most interpreters in preferring *echomen* to *echōmen*, despite its weaker attestation, on the grounds that early in the transmission process the latter could have been mistaken for the former in dictation, and that the former fits much better with the whole thrust of Paul's argument in 1:16 – 8:39.

[95]Best understood as an objective peace with God won through Christ's death and resurrection, but one which produces the subjective peace with God experienced by those who have been justified by faith.

[96]Dunn, *Romans 1 – 8*, pp. 249–250, identifies the sufferings as eschatological tribulations, and suggests that these are linked (through endurance and character-formation) to hope because the experience of such sufferings indicates that 'the process of salvation is under way'.

[97]Ziesler, *Romans*, pp. 138–139, suggests that the character which believers prove in affliction is God's good character, and this becomes the basis for their hope for the future. Attractive as this suggestion might be, it founders on the fact that in all Paul's other uses of the word *dokimē* the reference is to human character, not to the character of God (*cf.* 2 Cor. 2:9; 8:2; 9:13; 13:3; Phil 2:22).

[98]The gift of the Spirit is not to be thought of as one of the fruits of justification, but rather as something given with justification. Only in this way can the Spirit be said to have been 'already'

the guarantee of our participation in final redemption, *cf.* 8:23–25).

In verses 6–11 Paul seeks to bolster this hope in God on the part of those who are justified by faith. He points out that God's love has been demonstrated historically in Christ's death for us even when we were both weak and sinful (vv. 6–8). Then in two parallel statements Paul drives home this truth:

> Much more surely then, now that we have been justified by his blood, will we be saved through him from the wrath of God (v.9).

> For if while we were enemies, we were reconciled to God through the death of his Son, much more surely, having been reconciled, will we be saved by his life (v. 10).

While Paul's aim in these statements is to bolster hope, not to teach his readers about justification by faith, nevertheless certain important aspects of his understanding of justification are reflected here. First, justification is effected by the death of Christ ('by his blood'). The apostle does not say here *how* justification is achieved by Christ's death, he simply asserts the fact. Second, justification involves being saved from the coming wrath [of God].[99] Third, justification and reconciliation are closely related in Paul's thought. Believers are both justified and reconciled by the death of Christ ('by his blood'; 'through the death of his Son'), and being justified or reconciled they shall be saved by him on the last day ('saved through him from the wrath of God', or 'saved by his life'). This close relationship is also evident in the fact that the passage ends by saying that we boast in God through whom 'we have now received reconciliation' (v. 11), a statement very similar to the one with which the section started, 'since we are [already] justified by faith' (v. 1). While justification and reconciliation are closely related, they are not identical concepts. Justification highlights the forensic aspect and reconciliation the relational aspect of the salvation won through Christ's death, though, of course, justification cannot be said to be without its relational significance, and reconciliation presupposes a resolution of the forensic problem.

The humanity-wide implications of Christ's death

Following the pastoral application of the doctrine of justification by faith in

---

poured into our hearts and thus be able to bolster hope, which is one of the fruits of justification. Paul will return, in ch. 8, to the place of the Spirit in the life of those justified by faith.

[99]The bracketed words, missing from the Greek text, are supplied in the NRSV. They are consistent with what Paul says elsewhere about wrath being God's response to sinful human behaviour (*cf.* 1:18; 2:5–11).

5:1–11, Paul, in 5:12–21, picks up again the main theme of 3:21 – 5:21, *i.e.* that there are no distinctions between Jews and Gentiles in the matter of salvation, or more precisely, as far as 5:12–21 is concerned, that Christ's death has humanity-wide implications. In so doing, he touches upon three matters which are relevant to our present study: (i) the connection made between Christ's obedience and believers' justification, (ii) the giving of the law so that sin might be reckoned, and (iii) the giving of the law to increase the trespass.

Christ's obedience and believers' justification

In 5:12–19[100] Paul argues that the obedience of Christ affects all humanity in him (*i.e.* Gentiles as well as Jews), just as (or even more than) the disobedience of Adam affected all humanity in him.[101] The effect of Adam's disobedience was to bring condemnation, while the effect of Christ's obedience is to bring justification, acquittal and life.[102] Paul does not, in this passage, say *how* the obedience of Christ effects justification for those who are in him, or even *what*

---

[100]The structure of 5:12–19 has in recent times been most often understood to consist of the protasis of an incomplete conditional sentence intended to compare the effect of Adam's action with that of Christ (v. 12); a short digression to explain how sin could be said to affect all people as a result of Adam's action at a time when they were not under law (vv. 13–14); some statements contrasting Adam's act with the act of Christ (vv. 15–17); a restatement of the conditional sentence begun in v. 12 and the completion of the comparison between the effects of Adam's sinful action and Christ's righteous act (v. 18). So, *e.g.*, Cranfield, *Romans*, 1, pp. 272–273, *cf.* also Hans Weder, 'Gesetz und Sunde: Gedanken zu einen qualitativen Sprung im Denken des Paulus', *NTS* 31 (1985), p. 363. Chrys. C. Caragounis, 'Romans 5.15–16 in the Context of 5.12–21: Contrast or Comparison?', *NTS* 31 (1985), pp. 143–146, however, argues that if vv. 15–17 are regarded as contrasts made before the comparison is drawn, and then v. 18 is taken as a mere repetition of v. 12 without any arguments to support it, Paul would be asserting what he needed to prove. Caragounis argues convincingly that, in fact, vv. 15–17 are integral to Paul's argument, supplying the ground upon which the great conclusion of v. 18 stands.

[101]The way in which the acts of Adam and Christ respectively affect humanity is still disputed. Milne, 'Genesis 3 in the Letter to the Romans', pp. 13–15, argues in favour of the classical interpretation: that in his single act, Adam acted on behalf of all men and all are affected by Christ's act in the same way. Weder, 'Gesetz und Sunde', pp. 364–368, argues that the effect of Adam's sin is based upon the fact that his disobedience is repeated, but the effect of grace upon the many is based upon the fact that they allow the act of Christ to bring good. In the one case sinners are imitators, in the other recipients.

[102]That throughout vv. 16–19 Paul has justification in mind is confirmed by the facts that (i) *dikaiōma* and *dikaiōsin zōēs* both stand in contrast to *katakrima* in vv. 16, 18, and (ii) the making righteous of sinners in v. 19 is set in the future. *Contra* D. B. Garlington, 'The Obedience of Faith in the Letter to the Romans: Part III: The Obedience of Christ and the Obedience of the Christian', *WTJ* 55 (1993), pp. 288–293, who argues that much more than forensic acquittal from guilt is

exactly that obedience was, but only *that* his obedience does effect justification for all. In the light of 3:21–26, though, we can safely conclude that the obedience Paul has in mind here is primarily the obedience of the cross, by which atoning sacrifice for sins was made in Christ's blood.

The law given that sin might be reckoned

One of the problems Paul had (in using in his argument the fact that Adam's disobedience made many sinners) was that he could not assume that (all) his readers would agree that Adam's sin had that effect. How, for instance, could it be said that sin was in the world in the period between Adam and Moses when there was no law (of Moses) for people to break, thereby constituting themselves sinners? Paul's answer is that the fact that people died in this period (even though they had no specific law to break as Adam had) is proof that sin was in the world in this period (v. 14).[103]

In dealing with this problem, Paul implies that one of the purposes of giving the law was that sins might be reckoned by God against those who committed them. This applies to Israel (to whom the law was given), but not in the same way to the Gentiles (who did not have the law).

The law given to increase the trespass

In 5:20–21 Paul argues that the effect of Adam's sin upon humanity is more than counteracted by the effect of Christ's obedience upon those in him. This sweeping comparison leaves little place in salvation history for the giving of the law. It is perhaps with an objection along these lines at the back of his mind that Paul says, 'Law came in, with the result that the trespass multiplied' (v. 20a), even though his main purpose in stating this was to highlight the effects of grace, which he makes clear by adding, 'but where sin increased, grace abounded all the more' (v. 20b).

What does Paul mean here by saying, 'Law came in, with the result that the trespass multiplied'? A number of suggestions have been made. (i) The

---

involved in vv. 16, 18, 19, namely actual salvation from sin evidenced by an obedience of faith like Christ's.

[103]The unexpressed assumption here is that death is the consequence of and punishment for sin. This assumption is probably based upon the Genesis account of the Fall, where Adam and Eve are warned that if they eat of the forbidden fruit they will die. Those between Adam and Moses who had no specific commandment to break were nevertheless (as Garlington, 'The Obedience of Faith in the Letter to the Romans: Part III', pp. 283–284, points out) 'guilty of the violation of the law written on the heart by virtue of their creation in the image of God'.

increase of the number of commandments resulted in an increase in the number of trespasses. It is unlikely that anything as banal as this is intended. (ii) The law resulted in an increase in the number of trespasses by causing the Jews to take pride in the law so that they identified righteousness with distinctively Jewish actions.[104] This suggestion does not fit well with a passage where trespassing is conceived of as disobedience to God's commands (*cf.* v. 14), not Jewish pride. (iii) The law led to an increase in the number of trespasses in the sense that what were not known to be trespasses before the giving of the law were clearly recognized as such thereafter (*cf.* 4:15: 'where there is no law, neither is there violation'). (iv) The law actually incited rebellion against its own demands (*cf.* 7:8: 'But sin, seizing an opportunity in the commandment, produced in me all kinds of covetousness. Apart from the law sin lies dead'). (v) Paul could be referring, not to the individual's subjective experience of sin, but to an objective increase of transgressions in the whole world.[105] While the first two of these suggestions can probably be ruled out, it is difficult to decide between the last three because the apostle himself does not spell out what he means. One thing is clear, though: Paul sees the law as part of the human predicament, not the solution to it.

The examination of Romans is continued in the next chapter where relevant material in Romans 6 – 15 is examined, and where a summary of the findings of both this chapter and the next is provided.

---

[104] *Cf.* Dunn, *Romans 1 – 8*, pp. 299–300.
[105] Räisänen, *Paul and the Law*, p. 144.

6

Romans 6 – 15

Answering objections and explaining implications

Introduction

In Romans 1:18 – 3:20 Paul argued that God acts righteously in making no distinctions between Jews and Gentiles in the matter of sin, and therefore none in the matter of judgment either. In Romans 3:21 – 5:21 he went on to argue that, just as God reveals his righteousness in making no distinctions in the matter of sin and judgment, so too he reveals his righteousness in making no distinctions in the matter of salvation either. Jews and Gentiles alike are to be justified by the grace of God through faith in Jesus Christ, and that apart from works of the law. Such a thesis is open to a number of objections, and the apostle responds to these in Romans 6 – 11 before drawing out the ethical implications of his gospel in Romans 12 – 15.

Answering objections: morality and the law

Paul's gospel was susceptible to several strong objections, especially from his kinspeople, the Jews. Included among these objections are those concerning the effect of Paul's gospel upon moral standards and the status of the law. These matters are taken up in 6:1–23 and 7:1 – 8:11 respectively.

Objections to Paul's thesis: moral standards

Romans 6:1–23 is the first part of a long 'ethical excursus' which runs from 6:1 to 8:11.[1] It begins with the words, 'What then are we to say? Should we continue in sin in order that grace may abound?' (6:1). These words bring out the sort of criticism which Paul's words in 5:20 ('where sin increased, grace abounded all the more') seemed to invite, *i.e.* that his gospel of free grace is an invitation to moral anarchy. Paul answers this criticism by pointing out that Christian initiation involves being buried with Christ by baptism into death, so that having thus died to sin we might live to righteousness.[2] It is inconceivable that those who have died to sin should imagine that they could continue to live in it (6:1–11). They are to yield the members of their bodies, not to sin so as to be its servants, but to God as instruments of righteousness (6:12–13), 'for', Paul says, 'sin will have no dominion over you, since you are not under law but under grace' (6:14).

This last statement is surprising. We might expect a Jewish Christian (as Paul was) to say that sin would not have dominion over people if they *did* live under the law. As Dunn aptly puts it, 'for the loyal Jew the logic of grace was the law as God's provision against sin'.[3] But Paul says the opposite: sin will not have dominion over them because they are *not* under the law. The apostle does not develop this idea here, but in 7:1 – 8:13 he will argue that people need to be freed from the law so that the dominion of sin might be broken. He will argue that the law, though good and holy in itself, has been co-opted on to the side of sin and death because of the weakness of human flesh. There is an obvious continuity at this point between Paul's attitude to the law in Romans and in Galatians (*cf.* Gal. 5:18).

The surprising statement of 6:14 ('For sin will have no dominion over you, since you are not under law but under grace') is, of course, susceptible to gross

---

[1]Brendan Byrne, 'Living out the Righteousness of God: The Contribution of Rom 6:1 – 8:13 to an Understanding of Paul's Ethical Presuppositions', *CBQ* 43 (1981), p. 562, uses the term 'ethical excursus' to describe 6:1 – 8:13, which he identifies as a single unit.

[2]F. S. Malan, 'Bound to Do Right', *Neot* 15 (1981), pp. 133–134, correctly points out the change in Paul's use of *dikaiosynē* which occurs in ch. 6: 'In chs. 1–5 *dikaiosynē* is used of God who does right (ch. 3:5, 25); of Abraham whom God accepted as righteous because he believed (ch. 4:3, 6, 9, 11, 13 and 22) and especially to describe God's act to put man in a right relationship with himself (chs. 1:17; 3:21, 22, 26; 4:5 and 5:17). In ch. 6, however, *dikaiosynē* is used to describe right deeds and behaviour. The believers whom God has put into a right relationship with himself, are now bound to the right conduct which God requires.'

[3]James D. G. Dunn, 'Salvation Proclaimed VI. Romans 6:1–11; Dead and Alive', *ExpT* 93 (1982), p. 261.

misunderstanding. Aware of this, Paul immediately asks, 'What then? Should we sin because we are not under law but under grace?' (v. 15a). To this he responds, 'By no means!' (v. 15b). He goes on to argue that whichever master people choose to obey, they are the slaves of that master. Those who give themselves over to sin will be slaves of sin, and the end of that slavery will be death. But those who have obeyed the gospel, though they were formerly slaves to sin, have now been set free from sin and have become slaves of righteousness (vv. 16–18). Therefore they cannot conceivably yield the members of their bodies as instruments of sin any more.[4] In this way Paul answers the objection that not being under the law (as is the case with those justified in Christ) will lead to moral anarchy.

Objections to Paul's thesis: status of the law

As noted above, Paul's statement in 6:14 ('sin will have no dominion over you, since you are not under law but under grace') is surprising, because it implies that the law is something from which people must be freed in order to escape sin's dominion, rather than something which helps them to escape from it. In 7:1 – 8:13 Paul picks up this theme again to show that people must indeed be freed from the law in order to escape sin's dominion. In doing so he is careful to say that the law itself is not the problem, pointing out that sin, by taking the opportunity which the law afforded it, is the real culprit. The section 7:1 – 8:13 can be seen to consist of three parts, which are taken up in turn below.

Freedom from the law

The passage 7:1–6 foreshadows what will be argued in more detail in 7:7 – 8:13, and accordingly its programmatic nature has been noted by a number of scholars.[5] In particular, verse 5 foreshadows 7:7–25, where life in the flesh and under the law is depicted, and verse 6 foreshadows 8:1–13, where freedom and service in 'the new life of the Spirit' are explained.[6]

---

[4]At this point Paul is content to bring out the logical inconsistency of such an objection. Later on (especially in 8:1–13), he will argue that those who are justified in Christ are indwelt by the Spirit, who enables believers to put to death the sinful 'deeds of the body'.

[5]*Cf.*, *e.g.*, Bruce Morrison and John Woodhouse, 'The Coherence of Romans 7:1 – 8:8', *RTR* 47 (1988), p. 14; S. Voorwinde, 'Who is the "Wretched Man" in Romans 7:24?', *VoxRef* 54 (1990), p. 21.

[6]So Voorwinde, 'Who is the "Wretched Man" in Romans 7:24?', p. 21.

Paul addresses 'those who know the law' (7:1),[7] reminding them that 'the law is binding on a person only during that person's lifetime' (v. 1). He reinforces his reminder with an analogy based upon marriage law (vv. 2–4). Paul argues that just as the death of a husband discharges his widow from any obligation to observe the marriage law which bound her to him, so likewise the death of Christ discharges believers from their obligation to obey the law (of Moses). Paul's argument raises difficulties because of the lack of correspondence between the analogy itself and what Paul seeks to show from it.

Paul asserts that 'the law is binding on a person only during that person's lifetime' (v. 1), and in his application of the analogy he makes the same point: believers who have died (in Christ) are discharged from their obligation to the law (v. 4a). In the analogy itself (vv. 2–3), however, it is not the death of the wife which frees her from the law binding her to her husband (which we would expect and which Paul could have said to make this point), but it is the death of the husband which frees her. The reason Paul did not construct his analogy with the sort of exact correspondence which we would expect is that he wanted to use the analogy to make an additional point. He wanted to show not only that the death of believers in Christ frees them from obligation to the law, but also that it frees them to belong to Christ and 'bear fruit for God' (v. 4b). For the analogy to be able to be used to make this additional point, the wife must remain alive in order to be able to marry another man, and so it must be the death of the husband which discharges her from the marriage law. Paul does not seem to have been concerned about the lack of exact correspondence (as we, his modern readers, are), being satisfied with an analogy in which death (albeit the husband's and not the wife's) frees from the law so that the one freed can then belong to another.[8]

This analogy and its application constitute one of the clearest expressions

---

[7]This expression, taken on its own, could refer simply to people who know about any system of marriage law, but in the context Paul would seem to have in mind the Mosaic law from which, he argues, believers have been set free. Therefore the expression has significance for discussions about the readership and the purpose of Romans. It is not as helpful to us in this connection as it might first appear, however, because it is susceptible of several interpretations. Within the overall context of Romans 'those who know the law' could refer to (i) Christian Jews (who made up part of the Roman church); (ii) Gentile Christians who had formerly been proselytes; (iii) Gentile Christians who had formerly been loosely attached to the synagogue as God-fearers; (iv) Gentile Christians who had gained an understanding of the law and the Old Testament since they joined the church.

[8]Ziesler, *Romans*, pp. 174–175, notes that the analogy makes one straightforward point ('legal obligations are removed by death'), and that attempts to work out the illustration in detail run into confusion. Joyce A. Little, 'Paul's Use of Analogy: A Structural Analysis of Romans 7:1–6', *CBQ*

of Paul's belief that Christians (Jews as well as Gentiles) are completely freed from all obligations to the Mosaic law as a regulatory norm. Like a person who has died they have been discharged from all obligations to the law. Underlying this notion of freedom from the law is the assumption that the period of the law has been brought to an end with the coming of Christ.

For Paul, this death to the law's demands has two positive outcomes which can be seen in verses 5–6. In verse 5 he implies that believers' release from the law means they may escape the dilemma of having their sinful passions 'aroused by the law' (a dilemma which Paul expounds in 7:7–25). In verse 6 he says that believers' release from the law enables them to live 'the new life of the Spirit' (something he expounds in 8:1–13).

The law and sin

In 7:1–6, Paul claimed that believers have been, and needed to be, discharged from the law in order to 'bear fruit for God'. This, he said, was the case because our sinful passions were 'aroused by the law'.[9] Thus Paul's whole gospel is open to the objection that it involves a denigration of the law (God's good gift to Israel). The apostle's purpose in 7:7–25 is to defend his gospel by showing that it does not involve a denigration of the law itself. He does this by arguing that the root cause of the human dilemma is sin, not the law, but that the law was used (as an unwilling ally) by sin to bring death to those under the law. It is because the law has been co-opted on to the side of sin that people need to be free from the law to bear fruit to God.

In 7:7–25, Paul writes in the first person singular, and this raises a number of questions. Is he speaking autobiographically, and, if so, is he

---

46 (1984), p. 90, discusses the inconsistencies in Paul's use of the analogy. She disagrees with Dodd's conclusion that 'he [Paul] lacks the gift for sustained illustration of ideas through concrete images (though he is capable of a brief illuminatory metaphor). It is probably a defect of imagination.' Little argues instead that 'the defect Paul suffers from in the writing of this passage is, if anything, an excess of imagination which propels him through the above-noted succession of ideas so rapidly that he has neither the time nor the opportunity to bring his images to completion.' She adds that it is not certain that Paul could have brought his images to completion, even if he had been so inclined. But *cf.* John D. Earnshaw, 'Reconsidering Paul's Marriage Analogy in Romans 7.1–14,' *NTS* 40 (1994), p. 72, who argues that 'Paul's marriage analogy is properly understood only when *the wife's first marriage is viewed as illustrating the believer's union with Christ in his death and her second marriage is viewed as illustrating the believer's union with Christ in his resurrection*'.

[9] What Paul means by saying that sinful passions are 'aroused by the law' is discussed below.

speaking of his own experience before he became a Christian[10] (either representing how he felt then about his moral failures,[11] or how he thought later as a Christian about those failures),[12] or is he speaking of his experience as a Christian,[13] or both?[14] If he is not speaking autobiographically, then is he speaking rhetorically in order to portray the experience of humankind in general,[15] or of religious Jews in particular,[16]

---

[10]So, *e.g.*, Brice L. Martin, 'Some Reflections on the Identity of *egō* in Rom. 7:14–25', *SJT* 34 (1981), pp. 39–47.

[11]So, *e.g.*, D. J. W. Milne, 'Romans 7:7–12, Paul's Pre-conversion Experience', *RTR* 43 (1984), p. 12. Many modern scholars reject this position out of hand in the light of Phil. 3:6, where Paul describes his pre-conversion life in respect of righteousness under the law as 'blameless'. This, it is claimed, proves that Paul had a 'robust conscience' and felt no such sense of failure in his encounter with the law as that depicted in 7:7–25. This, however, pushes the evidence of Phil. 3:6 further than is warranted. In that context, Paul is matching the boasting of those who have confidence in the flesh and boast of outward things. He would seem, therefore, to be speaking there of outward observance of the law rather than claiming to be exempt from the sort of experience he depicts in Rom. 7:7–25.

[12]So, *e.g.* Cranfield, *Romans*, 1, pp. 344–347.

[13]Alan F. Segal, 'Romans 7 and Jewish Dietary Law', *SR/SR* 15 (1986), p. 365, argues that 7:9 depicts Paul's personal experience after giving up his allegiance to the ceremonial Torah and then having to observe it in part again for pragmatic reasons (*cf.* 1 Cor. 9:19–20). It was at that time that 'sin' again entered his actions, and he came under the condemnation of the law (*cf.* Gal. 2:17). Segal concludes that Romans 7 'is the *apologia* of a reasonable man who formulated a radical solution to the problem of food laws in Christianity, but who, as an apostle, was willing to compromise when his solution was not accepted by the more conservative members of the Christian community' (p. 371). Mark A. Seifrid, *Justification by Faith, The Origin and Development of a Central Pauline Theme* (Leiden: Brill, 1992), pp. 234–237, draws attention to the parallels between Paul's statements about the *egō* and Jewish penitential confessions and suggests, in the light of these, that the *egō* refers, not to what Paul once was, but to what he still is 'intrinsically considered', *i.e.* a fallen human being confronting the law apart from the resources now available through the saving work of Christ.

[14]Robert Banks, 'Romans 7.25a: An Eschatalogical Thanksgiving?', *AusBR* 26 (1978), p. 41, argues that the *egō* passages of Romans 7 are autobiographical, and that 7:7–25 portrays Paul's pre-conversion and post-conversion experiences, v. 14 being the transition between the two. He believes that the argument for the autobiographical interpretation is clinched by the presence of the additional reflexive pronoun *autos* (*egō*) in 7:25b. Parallel uses of this expression elsewhere in Paul's writings always refer to the apostle himself, being synonymous with the expression *egō Paulus*.

[15]So, *e.g.*, Morrison and Woodhouse, 'The Coherence of Romans 7:1 – 8:8', p. 14.

[16]Voorwinde, 'Who is the "Wretched Man" in Romans 7:24?', p. 23, argues that the 'I' of Romans 7 is 'the God-fearing, law-abiding Jew', one such as the rich young ruler. Hartmut Rosenau, 'Der Mensch zwischen Wollen und Können: Theologische Reflexionen im Anschluss an Röm 7, 14–25', *TP* 65 (1990), pp. 1–30, argues that Paul has in mind non-Christian (in particular Jewish) existence when he describes the experience of the 'I' in Rom 7:14–25.

or of both?[17] Is Paul speaking of Adam's encounter with the commandment of God in the Garden,[18] or is he speaking redemptive-historically of
Israel's encounter with the law at Sinai?[19]

It is hard to rule out any autobiographical element in the passage, for even if
the apostle is speaking of, *e.g.*, Israel or of humanity in general, he would
hardly exclude himself from what he says. And the strong existential overtones
of the use of 'I', in the latter part of the chapter (7:14–25), would suggest some
personal involvement in what is being described. Both the Adamic approach
and the redemptive-historical approach enable the interpreter to perceive some
autobiographical element in the passage, while also recognizing that Paul is
working on a broader canvas.

The Adamic approach has much to commend it. Verses 8–11 make sense
when read in terms of the serpent's temptation of Adam and Eve in the garden.
Of the first couple it is singularly true that they were 'once alive apart from the
law' but that 'when the commandment came, sin revived' and they died. For
them especially the words, 'sin, seizing an opportunity in the commandment,
deceived me and through it killed me', are true. The weakness of this approach
is that in this passage Paul is at pains to show that his gospel does not denigrate
the *Mosaic* law, and of course it was not the Mosaic law that caused the
problem for the primeval couple. Those who support this view, however, argue
that the Mosaic law and the commandment of God given in Eden were already
associated in Jewish thinking in Paul's day.[20] And it may be that Paul saw in
Israel's failure a recapitulation of Adam's sin.

According to the redemptive historical approach, Paul uses the first person
pronoun, 'I' (especially in 7:7–12), with Israel's encounter with the law at Sinai
in mind. This is consistent with the fact that the law which Paul has in mind in
Romans 7 is the *Mosaic* law (he cites the tenth commandment from the
decalogue), not the commandment given to Adam, or law in general. Further,
the redemptive-historical approach can account for the change from the aorist
tense used in 7:7–13 (Paul has the historic encounter of Israel with the law at
Sinai in mind) to the present tense in 7:14–25 (Paul has in mind the subsequent
struggles of Israel under the law). Paul's use of the present tense and the more
intense subjective tone in 7:14–25 are explained by the fact that, as a member

---

[17]G. Strelan, 'A Note on the Old Testament Background of Romans 7:7', *LTJ* 15 (1981), p. 24,
concludes: 'Either in solidarity with Adam, or in solidarity with Israel, or both, all people – Jew and
Greek together, and "I" – stand guilty as charged: all have sinned (Rm. 3:23a).'

[18]So, Dunn, *Romans 1 – 8*, pp. 400–402.

[19]Douglas J. Moo, 'Israel and Paul in Romans 7.7–12', *NTS* 32 (1986), pp. 129–130.

[20]*Cf.* Dunn, *Romans 1 – 8*, p. 400.

of Israel, he too was involved in the ongoing struggle of living under the law.[21] Thus, in the end, it seems that a combination of the redemptive-historical and autobiographical approaches is best. In this case, the 'I' of Romans 7:7–25 is not simply Israel, but Paul in solidarity with Israel.[22]

In the discussion of Romans 7:7–25 which follows, a combination of the redemptive-historical and autobiographical approaches is adopted because this seems to take best account of the fact that in this chapter Paul is defending his gospel against the charge that it involves a denigration of the *Mosaic law* and that he personally was involved in the struggle which he depicts. The debate over the best approach to Romans 7 will, however, continue. What does seem reasonably clear is that, while Paul defends his gospel against the charge that it denigrates the law God gave to Israel, he maintains, nevertheless, that the law had become the unwilling ally of sin, and as such it is something from which people do need to be freed in order to bear fruit to God. It is also reasonably clear that Paul himself at one stage (probably his pre-conversion days) experienced great frustration living under the law.[23]

The section 7:7–13 is marked by the use of the aorist tense, which is appropriate if Paul has in mind here Israel's encounter with the law at Sinai. If 7:7–13 is interpreted along these lines, a number of points emerge as far as Paul's view of the role of the law is concerned, all of which have their associated problems.

The law made sin known for what it was. Paul says, 'I would not have known what it is to covet if the law had not said, "You shall not covet"' (v. 7b, *cf.* v. 13). Ziesler has shown that while Paul's point holds in respect of the tenth commandment of the decalogue ('You shall not covet'), it does not apply generally to all the demands of the Mosaic law. For example, one could not say, 'I would not have known what it is to murder if the law had not said, "You shall do no murder."'[24] For Paul's purposes, however, it is not necessary to show that every single commandment functions in this way. It is enough to show that one of the functions of the law, operating through some of its commandments, is to make sin known.

The law became the (unwilling) ally of sin. Paul says that 'sin, seizing an

---

[21]*Cf.* Moo, 'Israel and Paul in Romans 7.7–12', pp. 129–130.

[22]So, Moo, *Romans 1 – 8*, p. 456.

[23]Phil. 3:6 does not negate such a view, because, as already noted, there Paul is speaking of his outward observance of the law, and it should not be taken as proof that he experienced no inward struggle.

[24]J. A. Ziesler, 'The Role of the Tenth Commandment in Romans 7', *JSNT* 33 (1988), pp. 48–49.

opportunity in the commandment, produced in me all kinds of covetousness' (v. 8). It is important to note what Paul does *not* say here. He does not say that the law produced in him the desire to covet, but rather that sin, seizing the opportunity afforded it by the commandment, produced in him all kinds of covetousness. It must be remembered that Paul's purpose in 7:7–13 (if not in the whole of 7:7–25) is to give an apology for the law as part of the defence of his gospel, so he is unlikely in that context to say that the law produced sin. As far as the apostle is concerned, the law is good (vv. 13, 16) and spiritual (v. 14). Sin, not the law, is the real cause of the human dilemma. Even so, we are still left with the task of seeking to understand in what way the law functioned as an (unwilling) ally of sin as it produced 'all kinds of covetousness'. Various suggestions have been made.

(i) The most influential of these is associated with Bultmann, who interpreted Paul's reference to the covetousness produced by sin through the law in terms of legalism. He argued that the law provided sinful humanity with an opportunity to justify themselves before God on the basis of their own achievements. They coveted a righteousness of their own, based on their own performance of the law. Räisänen, however, has shown convincingly that this approach to 'covetousness' does not hold water.[25]

(ii) Another approach was adopted by Dodd, according to which the law is involved in producing 'all kinds of covetousness' because, by issuing prohibitions, it makes the prohibited action attractive to sinful human beings.[26] This is an unsatisfactory solution, not only because it is just not true that law in general has this effect (people do not want to kill because the law says they should not do so), but more so because Paul portrays the Jews of his day as those who have a zeal for God, something they could not be said to have while consciously wanting to do what God prohibited.[27]

(iii) A third alternative suggested by Morris is that the law is involved in producing covetousness because, along with its demands, it makes people aware that they might fail to fulfil them. The natural response to this situation is to try to vindicate themselves – to establish their own righteousness, something people usually do by selectively focusing upon one law they feel they must

---

[25]Heikki Räisänen, 'Zum Gebrauch von *EPITHYMIA* und *EPITHYMEIN* bei Paulus', *ST* 33 (1979), pp. 89–99, argues that *epithymia* and *epithymein* in Rom. 7:7 are most naturally understood in a non-legalistic fashion, as in all other occurrences of the words in Paul's writings.

[26]C. H. Dodd, *The Epistle of Paul to the Romans* (London: Hodder and Stoughton, 1932), p. 109.

[27]*Cf.* T. F. Morris, 'Law and the Cause of Sin in the Epistle to the Romans', *HeyJ* 28 (1987), p. 286.

fulfil to justify themselves.[28] This appears to be a variation on Bultmann's view, and is susceptible to the criticisms Räisänen levelled against that view.

(iv) Gundry, recognizing that the key to interpreting Paul's claim that the law is used to produce sin is to be found in his reference to the tenth commandment, argues that Paul has in mind in particular the tenth commandment's reference to sexual desires. It was at puberty, which coincided with the apostle's taking upon himself the full obligation to obey the law, that he found that the law's prohibition of sexual desire only further aroused such desires.[29]

(v) Ziesler believes that Gundry's view 'comes close to being correct', but says that its critical mistake was to limit covetousness to sexual desire (this does not do justice to Paul's reference to 'all kinds of covetousness'). According to Ziesler, Paul chose the tenth commandment because it, unlike most other commandments, does illustrate what the apostle wants to prove, the inability of the law to deliver what it demands. Because it is one of but a few commandments which can be said to function in this way, Ziesler says, it is a faulty paradigm, though an apt one for Paul's purposes.[30]

(vi) More satisfactory are the views of Strelan and Moo. Strelan sees in the covetousness of 7:7 a reference to the primary sin of Israel which in a sense comprehends in itself all other sins (*cf.* Ps. 106; 1 Cor. 10).[31] Moo regards 7:7–13 as a theological interpretation of Israel's encounter with the law at Sinai.[32] It is this encounter with the law that Paul has in mind when he says: 'Apart from the law sin lies dead. I was once alive apart from the law, but when the commandment came, sin revived and I died' (vv. 8b–10a). Both Strelan and Moo recognize the primary importance of the tenth commandment in Paul's argument, as have several other scholars. By rooting their interpretation of 7:7–13 firmly in the historical context of Israel's encounter with the law at Sinai, however, and noting how covetousness can be seen to comprehend in itself all the other sins of Israel, they obviate the need to accuse Paul of using a faulty paradigm.

The law which promised life brought death. Paul says that 'the very

---

[28]Morris, 'Law and the Cause of Sin', pp. 286–287.

[29]Robert H. Gundry, 'The Moral Frustration of Paul before his Conversion: Sexual Lust in Romans 7:7–25', *Pauline Studies* (Festschrift for F. F. Bruce), ed. Donald A. Hagner and Murray J. Harris (Exeter: Paternoster, 1980), pp. 232–233.

[30]'The Role of the Tenth Commandment in Romans 7', pp. 43–49, 52.

[31]'The Old Testament Background of Romans 7:7', pp. 23–24.

[32]'Israel and Paul in Romans 7:7–12', p. 129. *Cf.* Moo, *Romans 1 – 8*, p. 461, where the example of Israel's making the golden calf after having received the law at Sinai (Ex. 32) is cited.

commandment that promised life proved to be death to me' (v. 10). The idea of the law promising life is based on Leviticus 18:5 (cited in Rom. 10:5: 'The person who does these things will live by them'). Although the law did hold out a promise of life (*cf.* also Dt. 27 – 28), as far as Paul is concerned, no-one could achieve what the law promised. His whole argument in 1:18 – 3:20 leads to the conclusion that ' "no human being will be justified in his sight" by deeds prescribed by the law, for through the law comes the knowledge of sin' (3:20), and 'all have sinned and fall short of the glory of God' (3:23). In 7:10, then, according to the redemptive-historical line of interpretation, Paul is saying that while the law given at Sinai promised life to Israel if she continued to obey it, in fact it brought death because she failed to do so.

All this raises the question whether Paul thought that God's purpose in giving the law was to make available an offer of life to those who obeyed it. Statements like that in 7:10 ('the very commandment that promised life proved to be death to me') and 10:5 ('Moses writes concerning the righteousness that comes from the law, that "the person who does these things will live by them"') do seem to imply that the law would have given life if anyone could have obeyed it perfectly, but this Paul believed had proved to be impossible (3:19–20).

Whereas 7:7–13 is marked by the use of the aorist tense, 7:14–25 is, by contrast, marked by the use of the present tense. According to the redemptive-historical approach, this change to the present tense takes place because Paul moves from his description of the historic encounter of Israel with the law at Sinai (described with the use of the aorist tense in 7:7–13) to his portrayal of the subsequent struggle of Israel with the law (described with the use of the present tense in 7:14–25). This subsequent struggle of Israel Paul describes with greater immediacy and subjectivity because it is a struggle which he himself once experienced.

Throughout the passage Paul depicts Israel's failure (and his own) in the struggle against sin, despite God's gift of the law. The law which he described earlier as holy and just and good (v. 12), he now further describes as spiritual (v. 14) and something in which Israel (and he himself) delighted (v. 22). Nevertheless, sinful Israel (and sinful Paul) could not perform the requirements of the law in which they delighted. Their plight is expressed vividly in vv. 22–24:

> For I delight in the law of God in my inmost self, but I see in my members another law at war with the law of my mind, making me captive to the law of sin that dwells in my members. Wretched man that I am! Who will rescue me from this body of death?

This accords with Paul's descriptions of first-century Jewish failures in Romans 2. There he spoke of his Jewish contemporaries' pride in the law and what it meant to them (vv. 17–20), but pointed out that they nevertheless did not perform what the law required (vv. 21–24). It is therefore likely that in 7:7–25, where Paul speaks redemptive-historically and subjectively, he should be understood to have in mind not only the failures of historic Israel and himself, but also those of his pious Jewish contemporaries as well.[33] They all delighted in the law, but found another law, 'the law of sin',[34] at work in them, so that they were prevented from doing what the law required. It is this frustration which gives rise to the cry, 'Wretched man that I am! Who will rescue me from this body of death?' (v. 24), and what follows: 'Thanks be to God through Jesus Christ our Lord!' (v. 25a). The latter prepares the way for what the apostle says in 8:1–13, where he picks up and expounds what he foreshadowed in 7:6, *i.e.* freedom from the law and service 'in the new life of the Spirit' made possible through the work of Christ and the coming of the Spirit.

Verse 25b ('So then, with my mind I am a slave to the law of God, but with my flesh I am a slave to the law of sin') is therefore, in its context, Paul's summing up of Israel's ongoing struggle with the law, a struggle which he himself experienced,[35] and which was experienced by other pious Jews in the first century. It was not intended to describe Paul's ongoing experience as a believer, even though modern-day believers might find it an apt description of the sort of experience they have from time to time in their struggle against sin. When Paul wants to describe that experience he speaks in terms of the conflict between the desires of the flesh and the desires of the Spirit (Gal. 5:16–19), not in terms of a conflict between wanting to do what the law says and being unable to do so.

---

[33]*Cf.* Rosenau, 'Der Mensch zwischen Wollen und Können', pp. 6–9, who argues that Paul is speaking of the non-Christian (*e.g.* Jewish) existence and about the conflict between 'willing' and 'doing'.

[34]Taking 'the law of sin' to refer, as in Qumran texts, to an evil force which rules the members of humankind (*cf.* Roland Bergmeier, 'Röm 7, 7–25a (8,2): Der Mensch – das Gesetz – Gott – Paulus – die Exegese im Widerspruch?', *KD* 31 (1985), pp. 169–171; Cranfield, *Romans*, 1, p. 364; Moo, *Romans 1 – 8*, pp. 490–492. *Contra* Dunn, *Romans 1 – 8*, pp. 395, 409 and Wright, *The Climax of the Covenant*, p. 198, both of whom see in the expression 'the law of sin' a reference to the Torah, which is used by sin to bring about death.

[35]As was noted above, Phil. 3:6 does not contradict such a view, because it does not deal with the presence or absence of an inward struggle between willing and doing, but simply serves as a counter to Paul's Jewish Christian opponents who claimed to have better 'credentials' than he had. Phil. 3:6 deals with outward commitment to Judaism.

The law and new life in the Spirit

If 7:7–25 may be seen as an exposition of Paul's statement in 7:5 ('While we were living in the flesh, our sinful passions, aroused by the law, were at work in our members to bear fruit for death'), then 8:1–13 may be seen as an exposition of his statement in 7:6 ('But now we are discharged from the law, dead to that which held us captive, so that we are slaves not under the old written code but in the new life of the Spirit').[36] A number of matters which Paul deals with in 8:1–13 are relevant to our present study and therefore call for comment.

No condemnation (8:1). It is noteworthy that Paul begins his exposition of life in the Spirit with a reference to the justification of believers: 'There is therefore now no condemnation for those who are in Christ Jesus' (8:1).[37] Those who are in Christ are freed from the condemnation of the law, and become recipients of the Spirit (*cf.* 8:9b). Justification and new life in the Spirit might be able to be separated in discussion; they cannot be separated in experience. For this reason also any objections that Paul's gospel promotes moral laxity are invalid.

The law of the Spirit of life and the law of sin and death (8:2). The expressions 'the law of the Spirit of life' and 'the law of sin and death' have both sometimes been interpreted as references to the Mosaic law,[38] and if this were the case they would provide us with important clues to Paul's understanding of the law. The two expressions would then reflect two aspects of the law. Dunn says:

> The law caught in the nexus of sin and death, where it is met only by *sarx*, is the law as *gramma*, caught in the old epoch, abused and destructive . . . but the law rightly understood, and responded to *en pneumati ou grammati*, is pleasing to God (2:29). The twofold law of v. 2 therefore simply restates the two-sidedness of the law expounded in 7:7–25.[39]

One of the problems with this view is that it implies that 8:2 is saying that the law rightly understood sets us free from the law wrongly understood. But this is not what Paul has in mind. In the very next verse (8:3) he speaks of God

---

[36]Cf. Voorwinde, 'Who is the "Wretched Man" in Romans 7:24?', p. 21. This approach would seem to be confirmed by the fact that 'the new life in the Spirit' mentioned in 7:6 drops out of sight in the rest of ch. 7 (which deals with life under the law) but re-emerges in ch. 8 (which is, for the most part, an exposition of life in the Spirit).

[37]The 'therefore' in this verse probably picks up what Paul said in 7:6. Such an approach is supported by the presence of the temporal 'now' in both 7:6 and 8:1.

[38]So, *e.g.*, Dunn, *Romans 1 – 8*, pp. 416–419.

[39]*Romans 1 – 8*, pp. 416–417.

sending his Son to deal with the problem of sin, something which the law (however understood) was unable to do. This, of course, was also in Paul's mind when he wrote 7:7–25, except that there the law was not only unable to effect the deliverance, but, as the unwilling ally of sin, was itself part of the problem.

It is therefore better to interpret the expressions 'the law of the Spirit of life' and 'the law of sin and death' as the liberating power of the Spirit and the dominion of sin respectively.[40] It was the power of sin (admittedly using the law as an unwilling ally) that caused the 'I' of 7:7–25 so much anguish. It is through (justification and) the reception of the Spirit that believers are delivered from sin's dominion.[41]

What the law cannot do (8:3–4). In 8:3a Paul speaks of 'what the law, weakened by the flesh, could not do', without explaining what exactly that was. In 8:3b–4, however, he proceeds to say that God has done what the law proved unable to do; that is, 'by sending his own Son in the likeness of sinful flesh,[42] and to deal with sin,[43] he condemned sin in the flesh[44] so that the just requirement of the law might be fulfilled in us, who walk not according to the

---

[40]So most commentators, including more recently Ziesler, *Romans*, p. 202; Cranfield, *Romans* 1, pp. 364, 373–376; Moo, *Romans 1 – 8*, pp. 504–508. *Cf.* Räisänen, *Paul and the Law*, pp. 50–52.

[41]This is not to say that in Romans Paul implies that believers no longer struggle with sin, but rather that this struggle does not have to end in the sort of defeat portrayed in 7:7–25. The new alternatives are expressed in 8:12–13: 'So, then, brothers and sisters, we are debtors, not to the flesh, to live according to the flesh – for if you live according to the flesh, you will die; but if by the Spirit you put to death the deeds of the body [here obviously a synonym for flesh], you will live.'

[42]There is ongoing debate whether Paul's 'in the likeness of sinful flesh' (*en homoiōmati sarkos hamartias*) implies a distinction or an identification between Christ's humanity and ours. *Cf.*, *e.g.*, more recently, Vincent P. Branick, 'The Sinful Flesh of the Son of God (Rom 8:3): A Key Image of Pauline Theology', *CBQ* 47 (1985), pp. 246–262; Florence Morgan Gillman, 'Another Look at Romans 8:3: "In the Likeness of Sinful Flesh"', *CBQ* 49 (1987), pp. 597–604.

[43]It is not necessary for our purposes to decide between the two possible interpretations of *peri hamartias* here, whether it means 'as a sin offering' (following the LXX usage of *peri hamartias*), or more generally 'to deal with sin'.

[44]Paul's expression 'he condemned sin in the flesh' (*katekrinen tēn hamartian en tē sarki*) is ambiguous. It could be taken to mean either 'God condemned the sin which is found in human flesh', or 'God condemned sin in the flesh of Christ'. The former is unlikely because, as Ziesler, *Romans*, p. 205, points out 'sin in the flesh' is a tautology. There is no other sort of sin on the horizon in this context. The latter is preferable as it makes sense to speak of God condemning sin in the flesh (of Christ), another way of saying that in the purpose of God, Christ in his death became a curse for us, bearing the burden and penalty of our sins (*cf.* Gal. 3:13). Ziesler, surprisingly, interprets the verse to mean that 'Christ, when in the flesh, condemned sin, either by his sinless life or by his death', failing (it seems) to recognize that God, not Christ, is the subject of the sentence.

flesh but according to the Spirit'. What the law cannot do, Paul implies, is to bring to fulfilment its own just requirement in the lives of those who lived under the law.[45]

The phrase 'the just requirement of the law' has sometimes been interpreted to mean 'all that the law requires'. Such an approach has obvious problems, because clearly Paul did not expect believers to fulfil all the demands of the law (circumcision, one of the basic demands of the law, Paul argued, was definitely not required of Gentile believers). A further difficulty for this view, often overlooked, is that Paul refers to the 'just requirement' (singular, *dikaiōma*), not the 'just requirements' (plural, *dikaiōmata*), and, while the plural is used in the New Testament and the LXX to refer to the sum of the law's demands, the singular is not.[46]

Ziesler, taking note of the singular *dikaiōma*, suggests that when Paul speaks of the just requirement of the law in 8:4 he means the tenth commandment, which he had in mind throughout 7:7–25. Because, on this view, 8:4 refers only to the command not to covet, it cannot be taken to refer to the sum of the law's demands (or the love command, or the moral law). Accordingly, Ziesler argues, it provides no help in answering questions about the ongoing function of the law for Christians.[47]

While it is important to note Paul's use of the singular form in 8:4, it is not at all certain that it should be interpreted as narrowly as Ziesler suggests. Even interpreting it in the light of Paul's reference to the tenth commandment in 7:7–25, we need to remember that there Paul used the tenth commandment as a paradigm for the whole law, as Ziesler himself acknowledges.[48]

A good case can be made out for interpreting 'the just requirement of the law' as the love commandment (despite Ziesler's dismissal of this view), especially in the light of the parallels between 8:4 and Galatians 5:13–16. It is precisely at these points in Romans and Galatians respectively that (i) the notion of the Spirit first comes to the fore, (ii) the antithesis of Spirit and flesh

---

[45]It is important to note that the law was unable to do this, not because of any imperfection in itself, but because its power to do so was weakened by the flesh. This is what Paul argues at length in 7:7–25. That Paul speaks of the law's inability to bring about the fulfilment of its own righteous demand because of the weakness of the flesh excludes (*contra* Morrison and Woodhouse, 'The Coherence of Romans 7:1 – 8:8', p. 15) any interpretation of 'the just requirement of the law' as death.

[46]*Cf.* J. A. Ziesler, 'The Just Requirement of the Law (Romans 8:4)', *AusBR* 35 (1987), p. 78.

[47]'The Just Requirement of the Law', p. 80.

[48]Ziesler, 'The Just Requirement of the Law', p. 80, notes that Paul generalizes from the tenth commandment, taking it as his paradigm for the whole law.

is mentioned for the first time, and (iii) there is a striking convergence of the concepts of freedom, fulfilment, walking in the Spirit and the negative aspects of the flesh.[49]

In the light of these striking similarities between Romans 8:4 and Galatians 5:13–16, it would seem desirable to interpret the former in the light of the latter, and to say that the fulfilment of the just requirement of the law (in the Romans text) is best understood in terms of the love of neighbour (in the Galatians text). Such a conclusion is strengthened by the fact that, in Romans 13:8–10, Paul says that all the other commandments are summed up in the commandment, 'Love your neighbor as yourself', and concludes: 'therefore, love is the fulfilling of the law.'[50]

It is significant that this text speaks about 'the just requirement of the law' *being fulfilled* (divine passive) in those who walk according to the Spirit, not about believers *fulfilling* (active) this requirement. The fulfilment of the law in believers is therefore not achieved because they are continuously careful to observe its many stipulations. Rather, it is fulfilled in them as they walk according to the Spirit and as by the Spirit they put to death the deeds of the flesh (8:13).

The hope of believers

In 8:18–30, Paul speaks of the Spirit being the firstfruits of our future redemption in the midst of present suffering (vv. 22–23), and of the Spirit helping us in our weakness in prayer (vv. 26–27). He concludes with an assertion that God's good purposes for believers will be worked out (vv. 28–30). In making this assertion he says: 'And those whom he predestined he also called; and those whom he called he also justified; and those whom he justified he also glorified' (v. 30). Paul uses the aorist tense in each of the verbs in this sentence, and this has puzzled commentators. How can it be said that believers are already glorified, as the use of the aorist would seem to imply? The least unsatisfactory solution is that the whole process of salvation is being viewed here from the perspective of its completion, perhaps to express the sense of certainty the apostle felt about its

---

[49] *Cf.* Richard W. Thompson, 'How is the Law Fulfilled in us? An Interpretation of Rom 8:4', *LS* 11 (1986), pp. 32–33, who cites the observations of H. W. M. van de Sandt, 'Research into Rom. 8:4a: The Legal Claim of the Law', *Bijdr* 37 (1976), pp. 252–269.

[50] *Contra* Wright, *The Climax of the Covenant*, pp. 211–212, who rejects this view, arguing instead that *to dikaiōma tou nomou* means 'the just decree of the law', *i.e.* 'the decree that gives life in accordance with the covenant'.

realization.[51] If this is the case, then for Paul, justification is one in a series of the acts of God for the salvation of believers which stretches from eternity (predestination) to eternity (glorification). From the viewpoint of the believer, justification depends as much on the grace of God as do predestination, calling and glorification.

The emotive climax to Paul's argument so far

In 8:31–39 Paul makes extensive use of the first person plural. By doing so he associates himself with his readers in affirming very emotively what together they hold to be true: that God is for us (v. 31), that having given up his own Son for us, he will freely give us all things with him (v. 32), that God justifies us (v. 33), that Christ died for us and, being now raised, intercedes for us (v. 34), and that nothing whatever can separate us from the love of God which is in Christ Jesus our Lord (vv. 35–39).

Snyman has argued that this emotive passage constitutes a peroration.[52] As such it does not recapitulate what has been said, or add any new arguments; rather, it appeals to the readers to affirm what they and the writer hold in common. But the function of a peroration at the end of a speech, according to classical rhetorical theory, was not simply to evoke an affirmation of things held in common, but to move the audience to accept the case made already in the speech, of which the peroration formed the climax. If, as seems likely, this is what Paul is seeking to achieve in 8:31–39, then this passage forms an important transition between Paul's response to objections that his gospel undermines moral standards and the status of the law (6:1 – 8:13) and his response to charges that his gospel does away with Israel's special place in the purposes of God (9:1 – 11:36). In other words, he seeks to gain his Jewish and Gentile Christian readers' agreement to what he has argued so far, and to carry them along with him in the argument he is about to mount in 9:1 – 11:36.[53]

The importance of this passage for our present study is that it roots justification squarely in the grace of God and reflects something of what being justified involves. It roots justification in the grace of God in so far as it stresses that it is the God who is for us, the God who did not spare his own Son[54] but gave him up for us all, and who justifies (vv. 31–33); and that it is Christ's

---

[51] *Cf.*, e.g., Dunn, *Romans 1 – 8*, pp. 485–486; Moo, *Romans 1 – 8*, pp. 572–573.

[52] A. H. Snyman, 'Style and Rhetorical Situation of Romans 8.31–39', *NTS* 34 (1988), p. 227.

[53] *Cf.* Snyman, 'Style and Rhetorical Situation in Romans 8.31–39', pp. 227–228.

[54] There is here, very probably, an allusion to Abraham's sacrifice of Isaac. When Abraham was tested by God he was willing to sacrifice his own son, but in the end Isaac was spared. When the

death, resurrection and intercession at God's right hand which silence all who could condemn God's elect (v. 34).

It reflects something of what being justified involves in so far as it stresses that when God justifies[55] believers he will entertain no charges brought against them (v. 33), and that, because of Christ's work, the voices of all who would condemn them are silenced (v. 34).[56] If human guilt (the one thing which could separate us from the experience of the love of God) has been dealt with by God's grace in Christ, then there is nothing left which can separate us from that love. Justification is then foundational to the experience of the love of God.

Answering objections: God's promises to Israel

In Romans 6 Paul answered the objection that his gospel opened the floodgates to moral laxity, and in Romans 7:1 – 8:13 he answered the objection that his gospel denigrated the law. In Romans 9 – 11 Paul answers the objection that his gospel negates the special place of Israel in the purposes of God. In doing so he shows how God has remained faithful to his promises. Romans 9 – 11 is then a defence of the righteousness of God, and in that sense can be regarded as the climax of Paul's theological argument in Romans 1 – 11.[57]

The exact way in which Paul approaches the problem in Romans 9 – 11 has been variously defined. For example, Getty says that Paul tries to reconcile two fundamental ideas: (i) that Israel is God's people, and (ii) that the Gentiles have been included in the plan of God for universal salvation.[58] Longenecker sees

---

salvation of sinful human beings was at stake, however, God did not spare his own Son. *Cf.*, *e.g.*, Dunn, *Romans 1 – 8*, p. 501; Ziesler, *Romans*, p. 228.

[55]Paul's use of the present participle, *dikaiōn*, here (contrast his use of the aorist participle, *dikaiōthentes*, in 5:1) shows that justification is not only to be regarded as an act in the past, but also an ongoing activity of God; having justified believers (at the time of their conversion), he continues to justify them.

[56]In the Old Testament it is Satan who brings charges against God's elect (Jb. 1:6–12; 2:1–6; Zc. 3:1–2), and it is probably Satan's accusations that Paul has in mind here. *Cf.* also Rev. 12:7–10.

[57]Wright, *The Climax of the Covenant*, p. 235, draws attention to the pervasive nature of this theme in Romans 9 – 11: 'The opening claim in 9.6 has to do with the unfailing character of God's word; 9.14 raises the question of whether God is unrighteous; 9.19, that of why he still finds fault; 9.19–23 of the rights of the potter over the clay, a metaphor taken directly from the discussions in Isaiah and Jeremiah of God's covenant behaviour with Israel. After the central and climactic statement of 10.3f., the argument of ch. 11 remains focussed not merely on the future of the Jews but on the character of God, as 11.22, 29 and 32 bear witness, and as is celebrated in 11.33–6.'

[58]Mary Ann Getty, 'Paul and the Salvation of Israel: A Perspective on Romans 9 – 11', *CBQ* 50 (1988), p. 468.

Paul as dealing with the question, 'How can God, whose people are presently marked out by their faith in Jesus Christ, be a faithful God if, in the past, he promised Israel a unique place as his covenant people?'[59]

It would be a mistake, however, to regard Romans 9 – 11 merely as Paul's endeavour to answer a theological objection to his gospel by stating his views about the place of Israel in God's purposes. The apostle had a deep, personal involvement in this issue. It distressed him that Israel had rejected her messiah. This is nowhere more poignantly expressed than in Romans 9:1–3:

> I am speaking the truth in Christ – I am not lying; my conscience confirms it by the Holy Spirit – I have great sorrow and unceasing anguish in my heart. For I could wish that I myself were accursed and cut off from Christ for the sake of my own people, my kindred according to the flesh.

The fact that Paul calls his conscience 'by the Holy Spirit' as witness to the depth of his anguish over Israel's failure suggests that he feels he must defend his patriotism. While preaching a law-free gospel to the Gentiles, his commitment to his own people must have been called into question.

The structure of Romans 9 – 11 has been variously analysed, but the essential elements appear to be: (i) 9:1–5, Paul's concern for Israel; (ii) 9:6–29, Israel's failure to accept the gospel is not evidence of the failure of God's promise; (iii) 9:30 – 10:21, Israel's failure is due to her unwillingness to submit to the righteousness that comes from God; (iv) 11:1–36, despite Israel's failure, God has not cast off his people. Within this overall structure there are several sections which are of particular importance as far as our investigation of Paul's understanding of law and justification is concerned, and these are discussed in turn below.

The privileges of Israel

In Romans 3:1, Paul mentioned as a privilege of the people of Israel the fact

---

[59]Bruce W. Longenecker, 'Different Answers to Different Issues: Israel, the Gentiles and Salvation History in Romans 9 – 11', *JSNT* 36 (1989), p. 95. Longenecker suggests that Paul emphasizes different things concerning Israel, depending on the issues he is addressing. When the apostle is thinking of the present stage of salvation history he strongly defends the freedom of the Gentiles from Jewish ethnic constraints. But when he has the grand plan of salvation-history in mind, he argues that the Gentiles cannot exist as believers except as participants in the promises of Israel. Put more briefly, the Gentiles do not have to adopt the ethnic symbols of the Jewish people, but nevertheless, God brings about the salvation of the Gentiles through an ethnic people, Israel (p. 113).

that they had been entrusted with 'the very words of God'. In 9:4–5 the apostle lists other great privileges enjoyed by them:

> They are Israelites, and to them belong the adoption, the glory, the covenants, the giving of the law, the worship, and the promises; to them belong the patriarchs, and from them, according to the flesh, comes the Messiah, who is over all, God blessed forever. Amen.

Two inferences concerning Paul's attitude to the law can be drawn from this statement. First, and more obviously, the law was a positive thing, something for which Israel could be grateful (a similar assumption underlies Rom. 2:17–20 and is stated explicitly in Rom. 7:12). Second, and less obviously, by referring to the 'giving of the law' (*nomothesia*), Paul implies that there was a time when it was not in Israel's possession.[60] There was a time when it was given, just as there was a time when it ceased to be operative (*cf.* Rom. 7:1–6). Thus we see that Paul's approach to the role of law in Romans is consistent with what he set forth more strongly in Galatians (where he says of the law, 'it was *added* because of transgressions, *until* the offspring would come to whom the promise had been made', 3:19).

The pursuit of righteousness and the law

Having expressed anguish of heart over his own kinspeople (9:1–3) and listed their great privileges as the people of God (9:4–5), and having argued that their failure was not due to the failure of God's word, but reflected God's election and freedom to show mercy to whomever he will (9:6–29), in 9:30 – 10:13 the apostle points out to his readers a striking historical paradox.

A striking paradox

Paul states the paradox in the following words:

> What then are we to say? Gentiles, who did not strive for righteousness, have attained it, that is, righteousness through faith; but Israel, who did strive for the righteousness that is based on the law, did not succeed in fulfilling that law (9:30–31).

---

[60] *Cf.* Eldon Jay Epp, 'Jewish–Gentile Continuity in Paul: Torah and/or Faith? (Romans 9:1–5)', *HTR* 79 (1986), p. 89, who further comments that by introducing a time limitation upon Torah, Paul was able 'to diminish its otherwise preeminent place among the factors of continuity for God's people, though without diminishing the "good" and "holy" nature of Torah'.

Before seeking to understand just what is being expressed through this paradoxical statement, it is important to note the imbalance in the paradox itself: Paul says that the Gentiles *did* get what they did *not* pursue (namely, righteousness), while the Jews did *not* get what they *did* pursue (namely, righteousness that is based on the law).[61]

Paul explains the reason for this surprising outcome in 9:32, which, rendered literally, reads: 'Why? Because not of faith but as of works'. Clearly a verb and subject have to be provided to bring out the sense of this elliptical statement. But what verb and what subject should be supplied?

Most modern commentators assume that the verb 'to pursue' (*diōkō*) is to be supplied, and its implied subject is 'the Jews'. These assumptions yield the translation, 'because they [the Jews] pursued it [the law of righteousness] not by faith but as it were by works (*hoti ouk ek pisteōs all' hōs ex ergōn*)'. When the text is construed in this way, the failure of the people of Israel is due, not to *what* they pursued (*nomon dikaiosynēs*), but rather to the *manner* of their pursuit (*ouk ek pisteōs all' hōs ex ergōn*).[62]

If the copular is provided and the implied subject is understood to be the law, however, we could end up with the translation, 'because it [the law] is not of faith, but as it were of works'. When the text is construed in this way, the reason for the failure of the people of Israel is not the manner of their pursuit, but what they pursued (*nomon dikaiosynēs*: law for righteousness). The people of Israel pursued the law for righteousness, but because the law is not of faith but of works, they were not able to attain righteousness.

Gordon offers the following reasons in support of this latter approach: (i) Galatians 3:12 attaches precisely the negated propositional phrase (*ouk ek pisteōs*) of Romans 9:32 to the Torah; (ii) Romans 10:5–6 refers to Torah's righteousness by citing the same Old Testament 'doing' (*poiēsas*) text cited by Paul in Galatians 3:12; and (iii) the paradox of Romans 9:30–31 involves saying that the Gentiles pursued *nothing*, rendering unlikely a translation of 9:32 which distinguishes correct pursuit from incorrect pursuit. Each of these considerations suggests that it is more likely that the negated prepositional phrase (*ouk ek pisteōs*) qualifies *nomos* itself, and not some mis-pursuit thereof.[63]

---

[61]*Cf.* T. David Gordon, 'Why Israel did not Obtain Torah–Righteousness: A Translation Note on Rom 9:32', *WTJ* 54 (1992), p. 165.

[62]So, *e.g.*, James D. G. Dunn, *Romans 9 – 16* (WBC; Dallas, TX: Word, 1988), p. 582; Ziesler, *Romans*, p. 254; Thomas Schreiner, 'Israel's Failure to Attain Righteousness in Romans 9:30 – 10:3', *TrinJ* 12 (1991), p. 214; Davies, *Faith and Obedience in Romans*, pp. 123–124, 180–185.

[63]Gordon, 'Why Israel did not obtain Torah-Righteousness', p. 166.

To say that the Jews pursued the law for righteousness is not to say that first-century Judaism was *in principle* a religion in which acceptance before God depended upon amassing merit by keeping the law. Rather, we should think of first-century Judaism as a covenantal and nomistic religion, within which the nomistic obligations of the covenant were sometimes over-emphasized at the expense of God's saving grace. And what was essentially a nomistic religion often degenerated, in practice, into a legalistic one. The Jews, Paul believed, being proud of their exclusive possession of the law, fell into the trap of believing that it was their observance of that law, rather than God's saving grace alone, which guaranteed their acceptance before God. This is not an uncommon phenomenon. Wherever people take their commitment to biblical religion with utmost seriousness, there is a tendency to end up in one form of legalism or another. (It is important to note that the saving grace available to Jews depended ultimately upon the death of Christ, something only foreshadowed in their cultus.)

It follows, then, that those Jews who were pursuing the law for righteousness would stumble at the preaching of Christ, an outcome which the apostle saw foreshadowed in Scripture: 'As it is written, "See, I am laying in Zion a stone that will make people stumble, a rock that will make them fall, and whoever believes in him will not be put to shame"' (9:33).

Zeal without knowledge

In 10:1–4 Paul explains further why, in his view, the people of Israel failed to attain the righteousness they sought. After expressing again great concern for his kinspeople (10:1), he identifies their problem: 'they have a zeal for God, but it is not enlightened' (10:2). He then explains what this means: 'For, being ignorant of the righteousness that comes from God, and seeking to establish their own, they have not submitted to God's righteousness' (10:3). The problem of the Jews, and the reason they failed to attain righteousness, was not their zeal, but zeal without knowledge. Paul's statement about their failure in knowledge has been understood in several ways.

First, the failure of knowledge on the part of the Jews here has been understood to mean that they were ignorant of the *manner* in which one should pursue law-righteousness. Schreiner adopts this approach and, by drawing upon 9:32 to illuminate 10:3, says:

> The charge leveled against the Jews in v. 3 is strikingly similar to 9:32, where the Jews' pursuit of the law is faulted because they did not pursue the law 'from faith'

but 'as from works'. To pursue the law 'as from works' is described in 10:3 as 'seeking to establish one's own righteousness' . . . The Jews stumbled over believing in Christ (9:32–33), and failed to submit to the saving activity of God which was revealed in Jesus Christ.[64]

Schreiner argues that the Jews were right to pursue the law for righteousness, but that they should have pursued it in faith. 'To pursue the law in faith', he says, 'is to recognize that the law cannot be obeyed sufficiently to obtain salvation, and that salvation can only be obtained by believing in Christ.'[65]

Schreiner's view is open to criticism on two counts. (i) He assumes that a form of the verb 'to pursue' (*diōkō*) is to be supplied in 9:32, and we have already noted reasons to question that assumption. (ii) Even if that assumption be granted, what Schreiner defines as pursuing the law in faith is in fact not pursuing the law at all; it is turning away from the law for righteousness and believing in Christ instead.

Second, the failure in knowledge on the part of the Jews has been construed as ignorance of the new thing which God was doing in Christ for both Jews and Gentiles. This meant an end to the time when the observance of the law was the defining mark of the people of God. Being ignorant of this fact, the Jews continued to cherish an exclusive righteousness predicated upon their privileges as the covenant people and their possession and observance of the law.[66]

By so explaining Paul's train of thought, an issue which is still the subject of much debate has been prejudged. When Paul says, 'For Christ is the end (*telos*) of the law so that there may be righteousness for everyone who believes' (10:4), is he implying that the law's role has been terminated as far as righteousness is concerned now that Christ has come,[67] or that the goal of the law (to bring about righteousness) has been reached in Christ?[68]

The issue cannot be settled on the grounds of lexicography, because it can be

---

[64]Schreiner, 'Israel's Failure', p. 214.

[65]*Ibid.*, p. 218.

[66]So, *e.g.*, Sanders, *Paul, the Law, and the Jewish People*, p. 38; Dunn, *Romans 9 – 16*, pp. 588–589; Ziesler, *Romans*, pp. 255–257; Wright, *The Climax of the Covenant*, p. 241.

[67]So, *e.g.*, François Refoulé, 'Note sur Romains IX, 30–33', *RB* 92 (1985), pp. 161–186; Werner Führer, '"Herr ist Jesus". Die Rezeption der urchristlichen Kyrios-Akklamation durch Paulus Römer 10,9', *KD* 33 (1987), pp. 137–149; Räisänen, *Paul and the Law*, pp. 53–56.

[68]So, *e.g.*, C. Thomas Rhyne, '*Nomos Dikaiosynēs* and the Meaning of Romans 10:4', *CBQ* 47 (1985), p. 498; Getty, 'Paul and the Salvation of Israel', pp. 466–467; Robert Jewett, 'The Law and the Co-existence of Jews and Gentiles in Romans', *Int* 39 (1985), p. 349. Jewett argues: 'If Christ is the "goal of the law", the path of faith can be pursued without repudiating the Torah. The crucial

shown that *telos* can have either of these meanings (and many more). Therefore the issue can be resolved only if one or other of the meanings can be shown to make better sense in the context. The following arguments can be advanced in support of the view that *telos* construed as 'termination' makes better sense here. (i) If it is correct to supply a form of the copula in 9:32 (and not some form of the verb *diōkō*, 'to pursue'), then the law is there defined as 'not of faith but of works'. Of such a law Christ must be the end. (ii) The verses (10:5– 6) which immediately follow 10:4 are logically connected to it by an explanatory 'for' (*gar*), and in these verses righteousness that is by faith in Christ is contrasted with righteousness from the law, and this in turn belongs with 'their own' righteousness which the Jews were seeking to establish (10:3). Of that sort of righteousness Christ can only be the end.[69]

Appealing to statements outside Romans itself, this view is further supported on the following grounds. (iii) It is consistent with Paul's use of the imagery of the disciplinarian (*paidagōgos*) and guardian (*epitropos*) in Galatians 3:23 – 4:7. This imagery is used to illustrate the freedom of Jewish believers from the law's jurisdiction, which, like the role of the disciplinarian or guardian, comes to an end at a specified time. (iv) It is also consistent with Paul's teaching in 2 Corinthians 3:7–11. There he contrasts the transitory nature of the ministry of Moses (associated with the 'letter' which kills) which has been set aside in favour of the permanent ministry (associated with the Spirit) entrusted to Paul (and the other apostles).[70] (v) It also has a parallel in 2 Corinthians 3:13–14, where Paul speaks of Moses' veiling his face so that the people of Israel might not see the end of the glory of the old covenant which was being set aside.[71]

There are significant arguments against this view, and in favour of construing *telos* as goal, however, and these need to be addressed.

(i) It is argued that if Paul were to admit that, according to his gospel, the law had been annulled by Christ, he would be placing at risk his credibility with the Jerusalem and Roman churches,[72] something he was seeking to establish by writing Romans. But it seems Paul is prepared to take this risk, because in Romans 7:1–6 he says quite straightforwardly that believers have been released from the jurisdiction of the law so that they are 'slaves not under the old written code but in the new life of the Spirit' (v. 6).

---

point is the avoidance of zealotism, the assumption that conformity to a particular standard guarantees superiority over those who do not conform.'

[69]*Cf.* Dunn, *Romans 9 – 16*, p. 590.

[70]*Cf.* Räisänen, *Paul and the Law*, p. 56.

[71]*Cf.* Dunn, *Romans 9 – 16*, pp. 590–591.

[72]Getty, 'Paul and the Salvation of Israel', p. 466.

(ii) It is said that because Paul argues (in 10:5–8) that the law itself testifies
to the righteousness by faith in Christ, he must have believed that there was a
positive relationship between Christ and the law, which in turn suggests that
Christ is the goal of the law, not its end.[73] There is a positive relationship
between Christ and the law in so far as the law testifies to the salvation effected
through Christ. It is quite another thing, however, to say that, because the law
testifies to Christ in this way, Christ cannot be the end of the law, but must
rather be its goal. Further, if it be admitted that 10:5–8 actually *contrasts* the
righteousness of the law with the righteousness through faith in Christ, then it
is unlikely that Paul saw Christ as the goal of the law as far as righteousness is
concerned. (It is also worth noting that the author of Hebrews bases his whole
argument on the Old Testament, and yet regards the old covenant as
superseded.)[74]

(iii) In the light of the many positive statements Paul makes about the law in
Romans (7:12, 14a; 8:4; 13:8–10), the categorical statement in 3:31 ('Do we
then overthrow the law by this faith? By no means! On the contrary, we uphold
the law'), and his appeals to the Pentateuch in 10:5–8 in support of his
arguments, it is highly improbable that Paul would want to say that Christ is the
termination of the law.[75] It is, of course, true that Paul makes many positive
statements about the law. As far as the apostle is concerned, sin is the real
culprit, not the law. In order that people may be delivered from sin's dominion,
however, they must be freed from the law's jurisdiction, so as to 'bear fruit for
God' (7:4–6). For believers, the role of the law has come to an end as far as
righteousness is concerned.

(iv) The law and obedience to its demands were never intended to provide
righteousness, therefore it would be a trivializing of the coming of Christ for
Paul to say that he came to bring to an end a wrong attitude to the law.[76] To this
objection it may be said that, on the view being advocated, the coming of
Christ marks not only the end of wrong attitudes to the law, but the end of the
jurisdiction of the law as far as believers are concerned. Free from the law, they
now 'bear fruit for God'.

The meaning of *telos* in 10:4 will continue to be debated and positions taken
will reflect the overall understanding that scholars have of Paul's attitude to the
law. I think Räisänen best sums up the situation when he says:

---

[73]Rhyne, '*Nomos Dikaiosynēs*', p. 498.

[74]Räisänen, *Paul and the Law*, p. 55.

[75]Cranfield, *Romans*, 2, pp. 518–519.

[76]Davies, *Faith and Obedience in Romans*, p. 188.

I believe that Paul *could* have written that Christ is the goal of the law. Some such statement would have been quite appropriate after 9.30–33; such a formula would also neatly summarize Paul's concern in Rom 3.21 or Gal 4.21. It is important to him that Christ and the righteousness through faith can be found already in Scripture. Yet Rom 10.4, in view of the immediate context of this verse, does not fit into *this* line of thought. In this verse Paul is concerned about the contrast between law and faith.[77]

In all this, it is important not to lose sight of the essential point Paul is making here: Christ is the end of the law *for righteousness*. Paul's purpose in 10:4 is a modest one. He is not here discussing whether the law has any role at all now that Christ has come, but rather asserting that it has no role now in establishing righteousness.[78] Righteousness before God is now offered on the same basis to Jews and Gentiles alike – through faith in Christ. The Jews who failed to attain this did so because they would not believe in him.

The testimony of the law to faith

The passage 10:5–13, introduced with the explanatory 'for' (*gar*), provides the basis for Paul's claim in 10:4 that the coming of Christ marks the end of the law for righteousness. Here Paul uses the law itself to explain why Christ is the end of the law.

In so doing, in 10:5 Paul cites Leviticus 18:5: 'Moses writes concerning the righteousness that comes from the law, that "the person who does these things will live by them."' Paul's point is that law-righteousness depends upon one's observance of the law. In its original context, Leviticus 18:5 forms part of an introductory exhortation before a list of sexual prohibitions. By obeying these, Israelites were to be distinct from both the Egyptians (from whom they had recently escaped) and the Canaanites (among whom they were soon to live). Those who failed to observe these laws would be cut off from the people (Lv. 18:24–30), but those who kept them would continue to enjoy physical life within the promised land (Lv. 18:5).[79]

---

[77]Räisänen, *Paul and the Law*, p. 56. By saying that 'Christ and the righteousness by faith can be found already in Scripture', Räisänen agrees with Robert Badenas, *Christ the End of the Law: Romans 10.4 in Pauline Perspective* (Sheffield: JSOT, 1985), pp. 148–150, but he rejects Badenas' claim that this is the point Paul makes in 10:4.

[78]So, too, Thomas R. Shreiner, 'Paul's View of the Law in Romans 10:4–5', *WTJ* 55 (1993), p. 124.

[79]Dt. 5:32 – 6:3 contains a similar promise of life in the promised land for Israel if she is careful to do what the Lord commanded her. And as Westerholm, *Israel's Law and the Church's Faith*, pp. 146–147, points out, there are dozens of other similar texts in the Old Testament.

In the context of Romans 10:5–10, Paul uses Leviticus 18:5 to depict a righteousness which is based on obedience,[80] which is then contrasted with the righteousness based on faith.[81] Christ had to be the law's termination as far as righteousness is concerned, because, as the apostle has laboured long to show, not even the people of Israel, who were the proud possessors of the law, had kept it, illustrating that the attainment of righteousness by the observance of the law was not possible (Rom. 2:17 – 3:20).

Quite surprisingly, however, Paul not only appeals to the law to depict righteousness based on obedience; he also appeals to it as a witness to the righteousness that is by faith. Thus he cites and interprets Deuteronomy 30:12–14 in the following way.

> But the righteousness that comes from faith says, 'Do not say in your heart, "Who will ascend into heaven?"' (that is, to bring Christ down) 'or "Who will descend into the abyss?"' (that is, to bring Christ up from the dead). But what does it say?
> 'The word is near you,
> on your lips and in your heart'
> (that is, the word of faith that we proclaim) (10:6–8).

In its original context, Deuteronomy 30:12–14 refers to the law (all the commandments of God conveyed to the Israelites at the time of the covenant renewal). The law, Moses told the Israelites, was not difficult or beyond their reach. They did not have to ascend into heaven to get it, or go beyond the sea to obtain it. On the contrary, he said, 'the word is very near to you; it is in your mouth and in your heart for you to observe' (Dt. 30:14).

When Paul cites Deuteronomy 30:12–14 in Romans 10:6–8, he adds to it his own comments (introduced in each case by 'that is . . .,' *tout' estin* . . .) by which he makes it speak of the gospel he proclaims. This seems, on first reading, to be a very arbitrary use of the Old Testament. Dealing with this problem, Ziesler argues, 'If Paul believes (v. 4) that Christ is the fulfilment of the Law, then he may also see him as the fulfilment of what the OT says about the Law, so that it is proper to make Deut. 30:12–14 refer to him.'[82] This makes sense if we construe *telos* in 10:4 as 'fulfilment', but if, as we are arguing, it makes better sense when construed as 'termination', then some alternative explanation of Paul's use of the Old Testament here is needed.

---

[80]Mark A. Seifrid, 'Paul's Approach to the Old Testament in Rom 10:6–8', *TrinJ* n.s. 6 (1985), p. 16, argues that the essential point Paul makes by citing Lv. 18:5 is that obedience is the prerequisite for a righteous status, and in this he reflects the concerns of the original text well.

[81]Paul uses Lv. 18:5 in the same way in Gal. 3:12. *Cf.* Ziesler, *Romans*, p. 259.

[82]*Romans*, p. 260.

One such alternative explanation is offered by Seifrid. He suggests that in Romans 10:6–8 Paul is stating the apostolic preaching and the events which make it up in such a way as to correspond to Deuteronomy 30:11–14, that it is the pattern of salvation-history which is fundamental, and that Paul's allusions to Deuteronomy 30 represent 'conformations to this scheme'.[83] Dunn offers another explanation, suggesting that the very wording of Deuteronomy 30:11–14 (ascending to heaven, descending to the abyss) invited a reference to the cosmic Christ by Paul, as it had invited earlier exegetes (Baruch and Philo) to make reference to divine wisdom.[84]

What is clear, however, is that Paul, in 10:5–8, uses different parts of the law (Lv. 18:5 and Dt. 30:12–14) to contrast faith-righteousness with law-right-eousness.[85] It is also clear that Paul uses Deuteronomy 30:12–14 to emphasize that, just as the law was not something hidden and distant from the Israelites, so also the gospel of faith-righteousness is not something hidden or distant – it is freely available to both Jews and Gentiles. Thus the apostle writes:

> But the righteousness that comes from faith says, 'Do not say in your heart, "Who will ascend into heaven?"' (that is, to bring Christ down) 'or "Who will descend into the abyss?"' (that is, to bring Christ up from the dead). But what does it say?
>
> 'The word is near you,
>
> on your lips and in your heart'
>
> (that is, the word of faith that we proclaim) (10:6–8);

and he adds:

> . . . because if you confess with your lips that Jesus is Lord and believe in your heart that God raised him from the dead, you will be saved. For one believes with the heart and so is justified, and one confesses with the mouth and so is saved. The Scripture says, 'No one who believes in him will be put to shame' (10:9–11).

Here Paul stresses that it is not doing the things of the law, but believing with the heart, and confessing with the mouth, that bring salvation.[86] This statement

---

[83]'Paul's Approach to the Old Testament in Rom 10:6–8', p. 27.

[84]Dunn, *Romans 9 – 16*, p. 614.

[85]*Cf.* J. S. Vos, 'Die hermeneutische Antinome bei Paulus (Galater 3.11–12; Römer 10.5–10)', *NTS* 38 (1992), pp. 254–270, who suggests that the hermeneutical oppositions discernible in Rom. 10:5–10 follow the principles laid down in Graeco–Roman rhetorical handbooks concerning *leges contrariae* – principles also adopted by Hillel and Philo.

[86]The believing with the heart and the confessing with the mouth are not separate activities. The separation is purely rhetorical. They are two aspects of the one believing in Christ (10:11), the one calling upon his name (10:13).

provides the basis for the conclusion to the section 10:1–13: 'For there is no distinction between Jew and Greek; the same Lord is Lord of all and is generous to all who call on him. For, "Everyone who calls on the name of the Lord shall be saved"' (10:12–13). Because justification does not depend upon fulfilling the demands of the law, salvation is available to all; it is not restricted to the Jews to whom the law was given. Just as there are no distinctions in the matter of sin and judgment, so also there are no distinctions in the matter of justification which leads to salvation.

A special way of salvation for Israel?

The Scripture cited in 10:13 ('Everyone who calls on the name of the Lord shall be saved') leads Paul on to highlight the need for the preaching of the gospel so that people may hear the good news and then call on the Lord (10:14–15). This in turn leads him to ask why Israel has not responded to the good news. Is it because they have not heard it? No, says the apostle, they have heard, but they were obstinate and disobedient (10:16–21). By saying that Israel was obstinate and disobedient, it could seem that Paul was implying that God had rejected his people. Anticipating an objection to his gospel along these lines, he says in 11:1a: 'I ask, then, has God rejected his people?'

In 11:1b–32 Paul answers the question by denying that God has rejected his people. Instead, he argues that God has preserved a remnant among them. As in the days of Elijah when God preserved a remnant of faithful Jews who would not bow the knee to Baal, so in the present, Paul says, God has preserved a remnant of believing Jews, among whom he himself is included (11:1b–5).

Paul's primary concern in chapter 11, however, is not with the *remnant* of believing Jews, but with the *rest* of Israel; with those who persist in unbelief. Nevertheless, the remnant is important because the existence of the remnant is the guarantee that eventually 'all Israel' will be saved. In the argument of 11:1b–32, verse 16 plays an important role:

> If the part of the dough offered as first fruits is holy, then the whole batch is holy; and if the root is holy, then the branches also are holy.

Here 'the whole batch' and 'the branches' denote all Israel, and 'the part of the dough' and 'the root' denote the remnant, so that the present existence of the remnant is the guarantee of the future salvation of 'all Israel'.[87] It is in

---

[87]Following the approach suggested by Dan G. Johnson, 'The Structure and Meaning of Romans 11', *CBQ* 46 (1984), pp. 98–99. So also Nils Alstrup Dahl, *Studies in Paul: Theology for the Early*

11:25–27 that the apostle speaks of the mystery of the salvation of 'all Israel':

> So that you may not claim to be wiser than you are, brothers and sisters, I want you
> to understand this mystery: a hardening has come upon part of Israel, until the full
> number of the Gentiles has come in. And so all Israel will be saved; as it is written,
>> 'Out of Zion will come the Deliverer;
>> he will banish ungodliness from Jacob.'
>> 'And this is my covenant with them,
>> when I take away their sins.'

A crucial question raised by the promise of eventual salvation for 'all Israel' is whether there is a *Sonderweg* (a special way of salvation) for Israel which is different from that provided in the gospel for Gentiles. Put another way: has God one way of justifying the Gentiles, and another for the Jews? Hvalvik provides a succinct description of the view that there is a *Sonderweg* for the Jews when he summarizes the views of Stendahl and Mussner:

> We can summarize the views of Stendahl and Mussner in three points: The Jews
> will be saved (1) without acceptance of Jesus as the Messiah (Stendahl), (2) without
> conversion to the gospel (Mussner) and (3) through the parousia of Christ (Mussner)
> . . . It should be clear that Stendahl and Mussner do not hold identical views.
> Nevertheless, they have two things in common: (1) they both tie their view to Rom
> 11.26f. and (2) they both hold that the Jews have a special way of salvation, a
> 'Sonderweg'.[88]

There are, however, other ways of explaining what Paul means by 'all Israel will be saved' which not only make better sense of the text, but also expose the weakness of the views of Stendahl and Mussner. For example, Johnson, who sees the metaphor of 'the remnant and the whole' as the dominating theme of Romans 11, argues that the way 'all Israel' is saved at the end of history must be the same as the way the remnant was saved within history, *i.e.* through faith in Jesus Christ. Otherwise Paul's whole argument would fall to the ground.[89]

Hvalvik argues that what is special about Israel's salvation is that she will be saved *as a people*, not that she will be saved *at once* (either at a particular

---

Christian Mission (Minneapolis: Augsburg, 1977), p. 151; J. Christian Beker, *Paul the Apostle: The Triumph of God in Life and Thought* (Edinburgh: T. and T. Clark, 1980), p. 90. *Cf.* Dunn, *Romans 9 – 16*, p. 659, who also interprets v. 16 along these lines, except that he argues that the remnant consists not just of believing Jews, but believing Gentiles as well.

[88]Reidar Hvalvik, 'A "Sonderweg" for Israel: A Critical Examination of a Current Interpretation of Romans 11.25–27', *JSNT* 38 (1990), p. 88.

[89]Johnson, 'The Structure and Meaning of Romans 11', pp. 102–103.

moment in history or at the parousia). He too argues that 11:25–27 cannot be used as a basis for belief in a *Sonderweg* for Israel.[90]

To elucidate what Paul means by the expression 'all Israel', Osborne draws attention to the repeated use of the term in the books of Chronicles.[91] He argues that, at the beginning of David's reign, 'all Israel' consisted of military leaders, but, after David's consolidation of power, other leaders such as judges, priests and levites (but not elders) were included in 'all Israel'. In the period of the divided kingdom the term was used of all those who were loyal to the king and the cult of Yahweh, including those of the northern kingdom who met these criteria. In the books of Chronicles, then, the term 'all Israel' usually means those who attach themselves to the Davidic house and to Yahweh. It is used only in connection with those kings who are loyal to Yahweh, and in theological terms it comes to mean 'the people of God'. This suggests that in Romans 11:26a 'all Israel' is a collective term denoting a majority of the people of Israel who give their loyalty to the Davidic messiah.[92] In the context of Romans, faith in the Davidic messiah can only mean faith in Jesus Christ. In this case also, there is no *Sonderweg* for Israel.

It must, however, be asked whether the time and means by which Israel will be brought to faith in Jesus Christ constitute something of a *Sonderweg* for Israel. Mussner, for example, argues that Israel will be saved at the parousia of Christ (11:26–27). But even then it will be by grace, through faith and apart from the law, in a way fully consistent with Paul's teaching on justification.[93] According to this approach, the way Israel is saved is special in so far as it is brought about by the appearance of Christ at the last day, but it is no different from the way in which the Gentiles are saved in so far as it still takes place by grace and through faith, apart from the law.

Others argue that Paul saw the mission to the Jews proceeding alongside the mission to the Gentiles, and the success of the latter would provoke the Jews to jealousy, and so cause them to repent. These things would occur concurrently and in the present age,[94] so that by the time the full number of the Gentiles had been brought in, it would be discovered that all the elect of Israel would also

---

[90]'A "Sonderweg" for Israel', pp. 87–107.

[91]William L. Osborne, 'The Old Testament Background of Paul's "All Israel" in Romans 11:26a', *AJT* (1988), pp. 282–293.

[92]Osborne, 'The Old Testament Background of Paul's "All Israel" ', p. 287.

[93]F. Mussner, 'Heil für alle. Der Grundgedanke des Römerbriefs', *Kairos* 23 (1981), pp. 207–214.

[94]D. Judant, 'A propos de la destinée d'Israel. Remarques concernant un verset de l'épître aux Romains XI,31', *Divinitas* 23 (1979), pp. 108–125, claims that no text-critical or theological

have been gathered into the people of God, and in this manner all Israel will be saved.[95] According to this approach there is, clearly, no *Sonderweg* for Israel.

Baxter and Ziesler shed some light on the matter by appealing to the ancient practice of arboriculture. They argue that Paul was aware of the practice of grafting scions of a wild olive on to an aged or diseased olive tree, to restore the latter to health and fruit-bearing.[96] The apostle used this practice to illustrate the way God would restore Israel. He would incorporate believing Gentiles into the people of God, and the people of Israel would then recognize that God was gathering the elect and that they themselves were not being included. 'This would make them repent, be forgiven, and return to being true Israel.' Baxter and Ziesler argue that it is the *ingrafting* of the Gentiles, rather than the Gentiles themselves, that will bring about the restoration of Israel: 'In the overall divine strategy, the ingrafting of Gentile scions is a crucial and necessary intermediate stage' leading to the salvation of 'all Israel'.[97] Such a view implies that there is no *Sonderweg* for Israel. She will be brought to repentance by seeing the Gentiles repent, and from this we may infer that 'all Israel' must come to salvation in the same way.

The one thing common to most of these various approaches to the salvation of 'all Israel' is their denial that God has provided a *Sonderweg* for Israel, a means of salvation different from that provided in the gospel for Gentiles (*i.e.* a salvation by grace through faith in Christ apart from the works of the law). That this common conviction is true to Paul's own views is confirmed by the way he concludes his argument in 11:28–32. He acknowledges that as far as the gospel is concerned the Jews are the enemies of God, but asserts that as far as election is concerned they are beloved on account of the patriarchs, God's gifts and calling being irrevocable. And because of their election, those who are the enemies of the gospel will, through the mercy shown to the Gentiles, themselves receive mercy. As Paul has previously indicated, this will occur as the Jews, seeing the Gentiles repenting and being gathered into the elect while they themselves are

---

argument can justify the removal of the word 'now' (*nyn*) from the phrase 'in order that they too may now receive mercy' (*hina kai autoi nyn eleēthōsin*) in 11:31. He argues that the mercy of God in 11:30–31 refers to faith in Christ; so the entrance of the Jews into the church should take place now.

[95]So, *e.g.*, D. W. B. Robinson, 'The Salvation of Israel in Romans 9–11', *RTR* 26 (1967), pp. 94–96; Wright, *The Climax of the Covenant*, pp. 249–250.

[96]A. G. Baxter and J. A. Ziesler, 'Paul and Arboriculture: Romans 11.17–24', *JSNT* 24 (1985), pp. 25–32.

[97]Baxter and Ziesler, 'Paul and Arboriculture', p. 28.

presently excluded, will also be brought to repentance and faith in Jesus Christ. In this way, God, having bound both Jew and Gentile over to disobedience, will have mercy on Jew and Gentile alike.

While there are no distinctions between Jews and Gentiles in the matter of salvation (no *Sonderweg* for Israel), that does not negate Israel's special place in the purposes of God. In 11:17–24 Paul reminds Gentile believers that the blessings they enjoy are derived from the root of Israel (the believing remnant), to which they have been joined. He also reminds them that God is able to graft back the rest of Israel 'if they do not persist in unbelief' (11:23). There is no place for Gentile Christian hubris.

The ethical implications of Paul's gospel

Having argued his main thesis (chs. 1 – 5) and defended it against various objections (chs. 6 – 11), Paul proceeds in 12:1 – 15:13 to draw out some of the ethical implications of his gospel. This section of the letter contains several statements relevant to our investigation of Paul's understanding of the law and justification. Before we take these up, brief comment is needed concerning the relationship between Paul's theological arguments in 1:16 – 11:32 and the ethical section, 12:1 – 15:13.

There are good reasons to believe that Paul intended this ethical section to be seen as the outworking of the theological thesis argued in 1:16 – 11:32. First, there is the inferential 'therefore' (*oun*) with which this section begins, and which relates it to what precedes. Second, the appeal for transformation in ethical living is made 'by the mercies of God' (*dia tōn oiktirmōn tou theou*), and Paul has just finished explaining how 'God has imprisoned all in disobedience so that he may be merciful to all' (11:32). Third, the idea of presenting one's body as a living sacrifice to God (12:1) picks up a similar concept in 6:12–19, and stands in contrast to the handing over of one's body to perform degrading acts mentioned in 1:24–27.[98] Fourth, the appeal for spiritual worship (12:1) and the renewal of the mind (12:2) constitutes a call to reverse the failure to worship the creator and the darkening of the mind spoken of in 1:18–32.[99]

But 12:1–2 not only links the ethical section to the earlier part of the letter, it also represents the basis of Paul's ethics in Romans: grateful response to God's

---

[98]Michael Thompson, *Clothed with Christ: The Example and Teaching of Jesus in Romans 12.1 – 15.13* (*JSNT*Sup 59; Sheffield: JSOT, 1991) pp. 79–83.

[99]Thompson, *Clothed with Christ*, pp. 81–82.

mercies in Christ.[100] In grateful response to God's mercies, believers are to
offer their bodies as living sacrifices, holy and pleasing to God, while refusing
to be conformed to the pattern of the world any longer. Instead, they are to be
transformed by the renewing of their minds. This means, in the words of 13:14,
that they must 'put on the Lord Jesus Christ, and make no provision for the
flesh, to gratify its desires'.

In 12:3 – 15:13 Paul draws out the implications of this grateful response for
various aspects of Christian living: 12:3–8, ministry in the church; 12:9–21,
love in action; 13:1–7, submission to rulers; 13:8–10, love of fellow believers;
13:11–14, life in the light of an imminent end; 14:1–23, no judging or causing
fellow believers to stumble; 15:1–13, following the example of Christ in
pleasing others. Two of these passages (13:8–10 and 14:1 – 15:13) have special
relevance for our investigation of Paul's understanding of the law and
justification, and these are discussed in turn below.

Love of fellow believers

As part of a grateful response to the mercies of God, Paul exhorts his readers:
'Owe no one anything, except to love one another' (13:8a). To bolster this
exhortation, the apostle adds:

> . . . for the one who loves another has fulfilled the law. The commandments, 'You
> shall not commit adultery; You shall not murder; You shall not steal; You shall not
> covet'; and any other commandment, are summed up in this word, 'Love your
> neighbor as yourself.' Love does no wrong to a neighbor; therefore, love is the
> fulfilling of the law (13:8b–10).

While we are interested in what this passage reveals of Paul's understanding
of the law, we must bear in mind that the apostle's intention here is to exhort his
readers to love one another. The idea that love is the fulfilment of the law is
brought in only to bolster that exhortation.[101] Nevertheless, it does reveal
something of his understanding of the role of the law in the life of believers.

[100]*Cf.* Hans Dieter Betz, 'Das Problem der Grundlagen der paulischen Ethik (Röm 12,1–2)',
ZTK 85 (1988), p. 218, who concludes: 'Letzlich ist die Grundlage der Ethik keine andere als die
der ganzen Theologie, nämlich die Gerichtigkeit Gottes, auf der nach Röm 1,17 alles aufgebaut ist'
('Finally, the basis of [Pauline] ethics is none other than that of [his] entire theology, namely, the
righteousness of God, upon which, according to Rom. 1:17, everything is built').

[101]Oda Wischmeyer, 'Das Gebot der Nächstenliebe bei Paulus. Eine traditionsgeschichtliche
Untersuchung', *BZ* 30 (1986), p. 182, goes too far when he says that Rom. 13:8–10 was part of
Paul's programme of abolishing the law by means of the law.

It is important to note that Paul is not saying that love will lead believers to carry out all that the law demands (which would have to include, *e.g.*, the practice of circumcision, obedience to calendrical rules, and the observance of food taboos – things which Paul clearly thought were not obligatory for believers, *cf.* 2:26; 14:2–6). What he says is that love *fulfils* the law, and that is clearly something different.

When Paul claims that love is the fulfilment of the law, he has in mind particularly those laws which relate to the neighbour's well-being. Thus he cites four commandments from the second table of the decalogue (only the commandment not to bear false witness is omitted from Paul's list), and says that these 'and any other commandment, are summed up in this word, "Love your neighbor as yourself"' (13:9). It is clear that what Paul is asserting here is of limited application: love is the fulfilment of the law in so far as the law is concerned to ensure that no harm is done to one's neighbour (13:10); he is not saying that love leads believers to observe all the demands of the Mosaic law.

This text has important implications for our understanding of the relationship of Paul's gospel to the Mosaic law. It indicates again that his gospel is not antinomian, for it results in a fulfilment of the law. This does not, however, mean a reinstatement of the law. Rather, the effect of Paul's gospel is that believers, by walking in the Spirit, are enabled to love one another, so that what the law sought, but was unable to produce, is fulfilled in them. Understood in this way, Paul's teaching does not involve inner contradictions or conflict. The apostle, having argued that believers have died to the law in 7:1–6 is not reinstating it again as a regulatory norm for them in 13:8–10.

Tolerance of the practice of other believers

While Paul's gospel makes it plain that God has obliterated the distinctions between Jews and Gentiles as far as sin, judgment and salvation are concerned, that does not mean that other distinctions may not be tolerated. There are good reasons to think that the aim of 14:1 – 15:13 is to deal with divisions of opinion between Gentile and Jewish believers[102] in Rome, and to exhort them to

---

[102]There are several indications that Paul has in mind a division of opinion between Jewish and Gentile believers: (i) Paul speaks of clean (*katharos*) and unclean (*koinos*) food (14:14, 20), categories which suggest a division between Jews and Gentiles. (ii) A tendency of the Gentile believers to look down upon 'weak' Jewish believers (14:3) is consistent with the fact that, in 11:13–24, Paul had to address himself to Gentile Christian pride over against Jews. (iii) In a letter which has been concerned throughout with the salvation of Jews and Gentiles, it would not be surprising to find the apostle dealing with the way they should relate to one another once they have

exercise mutual toleration. Because this passage deals with differences of opinion concerning the necessity or otherwise of observing various demands of the Mosaic law, it is significant for our understanding of Paul's view of the role of the law in the lives of believers.

In a word, Paul says here that the observance of food taboos and special days is a matter of choice (14:1–6). But once the choice is made, those who do not observe (*e.g.* food taboos) should not despise those who do, and those who do observe them should not condemn those who do not (14:3). On the other hand, those who feel free to eat anything should not insist on using their freedom if that is going to cause real distress to those who do not have that freedom. In this case, as always, love must prevail, and 'strong' believers should determine to put no stumbling-block in the way of 'weak' believers (14:13–18).

It is important to note that, even while Paul urges the 'strong' not to eat unclean food if that is causing distress for the 'weak', he nevertheless continues to maintain that 'nothing is unclean in itself'; it is unclean only to the one who thinks it is so (14:14).[103] Taken on its own, this passage shows that, for Paul, certain aspects of the law, at least, are no longer binding upon believers. In the light of Romans 7:1–6, however, we would have to add that this is but part of a total freedom from the law as a regulatory norm, something which is necessary if believers are to be 'slaves not under the old written code but in the new life of the Spirit' (7:6).

Summary

Having surveyed the relevant material in both chapters 1 – 5 and 6 – 15 of Romans, we are now in a position to summarize the findings.

Paul's *primary* purpose in writing Romans was to bring the Roman believers within the orbit of his apostolic ministry because he felt responsible for them. He wanted to ensure that their understanding of the gospel was such that they too would be included among those Gentiles who constitute an acceptable sacrifice to God, consecrated by the Holy Spirit. Beside this primary purpose,

---

been incorporated into the people of God. (iv) In 15:7–9 Paul exhorts Jewish and Gentile believers to 'accept one another'. If we recognize a connection between 15:7–13 and 14:1 – 15:6, then there is good reason to view Paul's call for toleration of different beliefs about clean and unclean food and special days as directed to Jewish and Gentile believers within the church. *Cf.* also discussion in Thompson, *Clothed with Christ*, pp. 161–163; Wedderburn, *The Reasons for Romans*, pp. 59–65.

[103]Thompson, *Clothed with Christ*, pp. 185–199, rightly identifies a dominical echo at this point (*cf.* Mk. 7:19).

the apostle had various *secondary* purposes in writing, including preparing the way for his visit to Rome and subsequent mission in Spain, and soliciting the Roman Christians' prayers for his impending 'collection visit' to Jerusalem.

To achieve these purposes, he felt it necessary to explain, in some detail, the gospel which he preached and how the righteousness of God was revealed in it. While the letter is intended to influence a Christian readership, much of the time the implied dialogical partner is a Jew who is critical of Paul's gospel on several grounds: it opened the floodgates to moral laxity, it denigrated the law, and it did away with Israel's privileged position in salvation-history because it failed to maintain appropriate distinctions between Jews and Gentiles in the matters of sin and judgment and salvation. In expounding his gospel against the background of such objections, Paul has much to say about the key themes of the law and justification. In the exploration of the letter just concluded, the focus of attention was upon those passages relevant to these two themes. The results of this exploration are summarized below.

The law and the Jewish people

Paul believed that it was a great advantage for the Jewish people to have the law, but if any of them entertained hopes of being justified on the grounds of 'the works of the law' they were deceiving themselves.

Jewish advantage: possession of the law

On several occasions Paul highlighted the advantages the Jews had in being the recipients of the law. In 2:18–20 he lists some of these advantages: being instructed out of the law, they know the will [of God], and, having in it the form of knowledge and truth, they are able to be guides to the blind, a light to those in darkness, instructors of the foolish and teachers of the young. In 3:1 the apostle stresses that there was indeed a great benefit in being a Jew, for to Jews were entrusted the promises of God. In 9:4–5 Paul lists the giving of the law (alongside the adoption as sons, the divine glory, the covenants, the temple worship, the promises, the patriarchs and the human ancestry of the Christ) as one of the great advantages of the Jewish people.

The failure of the Jews despite their advantage

In 2:17–24 Paul takes his unbelieving kinspeople to task because they boasted about having the law and yet, by disobeying it, dishonoured the God who gave it to them. He also says that their circumcision was of no value unless it was accompanied by obedience to the law, otherwise it was tantamount to uncircumcision (2:25).

They pursued the law for righteousness

Paul points to a paradoxical outcome in 9:30–31: the Gentiles who did not pursue righteousness obtained what they did not pursue, while the Jews who did pursue a law-righteousness did not attain what they pursued. This failure resulted, not from their ignorance about the proper *manner* in which to pursue law-righteousness, but rather from a failure to realize that the pursuit of law-righteousness itself was mistaken. This is confirmed by 10:3 where the apostle says that his kinspeople, being ignorant of the righteousness which comes from God, sought to establish their own (based on the law). It is mistaken, Paul asserts, because Christ has terminated the role of the law, as far as righteousness is concerned, for those who believe (10:4). This had to happen because law-righteousness depends upon human performance (10:5), and Paul had already gone to great lengths to show that neither Jews nor Gentiles attain righteousness before God by their own performance (3:9–20).

That Paul says the Jews pursued the law for righteousness does not need to be construed in such a way as to imply that Judaism in his day was *by definition* a legalistic religion, or that pious Jews were all intent upon amassing merit by keeping the law. It is better to regard first-century Judaism, like the religion of the Old Testament, as covenantal and nomistic in principle, *i.e.* a religion which was based on election and grace and lived out in grateful obedience to the law. It was when obedience to the law was over-emphasized at the expense of God's saving grace that covenantal nomism degenerated into the legalism which the apostle attacked. There is a fine line between pride in the possession of the law and the belief that one's acceptance before God is achieved by the observance of that law. In Paul's view, many Jews of his day were not only guilty of perpetuating Jewish exclusiveness based on the law, but also had fallen into the trap of believing that justification could be attained by carrying out what the law required. Such a view was, for Paul, untenable, for the law itself and the prophets testified that justification is by faith in Jesus Christ (3:21–22), and if that were not the case, then Christ would have died for no purpose (*cf.* Gal. 2:21).

The works of the law

The expression 'the works of the law' in Romans is used with a different primary reference from that in Galatians. In Galatians its primary reference is to circumcision and the observance of special days and seasons, the outward Jewish observances which the Judaizers were insisting the Galatians took on board.

In Romans, however, the primary reference is to moral achievement. Paul argues that no flesh would be justified by works of the law, because even the Jews who had the law failed to observe it. The Jews whom Paul accused of failing to observe the law had been circumcised (2:27), and the apostle gives no hint that they did not observe food taboos or keep sabbaths. Their failure was in the moral area (2:21–23; 3:9–20). Hence, when Paul says that no flesh will be justified by 'the works of law', he means that no-one will be justified on account of his or her moral achievements. Thus the expression 'the works of the law' in Romans, while not necessarily excluding those aspects of the law highlighted in Galatians (circumcision, special days and seasons), is used by Paul to denote primarily the moral demands of the law.

The nature and function of the law

If Paul believed that his kinspeople were mistaken when they pursued the law for righteousness, because it was not given for that purpose, then what did he understand to be the nature and function of the law? Romans provides us with a number of clues about this matter.

The strength and weakness of the law

Paul's purpose in Romans 7 is to defend his gospel against charges that it involves a denigration of the law. As far as the apostle was concerned, sin is the real cause of the human dilemma, not the law. The law is good (7:13, 16) and spiritual (7:14), and promises life to those who live by it (7:10; *cf.* 10:5).

If the law is good, why then is it necessary for believers to be released from the law through the death of Christ so that they might live by the Spirit (7:6)? The reason is twofold. First, the law became the unwilling ally of sin, in so far as sin took the opportunity which the law provided to bring the people of Israel into bondage. Second, once they had fallen into sin's bondage, the law which promises life then brought death, because it pronounced God's judgment upon them (4:15). People need deliverance both from the bondage to sin which goes with life under the law, and from the judgment which the law pronounces upon them because of their sins.

The function of the law

If the promise of life which the law holds out could not be attained because of sin, what then is the function of the law? In Romans this is seen to be twofold. First, the law has a function in respect of sin and transgression. It makes sin known to people, for otherwise they might not recognize it for what it is (7:7). Once they know what it is they can be held accountable for it (5:13–14). The law can be said actually to 'increase the trespass' (5:20–21) in the sense that it increases culpability by making sin known.

Second, the law functions as a witness to the gospel. In 3:21, where Paul speaks of a righteousness of God 'apart from the law', he insists that it is, nevertheless, a righteousness to which the law [and the prophets] bear witness (3:21b). Paul appeals to the testimony of the law to support his gospel in 4:1–25 (his treatment of the case of Abraham) and in 10:5–8 (where he interprets Dt. 30:12–14 as a witness to the righteousness which is by faith).

Limited time of the law's jurisdiction

There are indications in Romans of Paul's belief that the law was introduced for a limited period only. In the first place, he lists among the privileges of the people of Israel the 'giving of the law' (9:4), which implies that there was a time when the law was not in their possession. In the second place, Paul clearly teaches that, as far as believers are concerned, the role of the law as a regulatory norm has come to an end. Like a person who has died, they have been discharged from all obligations to the law. They have died to the law, so that they might belong to Christ (7:1–4). Further, there are good reasons to believe that *telos* in 10:4 ('Christ is the end [*telos*] of the law so that there may be righteousness for everyone who believes') is best construed as 'termination'. Thus in Romans Paul alludes to the time when the law was introduced, and to the time when its role as both an (ineffective) means for righteousness and a regulatory norm for believers came to an end.

Justification by faith for all

Paul, having concluded that neither Jews nor Gentiles will be justified in the sight of God by observing the law (3:20), argues that God has provided another way by which both might be accounted righteous. Romans reveals more of Paul's understanding of this way than any of his other letters.

Revealed in the gospel apart from the law

This other way of attaining righteousness in God's sight is being revealed through the preaching of the gospel (1:16), addressed first to the Jews and then also to the Gentiles (1:17). It is being revealed apart from the law (3:21), and for that reason is available to the Gentiles (who do not have the law) as well as to the Jews (who do).

To be received by faith

The righteousness revealed in the gospel apart from the law is received through faith, and is therefore available to all who believe, Gentiles as well as Jews (3:22). The principle of faith is a leveller. The one God is God of both Jews and Gentiles, and since he is one he justifies them both in the same way – through faith (3:29–30).

In his treatment of Abraham, Paul makes four points which emphasize that justification is by faith. First, he argues that a person who works for justification receives it not as a gift but as a due, whereas the one who 'trusts him who justifies the ungodly' has faith reckoned as righteousness (4:2–5). Abraham falls into the latter category as one who was justified without works.

Second, Paul shows that Abraham was justified without circumcision, which in his case functioned as a sign of the righteousness he already had by faith, and not as a prerequisite for it (4:10b–11a). The same righteousness will be reckoned to Gentiles who share the faith of Abraham even though they be uncircumcised, as well as to Jews who are not only circumcised but share Abraham's faith as well.

Third, the apostle makes the point that it was not through the law that Abraham received the promise that he would be heir of the world to come (4:13). The promises of God are realized by faith and not by the observance of the law, which means that the fulfilment of the promises may be guaranteed in respect of all who believe, Jews and Gentiles alike.

Fourth, in 4:17b–22 Paul describes the nature of Abraham's faith. It was essentially a belief that God was able to do what he promised, even though all the circumstances of his life seemed to make fulfilment of the promise impossible. 'Therefore', Paul says, 'his faith "was reckoned to him as righteousness"' (4:22), *i.e.* because he had faith in God. The lesson the apostle draws from this is that righteousness will be reckoned also to all those who similarly believe.

Based on the work of Christ

In 3:21–22 the apostle speaks of the righteousness of God which has been revealed *dia pisteōs Iēsou Christou*, which is best construed as meaning 'through the faithfulness of Christ'. Paul is saying here that it was through the faithful obedience of Christ that God's righteousness has been revealed, a righteousness which makes justification possible for both Jews and Gentiles. What Christ's faith-obedience involved is indicated in 3:24b–25a where Paul says that God set him forth *dia pisteōs* (through his [Christ's] faithfulness in his death [in his blood]) as an atoning sacrifice. Christ was obedient in becoming the atoning sacrifice which enabled God to be faithful to his own nature while overlooking former sins.

In 4:25 Paul describes Jesus as the one 'who was handed over to death for our trespasses and was raised for our justification', indicating that our trespasses are dealt with, and our justification secured, through the death and resurrection of Christ. In other words, it was Christ's obedience even to death, and his subsequent resurrection, which make possible the justification of Jews and Gentiles alike.

In 5:9 the apostle speaks of justification 'by his blood', indicating once again that the basis of justification is the death of Christ. He does not here say *how* Christ's death effects justification, he simply asserts the fact.

In 5:12–21 Paul shows that the obedience of Christ affects all humanity in him (*i.e.* Gentiles as well as Jews), just as (or even more than) the disobedience of Adam affected all humanity in him. The effect of Christ's obedience which Paul stresses most in this passage is the justification of those in Christ.

Because the main point Paul wishes to make in 5:12–21 is that Jews and Gentiles are on the same footing as far as salvation is concerned, he does not, in this passage, say *how* the obedience of Christ effects justification for those who are in him, or even *what* exactly that obedience was, but only *that* his obedience does effect justification for Jews and Gentiles alike. In the light of 3:21–26, though, we can safely conclude that the obedience Paul has in mind here is the obedience of the cross, in which atoning sacrifice for sins was made in Christ's blood.

Grounded in God's election and calling

When concluding a long section on the future hope of believers (8:18–30), Paul includes the following statement: 'And those whom he predestined he also called; and those whom he called he also justified; and those whom he justified he also glorified' (v. 30). Despite some difficulties which this text presents to interpreters, one thing is clear: for Paul, justification is one in a series of the acts of God for the salvation of believers which stretches from eternity (predestination) to eternity (glorification). From the viewpoint of the believer, justification depends as much on the grace of God as does predestination, calling and glorification.

What justification involves

Having argued at length in 1:16 – 4:25 that justification is by faith both for Jews and Gentiles, in 5:1–11 the apostle proceeds to draw out the pastoral implications of this conclusion. First among these is that, being justified by faith, 'we have peace with God'. This is best understood as an objective peace won through Christ's death and resurrection, yet one which produces the subjective peace experienced by those who have been justified by faith.

Though distinct metaphors, justification and reconciliation are very closely related in Paul's thought. The terms are used almost interchangeably in 5:1–11. Believers are both justified and reconciled by the death of Christ, and, being justified and reconciled, they shall be saved by him on the last day. This close relationship is also evident from the fact that the passage ends by affirming that 'we have now received reconciliation' (v. 11), a statement very similar to the one with which it started, 'we are [already] justified by faith' (v. 1). While justification highlights the forensic aspect of the salvation won through Christ's death and reconciliation the relational aspect, justification is not without its relational significance, and reconciliation presupposes a resolution of the forensic problem.

Justification involves, not only peace with God now, but salvation from the wrath of God to come: 'Much more surely then, now that we have been justified by his blood, will we be saved through him from the wrath of God' (5:9).

Justification results in confidence before God. Because God justifies believers, he will entertain no charges brought against them (8:33). Because of Christ's work, the voices of all who would condemn believers are ignored (8:34). If human guilt (the one thing which could separate us from the experience of the love of God) has been dealt with by God's grace in Christ, then those who have been justified may enjoy great confidence before God.

No Sonderweg *for the Jews*

While defending his gospel against the objection that it negated the faithfulness of God as far as his promises to Israel were concerned, Paul spoke of the mystery of the hardening of part of Israel and the eventual salvation of 'all Israel' when 'out of Zion will come the Deliverer' and 'banish ungodliness from Jacob' (11:25–27). This has prompted some to speak of a *Sonderweg* (a special way of salvation) for the Jews; one different from that preached to the Gentiles in Paul's gospel. An examination of the context of this passage, however, indicates that, while Israel does have a special place in salvation-history, there is for her no *Sonderweg*. The Jewish people will be gathered into the elect of God only through faith in Jesus Christ. There are, as Paul argues throughout Romans, no distinctions between Jews and Gentiles in the matter of salvation. Because all have sinned, all must be justified in the same way (3:23–24).

The law and the believer

In the letter to the Romans Paul not only argues that justification is independent of the works of the law, he also lets us see something of his belief about the place of the law in the life of the believer.

Freedom from the law

In two places in Romans Paul says that believers are free from the law. First, when responding to those who objected that his gospel is an invitation to moral laxity, he asserts that believers are those who no longer present their members to sin as instruments of wickedness, but to God as instruments of righteousness (6:12–13).To back this up, he makes a surprising statement: 'For sin will have no dominion over ycu, *since you are not under law but under grace*' (6:14). We might expect a Jewish Christian (as Paul was) to say that sin would not have dominion over them if they *did* live under the law. But Paul says the opposite: sin will not have dominion over them because they are *not* under the law.

In the second place, Paul reminds 'those who know the law' that 'the law is binding on a person only during that person's lifetime' (7:1). He reinforces his reminder with an analogy based upon marriage law, arguing that, just as the death of a husband discharges his widow from any obligation to observe the marriage law which bound her to him, so likewise the death of Christ discharges believers from their obligation to obey the law (of Moses). This passage (7:1–6) constitutes one of the clearest expressions of the apostle's conviction that believers (both Jews and Gentiles) have been freed from all obligations to the Mosaic law as a regulatory norm.

Freedom from the law is also implied by Paul's argument for toleration of other believers in 14:1 – 15:13. There the apostle assumes freedom in principle as far as food taboos and special days are concerned, and as long as that freedom is not compromised he allows voluntary observance as a matter of choice. This is part of the total freedom from the law; something which is necessary if believers would be slaves, not under the old written code, but in the new life of the Spirit (7:6).

Fulfilling the law

While Paul argues for the freedom of believers from the law, that does not mean they were free to live godless lives. In fact the apostle believed that it was precisely their freedom from the law which enabled them to escape bondage to sin (6:14). The paradox of the Christian life, as Paul understood it, is that, in a sense, the law is fulfilled in those who are not under the law. This comes out in two places.

First, in 8:3–4 we read that God sent his Son to condemn sin in the flesh so that 'the just requirement [singular] of the law might be fulfilled in us'. In the light of striking similarities between Romans 8:4 and Galatians 5:13–16, it seems best to understand 'the just requirement of the law' (in Rom. 8:4) as equivalent to the love of neighbour (in Gal. 5:14). It is significant that this text speaks about 'the just requirement of the law' *being fulfilled* (passive) in those who walk according to the Spirit, not about believers *fulfilling* (active) this requirement. This suggests that the fulfilment is essentially the work of God (the fruit of the Spirit) in the life of believers, although they must cooperate in the process by putting to death the deeds of the body by the Spirit (8:13).

Second, in 13:8–10, Paul says that the other commandments are summed up in the commandment, 'Love your neighbor as yourself', and concludes, 'therefore, love is the fulfilling of the law'. If the love of the neighbour is what Paul means by fulfilling the law in this context, then that reinforces the view that the fulfilment of 'the just requirement of the law' in 8:4 is also to be understood primarily in terms of the love of the neighbour.

Observing the law for the sake of the weak

While Paul insists on freedom from the law for believers as a matter of principle (7:1–6), he urges toleration towards those whose consciences do not yet allow them that freedom. The voluntary observance of food taboos and special days is a matter of choice (14:1–6). But once the choice is made, those who do not observe them should not despise those who do, and those who do observe them should not condemn those who do not (14:3). And those who feel free to eat anything should not insist on using that freedom if it causes real distress to others. In this case, as always, love must prevail, and 'strong' believers should determine to put no stumbling-block in the way of the 'weak' (14:13–18). In this way the apostle encourages voluntary observance of the law for the sake of the weak, as long as freedom from the law in principle is maintained.

Learning from the law

When Paul insists on the believer's freedom from the law, what he has in mind is freedom from the Mosaic law as regulatory norm for Christian living. This does not mean that there is no place at all for the law in the life of believers. They no longer live under the Mosaic law, but they still read it as Scripture and have much to learn from it. In Romans, as in most of Paul's other letters, there are examples of the way the apostle draws important lessons from his reading of the law as Scripture. (i) Human failure is depicted with allusions to the failure of Adam in Genesis 3. (ii) Appeal is made to the 'law' (meaning the Old Testament as a whole) in 3:1–20 to prove that God acts righteously in judging Israel. (iii) Both the law and the prophets are cited as witnesses to the righteousness of God made available through Christ (3:21–22). (iv) In 4:1–25 Paul points to the Genesis story of Abraham's being accounted righteous before God as a paradigm for the justification of both Jews and Gentiles through faith in Christ. (v) In 10:5–13 the apostle uses Leviticus 18:5 and Deuteronomy 30:12–14 to depict law-righteousness and faith-righteousness respectively. (vi) In 13:8–10 Paul lists commandments from the second table of the decalogue to show how love is the fulfilment of the law.

In the next chapter the relevant material in the remaining letters of the Pauline corpus is examined to fill out the picture of Paul's understanding of law and justification, before stating the general conclusions of this study.

7

Law and justification in the other Pauline letters

Introduction

Most of what Paul has to say about law and justification may be found in Galatians, 1 and 2 Corinthians and Romans, letters which have been discussed in previous chapters. There are, however, a number of relevant passages scattered through the other letters of the Pauline corpus. For the sake of completeness, these passages are picked up in this chapter.

The authenticity of some of these other letters is still the subject of debate. But even if some of them did not come direct from the hand of Paul, they are nevertheless heavily dependent upon Pauline tradition. This is not the place to review the debate about the authenticity of these letters or to engage in it further. For the sake of ease of reference in the discussion which follows, the author of the various letters is simply designated 'Paul', without necessarily assuming that each letter did or did not come directly from his hand.

1 Thessalonians

In 1 Thessalonians Paul responds to news received from Timothy concerning the steadfastness of the Thessalonian believers' faith under persecution (3:6–8).[1] He also defends his integrity as a gospel minister, denying that he had

---

[1] John M. G. Barclay, 'Conflict in Thessalonica', *CBQ* 55 (1993), pp. 513–514, points out correctly that this persecution emanated from the believers' Graeco-Roman, not Jewish,

acted with any ulterior motives, and reminds the Thessalonians of the impact his preaching had upon them (2:1–16). Paul exhorts his converts to live holy lives (4:1–12), and gives them instructions about the Day of the Lord (4:12 – 5:11). The letter concludes with various exhortations (including one that the readers should honour those set over them in the Lord) and final greetings (5:12–28).

It will be clear that 1 Thessalonians, then, is concerned particularly with the readers' persistence in faith despite persecution, and that the parousia is a major theme. It will be equally clear that the matters of law and justification are of no direct concern in this letter. In fact the word *nomos* does not occur in 1 Thessalonians at all. Nevertheless, the very fact that the apostle bases his theology wholly upon the death and resurrection of Christ in the perspective of futurist eschatology, and does not even hint at a role for the law in the Christian life, suggests that his arguments (in Galatians and Romans) for the freedom of the believer from the law are not merely responses to particular problems, but consistent with the content of his gospel as it was preached from the earliest time.[2]

Observing the commands of the Lord Jesus Christ

While 1 Thessalonians contains no reference to the Mosaic law, the importance of observing commands given through the Lord Jesus Christ is stressed:

> For you know what instructions we gave you through the Lord Jesus. For this is the will of God, your sanctification: that you abstain from fornication . . . For God did not call us to impurity but in holiness. Therefore whoever rejects this rejects not human authority but God, who also gives his Holy Spirit to you (4:2–8).

The instructions were those of Paul the apostle given 'through the Lord Jesus' to his converts, but to reject these instructions was to reject not only the apostle's authority, but God. The picture that emerges is one in which believers were definitely under obligation to obey commands believed to have been given 'through the Lord Jesus', even though no mention is made of any obligation to observe the law of Moses.

---

neighbours, for Paul says that his Gentile converts (1:9) experienced it at the hands of their fellow countrymen (2:14).

[2]*Cf.* Thomas Söding, 'Der Erste Thessalonicherbrief und die frühe paulinische Evangeliumsver-kündigung. Zur Frage einer Entwicklung der paulinischen Theologie', *BZ* 35 (1991), pp. 198–201.

The wrath of God has come upon the Jews

In 2:14–16, where Paul refers to the persecutions experienced by his converts, there is an uncharacteristic outburst by the apostle against unbelieving Jews:

> For you, brothers and sisters, became imitators of the churches of God in Christ Jesus that are in Judea, for you suffered the same things from your own compatriots as they did from the Jews, who killed both the Lord Jesus and the prophets, and drove us out; they displease God and oppose everyone by hindering us from speaking to the Gentiles so that they may be saved. Thus they have constantly been filling up the measure of their sins; but God's wrath has overtaken them at last.

This outburst seems so out of kilter with Paul's later sentiments in Romans 9 – 11 that some have argued that it is a non-Pauline interpolation into 1 Thessalonians.[3] Alternatively, it has been argued that, while 2:13–16 is Pauline, it is exegetically improper to try to harmonize it with Romans 9 – 11, because, unlike Romans 9 – 11, it was written against a background of belief in an imminent parousia. Such a belief did not allow for long-term rebellion or the opportunity for repentance for the Jews, who had opted to be on the side of the foes of God.[4] A better approach is to see that the relationship between 1 Thessalonians 2:13–16 and Romans 9 – 11 is not one involving inconsistency, but is rather a case of Romans 9 – 11 providing extra information for a different situation. The sentiments of 1 Thessalonians 2:13–16 are taken up in Romans 9 – 11 (*cf.* 9:22–44; 10:3, 21), but to these is added the further information about God's mercy towards Israel revealed at the last day.[5]

A related question thrown up by 2:13–16 is whether Paul here consigns all Jews (despite their dedication to observing the law) to the 'wrath of God'. Such an interpretation of the text seems implied by the insertion of a comma after the words 'the Jews' at the end of verse 14 in many English translations (NRSV: 'You suffered the same things from your own compatriots as they did from the Jews, who killed both the Lord Jesus and the prophets . . .' (vv. 14–15; *cf.* also RSV, NIV, JB, NEB). If the comma is removed, however, the passage can be read

---

[3]*Cf.*, *e.g.*, Birger A. Pearson, 'I Thessalonians 2:13–16: A Deutero-Pauline Interpolation', *HTR* 64 (1971), pp. 85–91; Daryl Schmidt, 'I Thess 2:13–16: Linguistic Evidence for an Interpolation', *JBL* 102 (1983), pp. 269–279.

[4]So, *e.g.*, G. E. Okeke, 'I Thessalonians 2.13–16: The Fate of the Unbelieving Jews', *NTS* 27 (1980–81), pp. 130–131. *Cf.* also John W. Simpson, Jr, 'The Problems Posed by 1 Thessalonians 2:15–16 and a solution', *HBT* 12 (1990), pp. 61–62, who concludes that the interpolation theory is inadequate, and that development in Paul's thinking is the best way to explain the difference.

[5]So Karl Paul Donfried, 'Paul and Judaism: 1 Thessalonians 2:13–16 as a Test Case,' *Int* 38 (1984), pp. 252–253.

in such a way that Paul is not condemning all Jews indiscriminately, but referring only to those Jews whom he specifies in verse 16: those who killed the Lord Jesus, those who persecuted the prophets, and those who drove Paul and his team out of Thessalonica.[6]

If it is right to say that Paul's statement that 'God's wrath has overtaken them at last' relates specifically to those Jews described in verses 15–16, then there is no need to interpret it in terms of punishment of the whole nation (*e.g.* in the destruction of the temple, with all the implications such a conclusion would necessitate). It may be taken to imply instead that these particular Jews had 'reached the point of no return in their opposition to the gospel and final, irremediable retribution is inevitable, indeed; it has to come'.[7]

2 Thessalonians

The second letter to the Thessalonians is also concerned with the readers' experience of persecution. In it Paul speaks of his pride in their patience and faith, explaining that God deemed it just to punish those who afflicted them, and at the coming of Christ to give rest to those who believed (1:3–12). The readers are urged not to be troubled by rumours, falsely claimed to have emanated from Paul, to the effect that the Day of the Lord has already come (2:1–2). This cannot be so, because the Day of the Lord will not appear unless the man of lawlessness has appeared beforehand (2:3–12). The letter concludes with a request for prayer that Paul himself might be delivered from the hands of evil men, an instruction that those who live in idleness should work to provide their own needs (3:1–15), and the final greetings (3:16–18).

It is clear, then, that 2 Thessalonians, like 1 Thessalonians, is concerned with the readers' persistence in faith despite persecution, that the parousia is a major theme, and that the matters of law and justification warranted no special

---

[6]*Cf.* Frank D. Gilliard, 'The Problem of the Antisemitic Comma between 1 Thessalonians 2.14 and 15', *NTS* 35 (1989), pp. 481–502. But *cf.* Simpson, 'The Problems Posed by 1 Thessalonians 2:15–16, pp. 54–59, who argues against this restricted view, because *inter alia* 'the Jewish motif of the killing of the prophets by their fellow Israelites came to be used in Christian writings as an indication of the continual sinfulness of the Jews [as a whole]'.

[7]F. F. Bruce, *1 and 2 Thessalonians* (WBC 35; Waco, TX: Word, 1982), p. 48. *Cf.* Simpson. 'The Problems Posed by 1 Thessalonians 2:15–16', pp. 59–61, who argues, *contra* Pearson, that 'wrath *eis telos*' does not have to be interpreted as a reference to a specific historical event such as the fall of the temple, and that 'the "final break" view of early Christian history is in simplest terms an assumption that Christians did not go beyond a certain level of polemical language until a certain historical impasse was reached. But intense polemics can have existed before total alienation.'

discussion (the word *nomos* does not occur in 2 Thessalonians either). The fact that the apostle, in this letter, does not even hint at a role for the law in the Christian life is consistent with his arguments (in Galatians and Romans) for the freedom of the believer from the law.

Keeping the charge given in the name of the Lord

While 2 Thessalonians contains no references to the Mosaic law, the importance of observing commands given through the Lord Jesus Christ is stressed again:

> Now we command you, beloved, in the name of our Lord Jesus Christ, to keep away from believers who are living in idleness and not according to the tradition that they received from us . . . Now such persons we command and exhort in the Lord Jesus Christ to do their work quietly and to earn their own living. Brothers and sisters, do not be weary in doing what is right.
>
> Take note of those who do not obey what we say in this letter; have nothing to do with them, so that they may be ashamed. Do not regard them as enemies, but warn them as believers (3:6–15).

Here the charge given is that of Paul the apostle, but the authority invoked is that of the Lord Jesus Christ. Paul's readers are to dissociate themselves from any believer who refuses to obey this charge. Once again it is clear that, as far as Paul was concerned, believers were definitely under obligation to obey commands believed to have the authority of the Lord Jesus Christ, even though he makes no mention of any obligation to observe the law of Moses.

Philippians

In the letter to the Philippians, written from prison, Paul informs his readers that even his imprisonment has had good effects (encouraging others to speak the word of God more fearlessly), despite the efforts of some who were preaching Christ in such a way as to stir up trouble for him during his incarceration (1:3–26). He urges readers not to be frightened by those who oppose them, and to be eager to maintain harmony among themselves, following the example of Christ, who did not serve his own interests. In the light of the example of Christ they are to work out their salvation with fear and trembling (1:27 – 2:18). After foreshadowing the impending visits of Timothy and Epaphroditus to Philippi (2:19–29), the apostle warns his readers of those who want to have them circumcised, claiming that he himself has just as much reason to put 'confidence in the flesh' as they have (3:1–6).[8] But all those things which once formed the basis of such confidence Paul now regards as loss, in comparison with the excellency of the knowledge of Christ (3:7–11). He urges his readers to press on towards the goal of obtaining their heavenly calling, and not to be led astray by the 'enemies of the cross of Christ' (3:12–21). He concludes his letter with an appeal for unity, various exhortations, expressions of thanks, and the final greeting (4:1–23).

While this letter does not deal at any length with the matter of law and justification, at two points the apostle does say things which are relevant to this study.

'Work out your own salvation with fear and trembling'

In 2:1–16 Paul urges his converts to strive for unity, exhorting each of them to put the interests of others first, following the example of Christ (2:1–5). To underline this, the apostle incorporates the famous Christ hymn (2:6–11), and then urges them to heed his exhortation and so to work out their own salvation with fear and trembling (2:12–13).

The exhortation to 'work out your own salvation', understandably perhaps, has sometimes been interpreted as implying that a person's acceptance by God depends, in part at least, upon his or her own work. To read the text in this way, however, is certainly mistaken. The whole context of this exhortation has to do with the well-being of the church, in particular the interrelationship of its members. It is possible then to understand 'salvation' here not as the eternal salvation of the individual, but rather as the well-being of the church. In this

---

[8]A good discussion of the identity of those causing this trouble is provided by Chris Mearns, 'The Identity of Paul's Opponents at Philippi', *NTS* 33 (1987), pp. 194–204, who concludes that they are best identified as Judaizing Christians whose nearest analogues are the Galatian opponents. A similar conclusion is reached by Mikael Tellbe, 'The Sociological Factors behind Philippians 3.1–11 and the Conflict at Philippi', *JSNT* 55 (1994), pp. 120–121, who suggests: 'The appeal of these [Judaizing] agitators to accept circumcision would have been theologically attractive for the Philippian believers as a means of securing their identity as true members of God's people and heirs to God's promises. Moreover, for a church which suffered from the clash with the surrounding [Roman] society, the same message would also have been sociologically attractive as a means of mitigating the conflict and obtaining recognition as a *religio licita* and protection from Rome'. David A. De Silva, 'No Confidence in the Flesh: The Meaning and Function of Philippians 3:2–21', *TrinJ* n.s. 15 (1994), pp. 31–32, argues that there were no opponents in Philippi. What Paul was doing in Philippians was seeking to build unity in the church by warning members of hostile forces outside, to which they must present a united front. In depicting these hostile forces Paul uses as examples opponents he experienced in Galatia and Corinth.

case the apostle's exhortation is directed, not to members of the church as individuals, but to the church as a corporate entity. They are to work at the well-being of their community, following the example of Christ's humility, because God himself is already at work among them to this end.[9] Another way of reading the text is to allow that 'salvation' here does refer to a person's eternal salvation, but to deny that the apostle is suggesting that the achievement of that salvation is dependent upon one's own work in any way. Instead, it is argued, Paul's exhortation here is to common action on the part of the Philippians 'to show forth the graces of Christ in their lives, to make their eternal salvation fruitful in the here and now as they fulfil their responsibilities to one another as well as to non-Christians.'[10] In neither case is there any suggestion that people's eternal salvation, including justification, depends upon their works.

We put no confidence in the flesh

In 3:2 Paul warns his readers to be on their guard against those who wanted them circumcised: 'Beware of the dogs, beware of the evil workers, beware of those who mutilate the flesh!' To underline the fact that they did not need to submit to circumcision, the apostle makes two points. First, he assures his readers that those who serve God by the Spirit, who glory in Christ Jesus and who place no confidence in the flesh constitute already the [true] circumcision.

Second, Paul points them to his own experience. Although he believes he has greater grounds for confidence in the flesh than his opponents (he was 'circumcised on the eighth day, a member of the people of Israel, of the tribe of Benjamin, a Hebrew born of Hebrews; as to the law, a Pharisee; as to zeal, a persecutor of the church; as to righteousness under the law, blameless', 3:6), he counts all this as loss in comparison to the knowledge of Christ which he now enjoys. The implication is that his readers should not listen to those who have fewer grounds for confidence in the flesh than he has. Rather, they should follow the example of their apostle who, though he had such strong grounds, turned his back on them all, once he realized the surpassing worth of knowing Christ.

What Paul says here includes statements about himself and his relationship

---

[9]So, *e.g.*, N. Baumert, '"Wirket euer Heil Mit Furcht und Zittern" (Phil 2,12 f.)', *GeistLeb* 52 (1979), pp. 1–9; Gerald F. Hawthorne, *Philippians* (WBC 43; Waco, TX: Word, 1983), pp. 98–99. *Cf.* S. Pedersen, '"Mit Furcht und Zittern" (Phil 2,12–13)', *ST* 32 (1978) pp. 1–31.

[10]So, *e.g.* Peter T. O'Brien, *The Epistle to the Philippians: A Commentary on the Greek Text* (Grand Rapids: Eerdmans, 1991), p. 280.

to the law which call for special comment. He says that as far as the law was concerned he was a Pharisee (*i.e.* one who sought to obey every minute detail of the law, and to carry out in every day life the purity regulations of the law that applied to the priests in their service in the temple),[11] and that in respect of the righteousness demanded by the law he was blameless.

As to righteousness under the law, blameless

The latter statement prompts many scholars to claim that Paul was not plagued by any sense of failure to keep the law in his pre-Christian days. This in turn leads them to argue that what the apostle wrote in Romans 7 about the inability of the 'I' to keep the law cannot be at all descriptive of Paul's pre-Christian experience.[12] But such conclusions go beyond what Paul's statements in Philippians 3 allow. For in this context Paul is dealing with what we might call his Jewish credentials. He claims to be a Jew whose pedigree and piety cannot be called into question. It is very unlikely that he is claiming never to have fallen short of what the law demanded, or never to have suffered the qualms of conscience because he had done so.[13] It is better, therefore not to use this text to argue that Romans 7 could reflect nothing of the apostle's own internal struggle with the law, or that Paul would want to exclude himself from those represented by the 'I' of Romans 7. Philippians 3 and Romans 7 are describing different things.[14]

Two kinds of righteousness

While the pre-Christian Paul valued so highly his Jewish pedigree and piety, the Christian Paul counts all these things as loss in comparison with the excellency of knowing Christ. His desire now is to 'be found in him [Christ], not having a righteousness of my own that comes from the law, but one that comes through faith in Christ, the righteousness from God based on faith' (3:9). Here the apostle contrasts two kinds of righteousness.

The first is what he describes as 'a righteousness of my own that comes from

---

[11]*Cf.* Jacob Neusner, *Judaism in the Beginning of Christianity* (Philadelphia: Fortress, 1984), p. 57.

[12]So, *e.g.*, recently, Hawthorne, *Philippians*, p. 135.

[13]*Cf.* discussion in O'Brien, *Philippians*, pp. 379–381.

[14]Moo, *Romans*, p. 477, describes the distinction in this way: 'In Philippians 3, Paul is describing his *status* from a Jewish perspective; in Romans 7, his *experience* from a Christian perspective.'

the law' (3:9a). What he means by this is best determined in the light of 3:4–6. There he lists those things in which he once took pride. These include his belonging to the people of the covenant ('a member of the people of Israel, of the tribe of Benjamin, a Hebrew born of Hebrews'), the sign of the covenant ('circumcised on the eighth day'), his meticulous observance of the demands of the law of the covenant ('as to the law, a Pharisee . . . as to righteousness under the law, blameless') and his zeal for the law and the traditions ('as to zeal, a persecutor of the church'). Thus, in terms of the modern debate concerning the meaning of righteousness based on works of the law, this passage suggests that the works of the law include *both* the badges of Jewish identity *and* the careful observance of the all that the law demanded.

The second righteousness of which Paul speaks is 'the righteousness which is through the faithfulness (*dia pisteōs*) of Christ,[15] the righteousness from God which depends on faith (*epi tē pistei*)' (3:9b). This is a righteousness which depends not upon the apostle's Jewish identity or his careful observance of the law, but upon the faithfulness of Christ in carrying out his Father's plan for the salvation of humankind. This righteousness, this right standing with God, comes from God himself, and, as far as human beings are concerned, depends on faith alone.

Colossians

The believers in Colossae heard the truth of the gospel through Paul's fellow worker Epaphras, probably during the apostle's extended ministry in Ephesus, when, according to Acts 19:10, 'all the residents of Asia, both Jews and Greeks, heard the word of the Lord'. Although Paul had not personally founded this church, he felt a great responsibility for it and had expended great effort on its behalf, as he had done for other churches which had not seen him face to face (2:1).

The church at Colossae was in danger of falling prey to what Paul called 'philosophy and empty deceit' based on human tradition (2:8). It was a philosophy which evidently demanded of its adherents submission to circumcision (2:11), observation of certain regulations concerning food and drink, keeping festivals, new moons and sabbaths (2:16), the practice of self-abasement and the worship of angels (2:18). All this, Paul said, while having

---

[15]Agreeing with O'Brien, *Philippians*, p. 396, *contra* Hawthorne, *Philippians*, pp. 141–142, that in this context *dia pisteōs* is best construed as 'through the faithfulness of', not 'through faith in' Christ.

the appearance of wisdom and intended to promote a rigour of devotion, was in fact useless in checking the indulgence of the flesh (2:23).

The exact nature of this 'philosophy' and the identity of those who introduced it into Colossae are the subjects of an ongoing debate.[16] What does seem clear is that the false teaching included an insistence that certain elements of the Jewish law be observed,[17] albeit alongside other demands of a non-Jewish character.

Christ the end of human traditions

What was wrong with this philosophy as far as Paul was concerned was that it was based on human tradition, human precepts and doctrines, and the elemental spirits of the universe, and not on Christ (2:8, 20–22). Its insistence upon circumcision had been made obsolete by the 'spiritual circumcision' experienced by those in Christ, by which the 'body of the flesh' had been put off 'in the circumcision of Christ' (2:11). Similarly, its food and drink laws and calendrical rules had been made obsolete, because they were but shadows of what was to come. The time for these 'shadows' had passed now that the 'substance', Christ, had appeared (2:16–17). Those in Christ, it is implied, should not have to submit to circumcision or observe food and drink taboos or keep special days, insistence on which was all part of the philosophy. Paul's defence of the freedom of the Christian in these matters is in keeping with his more extended arguments in Galatians 3 – 4, even though the false teaching which he was combating there was different. In Galatians he resisted the teaching of the Judaizers, who argued that Gentile believers should submit to circumcision and adopt parts of the Mosaic law as a regulatory norm. In Colossians he implies that circumcision is redundant and that believers should not submit to the ascetic regulations in respect of food, drink and special days which were part of the philosophy being spread around in Colossae.

---

[16]Peter T. O'Brien, *Colossians, Philemon* (WBC 44; Waco, TX: Word, 1982), pp. xxx–xxxviii, provides a succinct summary of the major views.

[17]It is noteworthy that in 4:10–11 Paul mentions Aristarchus, Mark, and Jesus called Justus as 'the only ones of the circumcision among my co-workers for the kingdom of God.' In this way Paul indicates his limited association with those of the circumcision. This is turn suggests that Paul's insistence in 2:11–12, that his baptized Gentile readers have been circumcised with the 'true' circumcision (made without hands), was intended to counteract Judaizing elements in the 'philosophy'.

The cross and the cancelling of the cheirographon

A remarkable statement in 2:13–14 shows why believers, though once 'dead' in their trespasses, are now forgiven and free from the legal indictments that once stood against them:

> And when you were dead in trespasses and the uncircumcision of your flesh, God made you alive together with him, when he forgave us all our trespasses, erasing the record (*cheirographon*) that stood against us with its legal demands. He set this aside, nailing it to the cross.

The believers Paul had in mind here were Gentiles who were once dead (in their trespasses and the *uncircumcision* of their flesh) but now had been made alive together with Christ. All this had been made possible because God had forgiven their trespasses, having erased the record that stood against them with its legal demands. This record God set aside by nailing it to the cross of Christ.

What Paul meant by the record (*cheirographon*) which stood against the Gentiles has been variously interpreted.[18] The major alternatives appear to be that it stood for (i) the law of Moses, (ii) a heavenly account book, or (iii) a certificate of indebtedness to God. It is unlikely that by *cheirographon* Paul meant the law of Moses, because elsewhere in his writings the Gentiles are never regarded as being under the Mosaic law, even though as those outside the law they were still held accountable to God for their moral failures.

There is some evidence for *cheirographon* being used to describe a heavenly book in which human sins are recorded,[19] but the widespread use of the word is to denote a certificate signed by the debtor acknowledging his or her indebtedness.[20] In the present context, then, and where Gentiles are in view, the *cheirographon* is best understood to denote an acknowledgment of indebtedness, of bondage to sin. This sense of indebtedness has been understood in terms of a failure either to live according to moral law written on people's hearts (*cf.* Rom. 2:14–15),[21] or to observe the voluntary and unnecessary obligations taken on by the Colossians in pursuit of a visionary

---

[18]Roy Yates, 'Colossians 2,14: Metaphor of Forgiveness', *Bib* 71 (1990), pp. 248–256, lists six different interpretations: the law of Moses, a pact with Satan, an IOU from mankind to God, the heavenly book, penitential stellae, and theophany visions.

[19]*Cf.* A. J. Bandstra, *The Law and the Elements of the World: An Exegetical Study in Aspects of Paul's Teaching* (Kampen: Kok 1964), pp. 158–163 (cited by O' Brien, *Colossians, Philemon*, p. 24).

[20]*Cf.* Yates, 'Colossians 2,14: Metaphor of Forgiveness', p. 258.

[21]So, *e.g.* O' Brien, *Colossians, Philemon*, pp. 124–125.

ascent.[22] Either way, the *cheirographon* denotes an awareness of guilt on the part of the sinner before God, rather than an indictment of the sinner by God.[23]

Here, then, Paul makes the point that, through the cross of Christ, God not only expiates human sins (something which he teaches elsewhere), but also makes possible the removal of the sense of guilt which humans feel because of their sins. We might even say that, for Paul, God's justification of sinners is an adjudication in their favour, not only in spite of their objective guilt in his eyes, but also in spite of their subjective guilt in their own eyes.

Ephesians

It is difficult to ascertain the provenance of the letter to the Ephesians. It lacks information concerning the particular Christian community (or communities) to which it was addressed,[24] and it does not deal with specific pastoral or theological problems which the readers might have had. Instead, it deals in general terms with great Christian themes. These include the eternal plan of God to unite all things in Christ, the breaking down of the ancient dividing wall between Jews and Gentiles, and the creation of one new humanity in Christ. Also included are Paul's role as an apostle in making known the mystery of the gospel (that Gentiles are fellow heirs with Jews of the promises of God) and the church's role in making the wisdom of God known to principalities and powers in heavenly places. The letter contains an extended paraenetic section in which readers are urged to lead lives worthy of their high calling. They are to maintain the unity of the Spirit, while pressing on to maturity in Christ. Instructions are given to wives and husbands, children and parents, and slaves and masters as to how they are to conduct themselves in their respective relationships. At three points in the letter there are important statements which touch upon the subject of law and justification.

Salvation by faith and not by works

Believers are reminded, in 2:1–3, of their pre-conversion life, when, being dead in trespasses and sins, and following the prince of the power of the air and the desires of the body and the mind, they were by nature children of wrath like the

---

[22]Yates, 'Colossians 2,14: Metaphor of Forgiveness', p. 257.

[23]*Cf.* Nikolaus Walter, 'Die "Handschrift in Satzungen" Kol 2:14', *ZNW* 70 (1979), pp. 117–118.

[24]Not only is there little specific information about the readers, but even the words *en Ephesō* ('in Ephesus') of 1:1 are omitted in some important manuscripts.

rest of humanity. This is contrasted with their present position as believers, which is set out in 2:4–6: through God's abundant love and mercy they have been raised up (from their former death in sin) to sit in heavenly places with Christ. All this has taken place, Paul is at pains to emphasize, not because of anything attributable to believers themselves, or because of their own works, but because of the immeasurable riches of God's grace and kindness towards them (2:5, 7–9). This is summed up in 2:8–10:

> For by grace you have been saved through faith, and this is not your own doing; it is the gift of God – not the result of works, so that no one may boast. For we are what he has made us, created in Christ Jesus for good works, which God prepared beforehand to be our way of life.

The first readers of Ephesians were Gentiles (3:11ff.), and there is no hint in this letter that they were thought to have once relied upon the performance of Jewish works[25] (whether these are understood as all that the Mosaic law demands or as Jewish identity markers) for their salvation. In the context of 2:1–10, the human works which could not save are not the Jewish works of the law however understood, but the general moral achievements of Gentiles,[26] who, Paul says, were dead in trespasses and sin and were children of wrath. And by insisting that it was not only the first readers of Ephesians (Gentiles) who could be described in this way but the rest of humanity as well (2:3),[27] Paul implies that no-one else is in a position to achieve salvation through their own works either.

The abolition of the law

In 2:11–22 Paul reminds his readers of their former state as unbelieving Gentiles, and then contrasts that with their present position in Christ. Formerly they were looked down upon as the uncircumcised by those who were circumcised (the Jews),[28] they were separated from Christ, alienated from the commonwealth of Israel, and strangers to the covenants of promise. They were

---

[25]*Cf.*, e.g., Rudolf Schnackenburg, *Ephesians: A Commentary* (Edinburgh: T. and T. Clark, 1991), p. 98.

[26]*Cf.* Andrew T. Lincoln, *Ephesians* (WBC 42; Dallas, TX: Word, 1990), p. 112.

[27]Agreeing with Lincoln, *Ephesians*, p. 99, that *hōs hoi loipoi* here means 'like the rest of humanity'.

[28]As Nils Alstrup Dahl, 'Gentiles, Christians, and Israelites in the Epistle to the Ephesians', *HTR* 79 (1986), p. 36, points out, pejorative terms are used of the Jews in this context: they are spoken of as 'the so-called circumcision', and their circumcision is disparagingly said to be 'in the flesh' and

without hope and without God in the world (2:11–12). But now in Christ, though once far off, they have been brought near; they are no longer strangers and sojourners; they are fellow citizens with the saints and members of the household of God (2:13, 19).

The inclusion of believing Gentiles together with believing Israelites (the saints) as members of the household of God was made possible, in part, by the removal of the hostility which separated the two groups, so that out of the two, one new humanity in Christ could be created. The key text is 2:14–16.

> For he [Christ] is our peace; in his flesh he has made both groups into one and has broken down the dividing wall, that is, the hostility between us. He has abolished the law with its commandments and ordinances, that he might create in himself one new humanity in place of the two, thus making peace, and might reconcile both groups to God in one body through the cross, thus putting to death that hostility through it.[29]

Here Paul says that it is the law of Moses itself which gives rise to the dividing wall of hostility between Jews and Gentiles.[30] Already in this passage (2:11) he has spoken of the uncircumcision (the Gentiles) being despised by

---

'made with hands'. The implied contrast is with circumcision of the heart, or the circumcision of Christ (*cf.* Rom. 3:29; Col. 2:11).

[29] It is widely believed that in this passage the author has adapted existing hymnic material to make his point about the reconciliation between Jewish and Gentile Christians. So, more recently, *e.g.*, Gerhard Wilhelmi, 'Der Versöhner-Hymnus in Eph 2.14 ff.', *ZNW* 78 (1987), p. 149; Lincoln, *Ephesians*, pp. 126–131. Calvin J. Roetzel, 'Jewish Christian–Gentile Christian Relations: A Discussion of Ephesians 2:15a', *ZNW* 74 (1983), p. 83, offers the following reconstruction of how the author made the hymn speak of the reconciliation of Jewish and Gentile Christians. The author's additions are shown in square brackets:

14 [For] he is our peace
   he who made both one
   and destroyed the barrier of the dividing wall [the enmity].
15 [Abolishing in his flesh the law of commandments in ordinances]
   in order that he might create the two into one new man in him [making peace]
16 and might reconcile both in one body [to God through the cross, killing the enmity in him]
17 And when he came, he preached peace [to you] to those far off and peace to those near.

[30] So, *e.g.*, Schnackenburg, *Ephesians*, p. 115, Lincoln, *Ephesians*, pp. 142–143. Roetzel, 'Jewish Christian–Gentile Christian Relations', p. 86, argues (on the basis that the words 'in ordinances', *en dogmasin* of 2:15a are missing from P[46]) that whereas the original author saw the law as the cause of the hostility, a later redactor added the words *en dogmasin* in order to remove the harsh rejection of the law suggested by the author's original wording. Instead, the redactor wanted to suggest that it was 'an improperly understood law overladen with misdirected human commandments or decrees which was invalidated'. Peter Balla, 'Is the Law Abolished According to Eph. 2:15?', *EuroJTh* 3 (1994), pp. 9–16, argues that it is not the Mosaic law as a whole that has been abolished, but only those regulations which separated Jews from Gentiles.

the circumcision (the Jews). This was one expression of hostility between Jews and Gentiles to which the law gave rise. To this could be added the effect of other elements of the law, such as the observance of the sabbath and the food taboos. But, Paul asserts, Christ made peace between Jews and Gentiles by destroying the dividing wall (that is, the hostility), and by abolishing the law of commandments [expressed] in ordinances which gave rise to the hostility.[31] As in earlier letters, Paul here indicates his belief that, with the coming of Christ, and in particular through the death of Christ, the time of the law had been brought to an end (*cf.* Gal. 3:23 – 4:7; Rom. 7:1–6). The difference between his use of this teaching here and its use in earlier letters is that here it is employed to show how Christ brought about peace between Jews and Gentiles, whereas in Galatians it was used to argue that Gentiles may become members of the true people of God without having to be circumcised or submit to the yoke of the law, and in Romans it was employed to argue that, while the law is good, people need to be free from it in order to serve God in the new life of the Spirit and bear fruit for God.

The first commandment with a promise

The paraenetic section of Ephesians includes instructions to children to obey their parents, and these instructions make reference to the fifth commandment of the decalogue:

> Children obey your parents in the Lord, for this is right. 'Honor your father and mother' – this is the first commandment with a promise: 'So that it may be well with you and you may live long on the earth' (6:1–3).

The injunction to children to obey their parents is reinforced in three ways. First, they are to obey them 'in the Lord'. That is, it is still proper for children as those 'in the Lord' (who have their own relationship to the Lord) to continue to fulfil their obligations to their human parents. To be children of the heavenly Father through faith in Christ does not negate the responsibilities of children to their human parents.[32] Second, they are to obey them because 'this is right'. That is, to do so is consistent with the correct forms of behaviour commonly

---

[31]*Contra* Yates, 'Colossians 2,14: Metaphor of Forgiveness', pp. 256–257, who interprets the expression 'the law of commandments' in terms of 'the ascetic rules, dietary regulations, and ordinances concerned with times, seasons and religious festivals referred to in Col 2, 16–23'.

[32]*Cf.* Colin Kruse, 'Human Relationships in the Pauline Corpus', *In the Fullness of Time: Biblical Studies in Honour of Archbishop Donald Robinson*, ed. David Peterson and John Pryor (Lancer: Homebush West, NSW, 1992), pp. 176–178.

expected of children in the Graeco-Roman world of the day.[33] Third, they are to obey their parents because this is also consistent with the fifth commandment of the decalogue (which has attached to it the promise of well-being and long life upon the earth for those who obey).

After the statement made in 2:15 that Christ has abolished in his flesh the law of commandments and ordinances (interpreted as suggested above), it could come as a surprise that here in 6:2–3 the apostle appeals to the law to reinforce his instructions to children of Gentile believers to obey their parents. But it should be noted that the appeal to the Mosaic law comes after his appeal to what is appropriate for those in the Lord, and what is commonly regarded as fitting in Graeco-Roman society. This suggests that Paul appeals to the law more as a paradigm of good behaviour for those in the Lord, than as a regulatory norm under which believers still serve.

1 Timothy

According to 1 Timothy, Paul had urged his younger colleague to remain behind in Ephesus when he himself went on to Macedonia. Timothy had been instructed to deal with those teaching false doctrine (1:3). The false teachers, Paul implies, occupied themselves with speculations based on myths and genealogies (1:4; 4:7), regarded themselves as teachers of the law (1:7), forbade marriage and enjoined abstinence from certain foods (4:3), while disputing over words and producing dissension (6:3–5). In 6:20 Paul warns Timothy to 'avoid the profane chatter and contradictions of what is falsely called knowledge (*gnōsis*)'. Clearly, certain Jewish elements were contained in the false teaching, but there were other elements which cannot be accounted for in terms of Judaism. It is therefore usually concluded that the false teachers purveyed a Hellenistic[34] or Gnosticising[35] form of Jewish Christianity.

The instructions to Timothy which this letter contains touch upon matters which concern our present study at a number of points.

The law is not for 'the just'

The false teachers of Ephesus are described as those who have deviated from

---

[33]*Cf.* Lincoln, *Ephesians*, p. 403.

[34]So, *e.g.*, Gordon D. Fee, *1 and 2 Timothy, Titus* (Peabody, MA: Hendrickson, 1988), pp. 8–9.

[35]So, *e.g.*, J. N. D. Kelly, *A Commentary on the Pastoral Epistles: I Timothy, II Timothy, Titus* (London: A. and C. Black, 1963), pp. 10–12; Martin Dibelius and Hans Conzelmann, *The Pastoral Epistles* (Philadelphia: Fortress, 1972), p. 66.

the truth, and want to be teachers of the law, but who understand neither what they are saying nor the things about which they make assertions (1:7). In 1:8–11 their defective understanding is contrasted with a proper understanding of the law:

> Now we know that the law is good, if one uses it legitimately. This means understanding that the law is laid down not for the innocent but for the lawless and disobedient, for the godless and sinful, for the unholy and profane, for those who kill their father or mother, for murderers, fornicators, sodomites, slave traders, liars, perjurers, and whatever else is contrary to the sound teaching that conforms to the glorious gospel of the blessed God, which he entrusted to me.

The mistake which the false teachers were making evidently was that they were continuing to lay upon their hearers certain demands of the Mosaic law, not realizing that, according to the gospel entrusted to Paul, the law, though good, was not intended to be used in that way for 'the innocent' (*i.e.* for those in Christ), but only for 'the lawless and disobedient'.

The justification of a notorious sinner

When the apostle Paul spoke of his conversion, what he emphasized was the abundant mercy of Jesus Christ his Lord to one who 'was formerly a blasphemer, a persecutor, and a man of violence' (1:13; *cf.* 1 Cor. 15:9). He realized that the grace of the Lord had overflowed for him with the faith and love that are in Christ Jesus (1:14). All this, the apostle believed, was to display the perfect patience of Jesus Christ as an example to all those who were to believe in him for eternal life (1:16). Clearly implied here is something Paul taught explicitly in earlier letters, *i.e.*, that one's acceptance before God is dependent, not upon one's performance, but upon the overflowing grace of God towards even notorious sinners.

The law provides a paradigm for financial support

Amid the instructions to Timothy there is a reminder that church leaders are worthy of honour and support: 'Let the elders who rule well be considered worthy of double honor, especially those who labor in preaching and teaching; for the scripture says, "You shall not muzzle an ox while it is treading out the grain," and, "The laborer deserves to be paid"' (5:17–18).

The first of these scriptural citations is from Deuteronomy 25:4, a text used previously in 1 Corinthians 9:9. In 1 Timothy 5:17–18 the apostle appeals to the law's prohibition concerning the muzzling of working oxen as a paradigm of God's care for all workers, both animal and human. As such it is instructive of the way believers should treat those who labour among them, especially those who labour in preaching and teaching. This paradigm is reinforced by a second 'Scriptural' citation, this time from the teaching of Jesus: 'The laborer deserves to be paid' (*cf.* Mt. 10:10 par.).

The use of the law here is consistent with Paul's approach in earlier letters, where, although he argues that believers need to be free from the law to bear fruit to God, nevertheless there is much for them to learn from the law, read paradigmatically, concerning God and the way in which he wants his people to live. In this context the apostle appeals to the teaching of Jesus in the same way.

Titus

A kind of false teaching similar to that alluded to in 1 Timothy (and 2 Timothy) was causing trouble in Crete. Thus in the letter to Titus Paul says that he left his fellow worker in Crete to deal with the troubles being experienced there. The circumcision party must be silenced (1:10–11), and those who give heed to Jewish myths and commands of men should be rebuked (1:13–14). Titus himself is to avoid foolish speculations, genealogies, dissensions, and quarrels over the law, which are unprofitable and futile (3:9). Titus, unlike 1 and 2 Timothy, lacks any reference to elements of the false teaching which could not be accounted for in terms of Judaizing Christianity. In the light of the otherwise close parallels between the false teaching reflected in each of the three letters, however, it would seem that in all cases we are dealing with the same sort of thing.

Justification by grace, not by deeds of righteousness

There is one passage in Titus which is particularly relevant to our present study. It follows instructions about how believers should behave towards those outside; they are 'to be subject to rulers and authorities, to be obedient, to be ready for every good work, to speak evil of no one, to avoid quarreling, to be gentle, and to show every courtesy to everyone' (3:1–2). They are to adopt this attitude and behaviour to those outside, remembering that they too once were foolish, disobedient, led astray, slaves to various passions, and so on (3:3). For believers, the great change came with the appearance of the loving kindness of God in Christ. This is described in one long sentence in the Greek:

But when the goodness and loving kindness of God our Savior appeared, he saved us, not because of any works of righteousness that we had done, but according to his mercy, through the water of rebirth and renewal by the Holy Spirit. This Spirit he poured out on us richly through Jesus Christ our Savior, so that, having been justified by his grace, we might become heirs according to the hope of eternal life (3:4–7).

The great change took place because God, in his goodness and loving kindness, saved them by the washing of regeneration and renewal in the Holy Spirit (3:4–5). This, it is emphasized, occurred, not because of any works of righteousness they had done, but because of the mercy of God himself (3:5). Their works of righteousness could not save them, for they too were once foolish, disobedient, led astray, slaves to various passions and pleasures, passing their days in malice and envy, hated by men and hating one another (3:1, 3). God's purpose in all this was that they might be justified by his grace and become heirs in hope of eternal life (3:7).

What is clear in this passage, then, is that justification depends solely upon the grace of God made known in Christ. It has nothing to do with the works of righteousness, *i.e.* the moral achievements of the human beneficiaries. Three points are worth making here. First, works of righteousness in this context have nothing to do with the national identity and privileges of Israel. Second, the theme of justification by grace without human works of righteousness is introduced here in a passage which has no direct application to the problem of Judaizing. If we allow that Paul was the author of the letter, or at least the Pauline basis of this passage, then it follows that Paul's doctrine of justification by grace through faith was not merely a fighting doctrine introduced to refute the teaching of the Judaizers, but was at the heart of his understanding of what God had done in Christ for the salvation of humankind. Third, there is a parallel to this passage in 1 Corinthians 6:9–11, where Paul reminds the Corinthians that some of them too had once been enslaved in all sorts of sinful behaviour, 'but', he says, 'you were washed, you were sanctified, you were justified in the name of the Lord Jesus Christ and in the Spirit of our God' (6:11). This parallel should give us pause before we write off as non-Pauline the rather unusual juxtaposition of washing and renewal in the Holy Spirit and justification here in Titus 3:5–17.[36]

---

[36] *Cf.* Fee, *1 and 2 Timothy, Titus*, p. 206.

2 Timothy

According to 2 Timothy 1:8, 16–17, Paul was already a prisoner in Rome when he wrote this letter. He had come through his first defence unscathed, having been rescued by the Lord from the lion's mouth (4:16–17). Nevertheless, he felt that for him the end was near (4:6). In his imprisonment the apostle was bereft of almost all human companionship, and therefore he urged Timothy to come to him, bringing Mark along with him (4:9–13).

This letter contains further instructions as to how Paul's younger colleague is to deal with false teachers. The false teaching appears to be the same as that alluded to in 1 Timothy (and Titus), involving disputes about words (2:14) which lead to senseless controversies (2:23). But there is an indication that it also involved a claim that the resurrection was past already, a claim that was upsetting the faith of some believers (2:18). At two points 2 Timothy touches upon matters of concern for the present study.

Saved by grace, not by works

First, while urging Timothy not to be ashamed of either the Lord or of his prisoner, but rather to share bravely in suffering for the gospel in the power of God, Paul reminds him that it was God who 'saved us and called us with a holy calling, not according to our works but according to his own purpose and grace. This grace was given to us in Christ Jesus before the ages began, but it has now been revealed through the appearing of our Saviour Jesus Christ, who brought life and immortality to light through the gospel' (1:9–10). Thus, even in a context which does not demand it, Paul's conviction that salvation is independent of human works, and dependent instead upon the grace of God manifested in Jesus Christ, is emphasized.

The positive role of the law

Second, when exhorting Timothy to continue in what he had learned and believed through acquaintance with the sacred writings, Paul says that these same sacred writings were able 'to instruct you for salvation through faith in Christ Jesus', adding that 'all scripture is inspired by God and is useful for teaching, for reproof, for correction, and for training in righteousness, so that everyone who belongs to God may be proficient, equipped for every good work' (3:14–17). Two factors are assumed here about Scripture, and therefore about the law: (i) it is able to point people to salvation through faith in Jesus

Christ, and (ii) although the law is not laid down for the innocent but for the lawless and disobedient (*cf.* 1 Tim. 1:9), nevertheless it still has an important role in the life of believers: it is profitable for teaching, for reproof, for correction, and for training in righteousness, all of which were important elements in Timothy's ministry.[37]

Summary

This survey has revealed that the main themes in relation to law and justification which are found in the major letters of Paul (Galatians; 1 and 2 Corinthians; Romans) are also present in most of the other Pauline letters. The different provenances of these other letters means that these themes are used in different ways, but their essential thrust remains the same. The results of this brief exploration can be set out under five headings.

Two kinds of righteousness

In most of the letters we have examined in this chapter, Paul contrasts righteousness based upon human status and achievement (mostly the latter) with that which comes from the overflowing goodness of God. In Philippians the apostle speaks of his own righteousness, by which he meant a righteousness based upon his Jewish pedigree and piety. This involved *both* his status as a Jew *and* his personal achievements in attaining (external) blamelessness in respect of the law. Yet this righteousness of his own he regarded as worthless in comparison with the excellency of knowing Christ and having in him the righteousness which comes from God (3:4–9). A similar point is made in Ephesians, 1 and 2 Timothy and Titus, where, again and again, Paul emphasizes that believers are saved, not by their own moral achievements, or by works or deeds of righteousness of their own, but only by the grace of God (and through faith).

As to the law, blameless

A key passage in any discussion of Paul and the law is Philippians 3:6. There the apostle says, while setting out his own (greater) grounds for boasting, that 'as to righteousness under the law' he was 'blameless'. It was noted that this statement has led many to assume that what Paul says about the despair

---

[37]*Cf. Ibid.*, pp. 279–280.

experienced by the 'I' of Romans 7, because of an inability to keep the law, can in no way be taken to apply to the apostle himself. What Paul claims in Philippians 3:6, however, is not that he has never fallen short of what the law demanded, or that he has never suffered the qualms of conscience because he had done so. Rather, he is drawing attention to something which is more external in nature: what we might call his Jewish credentials. He claims to be a Jew whose pedigree and piety cannot be called into question. Therefore, to conclude, on the basis of Philippians 3:6, that the experience of the 'I' of Romans 7 cannot refer at all to the pre-conversion experience of Paul is unwarranted.

The abolition of the law

In two letters, Colossians and Ephesians, Paul's teaching about the obsolescence and abolition of the law emerges again. In Colossians, the obsolescence of the law is stressed. Circumcision in the flesh has been replaced by a 'spiritual circumcision', and food laws and calendrical rules, being but a shadow of what was to come, have become obsolete now that Christ, the substance, has appeared. In Ephesians, Paul says that it is the law of Moses which gave rise to the hostility between Jews and Gentiles, and to make peace between the two Christ destroyed the hostility by abolishing the law through his own body on the cross. In addition, in 1 Timothy the apostle declares that the law is not intended for the innocent, but for the unrighteous – for those who persist in unbelief and sin.

Christ removes the human sense of guilt

In Colossians Paul makes use of a striking metaphor when he says that 'God . . . forgave us all our trespasses, erasing the record (*cheirographon*) that stood against us with its legal demands. He set this aside, nailing it to the cross' (2:13–14). The *cheirographon* was a certificate of indebtedness, and in its context in Colossians it denotes an awareness of guilt on the part of the sinner before God (rather than an indictment of the sinner by God). Paul then is saying here, not that God removes human sins through the cross of Christ (something which he does teach elsewhere), but that God removes the sense of guilt which humans feel because of those sins.

The role of the law

While the letters surveyed in this chapter do contain clear evidence of Paul's belief that the law is abolished, being made obsolete by the appearance of Christ and his death on the cross, nevertheless they also reveal, as do the major letters, that there remains a positive role for the law as far as believers are concerned. In 2 Timothy Paul says that the Scriptures (including the Mosaic law) are able to instruct people 'for salvation through faith in Jesus Christ', and they are profitable for teaching, for reproof, for correction and for training in righteousness (all of which were important elements in Timothy's ministry). In addition, Paul appeals to the law in both Ephesians (the fifth commandment of the decalogue) and 1 Timothy (the command not to muzzle working oxen) as a paradigm for Christian ethical behaviour.

Paul and the Jews

The great contrast between Paul's strong outburst against the Jews in 1 Thessalonians 2:13–16 and his later sentiments in Romans 9 – 11 is not simply a case of inconsistency. Rather, Romans 9 – 11 provides extra information for a different situation. The sentiments of 1 Thessalonians 2:13–16 are taken up in Romans 9 – 11 (*cf.* 9:22–44; 10:3, 21), but to these is added the further information about God's mercy towards Israel at the last day. Further, it is better to see this outburst as consigning to the wrath of God not all Jews, but only those who killed the Lord Jesus and the prophets and opposed the ministry of Paul and his colleagues by preventing them from proclaiming the gospel to the Jews.

The survey of relevant material in all the letters of the Pauline corpus now being completed, it is time to draw together, in the final chapter, the general conclusions of this study.

8

General conclusions

The results of the study of the various letters of the Pauline corpus have been summarized at the end of the respective chapters above. The present chapter goes on to offer (i) a brief overview of the different ways in which the themes of law and justification are introduced in the various letters, the reasons for which they are introduced, and the different approaches to the law and justification involved; (ii) a comprehensive summary of the various statements about the law and justification in the Pauline letters; (iii) a discussion of the problems raised by these statements; and (iv) some suggestions concerning the implications of Paul's teaching about law and justification for Christians today.

A brief overview

The purpose for which references are made to the law and justification vary from letter to letter, depending upon the different situations being addressed. Bearing in mind these differences, it is possible to account for many of the variations without recourse to accusations of inconsistency in Paul's thought.

Galatians

Paul wrote Galatians to save his converts from the spiritual abuse that he believed was being perpetrated against them by the Judaizers. He argued that those who have faith in Jesus Christ are the true children of Abraham, the true children of God, and they do not need to submit to circumcision or take upon themselves the yoke of the law. Under no circumstances must they submit again to a yoke of bondage by re-erecting the law as a regulatory norm for themselves, after it had been torn down through the death of Christ. If they did so, seeking to be justified by the law, they would be cut off from Christ and fall from grace. The law, Paul said, was never intended to annul the promise made to Abraham or to be added to it as an extra condition for justification. The purpose of the law was to act as a temporary moral restraint for the people of Israel until the coming of Christ. Thereafter, it was to function no longer as a regulatory norm for believers. They should recognize the educative role of the law, and learn from it (*e.g.*, from the story of Abraham that it is those who are justified by faith who are the members of the people of God, and from the story of Hagar and Sarah that no quarter should be given to those who would take away their freedom in Christ), but never again submit to it as a regulatory norm.

1 Corinthians

When we turn from Galatians to 1 Corinthians we find a very different use made of the law and very little mention of justification. In this letter Paul is combating not the influence of Judaizers, but rather the arguments and criticisms of his own converts in respect of a series of mostly behavioural issues. Accordingly, there are no warnings against seeking justification through the law, or against placing the demands of the law on Christian consciences. Rather, we find Paul making repeated appeals to the law as a paradigm for Christian behaviour. He appeals to the law in this way when, for example, he deals with the problem of incest in the congregation, the right of preachers of the gospel to receive financial support, the danger of compromise with idolatry by eating food offered to idols, and the way liberated women should relate to their husbands and behave in the Christian congregation. It is a mistake, however, to see in Paul's appeals to the law as a paradigm for Christian behaviour a reinstatement of the law as a regulatory norm.

While the majority of Paul's references to the law in 1 Corinthians are appeals to it as a paradigm for Christian behaviour, he does introduce references to the law in a couple of other places for other reasons. In one place, when highlighting the final victory over death which God will give to believers, Paul speaks of the sting of death being sin, and the power of sin being the law. In another place, where he defends his integrity by explaining his reason for adopting different attitudes to law-observance in different circumstances, Paul says that he lives as one outside the law to win to Christ those outside the law, and he lives as one under the law to win those who are under the law. The underlying assumption of these latter statements is that believers are free from the law as an *obligatory* norm for living, and once that is established they are free also to accommodate themselves to others' scruples by *voluntarily* observing the demands of the law for their benefit.

When dealing with the problem of incest, Paul makes brief reference to his readers' having been 'justified in the name of the Lord Jesus Christ and in the Spirit of our God'. Despite the passing nature of this reference, it is very significant because it is found in a letter which does not confront Judaizers, and therefore indicates that justification was for Paul not just a polemic doctrine, but a central element in the experience of grace.

2 Corinthians

The readiness of the Corinthians to criticize Paul and dispute his teachings (all of which is reflected in 1 Corinthians) later provided a climate in which Paul's authority could be rejected by one member of the congregation (the offender) and false apostles could deny the genuineness of Paul's apostleship and introduce another gospel. While explaining and defending the nature of his ministry in 2 Corinthians 3:4 – 4:6, Paul speaks of the letter (of the law) which kills in contrast to the Spirit who gives life. He contrasts the lesser splendour of the ministry of the law with the greater splendour of the ministry of the gospel. He implies that the ministry of the Mosaic law was one of condemnation, while the ministry of the gospel is one of justification, that the law brings death rather than life, and that the ministry of the law was temporary rather than permanent. These negative statements about the law are balanced by Paul's reminder that, when the veil that lies over the minds of Jewish readers of the law is removed, they will see in it the light of the gospel of the glory of Christ. Paul also introduces references to the law as a paradigm for Christian behaviour (abstention from idolatry, and equality in the sharing of resources). From one passage, where he mentions that five times he received the forty stripes less one at the hand of the Jews, it may be inferred that Paul taught believing Jews that they were under no obligation to continue observing all the demands of the Mosaic law.

Romans

In Romans Paul introduces his many references to the law and justification in the process of acquainting members of the church at Rome with the gospel as he preached it, in order that their own lives might be an offering acceptable to God, and that they, being drawn into his apostolic orbit, might support him in his imminent trip to Jerusalem and his planned mission to Spain. Romans is a less impassioned letter, and accordingly its many statements and arguments about the law are more nuanced than those in Galatians.

In presenting his gospel in Romans, Paul argues that there are no distinctions between Jews and Gentiles in respect of sin, judgment or salvation. Both Jews and Gentiles are under the power of sin, and therefore both must be justified freely by God's grace through faith. Those who believe in Christ are free from the law. In fact, freedom from the law is necessary for people to be able 'to bear fruit for God'. Paul balances this argument by insisting that the need for freedom from the law is not an indication that the law itself is evil. On the contrary, the law is holy, just and good. The law is not responsible for the human dilemma. It was only when sin took the opportunity provided for it by the existence of the law that the law ended up as part of the problem. Paul, placing the law, good though it is, on the side of sin, feels he must explain why the law was given in the first place. It was never intended that the law should be pursued for righteousness (a mistake some of his fellow Jews made). It was intended rather to make sin known so that people might be held accountable for their sins, and even to multiply the trespass (by which is probably meant 'to increase people's culpability for their sins by making them known'). Yet, despite the fact that the law became part of the human dilemma, and its function is to make sin known, Paul says that the law itself also bears witness to the gospel, and that, paradoxically, the 'just requirement' of the law finds fulfilment in the lives of those who are justified by faith and walk by the Spirit. In Romans, as in Galatians, Paul argues that the time of the law's rule over believers ended with the coming of Christ.

In Romans, as in Galatians and 1 and 2 Corinthians, Paul appeals to the law, not as a regulatory norm, but as a source of instruction for believers. It is a witness to the failure of humanity, to the righteousness of God in judging Israel, to the righteousness made available through Christ, and to faith as the means of justification. The commandments of the second table of the decalogue function paradigmatically to show how love is the fulfilment of the law. In Romans, having established freedom from the law for believers, Paul, as in 1 Corinthians, urges voluntary accommodation to the demands of the law for the sake of others.

The other Pauline letters

There was apparently no reason for Paul to introduce reference to the law and justification in 1 and 2 Thessalonians, and there is accordingly virtually nothing to learn from these letters about these matters, except perhaps that his very silence reflects his view that law-observance was not required of believers either as a precondition for justification or as an ongoing part of the Christian obedience.

In Philippians Paul contends with Jewish Christians who wanted his readers circumcised, and who put their confidence in things of the flesh. To counteract the influence of these people, Paul claims that he has greater reason to place confidence in the flesh than these people. To substantiate this claim, Paul makes a striking statement about his own blamelessness in respect of the law in his pre-Christian days, something which, upon first reading seems to stand in contrast to what he argues in Romans (that no human being will be justified in the sight of God by works of the law because all have sinned and fallen short of God's glory). On closer reading, however, it becomes clear that Paul has in mind an external form of righteousness of his own based on the law, which he then deems as rubbish in comparison to the righteousness made available to him through the faithfulness of Jesus Christ.

Colossians and Philemon have only a little to contribute to our understanding of Paul's approach to the law and justification. In Colossians, Paul combats an empty philosophy which involved demands to submit to circumcision and to observe various ascetic regulations. In his response, Paul implies that circumcision is redundant now that Christ has come, and argues that believers should not submit to the ascetic regulations which may have been derived in part from the Mosaic law. When urging his readers not to be taken captive through philosophy and empty deceit, Paul reminds them that they have been buried and raised with Christ, their sins have been forgiven and the record (*cheirographon*) that stood against them with its legal demands has been erased. This is a metaphor of justification, but one which relates primarily to the removal of the human sense of indebtedness and guilt.

In Ephesians, while seeking to instil in his Gentile readers a sense of gratitude, Paul reminds them that formerly they were children of wrath like the rest of humanity, but now they have been saved by God's grace and through faith, and that this had nothing to do with any works of which they could boast. He also reminds them they are now included among the new people of God, and that this has been made possible because the hostility that existed between Jews and Gentiles has been abolished through the cross of Christ. This hostility existed because the law functioned as a dividing wall between them, but now this wall has been broken down, as far as Jewish and Gentile believers are concerned, through the death of Christ.

In 1 Timothy, where Paul instructs his protégé to deal with false teachers in Ephesus who wanted to lay upon believers certain demands of the Mosaic law, he says that these false teachers did not know what they were talking about. They failed to realize that the law was not intended for 'the innocent' (those in Christ) but only for 'the lawless and disobedient'. Further, in 1 Timothy, as in 1 Corinthians, Paul introduces the law as a paradigm for Christian behaviour in the matter of financial support for those who teach and preach.

There was apparently no reason to introduce reference to the law in the letter to Titus, but, when speaking of the need for believers to be ready for every good work, Paul does refer to their justification by God's grace apart from works of righteousness.

In 2 Timothy Paul reminds his young colleague of the importance of the holy Scriptures for his ministry. They are profitable for teaching, reproof, correction and for training in righteousness. Even though there is no attempt in this letter to re-impose the Mosaic law as a regulatory norm, it is asserted that there is (as is assumed in most of the other letters of the Pauline corpus) much for believers to learn from the Scriptures (including the Mosaic law). Paul, while encouraging Timothy to share bravely in suffering for the sake of the gospel, reminds him that the salvation and calling of believers were not in virtue of their works, but in virtue of God's own purpose and grace.

A summary

What is provided below is a general summary of the many aspects of Paul's understanding of the law and justification which have emerged from the study of the letters of the Pauline corpus. These are arranged under four main headings.

The nature and function of the law

The temporary role of the law

In Galatians Paul argues that the law was intended only for a limited period (until Christ should come), by likening it to a custodian and governor (3:23 – 4:6). This temporary nature of the law is also implied in 2 Corinthians, where the splendour of the old covenant is said to be fading (3:7–11), and in Romans, where the reference to the 'giving of the law' (9:4) indicates that there was a time before it came into force, and where it is clearly stated that its role, as far as believers are concerned, has now ended (6:14; 7:1–4). In Colossians, the obsolescence of the law is stressed; being but a shadow, it has become obsolete now that Christ, the substance, has come (2:16–17). Ephesians speaks of Christ abolishing the law through his own body on the cross (2:15–16), and the abolition of the law as far as believers are concerned can be inferred from 1 Timothy, where it is said that the law is not intended for the innocent but for the unrighteous (1:8–11).

The law does not annul the promise

Galatians stresses that the introduction of the law was never intended to annul the promise given to Abraham (3:17), and this is reaffirmed in Romans, where Paul argues that the promise given to Abraham is still valid and applies to all, both Jews and Gentiles, who share the faith of Abraham (4:16–25). In Romans Paul says that, if the promised inheritance were to be given to the adherents of the law, then faith would be nullified and the promise made void (4:14). Clearly, then, the law does not annul the promise.

The law cannot give life

In Galatians Paul argues that the law was unable to provide the life it promised, and that righteousness could not come through the law because human beings were imprisoned under the power of sin (3:21–22). Similar arguments are found in Romans where Paul says that the law which promised life brought death to the 'I' (7:10). It was unable to bring its own just requirement to fulfilment in human lives because it was hindered from doing so by the sinfulness of human nature (8:4).

The law brings condemnation

Galatians speaks of the curse of the law under which those who fail to keep all its demands come (3:10). Analogous teaching is found in 2 Corinthians, where the effect of the law is described as bringing condemnation and death (3:6–9), and in Romans, where the function of the law is to make sin known so that all human boasting might be silenced and every human being held accountable before God (3:19).

The law as a witness to the gospel

That the law functions as a witness to the gospel is assumed in Galatians when Paul reminds his readers that 'the scripture, foreseeing that God would justify the Gentiles by faith, declared the gospel beforehand to Abraham, saying, "All the Gentiles shall be blessed in you"' (3:8). The role of the law as witness to Christ is implied in 2 Corinthians where the apostle says that a veil lies over the minds of many of his fellow Jews when they hear the old covenant read, but that when that veil is removed they see the light of the gospel of the glory of Christ (3:12 – 4:6). In Romans Paul claims that, although the righteousness of God has been revealed apart from the law, nevertheless the law and the prophets bear witness to this (3:21). In particular the law does so in its account of Abraham's believing response to the promise (4:1–25).

The law inferior to the promise

In Galatians Paul seeks to downplay the importance of the law in comparison to the promise by saying that it was 'ordained through angels by a mediator' (3:19). This does not mean that the law emanated from evil angels rather than from God, but simply that what is given directly by God (his promise) is superior to what was given through angels (the law) by a mediator (Moses).

The law is holy, just, good and spiritual

In Romans Paul stresses the inherent goodness of the law when he describes it as holy, just, good and spiritual (7:12, 14). He wants to make it crystal clear that, although the law may have become the unwilling ally of sin, he does not believe that the law itself is to blame. Accordingly, his gospel cannot be rejected as something which involves a denigration of the law of God.

The law is the unwilling ally of sin

In 1 Corinthians Paul says that sin derives its power from the law (15:56), and in Romans he speaks of the law as the unwilling ally of sin in so far as sin takes the opportunity provided by the giving of the law to bring people deeper into bondage (7:9–12). This goes beyond what the apostle writes in Galatians, but does not contradict it.

Justification

Justification has always been, and still is, 'by faith'

Galatians insists that people are justified through hearing the gospel with faith and without works of the law (3:1–5), in particular without circumcision (5:26). They are therefore justified in the same way as Abraham was (3:6–9). There have been no changes in the means of justification, despite the introduction of the law in the time of Moses. This means that the blessings of justification are available to Gentiles as well as Jews, for they too may become children of Abraham by faith alone. A similar emphasis is found in Romans. There, too, people are justified by faith apart from works of the law (3:21–22). Because Abraham was accounted righteous through his faith in the promise of God, before he was circumcised and without works of the law, it follows that the blessing promised to him is available to all who share his faith, both Jews and Gentiles (4:1–25). The same stress on justification by grace through faith is found in Ephesians, 1 and 2 Timothy and Titus, where, in various ways, it is affirmed that believers are saved, not by works, or by deeds of their own done in righteousness, but only by the grace of God through faith.

Justification rests upon the redemptive action of Christ

In Galatians it is made clear that the justification of those who believe rests upon the redemption won through the death of Christ. He died to redeem the Jews from the curse of the law so that they might be justified by faith, and so that justification might come to the Gentiles also (3:13–14). Justification is intimately related to the death of Christ, so much so that Paul can say that if there were any other means of securing justification for his people, Christ would have died in vain (2:21). This teaching is reaffirmed in Romans. It was through the faithful obedience of Christ when he was set forth by God as an atoning sacrifice that justification of sinners was made possible (3:21–25). Christ is the one who was put to death for our sins and raised for our justification (4:25). Justification comes through Christ's blood (5:9), and Christ's act of obedience (primarily his death) effects justification for all those who believe (5:12–21).

Justification and inclusion among the people of God

The letter to the Galatians is concerned primarily to show that the children of Abraham, the true people of God, are those who are justified by their faith in

Jesus Christ, not those who are merely circumcised and do what the law requires. The letter to the Romans demonstrates that there are no distinctions between Jews and Gentiles in the matter of sin, judgment or salvation. Since all alike are under the power of sin, all alike must be justified by God's grace. Those who are accepted by God and included in the covenant community are those who have faith in Christ. There is, then, an intimate connection between justification and inclusion in the covenant community. This does not mean, however, that justification can be defined simply as inclusion in the covenant community. Rather, it is better to say that justification is the gateway through which people enter the covenant community. Justification is God's decision to take no account of the many sins of believers, his refusal to entertain any charges brought against them, because Christ has died for them.[1]

Justification is incompatible with legalism and nomism

Galatians emphasizes that justification by faith is incompatible with legalism when it declares that those who want to be justified by works of the law cut themselves off from Christ and fall from grace (5:4), and implies that it is incompatible with covenantal nomism when it says that those who try to re-erect the law, once it has been torn down, only make themselves transgressors (2:18).

Justification is grounded in election and calling

In Romans justification is one of a series of the acts of God for the salvation of believers: 'And those whom he predestined he also called; and those whom he called he also justified; and those whom he justified he also glorified' (8:30). Here it is implied that justification is grounded in God's election and calling. But God's election and calling must be met with faith if people are to be saved. There is then no *Sonderweg*, no special way of salvation, for the Jewish people whereby they can be saved apart from faith in Jesus Christ.

The experience of justification

Romans, more than any other letter, spells out what is involved in justification.

---

[1] James D. G. Dunn, 'The Justice of God: A Renewed Perspective on Justification by Faith', *JTS* n.s. 43 (1992), pp. 1–22, provides a fresh and balanced statement of the nature of justification which emphasizes the communal purposes for which Paul employed the doctrine, without neglecting the personal aspects of justification which obviously meant so much to Paul.

It brings peace with God (5:1), and in this way is closely akin to reconciliation (the terms are used almost interchangeably in 5:1–11). In reconciliation, though, the relational aspect of salvation is emphasized and in justification the forensic aspect is to the fore. Nevertheless, justification cannot be said to be without its relational significance, and reconciliation presupposes a resolution of the forensic problem. Justification is also the basis of the believer's confidence. Because God refuses to entertain any charges brought against those whom he has justified, believers enjoy great confidence in their relationship with him (8:33). Analogous teaching is found in Colossians where Paul makes use of a striking metaphor, the cancellation of the *cheirographon*, the certificate of indebtedness, to show that through the cross of Christ God not only dealt with human sins, but also made possible the removal of the sense of guilt that humans feel because of their sins (2:13–14). Justification not only brings peace and reconciliation now but also guarantees salvation from the wrath of God which is to come (Rom. 5:9).

It may be added that, while many of Paul's statements about justification are made to combat the views of Jews and Judaizers, and constitute an attack on mistaken views about national privilege, it is quite inadequate to suggest that this is the extent of Paul's concern with the doctrine of justification. There are too many statements (see above) in which Paul celebrates the personal blessings of justification for this to be the case.

The place of justification in Paul's theology

Finally, it is worth noting that while in 1 and 2 Corinthians the matter of justification by faith was not an issue, still it was assumed to be a central part of the experience of grace in the one (1 Cor. 6:11) and a fundamental aspect of the ministry of the new covenant in the other (2 Cor. 3:9), suggesting that this doctrine occupied an important place in Paul's theology.

The law and the believer

Freedom from the law

The believer's freedom from the law is a pervasive theme in the Pauline corpus. In Galatians Paul tells his readers how he laboured hard to defend this freedom for the sake of Gentile believers (2:1–21), urges them not to submit again to the yoke of bondage, for this would mean cutting themselves off from Christ and falling from grace (5:2–4), and reminds them that if they are led by the Spirit they are not under the law (5:18). Freedom from the law is assumed in 1

Corinthians where the apostle tells how he lived as one outside the law to win those outside the law (9:21). It can be inferred from 2 Corinthians, where Paul recounts that five times he had received from the Jews the forty strokes less one (11:24), very likely because he was thought, rightly, to have encouraged Jews (Jewish Christians at least) to neglect the law. In Romans the believer's freedom is stated explicitly (6:14: 'you are not under law but under grace' *cf.* 7:6), illustrated with the analogy of the woman freed from any obligations to her husband once he has died (7:1–4), and implied when Paul says that the voluntary observance of food taboos and special days is a matter of choice for believers (14:1 – 15:3). Freedom from the law is implied by what is said in Colossians about the obsolescence of the law (2:16–17), and by what is said in Ephesians about destroying the enmity between Jews and Gentiles by the abolition of the law through the cross (2:14–16). It may be inferred from the statement in 1 Timothy that the law is not intended for the innocent but for the unrighteous (1:8–12).

Galatians has a unique and striking statement about the freedom of Jewish believers from the Mosaic law. Referring to the law, Paul says, 'But if I build up again the very things that I once tore down, then I demonstrate that I am a transgressor' (2:18). For the apostle, no matter what other role the law might have in the life of the believers, it was not to be re-erected to function as a standard by which believers, even Jewish believers, *must* live.

Learning from the law

While believers are free from the law as a regulatory norm, nevertheless they still have much to learn from it. Accordingly, throughout the Pauline corpus we find appeals to the law, not only as a witness to the gospel of Christ (as noted above in the section on the nature and function of the law), but also as a paradigm for Christian behaviour. In Galatians Paul expects his converts to learn from the story of Hagar and Sarah about the way to respond when their freedom in Christ is threatened (4:21–31). In 1 and 2 Corinthians there are many examples of this paradigmatic use of the law (listed in the summaries at the end of the chapters on 1 and 2 Corinthians, but too many to be repeated here). In Romans Paul uses the commandments from the second table of the decalogue to show how love is the fulfilment of the law (13:8–10). Appeal is made to the law in both Ephesians (6:1–3, the fifth commandment) and 1 Timothy (5:17–18: 'Do not muzzle the ox') as a paradigm for Christian behaviour. In 2 Timothy the Scriptures (including the law) are able to instruct people 'for salvation through faith in Jesus Christ', and are profitable for teaching, for reproof, for correction, and for training in righteousness (3:14–17).

The fulfilment of the law in the lives of believers

While Paul insists that believers are free from the law, and that they must maintain that freedom if they want to live holy lives that bear fruit for God, he argues, paradoxically, that the law nevertheless finds fulfilment in the lives of believers. It may be inferred from Galatians 5:13–14 that this occurs because all the law (meaning all the obligations the law places upon people in respect of their neighbours' well-being) is fulfilled through love, which is in turn produced in believers' lives by the work of the Spirit (5:22). This same point is made in Romans, where Paul says that the one who loves has fulfilled the law because love does no wrong to a neighbour (13:8–10). Paul probably has the same thing in mind when he writes of the just requirement of the law being fulfilled in those who walk not according to the flesh but according to the Spirit (Rom. 8:4).

The law of Christ

In Galatians alone we find mention of 'the law of Christ'. Paul urges his readers to bear one another's burdens and so fulfil the law of Christ (6:2). Paul, having fought to deliver Gentile believers from the yoke of the Mosaic law, is not placing upon them the heavier yoke of Christ's law. The law of Christ is the law of love, and love is the fruit of the Spirit produced in those who are no longer under the law.

Accommodation to those who live under the law

While Paul insists that the Mosaic law must never be re-erected to function as a regulatory norm which believers must obey, it is evident from 1 Corinthians that, once the principle is established, he is willing to allow accommodation. He is willing to live as one under the law himself to win Jews to Christ, and to live as one outside the law to win Gentiles (9:19–23). In Romans 14:15–21 Paul urges believers generally to practise such accommodation for the sake of those who might otherwise be caused to stumble.

Keeping the commandments of God

In 1 Corinthians there is a statement which, on first reading, appears to contradict Paul's insistence on freedom from the law: 'Circumcision is nothing, and uncircumcision is nothing; but obeying the commandments of God is everything' (7:19). Whatever 'obeying the commandments of God' in this text means, it cannot mean carrying out all that the law demands, for circumcision, one of the primary demands of the law, it says, is nothing! It is probably best understood in terms of the ethical imperatives of the gospel summed up in the command to love one's neighbour.

Obedience to the commands of Christ

If Paul taught that believers were under no obligation to the Mosaic law as a regulatory norm, 1 Corinthians reveals that there were two things which he did regard as obligatory for believers. The first was observance of the commands of Christ. Where there was a command of Christ (as, for instance, in the case of divorce) that was to be obeyed (7:10). And although the apostle believed he could live as one outside the Mosaic law to win those outside, he knew he was not free from God's law but was under the law of Christ (9:21). In this text Paul distinguishes between the Mosaic law (which he was not under obligation to observe) and God's law (which he equates with the law of Christ and which he must observe). To live by God's law in this sense probably included obedience to the commands of Christ, living by the law of love, and living for the sake of the one who died for him.

Observing the rules laid down in all the churches

The second thing which Paul mentions in 1 Corinthians as obligatory for his converts was observance of the traditions of behaviour that he had laid down for all his churches. These included the general rule of staying in the situation in which one found oneself when called (7:17–20), the need for women praying or prophesying in church to retain their head-coverings (11:16), and practice of women keeping silence in the churches (14:33b–34). In each case the context suggests that these ecclesiastical traditions had been developed, not to stifle the new freedom of the age of the Spirit which believers enjoyed, but to ensure that freedom was lived out in culturally (and theologically) appropriate ways while the present age was still running its course.

The law and the Jewish people

In Romans Paul was at pains to show that his gospel did not lead to a denial of the special place of Jewish people in the purposes of God. Accordingly, in several places, the apostle affirms the great privileges of the Jews, included among which is their possession of the law (2:18–20; 3:1; 9:4–5). Yet, despite this privilege, Paul says, his fellow Jews were susceptible to two opposing abuses of the law. Some dishonoured the God who gave them the law by disobeying it (2:17–24), while others made the mistake of trying to establish a righteousness of their own based on the law (10:3). It can be inferred from statements in Philippians that Paul himself was guilty of the latter abuse in his pre-Christian days. He too relied upon a righteousness of his own that comes from the law; a righteousness based on his Jewish pedigree and piety, involving both his status as a Jew and his personal achievements in attaining (external) blamelessness in respect of the law (3:4–9).

Problems

Anyone who seeks to understand Paul's approach to the law and justification encounters many problems. Not least of these is the fact that none of Paul's letters provides a systematic presentation of his views on the subject. One is then left with the task of trying to piece together a coherent picture of the apostle's views from a variety of occasional letters in which he introduces references to the law and justification to achieve a range of different purposes of his own (this is what was attempted above).

Some believe that the differences in what Paul says about the law and justification can be accounted for only by recognizing that the apostle himself modified his views over time to correct his earlier misunderstandings. Others think that because the differences are so great, and because many of the differences are found within the individual letters themselves, it is impossible to account for them in this way.

One of the purposes of this present study was to evaluate the claims made about irreconcilable inconsistencies in the apostle's statements about the law and justification. In what follows, the results of this study as far as the various areas of apparent inconsistency are concerned are brought together under four major headings.

The nature and function of the law

Ambiguous use of the term 'law'

The claim that Paul's use of the term *nomos* (law) oscillates between Torah as an undivided whole and something else (*e.g.* the demands of the Mosaic law or the entire Hebrew Scriptures), and is often reduced to moral law, is correct. In most places, however, the way the term is being used is made clear by the context, so that we do not need to charge the apostle with inconsistency on this count.

Contradictory statements about the origin of the law

Paul, it is claimed, holds two contradictory views about the origin of the law. On the one hand he ascribes its origin to God, on the other to (evil) angels. That Paul ascribes the origin of the law to God is unquestionably true. That Paul downplays the importance of the law relative to the promise by saying that 'it was ordained through angels' and not given directly as the promise was, is also true. It is not, however, necessary to say that being 'ordained through angels' is a bad thing, or to say that the angels through whom it was ordained were evil, still less to say that the law originated with evil angels.

Problematic statements about law and sin

It is claimed that Paul's statements to the effect that the law provokes people to sin and actually increases sins are at best problematic. It is just not true, it is argued, that the existence of a prohibition always incites people to violate that prohibition, or that the existence of laws increases the incidence of sinful behaviour. As a general observation it may indeed be true that laws do not generally provoke people to disobey them or actually increase the amount of sinfulness in the world. Paul does not say that the law produces sin, however, but that sin, taking opportunity provided by the commandment, produced in him all kinds of covetousness (Rom. 7:8). Two points need to be noted. First, this statement is probably to be understood as a theological interpretation of Israel's experience at Sinai, not just as a general observation about the effect of laws, or even of the Mosaic law. Second, Paul does not say that the law produced all kinds of covetousness, but that sin, taking the opportunity provided by the commandment, produced in him all kinds of covetousness. When Paul speaks of the law increasing sin (Rom. 5:20), it is not clear exactly what he means. Many suggestions have been made, one of the least problematic being that the law increased the sin in the sense that what was not known to be sin before the giving of the law was clearly recognized as such thereafter, thereby increasing human culpability.

Contradictory statements about human ability to keep the law

A real difficulty in Paul's statements about the law is that he insists that both Jews and Gentiles are equally under the power of sin, and that no-one will be justified by deeds of the law. Yet he also says that Gentiles, who do not have the law, do instinctively what the law requires, and in so doing put to shame Jews who have the law but do not keep it. The crux of the problem is how to interpret Paul's statement about the Gentiles doing instinctively what the law requires. Many suggestions have been made, and a number of these were discussed in the chapter on Romans 1 – 5 above. Of all the suggestions, only two are real possibilities. Either Paul was saying that some pagans conform formally and externally to some of the moral precepts of the law about which they are unaware, or that Paul has in mind pre-Christian Gentiles, who not only keep the law but who are also justified before God. In neither case is Paul saying that Gentiles, unaided by the grace of God, can escape the tyranny of sin so that they can properly fulfil all the demands of the law.

The power of sin attributed to both Adam and the law

It has been claimed that Paul is confused when in one place he attributes the power of sin over the human race to Adam's fall, and in another to the law. A closer examination of what the apostle says, however, suggests that he traced the *origin* of sin's dominion over human beings to Adam, but recognized in the law an unwilling ally of sin by which sin *increased its power* over them. Further, the law gives sin its power over sinners in so far as it pronounces God's judgment on them.

The law promised life, but lacks the power to provide it

In two places Paul quotes from Leviticus 18:5, which says of the law that 'the person who does these things will live by them', and yet, it is claimed, he denies to the law, even theoretically, the power to provide the life it promised. In its original context Leviticus 18:5 constitutes a promise of continued enjoyment of physical life within the promised land to an obedient Israel. Paul picks up the quotation, not to deny that the law could deliver what it promised, but to show that it operates on the principle of performance, unlike the promise which operates on the principle of faith. Paul does not deny that the law could deliver what it promised, but rather that the law, operating on the principle of performance, could not bring life and justification to those who broke it. On the contrary, it could only pronounce God's curse upon the disobedient. For Paul, the law could theoretically provide life to those who obeyed it, but it was prevented from doing so because human beings, in slavery to sin, could not fulfil its demands.

A dramatic act needed to terminate a temporary expedient

If, as Paul implies, God added the law as a temporary moral restraint for his people, then his argument that a dramatic act of God in the death of Christ was needed to liberate people from its dominion seems incredible. While it is true that the law functioned as a temporary moral restraint, it also had power over people because it pronounced God's judgment upon sinners. To provide escape from the latter, it was necessary for God to act dramatically through the death of Christ, for, while a rule of law may be introduced and terminated easily enough, the judgment of God which the law pronounced against sinners cannot be that easily swept aside. That requires an atoning sacrifice.

Justification

Justification was merely a polemic doctrine

It has been argued that the doctrine of justification by faith was merely a polemic doctrine employed by Paul in his campaign against the Judaizers, but which he was prepared to set aside once that campaign was over. For this reason, justification by faith looms large in Galatians and Romans, but drops out of sight in 1 Corinthians. It is true that justification is not a subject addressed directly or extensively in 1 Corinthians. But it is very significant that, in a passage that makes another point altogether, Paul alludes to justification by faith as a central aspect of the experience of grace when he says: 'And this is what some of you used to be. But you were washed, you were sanctified, you were justified in the name of the Lord Jesus Christ and in the Spirit of our God' (6:11). It is not only in 1 Corinthians, among letters other than Galatians and Romans, that we find reference to justification by faith. Incidental allusions to justification by faith or faith-righteousness are pervasive in the Pauline corpus, being found in 2 Corinthians, Philippians, Ephesians, 1 and 2 Timothy and Titus. Justification by faith was far more than a polemic doctrine for Paul, even though it may not function as the centre of his theology.

Contradictory statements about justification

In Romans 2:1–16 Paul makes some surprising statements which seem to contradict his teaching about justification by faith elsewhere. He says, for instance, that God will give to each one according to his works (v. 6); to those who work evil he will give trouble and distress (v. 9), but to those who work the good he will give glory and honour and peace (v. 10). It must be acknowledged that in this passage Paul *does* say that God will judge people according to their works. The question is: Can Paul say that people will be judged according to their works *and* justified by faith, without being guilty of inconsistency?

The resolution to this problem is to be found in Romans 2:1–16 itself. Two points can be made. First, Paul's purpose in this passage is to emphasize that God's judgment is entirely impartial, and this is in line with the overall purpose of 1:18 – 3:20 to show that Jews have no special immunity where God's judgment is concerned. In other words this passage is not a discussion of the means of justification.

Second, it is evident from this passage itself that the doing good which God will reward with glory and honour and peace is not perfect fulfilment of the demands of the law, but rather responding to God's goodness with repentance, and this leads to forgiveness according to his grace. What Paul is saying, then, is that God judges people impartially according to their works when he gives eternal life to the repentant (both Jews and Gentiles) who seek glory and immortality by persistence in well-doing. The residual problem is that this seems to leave justification dependent upon persistence in well-doing. But the problem is more apparent than real, for no-one would want to say that Paul taught that there would be final justification for those who persisted in evil-doing! Where there is true, justifying faith, there is also persistence in well-doing.

The law and the believer

Inconsistencies in the matter of freedom from the law

In Galatians 2:15–21 Paul claims that believers are no longer under the law, either as a means of justification or as a regulatory norm for ongoing Christian living. But in 1 Corinthians he appeals repeatedly to the law when giving ethical instructions (*e.g.* 5:6–8; 9:9, 13; 10:1–11; 14:21, 34) and even says that 'obeying the commandments of God is everything' (7:19). In Romans 7:1–6 Paul argues that believers are free from the law, yet in Romans 8:3–4 he says that Christ came so that the just requirement of the law might be fulfilled in those who walk according to the Spirit.

While on the surface of things it might appear that Paul, after throwing out the law in Galatians, readmitted it in 1 Corinthians, our study of the relevant texts in 1 Corinthians has shown that this is not the case. In all Paul's appeals to the law in 1 Corinthians, not once does he come anywhere near requiring his readers to observe all its demands. His use of the law is paradigmatic, *i.e.* he saw in the law (predominantly, but not exclusively, its narrative sections) examples of the way God dealt with, and what he expected of, his ancient people Israel. These examples Paul applied, not literally but analogically, to believers of his own day to show how God would deal with them, and what he expected of them, in analogous situations. Even Paul's statement, 'obeying the commandments of God is everything' (7:19), does not contradict what he taught in Galatians, for, as we saw, this cannot mean observing all that the law demands since the full statement in 7:19 runs: 'Circumcision is nothing, and uncircumcision is nothing; but obeying the commandments of God is everything.' There is no way that keeping God's commands here can involve the reinstatement of the law, when one of the fundamental demands of the law is said to be 'nothing', and so does not have to be observed.

It is more difficult to deal with the apparent inconsistencies in Romans. After all, Paul, having argued for freedom from the law in 7:1–4, does say that 'the just requirement of the law' is fulfilled in those who walk according to the Spirit, and he does imply that those who are in the Spirit do submit to God's law. As we saw (in the light of the many parallels between Rom. 8:4 and Gal. 5:13–16), however, a good case can be made for interpreting 'the just requirement of the law' in terms of the love of neighbour. Also, there is a difference between 'the just requirement [singular] of the law' being fulfilled in believers (divine passive) and believers doing all that the law demands. The fulfilment of the law in believers is accomplished, not by their scrupulous observance of all the demands of the law, but rather as they walk according to the Spirit and cooperate with the Spirit in putting to death the deeds of the flesh.

Later letters correct mistakes in earlier ones

Some have argued that Paul, having claimed that believers were no longer under the law when dealing with the Judaizing problem in Galatians, found it necessary to reintroduce the law when dealing with contentious ethical issues in 1 Corinthians. Then he became aware of the inconsistencies in his position and he began to correct his ideas by a process of synthesization. One stage in this process is reflected in 2 Corinthians and the final stage in Romans. It was in Romans that Paul achieved a balanced position between the two extremes which are reflected in Galatians and 1 Corinthians respectively.

Such a view depends for its cogency upon two debatable assumptions. It is assumed, first, that Paul does apply the law as a regulatory norm in 1 Corinthians, and second, that there are great differences between Galatians and Romans as far as Paul's teaching about the law is concerned. In 1 Corinthians, however, Paul does not reintroduce the law as a regulatory norm, but rather applies it paradigmatically; and Paul's teaching about the law in Romans, while going much further than that in Galatians, is consistent with what is found in that letter. (In both letters Paul teaches, for instance, that the law was introduced for a limited time only; that it is weak in the face of sin – it cannot make alive, and it cannot produce in people the fulfilment of its own just requirement, that believers are free from the law, but nevertheless have much to learn from it; and that the law finds a fulfilment in the lives of believers as they walk by the Spirit.)

Inconsistency in the matter of accommodation

In Galatians 2:11–14 Paul tells how he took Cephas to task for compromising the truth of the gospel when, in Antioch, Cephas accommodated himself to the beliefs of the Jews who came from James. Yet in 1 Corinthians 9:20 Paul said that he himself became as one under the law to win those under the law. Was he, therefore, guilty of inconsistency?

Our study of the relevant passages has shown that Paul was not guilty of inconsistency, as might at first appear to have been the case. It is one thing to accommodate oneself to the Jews when such accommodation promoted closer identification for the sake of the gospel. This is what Paul practised, and he would no doubt have approved of Cephas practising it also. It is quite a different thing to refuse to accommodate oneself to a particular group when that refusal implies that those who have accepted the gospel are still 'Gentile sinners'. When Paul rebuked Cephas in Antioch, he did so because Cephas was not acting in line with the gospel.

Jewish laws replaced by ecclesiastical practices

In Galatians 4:1–11 Paul taught that believers were no longer to be enslaved under the *stoicheia tou kosmou*, observing days and months, seasons and years. Rather, as those led by the Spirit and bearing the fruit of the Spirit, they were to live in love for their neighbours and so fulfil the law of Christ (5:1, 13–16, 22–25). But in 1 Corinthians, believers were reminded on three occasions of the traditions of behaviour accepted universally in the churches which they were expected to observe (7:17; 11:16; 14:33b, 36). Had Paul thrown out Jewish (or pagan) laws only to replace them with ecclesiastical traditions?

To this question we must respond with a qualified 'yes'. 'Yes', because a reading of 1 Corinthians does reveal that Paul expected his readers to follow the universal practices of the churches, in particular remaining in the state in life in which individuals found themselves when called, the retention of the head-covering by women when praying or prophesying in the congregation, and the observance of proper 'silence' by women in the worship service. A *qualified* 'yes', because these practices did not have the same function in the teaching of Paul as the Jewish laws had in the teaching of the Judaizers. Paul expected the Corinthians to follow the universal practices of the churches for the sake of the good order of the Christian community, whereas the Jewish laws were being laid upon the Galatians as a condition of their acceptance among the people of God.

The law and the Jewish people

The place of the law in Jewish soteriology

It has been claimed that Judaism is a better, happier and more noble religion than Paul portrays. It is a religion based upon God's elective grace, his great acts of salvation and his covenant with Israel. The law is God's gracious gift to Israel, her proud possession by which she orders her life and continues to enjoy God's blessing, and the law itself made provision for those who failed to observe all its demands. Paul was the one guilty of a legalistic moralization of the law, implying that it was a rival system of salvation opposed to grace and faith, and ignoring the fact that Jewish soteriology involves repentance, forgiveness and atonement.

Our study of the Pauline corpus has revealed that Paul did say a number of negative things about the law and the Jewish people. In Galatians 4, he does imply, by his use of the allegory of Hagar and Sarah, that the Jews were in bondage under the law (even though the main point Paul makes from the allegory is directed against the Judaizers, not the Jews). In 2 Corinthians he says that a veil lies over the minds of his fellow Jews when the law is read in their synagogues, and this prevents them from understanding the major purpose of the law – to bear witness to Christ. But it is in Romans that Paul's most devastating comments about the law and the Jewish people are made. He acknowledges the great privilege it is for them to have God's law, but blames them for a number of abuses of that privilege. First, they dishonour the name of God who gave them the law by disobeying it, and in this they are put to shame by Gentiles who, not having the law, actually carry out some of its demands without knowing it. Second, they mistakenly assume that their possession of the law, the most obvious sign of their being God's people, somehow makes them immune from God's judgment, which it does not. Third, some of them at least make the mistake of pursuing the law for righteousness (a mistake he admits that he himself made in his pre-Christian days when he sought to establish a righteousness of his own based on the law, *cf.* Phil. 3:9). Fourth, they mistakenly believe that the law still marks off those who belong to God's people from those who do not. This is taken a step further in Ephesians, where the law is seen as giving rise to the hostility that exists between Jews and Gentiles, a hostility that has been brought to an end by the abolition of the law through the death of Christ.

One way of explaining the difference between the nobler, happier approach to the law in Judaism and Paul's negative statements about it, is to argue that the apostle's starting-point was not Judaism and any shortcomings it might have had, but rather the new realization about the significance of Jesus Christ that came to him on the Damascus road. Accordingly, if the action of God in Christ was necessary as the basis for justification, then clearly no-one could be justified on the basis of works of the law. Yet this does not seem to be enough to explain Paul's criticisms of the attitude of his fellow Jews to the law. For Paul does imply that they were mistakenly trusting in their observance of the law for justification.

Another way of lessening the conflict between the Judaism which rejoiced in God's law as a gracious gift and trusted in God's forgiveness and atonement to cover sins on the one hand, and Paul's negative statements about Jewish attitudes to the law on the other, is to limit the apostle's critique to Jewish exclusivism based upon the law. Thus, it is argued, Paul does not criticize the Jews for trying to establish a righteousness of their own before God by their observance of the law's demands; rather, he criticizes them for their exclusivism in restricting membership among the people of God to those who observe the law. In practice this meant restricting it to those who submitted to circumcision, observed the sabbath and kept the dietary rules. Paul believed that this exclusivism was wrong because, now that Christ had come, the people of God were marked off by their faith in Christ, not by their observance of the law. But this too seems insufficient to explain Paul's criticisms of the attitude of his fellow Jews. Paul not only criticized their exclusivism, he also asserted that their own quest for righteousness before God was misdirected. They were striving for a righteousness of their own as if righteousness were based on works of the law, not realizing that it was to be attained only on the basis of faith.

If we are to take seriously the fact that the soteriology of first-century Judaism was not *in principle* based on the observance of the law, but on God's election and grace, and if we are not content simply to say that Paul got it wrong, then we must seek some other explanation of Paul's critique of Jewish attitudes to the law. Four observations can be made.

First, what is true of any religion in principle is often not true of its adherents in practice. While first-century Judaism may have taught that, *in principle*, inclusion among the people of God depended upon God's election and grace and not upon the observance of the law, *in practice* that teaching often degenerated into something else. We need not conclude that all Jews had adopted a works-righteousness approach to salvation, but only that some had done so, and that those whom Paul (and Jesus) criticized were numbered among them.

Second, the Jewish texts upon which our understanding of first-century Judaism rests reflect a spectrum of attitudes to the role of the law in soteriology. At one end of the spectrum there are texts in which the obligations of observing the law are stressed, while at the other end there are other texts in which the emphasis falls upon God's election and grace. These, of course, need not be in opposition to one another, but, human nature being what it is, there is always a tendency among devout people to focus upon obligations at the expense of grace, and to lay the burden of obligations upon others as well. It was this tendency which the apostle strenuously opposed.

Third, and most important, Paul had come to recognize that the coming of Christ marked the end of the period in which the people of God were distinguished by their circumcision and observance of the Mosaic law. Now they were to be distinguished by their faith in Jesus Christ and participation in his Spirit. Paul was critical of many of his kinspeople because they did not recognize what God had done in Jesus Christ and continued to act as if nothing had changed.

Fourth, Paul believed that many of his kinspeople were so committed to establishing their own righteousness based upon the law that they refused to submit to God's righteousness, a righteousness now manifested apart from the law through the saving work of Jesus Christ.

Law and justification today

It would be a shame to conclude this study of law and justification in the Pauline corpus with the discussion of the problems this matter raises for students of Paul's letters. So in what follows an attempt is made to point, albeit very cursorily, to some possible implications of the apostle's teaching about law and justification for Christians today.

The experience of justification

In two places especially (Rom. 5:1–11; 8:31–39) Paul says something of the experience of justification. Justification involves not only an objective peace with God won through the cross of Christ, but a subjective peace with God experienced by those who believe in Christ. It brings an assurance that nothing can separate us from the love of God. God is for us. He will entertain no charges brought against us, for God has justified us, Christ has died for us and he intercedes for us at the right hand of God. Such great truths are perennial in their application.

No unnecessary barriers for converts

Paul insisted that Gentiles could be accepted by God (justified) through faith in Jesus Christ without the need to submit to circumcision or carry out all the demands of the Mosaic law. In like manner, those who preach the gospel today should not add to it any other demands which must be met before people can be included among the people of God. This truth must be defended wherever cultural conformity or religious duties (or both) are taught as extra conditions for acceptance by God and thus for inclusion among his people. There is no place for this sort of legalism alongside the gospel.

No unnecessary burdens for believers

The apostle taught that, with the coming of Christ, the period of the law had come to an end. It was therefore inappropriate, not only to require people to observe the demands of the Mosaic law as a condition of acceptance by God, but also to reinstate the law as a regulatory norm for believers who had already been accepted by God through their faith in Jesus Christ. Today, also, believers need to guard against the tendency to relate to God through the Mosaic law, or any other set of rules, instead of relating to him directly through the Spirit and faith in Jesus Christ. Once people fall victim to law-related consciences in one respect, they will soon find their consciences making all sorts of other demands they should meet if they are to live well-pleasing to God. It would be like letting a camel get its nose in the door of the tent. Before long the rest of the camel is in the tent as well, and that makes life very uncomfortable!

The paradox of Christian living

Paul taught his readers that if they were to live well-pleasing to God and bear fruit for him in their lives, they needed to be free from the law. To cease from being slaves to sin, they needed to be liberated from the law. This is just the opposite of what one might expect. It seems logical that submission to the law should lead to the curbing of sin. But the apostle taught that the law was unable to achieve this, not because there was anything wrong with the law itself, but because of the weakness of human nature. Believers today need to take note of this paradox. They need to resist all temptations to relate to God through the law. To think that by trying to fulfil the demands of the Mosaic law, or following other rules and regulations, they can curb the power of sin, is an illusion. Paul says that such endeavours have 'an appearance of wisdom in promoting self-imposed piety, humility, and severe treatment of the body, but they are of no value in checking self-indulgence' (Col. 2:23). But if believers relate to God through faith in Jesus Christ, and look to the Spirit of God to produce his fruit in their lives, then they find that the 'just requirement of the law' is fulfilled in them by the Spirit's work. In this way the sort of life that the law envisages, a life characterized by the love for God and neighbour, begins to find its fulfilment in those who walk by the Spirit.

Reading the Old Testament as a Christian

While the apostle Paul taught clearly that believers were no longer under the Mosaic law, nevertheless he continued to read the Old Testament (including the Mosaic law) as Scripture. He found in it testimony beforehand to the gospel, and paradigms for Christian living. Believers today still need to be students of the Old Testament. They will read it in the light of what God has done in Christ. Although the Mosaic covenant is not their covenant, nevertheless they will still find the Old Testament (including the Mosaic law), read paradigmatically, 'useful for teaching, for reproof, for correction, and for training in righteousness' (2 Tim. 3:16).

Accommodation

Once the apostle Paul had established freedom from the law in principle, he was prepared to accommodate himself in practice to those under the law (either as an evangelistic strategy or so as not to encourage weaker brothers or sisters to act against their consciences). For Paul there was a very great difference between *limiting* one's freedom by accommodating oneself voluntarily to those who still felt bound by the law, and *sacrificing* one's freedom under pressure from those who denied the legitimacy of such freedom. The same principle applies to believers today. Once the principle of Christian freedom has been established, the mature believer will want from time to time to limit the exercise of that freedom for the sake of others. Whenever sacrifice of that freedom is demanded, however, believers must vigorously resist such demands. If that resistance causes offence, they must be prepared to let that occur in order to maintain the truth of the gospel. Not to do so would be to compromise, by their actions, the truth of the gospel that they preach, and so to reduce its effectiveness. Such compromise would also result in the loss of their Christian joy, which would, in turn, neutralize the effectiveness of their witness to the gospel.

Robust holiness

One of the consequences of believers' freedom from the law and justification by faith is that their holiness depends not upon their observation of rules and regulations in order to avoid contamination from the 'world', but rather upon their relationship with God through faith in Jesus Christ. This in turn means that they do not have to fear contamination by their involvement with the world, but rather by God's grace they may expect to be agents of transformation in the world (as, of course, was their Lord). This in turn means that believers do not have to be always preoccupied with concerns about their own holiness or spirituality, but may be freed from such preoccupation in order to serve others.

Bibliography

Achtemeier, Paul J., '"Some Things in them Hard to Understand": Reflections on an Approach to Paul', *Int* 38 (1984), pp. 254–267.

Badenas, Robert, *Christ the End of the Law: Romans 10.4 in Pauline Perspective* (Sheffield: JSOT, 1985).

Balla, Peter, 'Is the Law Abolished According to Eph. 2:15?', *EuroJTh* 3 (1994), pp. 9–16.

Bandstra, A. J., *The Law and the Elements of the World: An Exegetical Study in Aspects of Paul's Teaching* (Kampen: Kok, 1964).

Banks, Robert, 'Romans 7.25a: An Eschatological Thanksgiving?', *AusBR* 26 (1978), pp. 34–42.

Barclay, John M. G., 'Conflict in Thessalonica', *CBQ* 55 (1993), pp. 512–530.

——, 'Mirror-reading a Polemical Letter: Galatians as a Test Case', *JSNT* 31 (1987), pp. 73–93.

——, *Obeying the Truth: A Study of Paul's Ethics in Galatians* (Edinburgh: T. and T. Clark, 1988).

Barrett, C. K., *A Commentary on the Epistle to the Romans* (London: A. and C. Black, 1957).

——, *A Commentary on the First Epistle to the Corinthians* (London: A. and C. Black, 1968).

Bassler, Jouette M., 'Divine Impartiality in Paul's Letter to the Romans', *NovT* 26 (1984), pp. 43–58.

Baumert, N., '"Wirket euer Heil mit Furcht und Zittern" (Phil. 2, 12f.)', *GeistLeb* 52 (1979), pp. 1–9.

Baxter, A. G., and Ziesler, J. A., 'Paul and Aboriculture: Romans 11.17–24', *JSNT* 24 (1985), pp. 25–32.

Beker, J. C., 'The Faithfulness of God and the Priority of Israel in Paul's Letter to the Romans', *HTR* 79 (1986), pp. 10–16.

————, *Paul the Apostle: The Triumph of God in Life and Thought* (Edinburgh: T. and T. Clark, 1980).

Bergmeier, Roland, 'Röm 7,7–25a (8,2): Der Mensch – das Gesetz – Gott – Paulus – die Exegese im Widerspruch?', *KD* 31 (1985), pp. 162–172.

Best, Thomas F., 'The Apostle Paul and E. P. Sanders: The Significance of Paul and Palestinian Judaism', *ResQ* 25 (1982), pp. 65–74.

Betz, Hans Dieter, *Galatians: A Commentary on Paul's Letter to the Churches in Galatia* (Hermeneia; Philadelphia: Fortress, 1979).

————, 'Das Problem der Grundlagen der paulischen Ethik (Röm 12,1–2)', *ZTK* 85 (1988), pp. 199–218.

Borgen, Peder, 'Paul Preaches Circumcision and Pleases Men', *Paul and Paulinism: Essays in Honour of C. K. Barrett*, ed. M. D. Hooker and S. G. Wilson (London: SPCK, 1982), pp. 37–46.

Bornkamm, Gunther, 'The Letter to the Romans as Paul's Last Will and Testament', *The Romans Debate*, ed. Karl P. Donfried (Peabody, MA: Hendrickson, revised and expanded edn., 1991), pp. 16–28.

Bouwman, Gijs, '"Christus Diener der Sünde". Auslegung von Galater 2, 14b–18', *Bijdr* 40 (1979), pp. 44–54.

Branick, Vincent P., 'The Sinful Flesh of the Son of God (Rom 8:3): A Key Image of Pauline Theology', *CBQ* 47 (1985), pp. 246–262.

Brewer, D. Instone, '1 Corinthians 9.9–11: A Literal Interpretation of "Do Not Muzzle the Ox"', *NTS* 38 (1992), pp. 554–565.

Brinsmead, Bernard Hungerford, *Galatians – Dialogical Response to Opponents* (SBLDS 65; Chico, CA: Scholars Press, 1982).

Bruce, F. F., *1 and 2 Corinthians* (NCB; London: Oliphants, 1971).

————, 'The Curse of the Law', *Paul and Paulinism: Essays in Honour of C. K.*

Barrett, ed. M. D. Hooker and S. G. Wilson (London: SPCK, 1982), pp. 27–36.

————, *The Epistle of Paul to the Galatians: A Commentary on the Greek Text* (NIGTC; Exeter: Paternoster, 1980).

————, 'The Romans Debate – Continued', *BJRL* 64 (1982), pp. 344–359.

————, *1 and 2 Thessalonians* (WBC 45; Waco, TX: Word, 1982).

Bultmann, Rudolph, *Theology of the New Testament*, vol. 1 (ET, London: SCM, 1952).

Burton, Ernest De Witt, *The Epistle to the Galatians* (ICC; Edinburgh: T. and T. Clark, 1921).

Byrne, Brendan, 'Living out the Righteousness of God: The Contribution of Rom 6:1 – 8:13 to an Understanding of Paul's Ethical Presuppositions', *CBQ* 43 (1981), pp. 557–581.

————, '"Rather Boldly" (Rom 15,15): Paul's Prophetic Bid to Win the Allegiance of the Christians in Rome', *Bib* 74 (1993), pp. 83–96.

————, '*Sons of God – Seed of Abraham': A Study of the Idea of the Sonship of God of All Christians in Paul against the Jewish Background* (Analecta Biblica 89; Rome: Biblical Institute, 1979).

Callan, Terrence, 'Pauline Midrash: The Exegetical Background of Gal 3:19b', *JBL* 99 (1980), pp. 549–567.

Campbell, Douglas A., *The Rhetoric of Righteousness in Romans 3.21–26* (JSNTSup 65; Sheffield: JSOT, 1992).

————, 'Romans 1:17 – A Crux Interpretum for the *PISTIS CHRISTOU* Debate', *JBL* 113 (1994), pp. 265–285.

Campbell, W. S., 'Romans III as a Key to the Structure and Thought of The Letter', *NovT* 23 (1981), pp. 37–39.

Caneday, Ardel, '"Redeemed from the Curse of the Law": The Use of Deut 21:22–23 in Gal 3:13', *TrinJ* 10 (1989), pp. 185–209.

Caragounis, Chrys C., 'Romans 5.15–16 in the Context of 5.12–21: Contrast or Comparison?', *NTS* 31 (1985), pp. 142–148.

Carson, David, 'Pauline Inconsistency: Reflections on I Corinthians 9.19–23 and Galatians 2.11–14', *Churchman* 100 (1986), pp. 6–45.

Catchpole, David R., 'Paul, James and the Apostolic Decree', *NTS* 23 (1977), pp. 428–444.

Cavallin, H. C. C., '"The Righteous shall Live by Faith": A Decisive Argument for the Traditional Interpretation', *ST* 32 (1978), pp. 33–43.

Cohn-Sherbok, Rabbi Dan, 'Some Reflections on James Dunn's: "The Incident at Antioch (Gal. 2.11–18)"', *JSNT* 18 (1983), pp. 68–74.

Conzelmann, Hans, *1 Corinthians* (ET, Hermeneia; Philadelphia: Fortress, 1975).

Cope, Lamar, '1 Cor 11:2–16: One Step Further', *JBL* 97 (1978), pp. 435–436.

Cosgrove, Charles H., 'Arguing Like a Mere Human Being: Galatians 3.15–18 in Rhetorical Perspective', *NTS* 34 (1988), pp. 536–549.

——, 'Justification in Paul: A Linguistic and Theological Reflection', *JBL* 106 (1987), pp. 653–670.

——, 'The Mosaic Law Preaches Faith: A Study in Galatians 3', *WTJ* 41 (1978), pp. 146–164.

——, 'What If Some Have Not Believed? The Occasion and Thrust of Romans 3 1–8', *ZNW* 78 (1987), pp. 90–105.

Cranfield, C. E. B., '"The Works of the Law" in the Epistle to the Romans', *JSNT* 43 (1991), pp. 89–101.

——, *A Critical and Exegetical Commentary on the Epistle to the Romans*, vols. 1 and 2 (ICC; Edinburgh: T. and T. Clark, 1975, 1979).

Dahl, Nils Alstrup, 'Gentiles, Christians, and Israelites in the Epistle to the Ephesians', *HTR* 79 (1986), pp. 31–39.

——, *Studies in Paul: Theology for the Early Christian Mission* (Minneapolis: Augsburg, 1977).

Dahl, Nils A., and Sandmel, Samuel, 'Review of *Paul and Palestinian Judaism: A Comparison of Patterns of Religion* by E. P. Sanders', *RelSRev* 4 (1978), pp. 153–160.

Dalton, William J., 'Is the Old Covenant Abrogated (2 Cor 3.14)?', *AusBR* 35 (1987), pp. 88–94.

——, 'The Meaning of "We" in Galatians', *AusBR* 38 (1990), pp. 33–44.

Danby, Herbert, *The Mishnah* (London: Oxford University Press, 1933).

Davidson, Richard M., *Typology in Scripture: A Study of Hermeneutical Tupos Structures* (Andrews University Seminary Doctoral Dissertation Series 2; Michigan: Andrews University, 1981).

Davies, Glenn N., *Faith and Obedience in Romans: A Study in Romans 1 – 4* (JSNTSup 39, JSOT, Sheffield, 1990).

Davies, W. D., *Paul and Rabbinic Judaism: Some Rabbinic Elements in Pauline Theology* (1948; Philadelphia: Fortress, 4th edn., 1980).

Dawes, Gregory W., '"But If you Can Gain your Freedom" (1 Corinthians 7:17–24)', *CBQ* 52 (1990), pp. 681–697.

Derrett, J. Duncan M., '2 Cor 6:14 ff. a Midrash on Dt. 22:10', *Bib* 59 (1978), pp. 231–250.

————, 'You Abominate False Gods; but do you Rob Shrines?' *NTS* 40 (1994), pp. 558–571.

DeSilva, David A., 'No Confidence in the Flesh: The Meaning and Function of Philippians 3:2–21', *TrinJ* n.s. 15 (1994), pp. 27–54.

Dibelius, Martin, and Conzelmann, Hans, *The Pastoral Epistles* (Philadelphia: Fortress, 1972).

Dodd, C. H., 'ENNOMOS CHRISTOU', *Studia Paulina in honorem Johannis de Zwaan*, ed. J. N. Sevenster and W. C. Unnik (Haarlem: De Erven F. Bohn N. V., 1953), pp. 96–110.

————, *The Epistle of Paul to the Romans* (London: Hodder and Stoughton, 1932).

Donaldson, T. L., 'The "Curse of the Law" and the Inclusion of the Gentiles: Galatians 3.13–14', *NTS* 32 (1986), pp. 94–112.

Donfried, Karl P., 'Paul and Judaism: 1 Thessalonians 2:13–16 as a Test Case', *Int* 38 (1984), pp. 242–253.

————, ed., *The Romans Debate* (Peabody, MA: Hendrickson, revised and expanded edn., 1991).

Drane, John W., *Paul, Libertine or Legalist? A Study in the Theology of the Major Pauline Epistles* (London: SPCK, 1975).

Dungan, David L., *The Sayings of Jesus in the Churches of Paul: The Use of the Synoptic Tradition in the Regulation of Early Church Life* (Oxford: Blackwell, 1971).

Dunn, James D. G., 'The Incident at Antioch (Gal. 2:11–18)', *JSNT* 18 (1983), pp. 3–57.

————, *Jesus, Paul and the Law: Studies in Mark and Galatians* (Louisville, KY: Westminster John Knox, 1990).

————, 'The Justice of God: A Renewed Perspective on Justification by Faith', *JTS* n.s. 43 (1992), pp. 1–22.

————, '"A Light to the Gentiles", or "The End of the Law"? The Significance of the Damascus Road Christophany for Paul', *Jesus, Paul and the Law: Studies in Mark and Galatians* (London: SPCK, 1990), pp. 89–107.

————, 'The New Perspective on Paul', *Jesus, Paul and the Law: Studies in Mark and Galatians* (Louisville, KY: Westminster John Knox, 1990), pp. 183–206.

————, 'Once More – Gal 1:18: *historēsai Kēphan*. In Reply to Otfried Hofius', *ZNW* 76 (1985), pp. 138–139.

————, 'The Relationship between Paul and Jerusalem according to Galatians 1 and 2', *NTS* 28 (1982), pp. 461–478.

————, *Romans 1 – 8* (WBC 38a; Dallas, TX: Word, 1988).

————, *Romans 9 – 16* (WBC 38b; Dallas, TX: Word, 1988).

————, 'Salvation Proclaimed VI. Romans 6:1–11: Dead and Alive', *ExpT* 93 (1982), pp. 259–264.

————, 'Works of the Law and the Curse of the Law (Galatians 3.10–14)', *Jesus, Paul and the Law: Studies in Mark and Galatians* (Louisville, KY: Westminster John Knox, 1990), pp. 215–236.

Earnshaw, John, D., 'Reconsidering Paul's Marriage Analogy in Romans 7.1–4', *NTS* 40 (1994), pp. 69–88.

Elliott, John H., 'Paul, Galatians, and the Evil Eye', *CTM* 17 (1990), pp. 262–273.

Elliott, Neil, *The Rhetoric of Romans: Argumentative Constraint and Strategy and Paul's Dialogue with Judaism* (JSNTSup 45; Sheffield: JSOT, 1990).

Epp, Eldon Jay, 'Jewish–Gentile Continuity in Paul: Torah and/or Faith? (Romans 9:1–5)', *HTR* 79 (1986), pp. 80–90.

Fee, Gordon D., *The First Epistle to the Corinthians* (NICNT; Grand Rapids: Eerdmans, 1987).

————, *1 and 2 Timothy, Titus* (Peabody, MA: Hendrickson, 1988).

Flusser, David, '"Durch das Gesetz dem Gesetz gestorben" (Gal 2,19)', *Judaica* 43 (1987), pp. 30–46.

Froelich, Karlfried, 'Fallibility Instead of Infallibility? A Brief History of the Interpretation of Gal 2:11–14', *Teaching Authority and Infallibility in the Church*, ed. Paul C. Empie, T. Austin Murphy, and Joseph A. Burgess (Minneapolis: Augsburg, *c.* 1980), pp. 259–269.

Führer, Werner, ' "Herr ist Jesus". Die Rezeption der urchristlichen Kyrios-Akklamation durch Paulus Römer 10,9', *KD* 33 (1987), pp. 137–149.

Fuller, Daniel P., 'Paul and "The Works of the Law" ', *WTJ* 38 (1975), pp. 28–42.

Furnish, Victor Paul, *II Corinthians* (AB 32a; New York: Doubleday, 1984).

Gallas, Sven, ' "Funfmal vierzig weniger einen . . ." Die an Paulus vollzogenen Synagogalstrafen nach 2 Kor 11,24', *ZNW* 81 (1990), pp. 178–191.

Garlington, D. B., '*HIEROSYLEIN* and the Idolatry of Israel (Romans 2.22)', *NTS* 36 (1990), pp. 142–151.

————, 'The Obedience of Faith in the Letter to the Romans, Part III: The Obedience of Christ and the Obedience of the Christian', *WTJ* 55 (1993), pp. 281–297.

Gaston, Lloyd, 'Israel's Enemies in Pauline Theology', *NTS* 28 (1982), pp. 400–423.

————, *Paul and the Torah* (Vancouver; University of British Columbia Press, 1987).

————, 'Paul and the Torah', *Antisemitism and the Foundations of Christianity*, ed. Alan Davies (New York: Paulist, 1979), pp. 48–71.

Georgi, Dieter, *The Opponents of Paul in Second Corinthians* (Philadelphia: Fortress, 1986).

Getty, Mary Ann, 'Paul and the Salvation of Israel: A Perspective on Romans 9 – 11', *CBQ* 50 (1988), pp. 456–469.

Gilliard, Frank D., 'The Problem of the Antisemitic Comma between 1 Thessalonians 2.14 and 15, *NTS* 35 (1989), pp. 481–502.

Gillman, Florence Morgan, 'Another Look at Romans 8:3: "In the Likeness of Sinful Flesh" ', *CBQ* 49 (1987), pp. 597–604.

Goppelt, Leonhard, *Typos: The Typological Interpretation of the Old Testament in the New* (ET, Grand Rapids: Eerdmans, 1982).

Gordon, T. David, 'A Note on *PAIDAGŌGOS* in Gal 3.24–25', *NTS* 35 (1989), pp. 150–154.

————, 'Why Israel did not Obtain Torah-Righteousness: A Translation Note on Rom 9:32', *WTJ* 54 (1992), pp. 163–166.

Groesheide, F. W., *Commentary on the First Epistle to the Corinthians* (NICNT; Grand Rapids: Eerdmans, 1953).

Guerra, Anthony J., 'Romans 4 as Apologetic Theology', *HTR* 81 (1988), pp. 251–270.

Gundry, Robert H., 'The Moral Frustration of Paul before his Conversion: Sexual Lust in Romans 7:7–25', *Pauline Studies* (Festschrift for F. F. Bruce), ed. Donald A. Hagner and Murray J. Harris (Exeter: Paternoster, 1980), pp. 228–245.

Haacker, Klaus, 'Exegetische Probleme des Romerbriefs', *NovT* 20 (1978), pp. 1–21.

Hall, David R., 'Romans 3.1–8 Reconsidered', *NTS* 29 (1983), pp. 183–197.

Hammerton–Kelly, R. G., 'Sacred Violence and "Works of Law": "Is Christ Then an Agent of Sin?" (Galatians 2:17)', *CBQ* 52 (1990), pp. 55–75.

Hansen, G. Walter, *Abraham in Galatians: Epistolary and Rhetorical Contexts* (JSNTSup 29; Sheffield: JSOT, 1989).

Hanson, A. T., 'The Origin of Paul's Use of *PAIDAGŌGOS* for the Law', *JSNT* 34 (1988), pp. 71–76.

————, *Studies in Paul's Technique and Theology* (London: SPCK, 1974).

Hanson, R. P. C., *Allegory and Event: A Study of the Sources and Significance of Origen's Interpretation of Scripture* (London: SCM, 1959).

Hawthorne, Gerald F., *Philippians* (WBC 43; Waco, TX: Word, 1983).

Hays, Richard B., 'Christology and Ethics in Galatians: The Law of Christ', *CBQ* 49 (1987), pp. 268–290.

————, *The Faith of Jesus Christ. An Interpretation of the Narrative Substructure of Galatians 3:1 – 4:11* (SBLDS 56; Chico, CA: Scholars Press, 1983).

————, '"Have we Found Abraham to be our Forefather According to the Flesh?" A Reconsideration of Rom 4:1', *NovT* 27 (1985), pp. 76–88.

————, 'Psalm 143 and the Logic of Romans 3', *JBL* 99 (1980), pp. 107–115.

Heiligenthal, Roman, 'Soziologische Implikationen der paulinischen Rechtfertigungslehre im Galaterbrief am Beispiel der "Werke des Gesetzes". Beobachtungen zur Identitätsfindung einer frühchristlichen Gemeinde', *Kairos* 26 (1984), pp. 38–53.

Hengel, Martin, *The Zealots. Investigation into the Jewish Freedom Movement in the Period from Herod I until 70 A.D.* (ET, Edinburgh: T. and T. Clark, 1989).

Hester, James D., 'The Rhetorical Structure of Galatians 1:11 – 2:14', *JBL* 103 (1984), pp. 223–233.

————, 'The Use and Influence of Rhetoric in Galatians 2:1–14', *TZ* 42 (1986), pp. 386–408.

Hill, David, 'Salvation Proclaimed IV. Galatians 3:10–14: Freedom and Acceptance', *ExpT* 93 (1981), pp. 196–200.

Hofius, Otfried, 'Gal 1:18: *historēsai Kēphan'*, *ZNW* 75 (1984), pp. 73–85.

Hollander, H. W., and Holleman, J., 'The Relationship of Death, Sin, and Law in 1 Cor 15:56', *NovT* 35 (1993), pp. 270–291.

Holtz, Traugott, 'Der antiochenische Zwischenfall (Galater 2.11–14)', *NTS* 32 (1986), pp. 344–361.

Hong In-Gyu, 'Does Paul Misrepresent the Jewish law? Law and Covenant in Gal. 3:1–14', *NovT* 36 (1994), pp. 164–182.

————, *The Law in Galatians* (JSNTSup 81; Sheffield: JSOT, 1993).

Hooker, M. D., 'Adam in Romans I', *NTS* 6 (1960), pp. 300–301.

————, 'Beyond the Things that are Written? St Paul's Use of Scripture', *NTS* 27 (1981), pp. 295–309.

Horbury, W., 'Paul and Judaism', *ExpT* 90 (1979), pp. 116–118.

Houlden, J. L., 'A Response to James D. G. Dunn', *JSNT* 18 (1983), pp. 58–67.

Howard, George, *Paul: Crisis in Galatia: A Study in Early Christian Theology* (SNTSMS 35: Cambridge: Cambridge University Press, 1979).

Howard, J. K., '"Christ our Passover": A Study of the Passover–Exodus Theme in I Corinthians', *EvQ* 41 (1969), pp. 97–108.

Hübner, Hans, *Law in Paul's Thought* (ET, Edinburgh: T. and T. Clark, 1984).

Hultgren, Arland J., 'The *Pistis Christou* Formulation in Paul', *NovT* 22 (1980), pp. 248–263.

Hvalvik, Reidar, 'A "Sonderweg" for Israel: A Critical Examination of a Current Interpretation of Romans 11.25–27', *JSNT* 38 (1990), pp. 88–107.

Jervell, Jacob, 'The Letter to Jerusalem', *The Romans Debate*, ed. Karl P. Donfried (Peabody, MA: Hendrickson, revised and expanded edn., 1991), pp. 53–64.

Jervis, L. Ann, *The Purpose of Romans: A Comparative Letter Structure Investigation* (JSNTSup 55; Sheffield: JSOT, 1991).

Jewett, Robert, 'The Agitators and the Galatian Congregation', *NTS* 17 (1970–71), pp. 198–212.

————, 'The Law and the Co-existence of Jews and Gentiles in Romans', *Int* 39 (1985), pp. 341–356.

————, 'Romans as an Ambassadorial Letter', *Int* 36 (1982), pp. 5–20.

Johnson, Dan G., 'The Structure and Meaning of Romans 11', *CBQ* 46 (1984), pp. 91–103.

Johnson, Luke Timothy, 'Rom. 3:21–26 and the Faith of Jesus', *CBQ* 44 (1982), pp. 77–90.

Judant, D., 'A propos de la destinée d'Israel. Remarques concernant un verset de l'épître aux Romains XI, 21', *Divinitas* 23 (1979), pp. 108–125.

Kaiser, Walter C., Jr, 'The Current Crisis in Exegesis and the Apostolic Use of Deuteronomy 25:4 in 1 Corinthians 9:8–10', *JETS* 21 (1978), pp. 3–18.

Käsemann, Ernst, 'The "Righteousness of God" in Paul', *New Testament Questions of Today* (London: SCM, 1969), pp. 168–182.

Kelly, J. N. D., *A Commentary on the Pastoral Epistles: I Timothy, II Timothy, Titus* (London: A. and C. Black, 1963).

Kennedy, George A., *New Testament Interpretation through Rhetorical Criticism* (Chapel Hill: University of Carolina Press, 1984).

Kertelge, Karl, 'Gesetz und Freiheit in Galaterbrief,' *NTS* 30 (1984), pp. 382–394.

Kieffer, René, *Foi et Justification à Antioche; Interprétation d'un conflit (Ga 2,14–21)* (LD 111; Paris: Cerf, 1982).

Kim, Seyoon, *The Origin of Paul's Gospel* (Tübingen: Mohr, 1981).

King, Daniel Hayden, 'Paul and the Tannaim: A Study in Galatians', *WTJ* 45 (1983), pp. 340–370.

Klein, Günter, 'Paul's Purpose in Writing the Epistle to the Romans', *The Romans Debate*, ed. Karl P. Donfried, (Peabody, MA: Hendrickson, revised and expanded edn., 1991), pp. 29–43.

Koch, Dietrich-Alex, 'Der Text von Hab 2 4b in der Septuaginta und im Neuen Testament', *ZNW* 76 (1985), pp. 68–85.

Krentz, Edgar, 'The Name of God in Disrepute: Romans 2:17–29 (22–23)', *CTM* 17 (1990), pp. 429–439.

Kruse, Colin, 'Human Relationships in the Pauline Corpus', *In the Fullness of Time: Biblical Studies in Honour of Archbishop Donald Robinson*, ed. David Peterson and John Pryor (Lancer: Homebush West, NSW, 1992), pp. 167–184.

————, 'The Offender and the Offence in 2 Corinthians 2:5 and 7:12', *EvQ* 60 (1988), pp. 129–139.

310   *Paul, the law and justification*

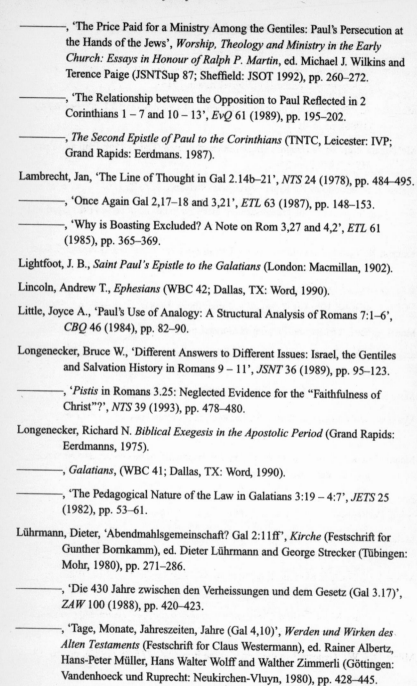

————, 'The Price Paid for a Ministry Among the Gentiles: Paul's Persecution at the Hands of the Jews', *Worship, Theology and Ministry in the Early Church: Essays in Honour of Ralph P. Martin*, ed. Michael J. Wilkins and Terence Paige (JSNTSup 87; Sheffield: JSOT 1992), pp. 260–272.

————, 'The Relationship between the Opposition to Paul Reflected in 2 Corinthians 1 – 7 and 10 – 13', *EvQ* 61 (1989), pp. 195–202.

————, *The Second Epistle of Paul to the Corinthians* (TNTC, Leicester: IVP; Grand Rapids: Eerdmans. 1987).

Lambrecht, Jan, 'The Line of Thought in Gal 2.14b–21', *NTS* 24 (1978), pp. 484–495.

————, 'Once Again Gal 2,17–18 and 3,21', *ETL* 63 (1987), pp. 148–153.

————, 'Why is Boasting Excluded? A Note on Rom 3,27 and 4,2', *ETL* 61 (1985), pp. 365–369.

Lightfoot, J. B., *Saint Paul's Epistle to the Galatians* (London: Macmillan, 1902).

Lincoln, Andrew T., *Ephesians* (WBC 42; Dallas, TX: Word, 1990).

Little, Joyce A., 'Paul's Use of Analogy: A Structural Analysis of Romans 7:1–6', *CBQ* 46 (1984), pp. 82–90.

Longenecker, Bruce W., 'Different Answers to Different Issues: Israel, the Gentiles and Salvation History in Romans 9 – 11', *JSNT* 36 (1989), pp. 95–123.

————, '*Pistis* in Romans 3.25: Neglected Evidence for the "Faithfulness of Christ"?', *NTS* 39 (1993), pp. 478–480.

Longenecker, Richard N. *Biblical Exegesis in the Apostolic Period* (Grand Rapids: Eerdmanns, 1975).

————, *Galatians*, (WBC 41; Dallas, TX: Word, 1990).

————, 'The Pedagogical Nature of the Law in Galatians 3:19 – 4:7', *JETS* 25 (1982), pp. 53–61.

Lührmann, Dieter, 'Abendmahlsgemeinschaft? Gal 2:11ff', *Kirche* (Festschrift for Gunther Bornkamm), ed. Dieter Lührmann and George Strecker (Tübingen: Mohr, 1980), pp. 271–286.

————, 'Die 430 Jahre zwischen den Verheissungen und dem Gesetz (Gal 3.17)', *ZAW* 100 (1988), pp. 420–423.

————, 'Tage, Monate, Jahreszeiten, Jahre (Gal 4,10)', *Werden und Wirken des Alten Testaments* (Festschrift for Claus Westermann), ed. Rainer Albertz, Hans-Peter Müller, Hans Walter Wolff and Walther Zimmerli (Göttingen: Vandenhoeck und Ruprecht: Neukirchen-Vluyn, 1980), pp. 428–445.

Lull, David J., '"The Law was our Pedagogue": A Study in Galatians 3:19–25', *JBL* 105 (1986), pp. 481–498.

Lütgert, W., *Gesetz und Geist: Eine Untersuchung zur Vorgeschichte des Galaterbriefes* (Gütersloh: Bertelsmann, 1919).

McEwan, A., 'Paul's Use of the Old Testament in 1 Corinthians 10:1–4', *VoxRef* 47 (1986), pp. 3–10.

McNamara, M., '*To de (Hagar) Sina estin en tē Arabia* (Gal. 4,25a): Paul and Petra', *MS* 2 (1978), pp. 24–41.

Malan, F. S., 'Bound to Do Right', *Neot* 15 (1981), pp. 118–138.

———, 'The Use of the Old Testament in 1 Corinthians', *Neot* 14 (1981), pp. 134–170.

Manson, T. W., 'St. Paul's Letter to the Romans – And Others', *The Romans Debate*, ed. Karl P. Donfried (Peabody, MA: Hendrickson, revised and expanded edn., 1991), pp. 3–15.

Martens, John W., 'Romans 2.14–16: A Stoic Reading', *NTS* 40 (1994), pp. 55–67.

Martin, Brice L., *Christ and the Law in Paul* (Leiden: Brill, 1989).

———, 'Some Reflections on the Identity of *egō* in Rom. 7:14–25', *SJT* 34 (1981), pp. 39–47.

Martin, Ralph P., *2 Corinthians* (WBC 40; Waco, TX: Word, 1986).

Marxsen, Willi, 'Sündige Tapfer. Wer hat sich beim Streit in Antiochen richtig verhalten?', *EvK* 20/2 (1987), pp. 81–84.

Matera, Frank J., 'The Culmination of Paul's Argument to the Galatians: Gal. 5.1 – 6.17', *JSNT* 32 (1988), pp. 79–91.

Mearns, Chris, 'The Identity of Paul's Opponents at Philippi', *NTS* 33 (1987), pp. 194–204.

Méhat, André, '"Quand Képhas vint à Antioche . . ." Que s'est-il passé entre Pierre et Paul?', *LumVie* 192 (1989), pp. 29–43.

Meile, Eva, 'Isaaks Opferung: Eine Note an Nils Alstrup Dahl', *ST* 34 (1980), pp. 111–128.

Metzger, Bruce M., *A Textual Commentary on the Greek New Testament* (London and New York: United Bible Societies, 1971).

Milne, D. J. W., 'Genesis 3 in the Letter to the Romans', *RTR* 39 (1980), pp. 10–18.

312   *Paul, the law and justification*

————, 'Romans 7:7–12, Paul's Pre-conversion Experience', *RTR* 43 (1984), pp. 9–17.

Mitchell, Margaret M., 'Concerning *peri de* in 1 Corinthians', *NovT* 31 (1989), pp. 229–256.

Mitton, C. Leslie, 'New Wine in Old Wine Skins: IV. Leaven', *ExpT* 84 (1972–73), pp. 339–343.

Montefiore, C. G., *Judaism and St Paul: Two Essays* (London: Max Goschen, 1914).

Moo, Douglas J., 'Israel and Paul in Romans 7.7–12', *NTS* 32 (1986), pp. 122–135.

————, *Romans 1 – 8* (The Wycliffe Exegetical Commentary; Chicago: Moody, 1991).

Moody, R. M., 'The Habakkuk Quotation in Romans 1:17', *ExpT* 92 (1981), pp. 205–208.

Moore, George Foot, 'Christian Writers on Judaism', *HTR* 14 (1921), pp. 197–254.

Morris, Leon, *The Apostolic Preaching of the Cross* (Grand Rapids: Eerdmans, 1965).

Morris, T. F., 'Law and the Cause of Sin in the Epistle to the Romans', *HeyJ* 28 (1987), pp. 285–291.

Morrison, Bruce, and Woodhouse, John, 'The Coherence of Romans 7:1 – 8:8', *RTR* 47 (1988), pp. 8–16.

Murphy-O'Connor, Jerome, 'The Divorced Woman in 1 Cor 7:10–11', *JBL* 100 (1981), pp. 601–606.

————, 'The Non-Pauline Character of 1 Corinthians 11:2–16', *JBL* 95 (1976), pp. 615–621.

Mussner, Franz, *Der Galaterbrief* (HTKNT 9; Freiburg: Herder, 1974).

————, 'Heil für alle. Der Grundgedanke des Römerbriefs', *Kairos* 23 (1981), pp. 207–214.

Neusner, Jacob, 'Comparing Judaisms', *HR* 18 (1978), pp. 177–191.

————, *Jews and Christians: The Myth of a Common Tradition* (London: SCM; Philadelphia: Trinity, 1991).

————, *Judaism in the Beginning of Christianity* (Philadelphia: Fortress, 1984).

Neyrey, Jerome H., 'Bewitched in Galatia: Paul and Cultural Anthropology', *CBQ* 50 (1988), pp. 72–100.

O'Brien, Peter T., *Colossians, Philemon* (WBC 44; Waco, TX: Word, 1982).

————, *The Epistle to the Philippians: A Commentary on the Greek Text* (NIGTC; Grand Rapids: Eerdmans, 1991).

Okeke, G. E., '1 Thessalonians 2.13–16: The Fate of the Unbelieving Jews', *NTS* 27 (1980–81), pp. 127–136.

Osborne, William L., 'The Old Testament Background of Paul's "All Israel" in Romans 11:26a', *AJT* 2 (1988), pp. 282–293.

Osten-Sacken, Peter von der, 'Geist im Buchstaben: vom Glanz des Mose und des Paulus', *EvT* 41 (1981), pp. 230–235.

————, *Römer 8 als Beispiel paulinischer Soteriologie* (Göttingen: Vandenhoeck und Ruprecht, 1975).

Pearson, Birger A., '1 Thessalonians 2:13–16: A Deutero-Pauline Interpolation', *HTR* 64 (1971), pp. 79–94.

Pedersen, S., '"Mit Furcht und Zittern" (Phil 2, 12–13)', *ST* 32 (1978), pp. 1–31.

Perriman, Andrew C., 'The Rhetorical Strategy of Galatians 4:21 – 5:1', *EvQ* 65 (1993), pp. 27–42.

Perrot, Charles, 'Les examples du desert (1 Co. 10.6–11)', *NTS* 29 (1983), pp. 437–452.

Piper, John, 'The Demonstration of the Righteousness of God in Romans 3:25, 26', *JSNT* 7 (1980), pp. 2–32.

————, 'The Righteousness of God in Romans 3, 1–8', *TZ* 36 (1980), pp. 3–16.

Räisänen, Heikki, 'Galatians 2.16 and Paul's Break with Judaism', *NTS* 31 (1985), pp. 543–553.

————, 'Zum Gebrauch von *EPITHYMIA* und *EPITHYMEIN* bei Paulus', *ST* 33 (1979), pp. 85–99.

————, 'Das "Gesetz des Glaubens" (Röm. 3.27) und das "Gesetz des Geistes" (Röm. 8.2)', *NTS* 26 (1979), pp. 101–117.

————, *Paul and the Law* (Philadelphia: Fortress, 1986).

————, 'Paul's Theological Difficulties with the Law', *The Torah and Christ: Essays in German and English on the Problem of the Law in Early Christianity* (Helsinki: Finnish Exegetical Society, 1986), pp. 3–24.

Ramsay, W. M., *A Historical Commentary on St Paul's Epistle to the Galatians* (London: Hodder and Stoughton, 1900).

Refoulé, Françoise, 'Note sur Romains IX, 30–33', *RB* 92 (1985), pp. 161–186.

Rhyne, C. Thomas, '*Nomos Dikaiosynēs* and the Meaning of Romans 10:4', *CBQ* 47 (1985), pp. 486–499.

Richardson, Peter, ' "I Say, Not the Lord": Personal Opinion, Apostolic Authority and the Development of Early Christian Halakah,' *TynBul* 31 (1980), pp. 65–86.

————, 'Pauline Inconsistency: I Corinthians 9:19–23 and Galatians 2:11–14', *NTS* 26 (1980), pp. 347–362.

Richardson, Peter, and Gooch, Paul W., 'Accommodation Ethics', *TynBul* 29 (1978), pp. 89–142.

Robinson, D. W. B., 'The Salvation of Israel in Romans 9 – 11', *RTR* 26 (1967), pp. 81–96.

Roetzel, Calvin J., 'Jewish Christian–Gentile Christian Relations: A Discussion of Ephesians 2:15a', *ZNW* 74 (1983), pp. 81–89.

Rosenau, Hartmut, 'Der mensch zwischen Wollen und Können: Theologische Reflexionen im Anschluss an Röm 7, 14–25', *TP* 65 (1990), pp. 1–30.

Russell, Walter B., 'An Alternative Suggestion for the purpose of Romans', *BSac* 145 (1988), pp. 174–184.

Sanders, E. P., *Paul, the Law, and the Jewish people* (London: SCM, 1985).

————, *Paul and Palestinian Judaism: A Comparison of Patterns of Religion* (London: SCM, 1977).

Sandmel, Samuel, *Judaism and Christian Beginnings* (Oxford: Oxford University Press, 1978).

Schlier, Heinrich, *Der Brief an die Galater* (KEK; Göttingen: Vandenhoek und Ruprecht, 1962).

Schmidt, Daryl, '1 Thess 2:13–16:. Linguistic Evidence for an Interpolation', *JBL* 102 (1983), pp. 269–279.

Schmithals, Walter, 'Judaisten in Galatien?' *ZNW* 74 (1983), pp. 27–58.

————, *Paul and the Gnostics* (ET, Nashville; Abingdon, 1972).

Schnackenburg, Rudolf, *Ephesians: A Commentary* (Edinburgh: T. and T. Clark, 1991).

Schoeps, H. J., *Paul: The Theology of the Apostle in the Light of Jewish Religious History* (ET, London: Lutterworth, 1961).

Schreiner, Thomas, 'Did Paul Believe in Justification by Works? Another Look at Romans 2', *BBR* 3 (1993), pp. 131–155.

————, 'Is Perfect Obedience to the Law Possible? A Re-examination of Galatians 3:10', *JETS* 27 (1984), pp. 151–160.

————, 'Israel's Failure to Attain Righteousness in Romans 9:30 – 10:3', *TrinJ* 12 (1991), pp. 209–220.

————, *The Law and Its Fulfilment: A Pauline Theology of Law* (Grand Rapids: Baker, 1993).

————, 'Paul's View of the Law in Romans 10:4–5', *WTJ* 55 (1993), pp. 113–135.

————, '"Works of Law" in Paul', *NovT* 33 (1991), pp. 217–244.

Schweitzer, Albert, *The Mysticism of Paul the Apostle* (London: A. and C. Black, 1931).

Segal, Alan F., 'Romans 7 and Jewish Dietary Law', *SR/SR* 15 (1986), pp. 361–374.

Seifrid, Mark A., 'Blind Alleys in the Controversy over the Paul of History', *TynBul* 45 (1994), pp. 73–95.

————, *Justification by Faith: The Origin and Development of a Central Pauline Theme* (Leiden: Brill, 1992).

————, 'Paul's Approach to the Old Testament in Rom 10:6–8', *TrinJ* 6 n.s. (1985), pp. 3–37.

Simpson, John W., Jr, 'The Problems Posed by 1 Thessalonians 2:15–16 and a Solution', *HBT* 12 (1990), pp. 42–72.

Smit, Joop, 'The Letter of Paul to the Galatians: A Deliberative Speech', *NTS* 35 (1989), pp. 1–26.

————, 'Naar een nieuwe benadering van Paulus' brieven. De historische bewijsvoering in Gal 3,1 – 4,11', *TijdT* 24 (1984), pp. 207–234.

Snodgrass, Klyne R., 'Justification by Grace – To the Doers: An Analysis of the Place of Romans 2 in the Theology of Paul', *NTS* 32 (1986), pp. 72–93.

Snyman, A. H., 'Style and Rhetorical Situation of Romans 8.31–39', *NTS* 34 (1988), pp. 218–231.

Söding, Thomas, 'Der Erste Thessalonicherbrief und die frühe paulinische Evangeliumsverkündigung. Zur Frage einer Entwicklung der paulinischen Theologie', *BZ* 35 (1991), pp. 180–203.

————, '"Die Kraft der Sünde ist das Gesetz" (1 Kor 15,56). Anmerkungen zum Hintergrund und zur Pointe einer Gesetzkritischen Sentenz des Apostels Paulus', *ZNW* 83 (1992), pp. 74–84.

Steinhauser, Michael G., 'Gal 4,25a: Evidence of Targumic Tradition in Gal 4,21–31?', *Bib* 70 (1989), pp. 234–240.

Stendahl, Krister, 'Paul and the Introspective Conscience of the West', *Paul Among Jews and Gentiles and Other Essays*, (London: SCM, 1977), pp. 78–96.

Stowers, Stanley K., '*EK PISTEŌS* and *DIA TĒS PISTEŌS* in Romans 3:30', *JBL* 108 (1989), pp. 665–674.

————, 'Paul's Dialogue with a Fellow Jew in Romans 3:1–9', *CBQ* 46 (1984), pp. 707–722.

Strelan, G., 'A Note on the Old Testament Background of Romans 7:7', *LTJ* 15 (1981), pp. 23–25.

Stuhlmacher, Peter, 'Der Abfassungszweck des Römerbriefes', *ZNW* 77 (1986), pp. 180–193.

Swetnam, James, 'The Curious Crux at Romans 4, 12', *Bib* 61 (1980), pp. 110–115.

Taylor, Nicholas, *Paul, Antioch and Jerusalem: A Study in Relationships and Authority in Earliest Christianity* (JSNTSup 66; Sheffield: JSOT, 1992).

Tellbe, Mikael, 'The Sociological Factors behind Philippians 3.1–11 and the Conflict at Philippi', *JSNT* 55 (1994), pp. 97–121.

Theissen, Gerd, *The Social Setting of Pauline Christianity: Essays on Corinth* (Philadelphia: Fortress, 1982).

Thielman, Frank, 'The Coherence of Paul's View of the Law: Evidence of First Corinthians', *NTS* 38 (1992), pp. 235–253.

————, *Paul and the Law: A Contextual Approach* (Downers Grove, IL: IVP, 1994).

————, *From Plight to Solution: A Jewish Framework for Understanding Paul's View of the Law in Galatians and Romans* (Leiden: Brill, 1989).

Thompson, Michael, *Clothed with Christ: The Example and Teaching of Jesus in Romans 12.1 – 15.13* (JSNTSup 59; Sheffield: JSOT, 1991).

Thompson, Richard W., 'How is the Law Fulfilled in us? An Interpretation of Rom 8:4', *LS* 11 (1986), pp. 31–40.

————, 'Paul's Double Critique of Jewish Boasting: A Study of Romans 3,27 in its Context', *Bib* 67 (1986), pp. 520–531.

Thornton, T. C. G., 'Jewish New Moon Festivals, Galatians 4:3–11 and Colossians 2:16', *JTS* 40 (1989), pp. 97–100.

Tomson, Peter J., *Paul and the Jewish Law: Halakha in the Letters of the Apostle to the Gentiles* (Assen and Maastricht: Van Gorcum; Minneapolis: Fortress, 1990).

Voorwinde, S., 'Who is the "Wretched Man" in Romans 7:24?', *VoxRef* 54 (1990), pp. 11–26.

Vos, J. S., 'Die hermeneutische Antinome bei Paulus (Galater 3.11–12; Römer 10.5–10)', *NTS* 38 (1992), pp. 254–270.

Vouga, François, 'La construction de l'histoire en Galates 3 – 4', *ZNW* 75 (1984), pp. 259–269.

———, 'Zur rhetorischen Gattung des Galaterbriefes', *ZNW* 79 (1988), pp. 291–292.

Wagner, G., 'Les motifs de la rédaction de l'Épître aux Galates', *ETR* 65 (1990), pp. 321–332.

Walker, William O., Jr, '1 Corinthians 11:2–16 and Paul's Views Regarding Women', *JBL* 94 (1975), pp. 94–110.

———, 'Why Paul Went to Jerusalem: The Interpretation of Galatians 2:1–5', *CBQ* 54 (1992), pp. 503–510.

Walter, Nikolaus, 'Die "Handschrift in Satzungen" Kol 2:14', *ZNW* 70 (1979), pp. 115–118.

Watson, Francis, *Paul, Judaism and the Gentiles: A Sociological Approach* (SNTSMS 56; Cambridge: Cambridge University Press, 1986).

Watson, Nigel M., 'Justified by Faith: Judged by Works – An Antinomy', *NTS* 29 (1983), pp. 209–221.

Wedderburn, A. J. M, 'Adam in Paul's Letter to the Romans', StudBib 1978 III: *Papers on Paul and Other New Testament Authors* (JSNTSup 3; Sheffield: JSOT, 1980), pp. 413–419.

———, 'The Purpose and Occasion of Romans Again', *ExpT* 90 (1979), pp. 137–141.

———, *The Reasons for Romans* (Edinburgh: T. and T. Clark, 1988).

Weder, Hans, 'Gesetz und Sunde: Gedanken zu einen qualitativen Sprung im Denken des Paulus', *NTS* 31 (1985), pp. 357–376.

Westerholm, Stephen, *Israel's Law and the Church's Faith: Paul and his Recent Interpreters* (Grand Rapids: Eerdmans, 1988).

Wiefel, Wolfgang, 'The Jewish Community in Ancient Rome and the Origins of

Roman Christianity', *The Romans Debate*, ed. Karl P. Donfried (Peabody, MA: Hendrickson, revised and expanded edn., 1991), pp. 85–101.

Wilhelmi, Gerhard, 'Der Versöhner-Hymnus in Eph 2.14 ff.', *ZNW* 78 (1987), pp. 145–152.

Wilkens, Ulrich, *Der Brief an die Römer*, 1. Teilband (EKKNT 6/1; Zurich: Benzinger; Neukirchen–Vluyn: Neukirchener, 1978).

Williams, Sam K., 'The Hearing of Faith: *AKOĒ PISTEŌS* in Galatians 3', *NTS* 35 (1989), pp. 82–93.

————, 'Justification and the Spirit in Galatians', *JSNT* 29 (1987), pp. 91–100.

————, 'The "Righteousness of God" in Romans', *JBL* 99 (1980), pp. 241–290.

Wischmeyer, Oda, 'Das Gebot der Nächstenliebe bei Paulus: eine traditionsgeschichtliche Untersuchung', *BZ* 30 (1986), pp. 161–187.

Wolff, Christian, *Der erste Brief des Paulus an die Korinther, Zweiter Teil: Auslegung der Kapitel 8 – 16* (THKNT; Berlin: Evangelische Verlagsanstalt, 1982).

Wright, Christopher J. H., *Living as the People of God: The Relevance of Old Testament Ethics* (Leicester: IVP, 1983).

Wright, N. T., *The Climax of the Covenant: Christ and the Law in Pauline Theology* (Edinburgh: T. and T. Clark, 1991).

————, *The New Testament and the People of God* (Minneapolis: Fortress, 1992).

Yates, J. C., 'The Judgement of the Heathen: The Interpretation of Article XVIII and Romans 2:12–16', *Churchman* 100 (1986), pp. 220–230.

Yates, Roy, 'Colossians 2,14: Metaphor of Forgiveness', *Bib* 71 (1990), pp. 248–259.

Young, Norman H., 'The Figure of the *Paidagōgos* in Art and Literature', *BA* 53 (1990), pp. 80–86.

————, '*Paidagōgos* The Social Setting of a Pauline Metaphor', *NovT* 29 (1987), pp. 150–176.

Ziesler, J. A., 'The Just Requirement of the Law (Romans 8.4)', *AusBR* 35 (1987), pp. 77–82.

————, *Paul's Letter to the Romans* (London: SCM; Philadelphia: Trinity, 1989).

————, 'The Role of the Tenth Commandment in Romans 7', *JSNT* 33 (1988), pp. 41–56.

Author index

Achtemeier, P. J., 179

Badenas, R., 229
Balla, P., 263
Bandstra, A. J., 260
Banks, R., 209
Barclay, J. M. G., 56, 66, 69, 250
Barrett, C. K., 57, 85, 134, 136, 140, 141, 173
Bassler, J. M., 174, 177, 178
Baumert, N., 256
Baxter, A. G., 235
Beker, J. C., 168, 233
Bergmeier, R., 215
Best, T. F., 37
Betz, H. D., 61, 63, 64, 66, 71, 72, 74, 77, 87, 89, 91, 92, 94, 95, 96, 97, 98, 100, 101, 103, 104, 106, 237
Borgen, P., 57
Bornkamm, G., 166
Bousset, W., 30, 54
Bouwman, G., 69
Branick, V. P., 217
Brewer, D. I., 127
Brinsmead, B. H., 56
Bruce, F. F., 55, 62, 64, 66, 71, 74, 77, 82, 85, 87, 88, 95, 141, 166, 213, 253
Bultmann, R., 44, 51, 54, 67, 212, 213
Burton, E. De W., 96
Byrne, B., 85, 168, 205

Callen, T., 92
Campbell, D. A., 173, 188, 189, 190
Campbell, W. S., 165
Caneday, A., 81, 85, 87
Caragounis, C. C., 201
Carson, D., 129, 130, 132
Catchpole, D. R., 61, 62
Cavallin, H. C. C., 172
Cohn-Sherbok, D., 61, 69
Conzelmann, H., 126, 130, 134, 136, 140, 265
Cope, L., 136
Cosgrove, C. H., 66, 82, 83, 90, 183
Cranfield, C. E. B., 167, 172, 179, 187, 192, 201, 209, 215, 217, 228

Dahl, N. A., 37, 232, 262
Dalton, W. J., 66, 152, 153
Danby, H., 124, 157
Daube, D., 102
Davidson, R. M., 135–136
Davies, G. N., 173, 178, 179–180, 184, 190, 224, 228
Davies, W. D., 31–32, 67
Dawes, G. W., 123
Derrett, J. D. M., 155, 181
DeSilva, D. A., 255
Dibelius, M., 265
Dodd, C. H., 128, 130, 208
Donaldson, T. L., 87–88, 95
Donfried, K. P., 163, 252
Drane, J. W., 33–34, 44, 124
Dungan, D. L., 127
Dunn, J. D. G., 40–42, 44, 51, 54, 55, 58, 59, 60, 61, 66, 67, 68, 78–79, 81, 85, 172, 173, 175, 179, 187, 189, 196, 199, 203, 205, 210, 215, 216, 220, 221, 224, 226, 227, 231, 233, 282

Earnshaw, J. D., 208
Elliott, J. H., 73, 74
Elliott, N., 167, 182, 184, 189
Epp, E. J., 223
Fee, G. D., 116, 118, 121, 122, 125, 126, 130, 133, 134, 136, 140, 265, 268, 270

Fitzmyer, J. A., 122
Flusser, D., 68
Froelich, K., 61
Führer, W., 226
Fuller, D. P., 82, 83, 84
Furnish, V. P., 150, 152, 155

Gallas, S., 157, 158
Garlington, D. B., 181, 201, 202
Gaston, L., 42–43, 87, 99, 100
Georgi, D., 152
Getty, M. A., 221, 226, 227
Gilliard, F. D., 253
Gillman, F. M., 217
Gooch, P. W., 129
Goppelt, L., 135–136
Gordon, T. D., 94, 224
Groesheide, F. W., 140, 141
Guerra, A. J., 194
Gundry, R. H., 213

Haacker, K., 166
Hall, D. R., 183, 184
Hammerton-Kelly, R. G., 66, 70–71
Hansen, G. W., 73, 75, 78, 87, 97, 99, 101
Hanson, A. T., 94, 126
Hanson, R. P. C., 97
Hawthorne, G. F., 256, 257, 258
Hays, R. B., 74, 106, 183, 185, 194, 198
Heiligenthal, R., 54, 68
Hengel, M., 65
Hester, J. D., 59
Hill, D., 87
Hofius, O., 59
Hollander, H. W., 143
Holleman, J., 143
Holtz, T., 61
Hong, I-G., 79, 82, 106
Hooker, M. D., 57, 85, 154, 175
Horbury, W., 37
Houlden, J. L., 61
Howard, G., 59, 62, 83, 95
Howard, J. K., 119
Hübner, H., 34–35, 44, 91, 192
Hultgren, A. J., 66, 67
Hvalvik, R., 233–234

Jervell, J., 166
Jervis, L. A., 163, 167
Jewett, R., 65, 166, 226
Johnson, D. G., 232, 233
Johnson, L. T., 190
Judant, D., 234–235

Kaiser, W. C., 126, 127
Käsemann, E., 185
Kelly, J. N. D., 265
Kennedy, G. A., 63
Kertelge, K., 104
Kieffer, R., 66
Kim, S., 58, 86
King, D. H., 57
Klein, G., 165
Koch, D-A., 171
Krentz, E., 181
Kruse, C. G., 116, 150, 151, 152, 155, 158, 264
Kümmel, W. G., 43, 130

Lambrecht, J., 66, 192, 194
Lightfoot, J. B., 75, 77

Lincoln, A. T., 262, 263, 265
Little, J. A., 207–208
Longenecker, B. W., 190, 191, 222
Longenecker, R. N., 64, 66, 69, 70, 71, 72, 74, 75, 76, 77, 84, 87, 89, 91, 92, 94, 95, 97, 98, 99, 101, 102, 105, 106, 126
Lührmann, D., 61, 90, 96
Lull, D. J., 94
Lütgert, W., 56

McEwan, A., 134
McNamara, M., 99
Malan, F. S., 205
Manson, T. W., 166
Martens, J. W., 180
Martin, B. L., 48, 209
Martin, R. P., 152, 154, 158
Marxsen, W., 61
Matera, F. J., 101
Mearns, C., 255
Méhat, A., 61
Meile, E., 194
Metzger, B. M., 96
Milne, D. J. W., 175, 201, 209
Mitchell, M. M., 116
Mitton, C. L., 119
Montefiore, C. G., 28–29, 31, 43, 67
Moo, D. J., 177, 179, 181, 184, 195, 210, 211, 213, 215, 217, 257
Moody, R. M., 172
Moore, G. F., 29–30, 67
Morris, L., 191
Morris, T. F., 212–213
Morrison, B., 206, 209, 218
Murphy-O'Connor, J., 122, 137
Mussner, F., 66, 84, 234

Neusner, J., 37, 257
Neyrey, J. H., 73, 74

O'Brien, P. T., 256, 257, 258, 259, 260
O'Neill, J. C., 176
Okeke, G. E., 252
Osborne, W. L., 234

Osten-Sacken, P. von der, 153, 192

Pearson, B. A., 252, 253
Pedersen, S., 256
Perriman, A. C., 100
Perrot, C., 134
Piper, J., 170, 186, 188, 189, 191

Räisänen, H., 38–40, 42, 44, 55, 66, 68, 76–77, 84, 87, 91, 103, 124, 130, 192, 203, 212, 213, 217, 226, 227, 228–229
Ramsay, W. M., 94–95
Refoulé, F., 226
Rhyne, C. T., 226, 228
Richardson, P., 122, 129, 131, 132
Robinson, D. W. B., 235, 264
Roetzel, C. J., 263
Rosenau, H., 209, 215
Russell, W. B., 167

Sanders, E. P., 24, 35–38, 39, 40, 41, 42, 43, 44, 51, 52, 72, 74, 80, 153, 175, 226
Sandmel, S., 37, 67
Sandt, van de, H. M. W., 219
Schlier, H., 71, 74, 77, 84
Schmidt, D., 252
Schmithals, W., 56
Schnackenburg, R., 262, 263
Schoeps, H. J., 32, 43, 67, 92
Schreiner, T. R., 51–53, 67, 68, 82, 83, 84, 180, 224, 226, 229
Schürer, E., 30, 54
Schweitzer, A., 30–31, 43, 45
Segal, A. F., 209
Seifrid, M. A., 82, 209, 230, 231
Simpson, J. W., 252, 253
Smit, J., 72
Snodgrass, K. R., 174, 176, 177, 178, 180
Snyman, A. H., 220
Söding, T., 143, 251
Steinhauser, M. G., 100
Stendahl, K., 33, 43, 67
Stowers, S. K., 183, 190, 191, 192

Strelan, G., 210, 213
Stuhlmacher, P., 168
Swetnam, J., 196

Taylor, N., 62
Tellbe, M., 255
Theissen, G., 127
Thielman, F., 45–48, 124, 129
Thompson, M., 236, 239
Thompson, R. W., 191, 192, 219
Thornton, T. C. G., 96
Tomson, P. J., 49

Voorwinde, S., 206, 209, 216
Vos, J. S., 231
Vouga, F., 72

Wagner, G., 56
Walker, W. O., 59, 136
Walter, N., 261
Watson, F., 62
Watson, N. M., 177
Weber, F., 30, 54
Wedderburn, A. J. M., 165, 166, 175, 239
Weder, H., 201
Westerholm, S., 43–45, 84, 87, 103, 104, 229
Wiefel, W., 165
Wilhelmi, G., 263
Wilkens, U., 44, 165
Williams, S. K., 75, 77
Wischmeyer, O., 237
Wolff, C., 140, 141
Woodhouse, J., 206, 209, 218
Wrede, W., 43
Wright, C. J. H., 119
Wright, N. T., 49–51, 81, 86, 88–89, 90, 92, 154, 215, 219, 221, 226, 235

Yates, J. C., 179
Yates, R., 260, 261, 264
Young, N. H., 94

Ziesler, J. A., 167, 188, 191, 199, 207, 211, 213, 217, 218, 221, 224, 226, 230, 235